Date Due

MAY 1 0 '74			
APR 31 '75			
MAY 16 '75			
MAY 1 1 1987			
FE 2 8 '04			

POPULATION GROWTH AND LAND USE

By the same author

THE CONDITIONS OF ECONOMIC PROGRESS

THE ECONOMICS OF SUBSISTENCE AGRICULTURE
(*with Margaret Haswell*)

STARVATION OR PLENTY ?

POPULATION
GROWTH AND
LAND USE

COLIN CLARK
M.A. (Oxon.), M.A. (Cantab.), Hon. D.Sc. (Milan), Hon. D.Ec. (Tilburg)

Research Fellow at Mannix College,
Monash University

MACMILLAN
ST MARTIN'S PRESS

First published 1967
Reprinted with alterations 1968
Reprinted 1969, 1970

Published by
MACMILLAN AND CO LTD
London and Basingstoke
Associated companies in New York Toronto
Dublin Melbourne Johannesburg and Madras

Library of Congress catalog card no.67–15941

SBN (boards) 333 01126 0

Printed in Great Britain by
REDWOOD PRESS LIMITED
Trowbridge & London

À Alfred Sauvy

du Collège de France

auteur d'études démographiques objectives

homme des idées fertiles

CONTENTS

PREFACE

THE student of population growth and its consequences finds himself compelled, whether he likes it or not, to assemble information from the diverse fields (to name them in the order in which they are examined) of biology, medicine, mathematics, archaeology, history, nutrition, agriculture, geography, sociology, politics, economics, town planning, and traffic engineering — to say nothing of questions of morals and religion. This book is only a preliminary attempt to survey the necessary range of material and should be soon superseded. But it suffices to show that the principal questions of population growth are not what many people think.

Population growth has taken place, and will continue, because of improvements in medical knowledge and practice. It brings economic hardship to communities living by traditional methods of agriculture; but it is the only force powerful enough to make such communities change their methods, and in the long run transforms them into much more advanced and productive societies. The world has immense physical resources for agricultural and mineral production still unused. In industrial communities, the beneficial economic effects of large and expanding markets are abundantly clear. The principal problems created by population growth are not those of poverty, but of exceptionally rapid increase of wealth in certain favoured regions of growing population, their attraction of further population by migration, and the unmanageable spread of their cities. Measures are proposed for curing these evils.

I am very grateful to Miss Christine Ireland for the accuracy and patience with which she has performed the main part of the great amount of typing required for this book; and to Mr. Peter Martin for drawing many flawless diagrams, and for the care and skill with which he has handled masses of statistical material.

C. C.

CHAPTER I

The Reproductive Capacity of the Human Race

THOUGH not to be compared with the elephant, hippopotamus and rhinoceros, whose slow reproductive cycles are celebrated in medical students' songs, nevertheless man, in comparison with most other organisms, is 'a slow-breeding organism of low fertility', as the distinguished biologist Hogben has put it.

The meaning of the word 'fertility' has now unfortunately become obscured. It is sometimes used to mean willingness to reproduce, sometimes physical ability to do so. To denote the latter concept clearly we use the neologism 'fecundability', awkward but free from obscurity.[1] We keep the word 'fertility' to denote offspring actually born, the consequence of fecundability combined with willingness to reproduce. Applied to women (there is no agreed counterpart word to describe the physical capacity for reproduction of men; but their capacity in any case appears to be much less variable) fecundability is defined as the mathematical probability of a woman, cohabiting with a husband fully capable of reproduction, and not restricting conception in any way, conceiving during any given single menstrual cycle (menstrual cycles, averaging about 13 to the year, being clearly the natural units in terms of which fecundability is best measured).

The measurement of fecundability is not at all easy. It involves asking questions of women on matters which they are usually only willing to discuss with their doctors, if with them; and in any case most medical practitioners and gynaecologists are too busy to have much time for research in this subject; such researches must of their nature be costly and time-consuming.

The pioneer of research in this field appears to have been Matthews Duncan, a Glasgow medical practitioner who collected statistics of a large number of cases and published in 1866 a book showing the probability of

---

[1] This word had its origin as 'fécondabilité' in the work of the Institut National des Études Démographiques in Paris, publishers of the Journal *Population*, and the world's most important centre of demographic research.

conception within two years of marriage, among people who probably practised little if any deliberate restriction of conception.[1]

Pearl developed a technique[2] of measuring probability of conception per woman–year (or woman–menstrual cycle) of 'exposure', defined as the time when she is cohabiting with a husband fully capable of reproduction, not attempting in any way to restrict conception, and not already pregnant. It was not until considerably later that Henry, of the Institut National des Études Démographiques, pointed out[3] that this method concealed a subtle and serious statistical bias — the relatively less fecundable women spend a much larger proportion of their married lives in a state of 'exposure' than do the more fecundable, and in consequence measurements by Pearl's method must give fecundabilities which are *below* the true average.

Pearl[4] collected a large number of data among women (predominantly American) who had been married once only, who had never used contraceptives, and who were free from any discernible gynaecological disease. He was puzzled by the fact that the means of his results were much higher than the medians, particularly among the younger women (we now know that this can be explained by the inclusion of first births immediately after marriage, when fecundability is much higher than it is later). Though his medians were too low, because of the bias which Henry points out, they did give the interesting result that for those women who were still conceiving, and had not yet become totally infecundable, fecundability did *not* fall with increasing age. He also found Negro fecundability not discernibly different from white.

While still using the 'exposure' method, and therefore obtaining results which were too low, Stix and Notestein[5] first brought out a number of important points (i) that fecundibility was much higher for first conceptions than subsequently, (ii) that in couples who had been using contraceptives and had discontinued them because they desired a conception, fecundability was also very high,[6] (iii) that those attending contraceptive clinics, who have provided material for many statistical investigations, provide a highly biased statistical sample. It is the more fecundable who are more likely to seek contraception.

---

[1] His results showed:

	Age of mother	20–24	30–34	40–44
Probability of conception within 2 years of marriage		0·90	0·63	0·15

[2] *Natural History of Population.*
[3] *Revue de l'Institut International de Statistique*, Vol. 21, No. 3.
[4] *Milbank Memorial Quarterly*, July 1936.
[5] Stix & Notestein, *Milbank Memorial Quarterly*, April 1935, and Stix, ibid. January 1939 (original results expressed per year, and divided by 13).
[6] A similar result was obtained by Tietze (*Population Index*, July 1950), who, however, placed the average figure, lower than Stix & Notestein, at 0·275.

Some alternative results for a remote rural community in Kentucky[1] may however be less biased, because in such a community, at that time, there may have been less differential selection of the more fecundable to the use of contraceptives (Table I.1). It was another study by Stix[2] which first suggested that the apparent decline of fecundability with duration of marriage (as a consequence of advancing age probably) might be only 'statistical', in the of an sense increasing proportion of infecundable, but with a more or less constant figure for those who remained fecundable (Table I.2). Sauvy[3] generalizes boldly that, while subject to small fluctuations, fecundability remains fairly constant in the neighbourhood of 0·12 throughout the period from menarche to menopause, until it 'drops suddenly, on a given day, to zero'. The idea that fecundability is something which can vary for a population, but which, for an individual woman, is something which is either fully present or fully absent, is now generally (though not universally) accepted by those who have studied the subject, with some qualifications.

During the 1920's, when the size of family in France was at its lowest, there was established a prize fund for parents who brought up the largest families. It can be assumed, that, in their case, there was little or no restriction of conception. Applications to this fund provided a good set of statistical records on fecundability, which were analysed by Vincent.[4] He concluded that fecundability at the time of marriage, and also at the time of the renewal of fertile intercourse after a period of interruption, was 0·25. Similar conclusions were obtained from American data by Potter,[5] both at the beginning of marriage and 'after stopping contraception'.

For women who marry very young however, initial fecundability is lower. At the age of 15 Vincent estimates it at only 0·15 — a similar figure is estimated by Henry.[6] Vincent puts the figure at over 0·2 at the age of 18, and at 0·27 for women in their 20's.

For conceptions after the first normal childbirth (the situation is somewhat uncertain when the first conception does not result in childbirth) the rate of fecundability is put at 0·1 for women at 18, rising to a maximum of 0·13 for women in their 20's, falling slowly and regularly to 0·1 in the 30's, and to rather less than 0·1 for those who are still fecundable at the age of 43.

The high figures of fecundability of the newly married, and also for those

[1] Beebe & Geisler, *Human Biology*, February 1942.
[2] *American Journal of Obstetrics and Gynaecology*, April 1938. Data obtained in Bronx, 1931–2.
[3] *Fertility and Survival*.
[4] International Statistical Conference, 1957, and *Population*, January–March 1961.
[5] *Milbank Memorial Quarterly*, January 1961.
[6] *Population*, October 1961.

TABLE I.1. PROBABILITY OF CONCEPTION PER MENSTRUAL CYCLE (STIX & NOTESTEIN)

	Couples who had never used contraceptives	Do. for rural community (Beebe & Geisler)	Couples who had used contraceptives only after 10 years of marriage	Couples using contraceptives intermittently throughout marriage	Couples who had recently discontinued contraceptives with a desire to conceive
First conceptions	0·128	0·108	0·088	0·134	0·361
Subsequent conceptions:					
Marriages of 0— 4 years' duration	0·076	0·062	0·063	0·079	0·324
,, ,, 5— 9 ,, ,,	0·072	0·054	0·058	0·095	0·323
,, ,, 10—14 ,, ,,	0·061	0·044	0·061		0·348
,, ,, 15—19 ,, ,,	0·052	0·049	0·052		
,, ,, 20—29 ,, ,,		0·048			

who have resumed fertile intercourse with a desire to conceive, lends weight to the suggestion[1] by Stallworthy, the Oxford gynaecologist, that there is a considerable psychosomatic factor, arising from the strength or otherwise of the desire to conceive, in a woman's fecundability under any given circumstances.

TABLE I.2.   STIX — PROBABILITY OF CONCEPTION PER MENSTRUAL CYCLE
(Couples who had never used contraceptives)

	General average	Average excluding all those in which any pathological[a] condition of the reproductive organs had been found
First conceptions	0·208	0·233
Subsequent conceptions:		
Marriage of 0– 4 years	0·088	0·096
„ „ 5– 9 „	0·078	0·096
„ „ 10–14 „	0·062	0·090
„ „ 15–19 „	0·053	0·101

a The word 'pathological' here appears to include many minor disabilities.

It may be suggested alternatively however that coital frequency may be a determining factor. Potter[2] worked out an interesting but a rather theoretical biological model. The woman's fertile period (after allowing for certain defects of the ovum) is now believed to be as short as 18–36 hours during each menstrual cycle (some gynaecologists would estimate even less). The life of the spermatozoon is also known — there seems to be no authenticated case of its surviving more than five days, and most of them die much more rapidly. Potter concluded that, on the basis of these known facts, and certain other evidence, observed fecundabilities were compatible with a coital rate between 7 and 11 per menstrual cycle. Attempts to test this theorem empirically come up against the extreme uncertainty of the evidence about coital frequency. To quote Hogben again, evidence on this subject is all 'anecdotal'; and, moreover, it is a subject on which people are untruthful, not randomly, but systematically. However, so far as it goes, the evidence does give some confirmation of Potter's theories. Stix found no relation between fecundability and recorded coital frequency in the Bronx study, but a marked relationship in Cincinnati, as also did McLeod and Gold (Table I.3).[3]

[1] Private communication.
[2] *Milbank Memorial Quarterly*, January 1961.
[3] *Fertility and Sterility*. Data obtained in 1953.

TABLE I.3.   COITAL FREQUENCY AND FECUNDABILITY

Coital frequency per menstrual cycle	Fecundability (Stix)	Percent conceiving within 5 months (McLeod & Gold)
Under 8	0·110	29
10		46
12	0·134	
14		52
16	0·180	
Over 18	0·206	83

Theoretical calculations by Bourgeois-Pichat[1] for varying coital frequencies (the relationship is highly curved with greatly increased frequencies having comparatively less effect), with the life of the ovum variously assumed at 24, 48 and 72 hours, also conflict with Stix's results. Some recent medical researches, suggesting that the life of the ovum may, however, be as short as 12 hours, may reconcile the conflict between his results and Stix's. Alternatively, there may be a substantial rate of failure to nidate on the part of already fertilized ova, which the calculations have not taken into account.

Some authorities however, particularly Tietze and Potter, have contended that the orders of magnitude of true fecundability were really much higher than these proposed above, while at the same time the rate of foetal mortality (miscarriage), quite apart from deliberate abortion, was also much higher than previously supposed, the two together thus giving a misleading impression of low fecundability. The rate of miscarriage was estimated by Stix at 10–12 per cent, excluding deliberate abortion; by Pearl at 13 per cent, of which about one-fifth represented deliberate abortion (3 per cent for first pregnancies, and 15 per cent for subsequent). The British Royal Commission on Population (1949) estimated 9 per cent, plus 4 per cent still births.

Shapiro, Jones and Decker[2] in New York recorded 6,844 pregnancies, in which they found 14 per cent of intrauterine deaths. For no known reason, the frequency of these miscarriages was sharply peaked in the eleventh week of pregnancy. 72 per cent of them occurred in the fifteenth week or earlier. An inquiry in Hawaii[3] in 1953–6 gave 9 per cent for reported miscarriages. It appeared however that there might be a great deal

[1] Population, May–June 1965.
[2] Milbank Memorial Quarterly, 1962, No. 1.
[3] French & Bierman, U.S. Public Health Reports, 1962 (quoted in Population, June–July 1964).

of undeclared intrauterine mortality, and a complete table of rates was suggested as follows (Table I.4):[1]

TABLE I.4. INTRAUTERINE MORTALITY

Age of mother	Below 20	20–24	25–29	30–34	35–39	40–44
Ratio of intrauterine deaths to live births	0·357	0·258	0·323	0·395	0·672	0·873

The rate of foetal mortality appears[2] to be very high, at the rate of 11 per cent *per month*,[3] at the end of the first month of pregnancy, falling to a level of 0·3 per cent (Shapiro gives 2 per cent) per month at the sixth month of pregnancy, after which it stabilizes. The records of foetal mortality published by many countries appear to refer only to the rate for the later months. It would of course be very interesting to have estimates of foetal mortality in the first weeks, days or even hours of pregnancy, when some authorities think that it may be very much higher: but the bio-chemical methods now known for ascertaining whether conception has taken place do not work reliably for pregnancies of less than a month's duration, and we cannot hope to obtain further information on this interesting subject until we have a method which is reliable during this early period for detecting whether conception has taken place. But even

TABLE I.5. FOETAL MORTALITY IN FRANCE

Age of mother	Foetal mortality	Age of mother	Foetal mortality
15	0·329	20–24	0·164
16	0·279	25–29	0·172
17	0·209	30–34	0·224
18	0·197	35–39	0·320
19	0·178	40–44	0·474
		45–49	0·793

without including any estimate for possible high rates at the very beginning of pregnancy, it appears that we must put average foetal mortality at 30 per cent of conceptions at least.

Bourgeois-Pichat also gives estimates of the rate of foetal mortality to live births for France in 1960–3, which are much lower than those for Hawaii (Table I.5).

Childbirth is usually followed by a period of lactation, of varying length. For the first few months after childbirth Vincent finds that fecundability is

---

[1] *Milbank Memorial Quarterly*, Vol. XL, No. 1, and *Population*, May–June 1965, p. 413.

[2] Bourgeois-Pichat, World Population Conference, 1965. His estimate is for the human race in general, not only for Hawaii, which has, he believes, a below average rate of foetal mortality in the later months of pregnancy.

[3] Throughout these paragraphs the word 'month' is used in the sense of 28 days, or the supposed average menstrual cycle.

almost zero. That this infecundability is physiologically linked with lactation can be demonstrated from the fact that it does not occur after a stillbirth or a neo-natal death. For the subsequent months the situation is more complex. After the first two months, there follow three or four months during which fecundability seems to vary with age. After six months, fecundability appears to vary with age for women under 30, but only varies slightly above the age of 30. However the effect of childbirth on subsequent fecundability only disappears altogether after a lapse of twenty-four months. Henry[1] considers that the variability of the length of this infecundable period after childbirth has a more important effect on the total number of children born than does the variability of fecundability itself. This indeed is confirmed by Vincent's results, which show that there are many women with fecundability below 0·10[2] who have nevertheless borne more than nine children. Henry points out that this infecundable period tends to lengthen with age, and probably also with the number of children previously born, independent of age. Some eighteenth-century data from the village of Crulai (discussed subsequently) appear to indicate that women who had borne six or more children averaged an infecundable period of about 21 months after childbirth.

Henry in a more recent study[3] estimated from a general review of eighteenth-century birth register data that the infecundable period (measured *inclusive* of the period of gestation) is at a minimum of 20 months for women of age up to 30 and that it rises by 0·6 months for each subsequent year of age. The early death of the child may reduce it by anything between five and nine months. In Rwanda[4] 50 per cent of the women were found to show post-partal amenorrhea of 18 months or more (also numerous anovulatory cycles). Ferin thinks that the infecundable period is lengthened not only by the number of children previously born, but also by underfeeding of the mother, and when she does heavy agricultural labour. Dandekar[5] also finds in India a long period of suppression of menstruation after childbirth: this is usually, though not certainly, linked with infecundibility (Table I.6).

If fecundibility averages 0·12 (for approximation we can use this figure and apply the previously supposed rate of foetal mortality), we should nevertheless allow 10 calendar months as the average time required for

---

[1] *Population*, October 1961.
[2] Measured according to previous conceptions of foetal mortality.
[3] *Population*, June–July 1964. He follows this with a further study (*Population*, Oct.–Dec. 1964) in which he designs an ingenious mathematical model to analyse the heterogeneity of fecundabilities, of intrauterine mortality, and of the duration of the infecundable period after conception.
[4] Professor Ferin, University of Louvain, private communication.
[5] *A Demographic Survey of Six Rural Communities*, Gokhale Institute, Poona, 1959.

THE REPRODUCTIVE CAPACITY OF THE HUMAN RACE 9

TABLE I.6. POST-PARTAL AMENORRHEA IN INDIA

Duration of period	Percentage distribution
Under 3 months	11
3– 6 „	7
6–12 „	30
12–18 „	19
18–24 „	23
Over 24 „	10

successful conception, after allowing for miscarriages. This is followed by an infecundable period averaging (inclusive of 9 months' gestation) 20 months, or 30 months in all, i.e. we expect on the average 0·4 births per year of married life, when both husband and wife are fully capable of reproduction, and no attempt is made to restrict conception. A higher rate however is to be expected in a population containing a substantial proportion of newly married.

Bourgeois-Pichat[1] undertakes this calculation more thoroughly, with the new and much higher measures both of fecundability and of foetal mortality, using Potter's estimates of fecundability (which he considers to vary with coital frequency), Dandekar's figure of 14 menstrual cycles for post-partal infertility, and Hawaian foetal mortality figures (Table I.7).

TABLE I.7. COMPUTED BIRTHS PER YEAR OF MARRIAGE

Age of mother	15–19	20–24	25–29	30–34	35–39	40–44	45–49
Fecundability	0·62	0·52	0·47	0·43	0·39	0·33	0·28
Expected live births per year of marriage	0·471	0·474	0·463	0·441	0·420	0·392	0·371

The average of expected live births per year of marriage (with a fertile husband and with no restriction on conception) is 0·433. If there were no foetal mortality it would be 0·492. The proportionate difference is of course much less than the 30 per cent foetal mortality rate (because with a miscarriage the subsequent months of pregnancy and of post-partal infertility are missed).

A rate of precisely 0·4 births per year of marriage is shown by the Hutterites,[2] a rural community of devout Lutherans of German descent in U.S.A., who practise community of goods, and who believe it to be a religious duty to bear as many children as possible. This figure is computed on *all* marriages. It would not however be seriously affected by the exclusion of the 2 per cent found to be infecundable. A lower but

[1] World Population Conference, 1965.
[2] Eaton & Mayer, *Man's capacity to Reproduce*, Glencoe, Illinois, 1954.

uniform rate was found among the rural population of Formosa,[1] who averaged 2·1 years from marriage (probably very early, and not immediately consummated) to first birth, and 2·7 years between subsequent births (i.e. 0·37 births per year of marriage, irrespective of birth order). A study in Delhi in 1952 showed an average of 31 months for all birth intervals after the first, not significantly affected by age at marriage.[2]

A comparative constancy of fecundability was also shown by the small Swedish community in nineteenth-century Estonia,[3] believed not to practise any restriction of conception, living isolated lives, and keeping very precise records, so that each woman's last child (and presumed termination of fecundability, or loss of husband) could be identified. Within the woman's fecundable period, live births per year of marriage remained within the range of 0·31–0·38: these figures appeared to be independent both of age and of duration of marriage.

Girard[4] held that fecundability varied somewhat with age, but considered that evidence from eighteenth-century France, Geneva and Canada showed it to be independent of marriage duration. Blanc and Théodore,[5] analysing African data from Guinea, considered it also to be independent of sequence of birth (except for women aged 20–24).

Statistics of births per year of marriage for any given population will include some first births. Their effect is brought out very clearly in some results[6] for eighteenth-century France, when we compare first entries in each line with those next to the right of them (Table I.8). Henry[7] compiled

TABLE I.8. BIRTHS PER YEAR OF MARRIAGE,
EIGHTEENTH-CENTURY FRANCE

Mother's age at time of marriage	Mother's age at time of birth				
	20–24	25–29	30–34	35–39	40–44
20–24	0·47	0·42	0·42	0·25	0·12
25–29		0·48	0·42	0·29	0·15
30–34			0·44	0·33	0·12
35–39				0·21	0·06

a general average for eighteenth- and nineteenth-century Europe, which is found to be lower than in eighteenth-century Canada,[8] but higher than for

[1] Tuan, *Population Studies*, July 1958.
[2] Thapar, World Population Conference, 1965.
[3] Hyrenius, *Population Studies*, November 1958.
[4] *Population*, July–September 1959.   [5] *Population*, June–July 1960.
[6] Girard, loc. cit., data for Sotteville, averaged with data for Ingouville (*Population*, April–June 1961). Pre-marital conceptions excluded.
[7] *Population*, October–December 1961.
[8] Henripin, Institut National d'Études Démographiques, Cahier No. 22, Travaux et Documents. Marriages of 1700–29.

Guinea,[1] Jamaica,[2] Persia[3] and India.[4] Henry restates his European average for reproductive marriages only (allowance has been made for the estimated increasing proportion of male infertility with advancing age, as well as for female infecundability, using data given later in this chapter). Recently also some early English figures have become available[5] for the parish of Colyton in Devon, for the period 1560–1629 (Table I.9).

TABLE I.9. BIRTHS PER YEAR OF MARRIAGE, VARIOUS POPULATIONS

	Age of Mother						
	15–19	20–24	25–29	30–34	35–39	40–44	45–49
Canada		0·51	0·50	0·48	0·41	0·23	0·03
Delhi	--	0·35	0·31	0·27	0·18	0·08	0·01
Guinea	0·18	0·42ᵃ	0·30	0·25	0·20	0·05	
Jamaica: Married Women	0·37	0·37	0·26	0·18	0·12	0·03	0·01
Unmarried Women cohabiting with men	0·45	0·32	0·19	0·13	0·08	0·03	0·01
Persia		0·40	0·38	0·35	0·30	0·20	
18th- and 19th-century Europe		0·435	0·407	0·371	0·298	0·152	0·022
Do. reproductive marriages only			0·494	0·483	0·443	0·389	
England	0·412	0·467	0·403	0·369	0·302	0·174	0·018

ᵃ For third and subsequent births this falls to 0·25.

Irish data for 1831–41 are available,[6] classified however only by age at marriage, and referring to the first ten years of married life. They appear to be a little lower, about 0·37 births per year of marriage for women in their 20's, and 0·33 for women in their 30's. Japanese data[7] for peasant women, among whom contraception and abortion appear to have been little used, excluding the fully infecundable, still only give a figure of 0·32. An Indian rural sample[8] shows also a figure of 0·32, irrespective of age, so long as fecundability lasts.

Against the above conclusions, however, a study[9] of eighteenth-century data for Saint-Agnan appears to indicate quite a strong relationship between offspring per year of marriage and sequence of birth; though this latter is

[1] Blanc & Théodore, *Population*, June–July 1960.
[2] Roberts, *The Population of Jamaica*.
[3] *Population*, January–March 1954.
[4] Thapar, World Population Conference, 1965 (figures for Delhi).
[5] Wrigley, Economic History Conference, Munich, 1965. The parish suffered a devastating epidemic in 1645 which was followed by a period of two generations or more of late marriage and also of reduced marital fertilities.
[6] K. H. Connell, *The Population of Ireland*.
[7] *Population*, October–December 1953.
[8] J.K. Institute of Sociology and Human Relations, Lucknow, Monograph 6.
[9] *Population*, April–June 1961.

strongly correlated with age, and it is hard to really distinguish the factors at work (Table I.10).

TABLE I.10. AVERAGE INTERVALS BETWEEN BIRTHS (MONTHS)

1st and 2nd	25·5
2nd and 3rd	25·2
3rd and 4th	28·7
Last but three and last but two	29·7
Last but two and last but one	30·5
Last but one and last	32·0

Another interesting historical study in this field was made by Krause.[1] In the Protestant Saxon village of Reinhardtsgrimma he found that the average number of children per marriage (contracted and terminated by death in the village) did not vary significantly between 1597 and 1799 (Table I.11).

TABLE I.11. SEVENTEENTH- AND EIGHTEENTH-CENTURY FERTILITIES

	1600–50	1650–1700	1700–50	1750–99
Average months from marriage to birth of 1st child	23	23	23	18
Do. from 1st to 2nd child	34	32	31	25

The average age of women at marriage rose from 23·6 in 1661 to 25·4 in 1755.

Re-expressing these results in the form of the probability of conception per ovulation, these figures represent, for first births, a probability of only 0·066 before 1750 and of 0·102 after that. The former ratio is much lower than that found nowadays. As we are dealing with first births, it is not likely that conception was restricted, and it is quite possible, from these figures, that there was some actual increase in biological fertility about 1750.

Regarding second births, the probability of conception stood at 0·037 in the first period, rising to 0·057 in the second half of the eighteenth century. These rates are also considerably below those found at the present time. The apparent increase in fertility which took place about 1750 was, in respect of first births, fully accounted for by an increase in fertility among those described as 'cottagers and servants'; but in the case of second births, among all classes. We do not really yet know whether this was just an

---

[1] *Unterschiedliche Fortpflanzungen in 17 und 18 Jahrhunderts.* The probabilities of conception per ovulation mentioned below were calculated on the now obsolete low estimate of foetal mortality.

accidental result for this particular village, and it is to be hoped that further studies in this field will soon be available.

Koller[1] found for Saxony in 1901–2 an average interval of 26·7 months between the first and second child, 28–30 months for all other sequences. He traced the lengthening of these *average* intervals in subsequent years: but both then and now there was a pronounced peak in the frequency distribution of intervals at 14 months (for all sequences up to 10th births in 1901–2). If we accept Vincent's conclusion that the first two months after childbirth are completely infecundable, and deduct these as well as the nine gestation months from Koller's fourteen, we are left with the conclusion that there must be quite a high proportion of conceptions requiring only three months' coition.

In Japan, after abortion had been legalized (during the American occupation), a study[2] of a number of women, two-thirds of whom were over the age of thirty, who had had abortions, showed that about 37 per cent of them again became pregnant within a year. This also represents a high fecundability — no doubt however it had been the most fecund women who had been the principal clients of the abortion clinics. (Muramatsu went on to record that about half of those who so conceived had a second abortion, at a price of about $6.)

In any case, the description of fecundability as constant, or more or less constant, over a considerable range of ages, is only true as a statistical average of a population from which the infecundable have been excluded, and there are clearly great individual variations about the mean. Potter[3] has set out to calculate a coefficient of distribution.

Three distributions of fecundabilities (measured by total offspring in communities which place little or no restriction on conception) about modes of approximately 8 for Brazil and the Hutterites, and a much lower mode for Sudan, are shown in Diagram I.A.

Brass[4] thinks that the distribution of fecundabilities among a population of women, excluding those totally infecundable, defining fecundability as E, is described by a curve of Pearsonian Type III.

$$f(E) = (a^k/\Gamma k)e^{aE}E^{k-1}$$

He then transforms this ingeniously to obtain the expected distribution of total children born throughout the reproductive period; and gets a moderately good fit to some data for African and other 'unplanned'

[1] World Population Conference, 1954.
[2] Muramatsu, World Population Conference, 1954.
[3] *Milbank Memorial Quarterly*, 1960, p. 140.
[4] International Statistical Conference 1957 and *Population Studies*, July 1958.

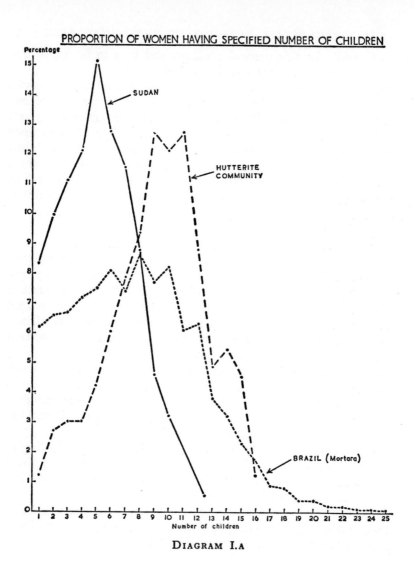

DIAGRAM I.A

populations. However he has to vary his k from 3 to 448, and his a similarly, to fit a pair of neighbouring African tribes.

There is no recognized and reasonably easy technique for fitting curves of Pearsonian Type III. If it could be done, it would be interesting to fit. Some data[1] which might fit Brass's function, of the distribution of the numbers of the months required for conception (i.e. the reciprocal of E)

[1] D. L. Jones, *British Medical Journal*, 25 July 1953.

from a number of *newly married* women interviewed, and expressing the desire to conceive (fecundability being considerably higher for newly married than subsequently), are shown in Table I.12. Those not conceiving in 36 months are regarded as infecundable and excluded. In view of the high proportion of premarital conceptions it is assumed that the average coition began three months before marriage.

TABLE I.12. PERCENTAGE DISTRIBUTIONS OF NUMBER OF MONTHS REQUIRED FOR CONCEPTION IN ENGLAND

	Women Aged			
	20–24	25–29	30–34	35–39
0– 3 months	16	6	9	17
3– 6 ,,	44	40	26	12
6– 9 ,,	20	22	17	12
9–12 ,,	9	11	20	25
12–15 ,,	7	10	7	30
15–21 ,,	2	4	8	4
21–27 ,,	1	3	10	
Over 27 ,,	1	4	3	
Mean months required (approximately)	6·5	8·8	10·4	9·0

Further data on percentage distribution of number of months required for conception are available for Rwanda (Central Africa)[1] (Table I.13).

TABLE I.13. PERCENTAGE DISTRIBUTIONS OF NUMBER OF MONTHS REQUIRED FOR CONCEPTION IN RWANDA

	Non-lactating women[a]	Women lactating for whole interval between births	
	50 Hospital Records	207 Hospital Records	109 Interviews
0– 3 months	38	$\frac{1}{2}$	0
3– 6 ,,	30	$1\frac{1}{2}$	1
6– 9 ,,	6	$5\frac{1}{2}$	3
9–12 ,,	6	$7\frac{1}{2}$	15
12–15 ,,	4	14	8
15–21 ,,	8	38	20
21–27 ,,	6	29	30
27–36 ,,	2	4	16
36–48 ,,	—	—	7

[a] Previous infant died within a week of birth.

The effects of lactation, and also the quicker conception of non-lactating women in Africa than in England, are striking.

The considerably slower conception among older women in England

[1] Professor Ferin, University of Louvain, private communication.

may be due, it has been suggested, to slower resumption of activity of the pituitary gland.

Applicants[1] to contraceptive clinics 'of little prior contraceptive experience', in U.S.A. and Puerto Rico in the 1930's (these data are biased towards the higher fecundabilities, and the authors estimate that their results may be 30–40 per cent too high) show the results given in Table I.14.

TABLE I.14. BIRTHS PER YEAR OF MARRIED LIFE

Urban:		Rural:	
Nashville whites	0·41	W. Virginian whites	0·44
Nashville Negroes	0·46	Tennessee whites	0·41
Puerto Ricans	0·41	Kentucky whites	0·40
		Puerto Ricans	0·47

It is often held that three or more years of married life without conception, when no attempt has been made to prevent it, is evidence of complete incapacity to reproduce, in one spouse or the other. But cases are reported of first conceptions after as long as twenty years of married life — their significance however, depends on the validity of the evidence of absence of contraception, separation, etc. However Dandekar's figures[2] for India, where it can be assumed that there is virtually no restriction of conception, show that there may be a very wide distribution of fecundabilities — even after we have allowed for the fact that some (by no means all) marriages are contracted very young, and not consummated until the wife has reached 16 or 17 (Table I.15).

TABLE I.15. PERCENTAGES OF MARRIAGES INFERTILE

Duration of marriage in years	Without childbirth	Without conception
5– 9	17·5	
10–14	7·3	
15–19	5·2	
20–24	4·7	4·3
25 and over	4·7	4·3

Infecundibility is generally measured, in view of the limitations of data available, by classifying, according to the woman's age at time of marriage, marriages found to be ultimately childless — assuming that no fecundable couple carry contraception to the point of voluntarily leaving themselves completely childless. Even if this assumption is true, there remain however the possibilities that contraception may have been used for a number of years of marriage and only terminated after the woman's fecundable period

---

[1] Beebe & Overton, *Journal of the American Medical Association*, 28 March 1942.
[2] *A Demographic Survey of Six Rural Communities*, Gokhale Institute, Poona

had ended; also that in some cases fecundability is present, but low, and the marriage may not have lasted long enough for it to be effective; and that childle$s women may have had conceptions, followed by miscarriage or abortion.

But there is a graver objection to this method than any of these. The measurement of infecundability by the proportion of women ultimately found childless is biased because the most fecund tend to marry early (there is more than one possible reason for this), the least fecund to marry late. This difference is brought out very clearly in the Swedish–Estonian study by Hyrenius,[1] when he measured the ages at which conception ceased, in a population believed to practise no contraception (Table I.16).

TABLE I.16. ESTIMATED AGES OF CEASING CONCEPTION

Age-group	Women found ultimately childless as percentage of age-group for specified age at first marriage	Marriages at which offspring ceased at specified age as percentage of all married women in that age-group
15–19	2	0
20–24	6	1·4
25–29	15	1·6
30–34	}20	2·4
35–39		7·9
40–44		28·4
45–49		63·0

The weighted mean age at which offspring ceased was 45. In the first column, there seems to be a clear bias, with the relatively infecundable marrying later. The second column is of course also biased — a woman has to have at least one child in order to enter it, and the permanently infecundable, and those who had become infecundable by the time of their marriage, are therefore excluded. The general average lies somewhere between the columns: but we can see how far apart they are. The only hope of good information appears to be from small samples examined by expert interviewers, to whom women are willing to disclose the extent of voluntary restriction of conception.[2]

We may now assemble the evidence about the proportions of infecundability among women at various ages. The proportions for French Canada are believed by some French demographers to be exceptionally low: it was a population which had been specially selected for vigour and vitality. It is

[1] *Population Studies*, November 1958.
[2] Part of the difference may be accounted for by the fact, attested by gynaecologists, that certain minor pathological conditions destructive of fecundability are much more likely to occur in women who have long delayed childbearing.

interesting to see that the proportion of infecundability in Japan appears to be considerably higher than in England or the United States (Table I.17).

The British Royal Commission on Population estimated that 8 per cent of all marriages were completely infertile, and that this proportion had not changed since the 1860's, in a community which, throughout the period under review, had been comparatively late-marrying. Vincent[1] obtained similar results for England and Wales in 1911 and for rural Quebec in 1941, namely that 6 per cent of all married women were infecundable at the age of 20–24, 18 per cent at 30–34, and 33 per cent at 35–39. He also made a search among the conjugal condition tables in the census records of various countries, distinguishing occupations where possible, to find minimum figures of the proportions of childless marriages. Among the white population of South Africa in 1921, for women marrying under the age of 20, the percentage was only 2·3. For women marrying under the age of 25, for Dutch farm workers in 1930 and for French miners in 1906, the percentages were 2·3 and 2·8 respectively. These results, however, he considered to be generally too low, and to exemplify the bias already discussed, of the more fecundable women tending to marry early. Particularly in the case of women marrying below the age of 20, such groups may contain a substantial proportion of women who have married because they have become pre-maritally pregnant. He considered that such results are more likely to be found among miners and farm workers than among other social groups. The order of magnitude of total infecundability appears to be at least 3 per cent, even at the most favourable age.

The Census of the State of Travancore in India shows about 4 per cent totally infecundable in 1941, as did Dandekar's figures. A sample[2] of Annamite women in Vietnam showed only 2–3 per cent who had never borne a child. Among the Hutterites,[3] the proportion was found to be 2·7 per cent among those born before 1896 and only 1·8 per cent among those born 1896–1905. The Hutterites are one of the communities who are 'breeding out' their infecundable strains.

Much higher figures of infecundability however may sometimes prevail. Among the primitive tribesmen of the Andaman Islands,[4] who have been rapidly dying out, the proportion of childlessness appears to have been quite exceptional. A special inquiry in the Census of 1901 showed 45 per cent (average total offspring only 1·2) among women who had only one husband, 35 per cent (average total offspring 1·9) among those who had two or more. Male infertility may have been an important factor here. A

---

[1] *Population*, January–March 1950.   [2] *Population Index*, April 1945.
[3] Eaton & Mayer, *Man's Capacity to Reproduce*, Glencoe, Illinois, 1954.
[4] Cappieri, World Population Conference, 1954.

TABLE I.17. PERCENTAGES OF INFECUNDABILITY IN MARRIED WOMEN BY AGE

	Japan present day[b]	Delhi 1952[h]	French Canada 18th century	U.S.A. 1931-2[c]	Estonian[a] Swedes	Average based on European historical data[e]	England and Wales		
							1951-2[g]	1851[a]	Do. expressed as average number of years of fertile married life expected by women marrying at age specified
15–19			3·7				3·7	0·5	25·8
20	4½	4							20·9
20–24			2·5		2	3	6·5	3·0	16·1
25	10	12							
25–29			5·0	8	9	6	8·8	6·5	11·6
30	21	23							
30–34			8·1	19	16	10	10·4	11·5	7·3
35	33	44							
35–39			17·2	31	26	16		19·0	3·6
40	53	69							
40–44			29·6	48	52 / 80[f]	31		32·5	0·8
45	85	95							
45–49			—		95			60·5	
50	100							100·0	

[a] Henry, *Population*, October–December 1961.
[b] *Population*, October–December 1953.
[c] Deduced from Stix's results (see Table I.2.), assuming age at marriage 25.
[d] Hyrenius, *Population Studies*, November 1958.
[e] Henry, World Population Conference, 1954.
[f] Age 43.
[g] D. L. Jones, *British Medical Journal*, 25 July 1953.
[h] Thapar, World Population Conference 1965.

study[1] in 1935 on the island of Yapca showed that 31 per cent of the women were infecundable, and that those who had conceived had only averaged 3 conceptions by the age of 40. Gonorrhea was found in 25 per cent of the men and 43 per cent of the women. The proportion of childless marriages shown by the Census of Sudan was also high, with figures ranging from 2·5 per cent to 10 per cent for various districts, and a median amount of 6·2 per cent.

Ardener[2] found in a Cameroon village (Bakweri Tribe) an ominous increase in the proportion of infecundability from 9·6 per cent among the women over 45 to 16·2 per cent among the women aged 35–44, which he thought might be due to the spread of venereal disease. Morgantini[3] in Italian Somaliland found 10 per cent and 14 per cent for the respective age-groups, and also 12 per cent still births. Blanc and Théodore[4] found 8 per cent in the Niger Delta.

In a recently completed study[5] Bourgeois-Pichat, from data of distribution of families by size, and assuming a 2½-year interval between births,

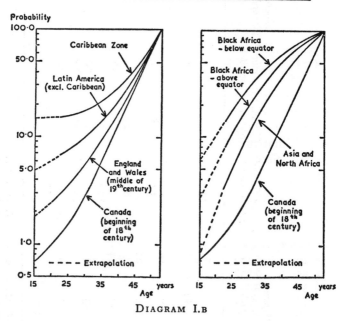

PERCENTAGES OF INFERTILE MARRIAGES AT DIFFERENT AGES
AS SHOWN BY MOTHER'S AGE AT BIRTH OF LAST CHILD.

DIAGRAM I.B

[1] Quoted by UNESCO, *Culture and Human Fertility*, p. 137.
[2] *Divorce and Fertility* and *Plantation and Village in the Cameroons*.
[3] World Population Conference, 1954.   [4] *Population*, June–July 1960.
[5] *Population*, May–June 1965.

boldly generalizes the proportions of infecundability by age for different regions of the world. Eighteenth-century Canada shows outstandingly low figures; Africa and the Caribbean countries the highest (Diagram I.B).

An interesting indication of the relative significance of male infertility with increasing age is shown in Table I.18. for Ireland, a country of customary late marriage, but of very little restriction of conception within marriage, where the (comparatively few) early marriages produce large families. By reading down the columns, the effect of male infertility increasing with age is discernible, though not very marked.

TABLE I.18. MALE AND FEMALE FERTILITY BY AGE

Average number of children born (excluding children from previous marriages) to married women, with marriages of 30–35 years' duration, and with husbands still living, classified by age of wife and of husband at marriage, Census of Ireland 1946.

Husband's age at marriage	Wife's age at marriage				
	15–19	20–24	25–29	30–34	35–39
15–19	7·15	6·17	4·68	4·72	
20–24	7·79	6·37	5·23	4·09	2·82
25–29	6·96	6·04	4·87	3·94	2·38
30–34	6·79	6·15	4·99	3·83	2·47
35–39	6·82	6·12	5·05	3·92	2·53
40–44	5·66	5·86	4·95	3·93	2·25
45–54	5·92	6·38	4·69	3·63	2·44

In India[1] Sovani examined the frequency of births per year per married woman in age groups. Having shown that it appeared to be predominantly a function of the age of the woman and that, for a given age, it seemed to be independent of duration of marriage or age at marriage, he then proceeded to examine the effect of differences of age between husband and wife (Table I.19).

TABLE I.19. EFFECT OF HUSBAND'S AGE ON FERTILITY
Excess of age of husband over wife

Mother's age	Negative	0–9 yrs.	10–14 yrs.	15–19 yrs.	20 yrs. & over
16–20	0·189	0·232	0·214	0·197	0·163
21–25	0·230	0·273	0·255	0·238	0·204
26–30	0·208	0·251	0·233	0·216	0·182
31–35	0·157	0·200	0·182	0·165	0·131
36–40	0·076	0·119	0·102	0·085	0·050
41–45	0·008	0·051	0·033	0·016	—
46–50	—	0·016	—	—	—

[1] *Social Survey of Kolhapur City*, Gokhale Institute, Poona.

The effects of increasing age of husband are discernible, though the reducing effect of young husbands on the fecundability of women in all age groups is rather puzzling.

Very early marriage (as in India) appears[1] to increase the proportion of childlessness, partially offset by the longer duration of fecundability (measured by the number of years between the first and last childbirth — it is presumed that the sample is confined to those whose husbands remained alive throughout the fecundable period): those whose first childbirth was at the age of 16 or less showed an average duration of fecundability of 20 years, others 18 years. Sinha[2] obtains the following figures for India (Table I.20).

TABLE I.20.   EFFECTS OF AGE AT MARRIAGE

Age	Interval before first live birth, years	Total births
Under 13	5·0	7·8
13–15	3·2	8·1
16–18	2·5	8·4
19–21	1·7	7·5
22–24	1·7	7 approx.

N.B. The interval is measured from consummation, not from the formal date of marriage.

Likewise Bourgeois-Pichat[3] points out that women recorded in the Census of Scotland of 1911 who had completed their reproductive period showed average total offspring of 8·5 if married at 16 or less (apparently legal in mid-Victorian Scotland), 9·5 if married at 17, less if married later.

By multiplying together the average number of children which can be expected per year of marriage, and the expected duration of fecundable married life, we can obtain the maximum expected family — not the maximum expected for any individual woman which, as the figures for Brazil show, may be nearly as high as 25 — but the maximum which can be expected as an average for a population, in which every woman marries as early as possible, and does not restrict conception; and subject to the further condition that both she and her husband live to the end of her fecundable period — which is by no means always the case. Sauvy[4] estimates this figure, on data for white populations, at 10–12; on evidence which we have for Asian populations, with the average period of fecunda-

[1] J.K. Institute of Sociology and Human Relations, Lucknow, Monograph No. 6 — based on 202 rural mothers of completed fertility.
[2] International Statistical Institute Proceedings, 1951 Conference.
[3] *Mesure de la Fécondité des Populations*, 1950.   [4] *Fertility and Survival.*

bility apparently only of 20 years, and probably a lower figure of expected births per year of marriage, it may be put at only 7 or 8.

Some generalization is possible[1] about the average durations of fertile married life in different parts of the world for women who survive to the end of their reproductive period (though their husbands may not always do so (Table I.21).

TABLE I.21. AVERAGE DURATION OF FECUNDABLE
MARRIED LIFE

	Percentages of women married at ages:						Average duration of married life between ages 15 and 45
	15–19	20–24	25–29	30–34	35–39	40–44	
Africa south of Sahara	60	92	95	95	95	87	26·1
North Africa	30	75	88	88	86	78	27·5
Asia	35	80	92	92	90	85	23·4
Latin America	20	55	70	75	75	70	18·2
Europe and other countries of European civilization	5	45	70	80	80	80	18·0

Late marriage in Latin America is noticeable.

In most cases it is difficult to obtain records showing in how many cases the husband survived, and lived with the wife, until the end of their fecundable period. It is on the other hand comparatively easy to obtain large numbers of data of the total number of children born (whether surviving or not) to women who have reached the end of their fecundable period. These figures are defined as 'total fertilities'. The colloquial phrase 'average family' may also be used here, so long as the user makes it clear that it refers only to average *completed* family, and does not include in this average any families of those wives who are still young and may have an expectation of further increasing them. This figure will be lower than the theoretical figures considered above to the extent that some women may have been without husbands for the latter part of their fecundable period — or, for that matter, at intervals during it. This difference will be of less significance in some communities, e.g. in Africa where there is a large surplus of males, and widowed women can expect quick re-marriage; it will on the other hand be of great significance in India, where the re-marriage of widows is forbidden in practising Hindu families. It should be remembered also that the quoted figures of total fertility, unless they

[1] Bourgeois-Pichat, *Population*, May–June 1965.

TABLE I.22. TOTAL FERTILITIES

AFRICA[a]

Angola	3·6–4·2	Ethiopia[cc] rural	5·1	Republic of the	
Ashanti[b]	6·2	,, urban	3·3	Congo (formerly	
Buganda[b]	2·9	Fouta Djallou[e]	5·5	French)	4·6
Buhaga[b]	3·3	Ghana	5·1–6·6	Reunion[p]	6·4
Cameroons[c]	6·3	Guinea	5·5	Senegal[q]	6·5
Central African		Ivory Coast[f]	6·5	South Africa	
Republic	4·2	Kenya	5·3	(urban Bantu)	4·9
Congo (formerly		Mauritius[p]	5·5	Rhodesia	5·7
Belgian)	4·2	Mozambique	3·5–3·8	Sudan[h]	4·9
Egypt[d]	6·2–6·4	Niger Delta[g] rural	4·7	Swaziland	4·5
do. for		,, ,, urban	4·5	Tanganyika	4·4
married women		Portuguese Guinea	3·3	Togo	6·2
with surviving				Uganda	4·8
husbands	7·4			Zambia	5·9

AMERICA

Barbados[n] 1909–13		5·5	British Guiana[n, o] 1909–13		3·6
1950–2		4·5	1950–2		6·4
Brazil[i] 1940		6·3	El Salvador[p] 1961		6·6
Do. exc. childless women[j]		7·4	French Canada, marriages of		
Do. married below 20[k]		8·8	1666–81[k, l]		9·0
Do. married below 20–24[k]		7·6	Do. 1941, rural		
French Guiana[r]: Boni		7·9	married under 20[k, m]		9·9
Oayana		3·7	Trinidad 1889–1933[v]		4·2
Grenada[s, t]		6·1	1941–52[v]		5·4
Jamaica[s] 1844–1923		5·4	1960[u]		5·5
1950–52		4·7	United States, rural farm coloured		
Mexico[u] 1960		6·4	women born before 1865[w]		7·3
Panama[u] 1961		5·3	Hutterites[x] born before 1896		10·2
			Hutterites[x] born 1896–1905		10·6

ASIA

Ceylon[y]	4·8
China[z]	6·35
Manchuria[aa]	5·3–7·3
Formosa[bb]: women born	
1888–97	6·9
1898–1907	7·2
1908–1917	7·0

[a] Data assembled by Spengler in *Economic Development for Africa South of Sahara* (International Economic Association), pages 288–9 unless otherwise specified. See also Myburgh, *Population Studies*, 1956.

[b] Lorimer, *Demographic Information on Tropical Africa*, Boston, 1961.

[c] Republic of Cameroon, Ministry of Economic Affairs, *The Population of West Cameroon*, 1964. However Ardener (*Plantation and Village in the Cameroons*) finds 2·9 for the older women of the Bakweri tribe, less for the younger.

[d] El Badry, *Milbank Memorial Quarterly*, January 1956. Includes children by earlier marriages of divorced women.

[e] In West Africa. Blanc, *Problems in African Demography*, Union Internationale pour l'Étude Scientifique de la Population, 1960.

[f] *Enquête Nutrition — Niveau de Vie* 1955–6. 39 per cent of the women recorded were polygamous.

[g] Blanc & Théodore, *Population*, June–July 1960.

[h] Census shows regional figures ranging from 4·2 to 5·4.

[i] Mortara, *Revista Brasiliera de Estadística*, 1947 and 1948. In the industrialized state of São Paulo figures were not significantly different (ibid. January–March 1954). Total fertility had fallen a little by 1950 (ibid. July–September 1956).

[j] The proportion childless at age 45–49 in 1950 was 16 per cent for the population as a whole, 20 per cent for negresses and 7 per cent for women of Japanese descent. These differences however may only represent varying probabilities of marriage (Mortara, International Population Conference, Vienna, 1959).

[k] UNESCO, *Culture and Human Fertility*.

[l] An earlier estimate of 10·3 by Sabagh (*American Journal of Sociology*, Vol. 47, No. 5) is criticized.

[m] Charles, *Trends in Canadian Family Size* (Report of 1941 Census), finds average of 10·3 and mode of 13 for women over 65 in 1941.

[n] Roberts, *The Population of Jamaica*.

[o] The Census of 1946 (quoted in *Population Index*, June 1952) showed that, at age 45–54, women of East Indian descent who had ever conceived had 5·8 children, of African descent 4·75. The proportion childless (whether through infecundability or through remaining unmarried) was 10 per cent for East Indians and 21 per cent for Africans.

Comparison of age groups also appears to show rising Indian and declining African fecundability:

Age at time of Census	Total fertility per woman		Total fertility per married woman	
	African	Indian	African	Indian
40–44	3·5	5·4	4·4	5·9
45–54	3·75	5·2	4·75	5·8
55–64	3·95	4·75	4·95	5·35
65 and over	4·5	4·85	5·45	5·4

[p] Computed from specific fertilities of age groups.

[q] Cantrelle, World Population Conference, 1965.

[r] Hurault, *Population*, July–September 1959. The Oayana are indigenous, and the Boni descended from escaped African slaves: however they live side by side under similar conditions.

[s] Roberts, *The Population of Jamaica*.

[t] About the same level of total fertility has prevailed since 1879.

[u] Computed from specific fertilities of age-groups given in UN Demographic Year Book.

[v] Roberts, *The Population of Jamaica*.

[w] Grabill and others, *The Fertility of American Women*.

[x] Eaton & Mayer, *Man's Capacity to Reproduce*, Glencoe, Illinois, 1954.

[y] Census of 1946.

[z] *An Experiment in the Registration of Vital Statistics in China*, Scripps Foundation, 1934.

[aa] Taeuber, *Milbank Memorial Quarterly*, January 1947.

[bb] Tuan, *Population Studies*, July 1958. Rural families only. A further study (*Population Studies*, March 1963) shows that the total fertility of subsequent generations will be considerably lower. The fall in specific fertilities began quite suddenly about 1956. A further study, however, (Fan, World Population Conference, 1965) shows that this is mostly due to a sudden change in age at marriage. Between 1959 and 1964 fertility in marriage has been increasing for women under 30, and decreasing rapidly above that age. The older women however make a relatively much smaller contribution to the total.

[cc] Central Statistical Office of Ethiopia, *Report on a Survey of Shoa Province*, 1966. Marital fertilities for women over 15 were 5·1 rural and 8·1 urban — in the towns the divorce rate is very high.

ASIA—*contd.*
India[n]

	All women			Married women			Married women not widowed		
	1931	1941	1951	1931	1941	1951	1931	1941	1951
All India	5·5[k]								6·4[o]
States: Ajmer-Merwara		5·78						6·1	
Bengal	6·3[d]	5·5[k]							
Cochin (Kerala)[l]					6·37				
Kashmir								4·91	
Mysore					5·17			6·20	
Travancore (Kerala)					5·29		6·50	6·65	
Cities: Ahmedabad[m]		4·88							
Bangalore		3·88							
Bombay[m]		3·68							
Delhi								4·91	
Kolhapur[m]					5·43				
Urban Areas[a]:			5·14			6·52			
Rural Areas:									
Maharashtra[o]			5·0						
Uttar Pradesh[b]			5·5			6·0[p]			
Primitive Tribes[e]									6·3

Indonesia, rural[f] married women (approx.) 6·2　　Philippines[q] 6·5
　　　　　　　all women (approx.) 5·6　　Singapore 1959[v, g] 6·75
　　　　　　　　　　　　　　　　　　　Vietnam[r] 5·2

Japan (1868)[w] 6·5-7·3
Korea[s] 1925 7·1
　　　　1930's 6·9
Palestine Arabs 1931[t] 6·8

EUROPE
18th and 19th centuries[h] 8·4
Married women
Bulgaria[u]　1900-4 6·7
　　　　　　1905-9 6·5
England and Wales[t]
Married women
　(married 1861-71)
　married 15-19 8·4
　married 20-24 7·0
Russia (Ukraine)[u] 1897- 7·5
Azerbaijan　　1910-41 8·15
Armenia　　　1910-41 8·30

OCEANIA
Fiji[j]: Fijians:　1946 5·0
　　　　　　　　1956 5·2
　East Indians: 1946 6·6
　　　　　　　　1956 6·8

[a] Jain, *Indian Journal of Medical Research*, April 1951 andWorld Population Conference, 1954, (sample for 1946–8).
[b] Institute of Sociology, Lucknow, Monograph No. 6.
[c] J. K. Dandekar, *A Demographic Survey of Six Rural Communities*, Gokhale Institute, Poona.
[d] Ghosh, *Population Studies*, March 1956.
[e] Mujumdar (Department of Anthropology, Lucknow University), World Population Conference, 1954. This total fertility is measured for cases where both husband and wife survive to the end of the woman's fecundable period. Abortion is said to be frequent among them. One tribe which is polyandrous had a total fertility of 5·2.
[f] Village of Djabres, Central Java, 1955 (*Economics and Finance in Indonesia*, December 1956).
[g] Since 1959 there has been a rapid fall in the number of births in Singapore.
[h] Obtained by summing Henry's general average of specific fertilities (*Population*, October–December 1961) assuming 20 as average age of marriage.
[i] UNESCO, *Culture and Human Fertility*, Data confined to marriage where wife *and* husband survived until 1911.
[j] McArthur, *Population Studies*, March 1959. The descendants of the Indian immigrants (who now outnumber the Fijians) not only marry earlier but also show higher fecundity in marriage.
[k] Approximate from small sample.
[l] Rama Varna, unpublished thesis, privately communicated (sample inquiry, 1937).
[m] Samples for 1940–2 (1941–5 for Kolhapur) Gokhale Institute, Publication No. 18. 1954 (sample for 1946–8).
[n] Census data (including some data for Princely States in 1941) where not otherwise stated.
[o] Census sample for Eastern, Western and South Western Districts of Madhya Pradesh, and for Travancore-Cochin (Kerala).
[p] Excluding childless marriages.
[q] *Public Health and Demography in the Far East*, Rockefeller Foundation, 1950.
[r] *Population Index*, April 1945.
[s] *Population Index*, October 1944.
[t] Hinden, *Sociological Review*, January–April 1940.
[u] Kuczyński, *Economica*, May 1935.
[v] Computed from specific fertilities of age-groups given in UN Demographic Year Book.
[w] Taeuber, *Milbank Memorial Quarterly*, January 1947.

are specified as applying to fertile married women only, will generally be for the total female population, including some who have remained unmarried, and some of whom who have been permanently infecundable in marriage.

In Table I.22 are given a number of data of total fertility for communities in Africa, Asia and Latin America now, and some in Europe in the past, where little or no restriction of conception is believed to have been practised. In almost every case they are considerably below the theoretical figures. This may indicate that, even in these communities, marriage is often later than the theoretical minimum age, that a certain proportion of women may remain unmarried, that the proportion of infecundability may be higher than expected — or that conception is in fact to some extent restricted by various methods.

Total fertility can only be measured directly at the end of the reproductive period of the women to whom it refers, and therefore a number of years after the actual time of its occurrence. A more sophisticated method, which makes it possible to estimate contemporary total fertility, depends upon the availability of statistics of the number of women in each age group — in communities of high total fertility these are not often available for the whole country, but may be available for sample populations. The number of births to mothers in each age group, divided by the total number of women in the age group, is defined as the specific fertility of the age group. The alternative definition of total fertility is the number of children born to a hypothetical woman who had passed in succession through each of the age groups, undergoing the specific fertility which each age group shows *at the present time*. This is computed by adding together the specific fertilities of the age groups, and then multiplying the sum by five (because it is customary to prepare records in quinquennial age groups, and the hypothetical woman in question is to be supposed to have spent five years in each age group).

Sauvy's theoretical figure is hardly ever obtained, except among the Hutterites, and in eighteenth-century French Canada. It seems clear that there are hardly any communities where every girl marries at the lowest possible age. Even where we do isolate early marrying groups, as in Europe, total fertilities still appear to be only of the order of 8. After all, it must be remembered that there are distinct probabilities of widowhood without re-marriage.

In comparison with Europeans not restricting conception, Asians definitely show lower total fertilities. They appear to have a higher proportion of infecundable women at any given age, and also a lower rate of fecundability in marriage. The figures for India are brought lower still by the Hindu religious prohibition on the re-marriage of widows.

Total fertilities are at their lowest in Africa — in some countries quite surprisingly so. We have already seen some information which gives us some idea of the cause. There appear to be quite high proportions of total infecundability (Myburgh gives as much as 17 per cent for Tanganyika) and probably many more couples whose fecundability is reduced by disease. Total infertility in Egypt in 1960[1] was 11 per cent in the large cities and 7 per cent in the rest of Egypt.

Hurault[2] gives us the converse picture, of an area in French Guiana for which we happen to have precise mission records of births in the eighteenth century, where health, and consequently fecundability, is improving (Table I.23).

In addition, the continued prevalence of polygamy in West Africa probably has a substantial effect in reducing the average total fertility. (It

[1] Zikry, World Population Conference, 1965.
[2] *Population*, September–October 1965.

TABLE I.23. MARITAL FERTILITIES IN FRENCH GUIANA

		Mothers born	
Ages	Births of 1731–63	1890–1920	Since 1920
13–17	0·297		
18–22	0·310	0·317	0·386
23–27	0·305	0·365	0·417
28–32	}0·274	0·369	0·481
33–37		0·323	
38–42		0·272	
43–47		0·129	
48–52		0·029	

might possibly have the opposite effect in a community in which the number of males had been quite abnormally reduced by war; but these circumstances do not often arise). Thus the Likonala Tribe in the French Congo[1] were estimated to show 25 per cent complete infertility (possibly due to drugs), and a total fertility of 4 per fertile woman, or 3 in all. The tribe was polygamous, which French administrators in general regarded as a factor reducing fertility (on the grounds that the older women in a polygamous family are not given a fair chance of conceiving — however in some cases the customs of the tribe require that, in a polygamous marriage, the wives should have access to the husband in strict rotation). The customs of this tribe also require complete abstinence during lactation.

With this low fertility, and an African mortality rate, the tribe is decreasing, and lost 17 per cent of its numbers between 1933 and 1952.

It is unlikely that these wide differences in total fertility can be explained by differences in climate and diet — few, if any, have in fact suggested that they could be. We have seen in fact a remarkable series of examples of very different total fertilities in different communities living side by side under more or less similar conditions — the Indians and Africans in British Guiana, the Indians and the Polynesians in Fiji, and, most striking of all, the Boni and Oayana in French Guiana. Another striking difference is in Malaya,[2] where *net* reproduction rates are estimated at 1·7 for the population of Malay descent, 2·6 for those of Chinese descent, and even higher for those of Indian.

It does not suffice to describe these differences as due to 'race': they are not necessarily genetic in origin (though they might be). They may also be

[1] Croquevielle, *Population*, July–September 1953.
[2] Smith, *Population Growth in Malaya* (Royal Institute of International Affairs, London, 1952). For definition of net and gross reproduction rates see Chapter II.

of social origin, and may reflect differences between the inherent desires of the different peoples to multiply, if psychosomatic factors are important in explaining differences of individual fecundability.

This theory is indeed borne out by some recent figures for Singapore,[1] where the Malayan situation is reversed, and the Chinese are the majority. The great fall in fertility which has taken place since 1957 has affected them differentially (Table I.24).

TABLE I.24. GROSS REPRODUCTION RATES IN SINGAPORE

	Chinese	Malaysians	Indians and Pakistanis
1957	3·17	3·03	3·58
1961	2·64	3·29	3·24

There remain for solution several problems of a strictly biological nature concerning human reproduction, of considerable intrinsic interest, concerning which it appears that there is much research still to be done.

The ratio of male to female births is usually about 1·05, but it is subject to strange variations with both time and place. Some very high figures for the male ratio at birth have been quoted occasionally for some Asian countries. Some demographers have believed that these conceal a certain amount of female infanticide. Chi-Ming Chao, who was associated with Buck's large-scale agricultural inquiry in China, recorded however[2] that a sample taken in a hospital, under strictly controlled conditions, still showed a ratio of 1 : 10.

Among the African studies, Ardener's figure for the Bakweri in the Cameroons was 1·06, but Morgantini's figure for Somaliland was 1·09 and Cantrelle's was 1·10.

This subject of sex ratios was reviewed by Parkes.[3] He pointed out that, in pigs and hamsters, the male ratio at the time of conception was approximately 1·5. (It is however known that the sow and the rabbit, as compared with all other animals, have very high rates of intrauterine mortality). He thought that, for human beings, the ratio at conception might be somewhere between 1·25 and 1·5: and expressed a hope that he might receive material for further researches from 'mass abortion programmes'.

[1] Chung, World Population Conference, 1965.
[2] *Milbank Memorial Quarterly*, October 1933 and April 1934. However, Ramachandra and Deshpande (*Milbank Memorial Quarterly*, April 1964), point out that hospital figures may be biased upwards because male infants, being larger, are more likely to be subject to difficult birth, and therefore brought to hospital.
[3] *Man and His Future*, CIBA Foundation, 1963.

It will be seen from Diagram I.c that in England and Wales (and it has also been observed in other countries), there is a tendency for the male ratio to show a rise in war periods. This interesting and undoubted fact has tempted biologists to speculate over some meta-biological force (to use one of Bernard Shaw's phrases) at work, attempting to redress the losses of war.

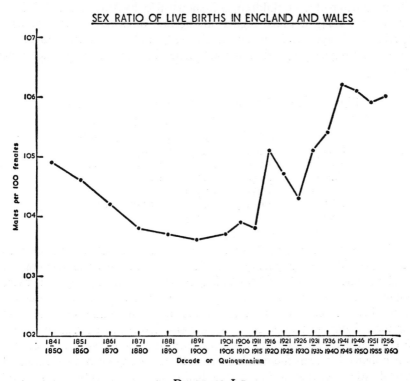

DIAGRAM I.c

In 1915 Tschuprow, who was aware that pre-natal mortality was much higher for males than for females, suggested that variations in the sex ratio might be explainable by changes in the proportions of miscarriages and still births, and that for some reason the amount of pre-natal mortality might decline in war-time.

It was also suggested that the age of the mother might play a part. The statistics of births in England and Wales in 1939, for instance, show a ratio of 1·06 when the mother is under 25, falling steadily to 1·025 for mothers aged 40–44, and 0·96 for the few births which occur to mothers of 45 and over. But a more thorough study by W. T. Russell,[1] using American data, showed that, where other variables were controlled, the ratio appeared to be independent of the age of the mother, but might fall slightly with increasing age of the father. Myers[2] stated categorically that sex ratio was determined by birth order, independently of mother's age. The mystery of the war-time ratios appears to have been finally cleared up by W. J. Martin.[3] The proportion of male children, as is shown alike by American and French data (Table I.25), is much higher among first births. In periods of war, marriages always tend to be accelerated, and first births therefore represent a bigger proportion of total births than they do in a peace-time year.

TABLE I.25. SEX RATIO BY ORDER OF BIRTH

	U.S.A.	France (1912)	U.S.A. (white)	U.S.A. (coloured)
First	1·061	1·075	1·067	1·024
Second	1·060	1·037	1·061	1·031
Third	1·050	1·051	1·054	1·026
Fourth	1·055	1·039		
Fifth	1·051	1·035	1·052	1·018
Sixth		1·022		

The other problem is that of twinning and multiple births. This has been the subject of an excellent scientific review by the Registrar General for England and Wales.[4] The monozygotic, less frequent, type of twins originate from the splitting of a single ovum. Monozygotic twins resemble each other very closely indeed, and are always of the same sex. The more common dizygotic type arises from the simultaneous fertilization of two ova. There is no necessity for dizygotic twins to be of the same sex, and the resemblance between them is less close. By assuming even distribution of probabilities, i.e. that approximately half of all the dizygotic twins would be of the same sex, the Registrar General has estimated the proportion of monozygotic twins.

Over a long period of years it has shown no measurable trend. Monozygotic twins have averaged 3·52 per 1000 legitimate births (3·29 per 1000 illegitimate births). This proportion is however affected by age of mother, rising gradually from 3·24 for mothers under the age of 20 to 3·61 for mothers aged 40–44.

[1] *Journal of Hygiene*, 1936.
[2] *Milbank Memorial Quarterly*, July 1954.
[3] *The Lancet*, 25 December 1943.
[4] Annual Report 1956.

The proportion of dizygotic twins, on the other hand, for some reason unknown, has shown a marked rising tendency since 1938. This is also a function of the mother's age, but in quite a different manner, standing at 3·2 per 1000 legitimate births for mothers under the age of 20, rising to a maximum of 13·5 for mothers aged 35 to 39, and then again falling rapidly to 2·7 for mothers aged over 45.

The corresponding illegitimate figures are 2·0, 16·6, and 5·4. Why these ratios should show this curious peak for women in their late 30's is not known.

NOTE

Some estimates have been collected[a] of probabilities of conception under various circumstances. They have been calculated by the 'exposure' method and therefore (for the reason given on page 2) understate the fecundability of those who are not trying to avoid conception.

	Rate of conception per year
No attempt to avoid conception	0·80
Using contraceptives: male apparatus	0·11 –0·28
„ „ female apparatus	0·08 –0·33
„ „ intra-uterine devices	0·005–0·037
„ „ pills	0·004–0·017
Confining coitus to agenetic period	0·14
„ „ only after ovulation	0·01 or less

The belief frequently expressed that female desire is at its maximum during the period of ovulation is discountenanced by some inquires by Hart.[b]

[a] Drs. Tietze and Marshall, private communications.
[b] *British Medical Journal* 1960, p. 1023.

CHAPTER II

Survival and Growth

THE first step in demographic analysis was to compute so-called birth rates and death rates, or numbers of births and deaths per year, expressed per thousand of existing population. For much of the world even this simple information is still not available. It can only be obtained by a system of registration of births and deaths, which we take for granted, but which in fact is only possible with a reasonably literate population, and a widely diffused network of responsible public officials. Complete systems of birth and death registration are still found in only six countries in Asia (Japan and five small countries), three in Africa and three in Latin America. For other countries (for most of the world, in fact) we have to rely upon estimates, based on samples or on indirect sources of information, which sometimes may be quite wide of the mark.

Birth and death registration was first introduced in Sweden, in the mid-eighteenth century. It came with compulsory military service, universal education, maintenance of police registers, and the other ambivalent characteristics of the modern state. It did not come to Britain until 1834, near the beginning of the Victorian Era. In the United States, where it was a matter of State Law, the system of registration was not complete until 1933.[1]

However, even where we have birth and death rates per thousand of population — 'crude' birth and death rates — their use for purposes of analysis of population trends is, in most circumstances, not merely inadequate, but positively misleading. The number of births, we have seen, depends principally on the number of women in certain age groups, and the proportions which these bear to the total population may vary very considerably. Differences in the relative numbers in different age-groups have an even more marked effect upon the crude death rate. Demographers became aware of the need to refine crude death rates before the necessity of refining crude birth rates was understood. This was first attempted through the cumbrous device of a 'standard population'; the age-composition of the population of Sweden in 1900 was taken as a standard, with the intention that the mortalities found for specific age groups in other countries should be weighted and combined in the proportions

---

[1] The last state outstanding was, of course, Texas.

indicated by the standard population, so as to express the general level of mortality in a single figure.

This device, however, was soon abandoned. The best general view of a country's mortality is obtained by plotting the 'survival diagram', i.e. taking age as the horizontal co-ordinate, and showing the expected survivors to each age of 10,000, or other convenient round figure, of births. If it is desired to express a country's whole mortality experience in a single figure, the best one to use is 'average expectation of life at birth', obtained from the survival diagram. A still simpler single figure is the proportion of each female generation surviving to the age of 15, which provides a good measure of the numbers available to beget the next generation, and also has been found to be a useful basis for formulae for estimating other survival rates. A collection of these data is given in Table II.1.

A complete collection of all available survival tables since 1900 has been made by the Population Division of the United Nations, in the Demographic Yearbook 1953, and kept up to date in subsequent issues. Available information for the nineteenth century was assembled in a convenient compilation in 1907.[1]

The information on survival available from official registrations is naturally heavily concentrated in the more advanced countries. In seeking information about the comparatively low survival rates which have always prevailed among the greater part of mankind, we have to rely upon samples and partial inquiries. Of all rates of survival, the first recorded were the worst. Graunt[2] pioneered demographic analysis, using data from seventeenth-century London. In 1692 Halley, the Astronomer-Royal (best known for the conspicuous comet named after him) prepared a more plausible life table, on some incomplete data from the city of Breslau. The first life table prepared from adequate death registrations, referring to Sweden for the period 1757–63, was prepared by another astronomer, Wargentin. Even after excluding the plague year of 1665, London survival rates then, we now know (and Gregory King indeed thought so at the time), were much lower than for rural areas. It is clear, however, that Graunt considerably overstated London mortality, with only 40 per cent of each generation believed to reach the age of 16.

From the ages recorded on tombstones, some attempts have been made to estimate mortality and survival rates at different ages in the Graeco–Roman world. But these results do not appear yet to have been adequately criticized and analyzed. In any case such a source will certainly understate

---

[1] *Statistique Internationale du Mouvement de la Population* (Statistique Générale de la France).
[2] See *Journal of Royal Statistical Society*, 1963, Part 4.

TABLE II.1. SURVIVALS TO AGE 15

Date (about)	1757–1763	1816–1840	1840	1850	1860	1870	1880	1890
AFRICA:								
Egypt								
Guinea								
Mauritius								
Reunion								
South Africa (whites)								
AMERICA, NORTH:								
Canada								
Greenland								
U.S.A.								
AMERICA, CENTRAL:								
British Honduras								
Costa Rica								
El Salvador								
Guatemala								
Haiti								
Jamaica								
Mexico								
Panama								
Puerto Rico								
Trinidad & Tobago								
AMERICA, SOUTH:								
Argentina								
Bolivia								
Brazil								
British Guiana								
Chile								
ASIA:								
Cambodia								
Ceylon								
China (Taiwan)								
Cyprus								
India								
Israel								
Japan								
Malaya								753
Palestine Arabs								
Philippines								
EUROPE:								
Austria								
Belgium					670(1841–50)			555	
Bulgaria								737(1880–90)
Czechoslovakia								
Denmark			699	711	700	713	727	734
Finland								699(1881–90)
France				676	676		703	
Germany					636(1850–64)	636		677
Greece								
Hungary								
Iceland								
Ireland								789
Italy								
Netherlands				648(1840–51)				
Norway								760(1890–99)
Poland								
Portugal								
Spain								
Sweden	602	719		736(1841–55)			564	
Switzerland							755(1881–88)	740
U.K. (England & Wales)				697(1838–54)			725(1871–80)	
Yugoslavia								
U.S.S.R. (Europe)								
OCEANIA:								
Australia								
New Zealand								807(1881–90)

1900	1910	1920	1930	1940	1950	1955	1959
				626(1936-8)		583 (male & female)	
				688(1942-6)	827(1951-3)		
					796(1951-5)		
	849	873	900	924	955		
			895	927	954	963	
					698	863	
803	828	882	914	940	965	969	970
					797		
					840		
					791		
					725		
					602 (male & female)		
	696	676		843	874		
			581	671	748		
				835	888(1952-4)		
			738	765	875		
			805		887(1945-7)		
707	738	737					
	774(1914)				887(1947)		
					794		
		675			685(1940-50, male)		
	655	698	792		858(1945-47)		
			828		808(1952)		
		576					751
					815	848	919
				735	843		
				863(1931-46)	908		
					591(1941-50)		
		801(1926-7)	875	926(1942-4)	938	956	966
		733(1921-5)	765	801(1935-6)	889	940	953
							876(1956-8)
		554(1926-7)	609	716(1942-4)			
					794(1946-9)		
745	739						
674(1901-5)			864		924		
762(1891-1900)			880		933(1946-9)		
661			719(1925-8)				
679			823				
820	863	885	909	935	962	960	967
	751(1901-10)	778(1911-20)	846(1921-30)	892	952	969	
	816	856	884		946	961	
772	779	860(1924-6)	903(1932-4)		937	958	
701		728	770				970
		685	788	854	892	938	939
633	806(1901-10)	876(1911-20)	900(1921-30)	929(1931-40)	954(1941-50)		962
			881(1925-7)	903	946		
686	736	775	822		919	938	
803(1900-09)		851(1910-20)	913(1921-30)	943(1931-40)	969	973	
822(1891-1900)	867(1901-10)	886(1911-20)	924(1921-30)	942(1931-40)	967		
			787		877		
				776	845	922	923
						872	877
598	687	674	787	799	973		
809(1891-1900)	851(1901-10)	877(1911-20)	913(1921-30)	938(1931-40)	961		
786	839	879	926	942			981
755(1891-1900)	828	871	904		966	972	975
			816		845(1952-4)		
542(1896-7)			696(1926-7)				
823	876(1901-10)	907	940(1932-4)		967		
892(1901-5)	912	934	955		963	969	

the relative number of deaths of children. We can however go further back to some interesting results deduced for earlier periods, by the excavation of Stone Age and Bronze Age burial grounds.[1] In this case, of course, the ages of death were not recorded on any sort of monument. But they can be estimated, within a certain margin, by anatomical examination of the skeletons. In this way we can obviate some of the difficulty which arises in any examination of tombstones in historical times, namely the tendency to bias in the result through the younger and less important people being less likely to have a tombstone, which must have been comparatively costly, erected over their graves.

The results obtained from the excavation of primitive burial grounds are however also clearly defective in that the proportion of children under 14 is found to vary very much between different studies, and in any case is obviously understated. In those times there was, apparently, no certainty that the bodies of children would be given the customary burial. If however we construct the tables on the assumptions (based on the Samburu data, considered later) that in the Bronze Age 50 per cent, in the Stone Age 55 per cent of those born in each generation would have died by the age of 14, we obtain a curve which, for Bronze Age Europe, bears a considerable resemblance to the lowest known survival curve for any present day population.

Some data are also given[2] for *Sinanthropus* skeletons, which at least have the merit of apparently including a due proportion of deaths under 14. Some doubts however have been expressed as to whether *Sinanthropus* was human: and, whatever he was, he may have had a much quicker reproductive cycle than man as we know him (Table II.2). The shape of

TABLE II.2. RELATIVE NUMBERS OF DEATHS AT DIFFERENT AGES FOR PRIMITIVE MAN

	Number of cases	Percentages of deaths under age 14		Percentage proportions of deaths at other ages, if assumed figure for deaths under 14 is correct			
		As originally given	Now assumed	14–20	21–40	41–60	over 60
Sinanthropus	22	68	68	14[a]	14[b]	4[c]	
Neanderthal man	20	40	55	11	30	4	—
Upper Palaeolithic man	102	24	55	6	32	7	—
Mesolithic man	65	31	55	4	38	2	1
Early Bronze Age							
Austria	273	8	50	9	22	15	4
Cyprus	38	28	50	11	19	20	—

[a] 15–29.   [b] 40–50.   [c] Over 50.

[1] Vallois, *L'Archéologie*, 1937, pp. 499–532, except for the results for Cyprus (Stewart, University of Sydney, privately communicated).
[2] *The Shorter Anthropological Papers of Franz Weidenreich*, New York, 1949.

ancient and some low modern survival curves (with curves for two high survival countries) can be studied in Diagrams II.A and II.B.

The lowest known survival rates for any contemporary community are for the Samburu,[1] a very primitive pastoral tribe inhabiting arid country

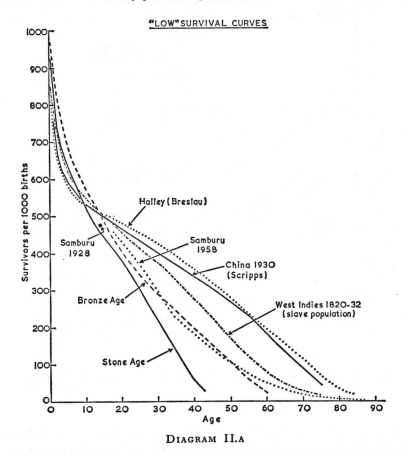

DIAGRAM II.A

in East Africa, who, however, keep records of their ages (because of the parts which the different age-groups have to play in intricate tribal ceremonies). Recent French sample studies of survival in Guinea and Ivory Coast are now quoted in U.N. *Demographic Yearbook*.[2] Survival tables have also

[1] Information privately communicated by Paul Spencer, University of Oxford, Department of Anthropology, who became a 'blood brother' of the tribe.

[2] A study, also quoted there, for Belgian Congo (as it was then) in 1950–2, showing a very anomalously-shaped survival curve, appears to have been based on a defective registration system.

been prepared[1] for the Boni and Oayana, Negro and indigenous tribes
living side by side in French Guiana, whose mortality shows as surprising
a difference as does their reproductivity (the immunity of the Boni to malaria

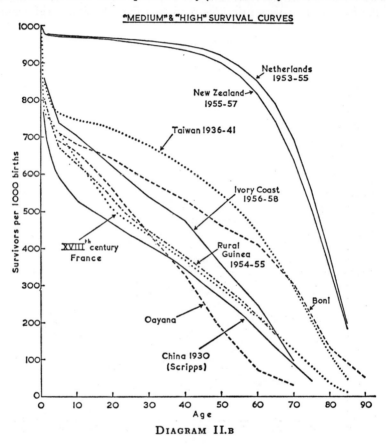

DIAGRAM II.B

may however have assisted them in both respects). Data are available[2] for
the slave population in the West Indies, 1820–32. For China, a substantial
sample[3] was taken in 1932. For eighteenth-century France a general
survival table was computed by Duvillard.[4]

[1] Hurault, *Population*, July–September 1959.
[2] Roberts, *Population Studies*, March 1952.
[3] Chiao Thompson and Chen, *An Experiment in the Registration of Vital Statistics in China*, Scripps Foundation, Oxford, Ohio. An alternative survival table (*Milbank Memorial Quarterly*, July 1935) prepared by Seifert, also associated with Buck's extensive study *Chinese Farm Economy*, appears to be defective (Clark, *Population*, June–July 1964).
[4] Quoted by Sauvy in *Fertility and Survival*. More detailed studies (Girard, *Population*, July–September 1959, and *Population*, April–June 1961) are now available for some

Account has not been taken of the supposed survival tables for India for the periods 1891–1901 and 1901–11, although these survival tables and calculations of average expectation of life were published in the Census of India. These calculations (prepared by English actuaries) which purported to show that the average expectation of life of an Indian was only 23, became world-famous, and to this day many people who take any interest in demography still have the impression that something like this figure represents the average Indian's expectation of life, in spite of the fact that these tables have recently been replaced by a new calculation which probably now errs in understating mortality. These results for 1891–1901 and 1901–1911 purported to be based upon the Census, and not upon any demographic sample inquiries, which indeed were almost entirely lacking at that time. The critic may well ask how, using a Census which is obviously full of the wildest mis-statements of age, with hopelessly incomplete death registrations and no recording of ages at death, even the most skilful actuary can hope to compile a survival table and calculate an average expectation of life. A review of methods used is given in an article of the Journal of the Institute of Actuaries, 1913, which leaves the reader amazed that even the rashest member of a learned profession could make such unsupported speculations and publish deductions from them as an ascertained result. We can, if we wish, test these supposed survival tables by applying to them what information we have about Indian reproductivity; and are led to the conclusion that if they were true the Indian population during these periods must have been rapidly declining.

Diagram II.c, showing the progress of Swedish survival data from the eighteenth century to now, conveys an idea of the manner in which the shape of the survival curve changes, as we pass from low-survival communities, in which half or more of each generation is lost by the age of 15, to the most advanced modern communities, where 95 per cent of a generation may survive to the age of 40.

We still know far less than we should about the survival rates applying to the majority of mankind, in those areas where death registration is still incomplete or absent. We have a certain amount of further information confirming one important feature, namely the exceptionally high mortality in infancy. A medical study in North West Nigeria by Nicol in 1948[1] showed an infant mortality of 294 per 1000 children born. Total losses up to the age of five, including pre-natal losses (presumably of the order of magnitude of 100) were estimated at 472.

seventeenth- and eighteenth-century villages, which show considerable differences between themselves, but at any rate do not appear to invalidate Duvillard's results.

[1] Quoted Baldwin, *The Niger Agricultural Project*, page 25.

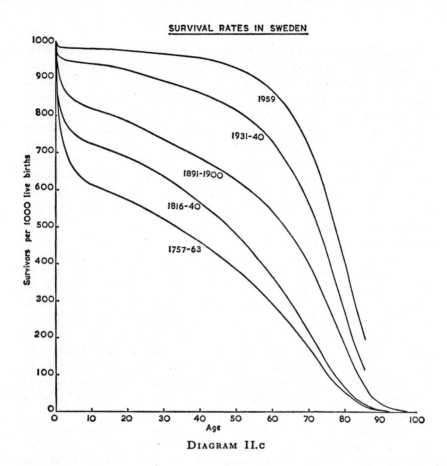

DIAGRAM II.c

Nineteenth-century figures show a very high infant mortality in Europe, particularly in urban areas, where infectious disease was very prevalent. The rural populations, though poorer and almost without medical attention, nevertheless enjoyed some hygienic advantages in comparison with the towns. Meuriot[1] quotes the figure for the *arrondissements* of Paris about 1890. In the worst area, the XIVth, infant mortality stood at 327, 290 in the XXth, and 253 in the XIIIth. In the best areas (I, VIII, IX, XVI), the figure at that time stood below 150. He also quotes some grim figures for Sweden (Table II.3).

For Ireland in 1840 on the other hand[2] the figures were surprisingly low, namely 81 in the rural areas, and 138 in towns over 2000 population.

[1] *Des grandes agglomérations urbaines*, 1898.
[2] Connell, *The Population of Ireland.*

TABLE II.3. NINETEENTH-CENTURY INFANT MORTALITY
IN SWEDEN PER THOUSAND BIRTHS

	Stockholm	Other Cities	Rural
1816–40	307	192	163
1851–60	318	181	137
1881–90	194	131	102

We have further data about some areas of high infant mortality (Table
II.4) (deaths under one year of age per thousand births).

TABLE II.4. INFANT MORTALITIES

AFRICA

Algeria[a]		200
Cameroon[b]		180
Central African Republic[b]		191
Congo (Brazzaville)[b]		200
Dahomey[b]		110
Gabon[b]		160
Ghana[b]		90
Guinea[a]	Rural	200
	Urban	140
Haute Volta[b]		174
Kenya, 1948[c]		184
Mali[b]		147
Somalia[d]	Male	199
	Female	194

AMERICA

Barbados[e]	1926–30	300
	1931–5	260
	1936–40	210
Jamaica[e]	1881–1930	173
	1931–5	143

ASIA

India[f]	1920[g]	190
	1946[g]	150
	1951[h]	124
Japan[i]	1900–24	161
	1925–29	141
	1930–34	126
Vietnam[j]		300

EUROPE

Greece[k]	1860–90	194
	1890–1910	175
	1920–24	148
Rumania[l]	1938	179

[a] *Population*, July–Sept. 1956.
[b] Gerardin, *La Développement de la Haute Volta*, I.S.E.A. Supplement 142, 1963.
[c] East African Royal Commission.
[d] Morgantini, World Population Conference, 1954.
[e] Roberts, *The Population of Jamaica*.
[f] Chandrasekhar (World Population Conference, 1965) has records back to 1900 for Madras City, which he believes to be fully comprehensive. We should expect for a large city rates higher than the Indian average. Approximate averages are:

1900–09	298	1930–39	234
1910–19	300	1940–49	201
1920–29	272	1950–59	154
		1960	120

The fall began quite sharply about 1920.
[g] Swaroop, Census of India, Paper No. 3.
[h] 'India 1955' (Ministry of Information).
[i] Mainichi Publications, *Population Problems* Series II.
[j] *Population Index*, April 1945.
[k] *Population*, October 1960.
[l] World Population Conference, 1954.

European Russia	1874–83	327	Novoselsky & Paevsky, *Mortality & Expectation of Life of the USSR*, 1927
	1896–7	303	Novoselsky & Paevsky, *Mortality & Expectation of Life of the USSR*, 1927
	1907–10	276	

In a special survey[1] of villages below 1000 population in Lebanon in 1953, the infant mortality rate was found to be 195 for males and 315 for females. In face of these rather shocking figures it is difficult to resist the conclusion that, while deliberate female infanticide may not occur, nevertheless there must be a certain amount of 'thou shalt not kill but needst not strive officiously to keep alive'.

Diagram II.D plots a number of significant points[2] showing improvements in survival rates through time, including a Catalonian study which, while only for a single parish, nevertheless gives a longer continuous record than any other at present available. The figures have all been calculated on female *non-survivors* to the age of 15; it should not make any significant difference whether we take 15, 20 or any adjacent age.[3] It is seen that the rate of improvement has clearly accelerated dramatically since the 1930's.

Our eighteenth-century studies so far show, in Catalonia, a fall in mortality (non-survivors to age 14) at the rate of only 0·2 per cent a year from the beginning to the middle of the eighteenth century, and 0·4 per cent a year from the middle to the end of the century. The Swedish data from 1760 to the 1820's show a fall of 0·6 per cent per year. Nadal pointed out that vaccination was adopted quite early in Catalonia, but not in the rest of Spain; the survival rates shown for his parish in the 1830's are in fact much higher than those estimated for the rest of Spain in the 1880's.

For the first decades of the nineteenth century we have at present less information. In the Catalonian parish, mortality was declining at the rate of 1·3 per cent per year (presumably this was the time when vaccination was being introduced); the Swedish figure, between the 1820's and the 1840's, declined at the rate of only 0·2 per cent per year (perhaps due to infant mortality rising with urbanization).

---

[1] Khamis, International Statistical Conference, 1957.

[2] From the sources already quoted, with the addition of a study of the Catalonian village of Palamos going back to 1735 (Nadal, *Population*, January–March 1961). There is also a statement by Grabill, *Fertility of American Women*, p. 10, that the U.S.A. in 1800 was fitted approximately by the English survival table for 1838–54. This datum is rather uncertain however and is not included in the diagram.

[3] The Catalonian figures refer to male and female survival combined to age 14. A few other data refer to combined sexes (these have been indicated in Table II.1).

From the later nineteenth century, survival data for a substantial number of countries are now available. It is interesting to see whether rates of improvement bear any relation to initial levels of survival (Diagrams II.E, F, G). It appears that in the later nineteenth century, the rate of progress

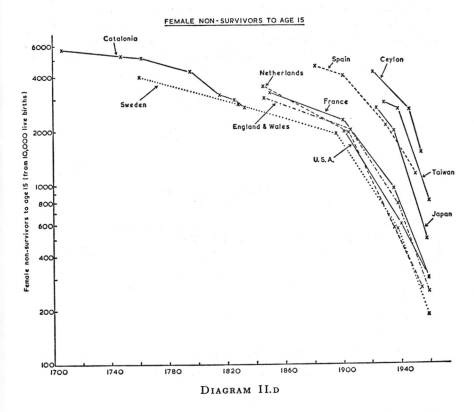

DIAGRAM II.D

was more or less uniform, independent of whether the level of mortality at the beginning of the period was high or low; and that the average rate of improvement was only 0·7 per cent per year.

For the first 35 years of the present century it is seen that, in some countries, very large improvements were obtained. Diagram II.F shows that there is a strong association for this period (though not for the preceding period) with the initial mortality, in the direction of 'to him that hath may more be given', i.e. that the countries which had already had comparatively good health records by 1900 were those which subsequently improved them most rapidly. During this period some of the least fortunate countries were improving at a rate of only 0·9 per cent per year — though even this figure was above the world average for the later nineteenth century — but the best countries, by this time, were improving at the rate of 4 per cent per year.

Diagrams II.D and II.G make clear the still more dramatic changes which began, with chemotherapy, about 1935. For the last period an association between initial mortality and rate of improvement is again important — but this time slightly in the opposite direction, with the countries of higher mortality in 1935 showing a median rate of improvement of 6 per cent per year, the more advanced countries 5 per cent.

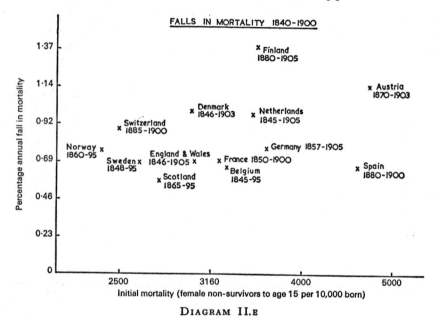

DIAGRAM II.E

Let us now return to our lowest survival rate, of Bronze Age man, or the modern Samburu. It is possible to demonstrate the interesting conclusion that with this rate of survival the biological maximum of reproductivity still only just suffices to maintain the population; or, if we like to use the phrase, keeps man in ecological equilibrium.

In Table II.5 are first given the survivors at the various ages per 1000 births. In the second column these figures are somewhat arbitrarily reduced to give the estimated female survivors from 1000 births. Some anthropologists indeed consider that, in primitive communities, a certain amount of deliberate infanticide affecting females more than males, together with the considerable hardships of primitive life which may bear more severely upon women than men, may have the effect of reducing the proportion of marriageable women to 20 per cent below what it would be for a normal population.

To these estimated numbers in the various age-groups surviving from 1000 female births we may apply the rates of specific fertility found for Guinea (of the countries for which we possess fertility tables the one

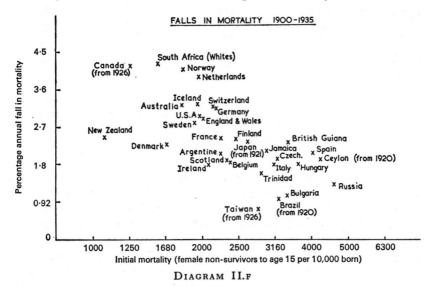

FALLS IN MORTALITY 1900-1935

DIAGRAM II.F

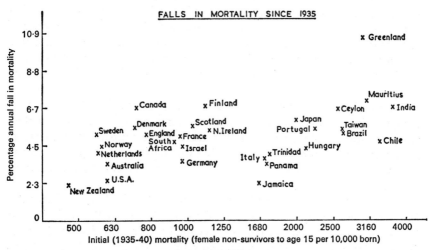

FALLS IN MORTALITY SINCE 1935

DIAGRAM II.G

TABLE II.5. NET REPRODUCTION MODEL AT LOWEST
SURVIVAL RATES

Age	Survivors of 1000 births	Estimated survivors of 1000 female births	Births per year of married life[a]	Estimated annual births from mothers in age-group
15–19	448	414	0·18	75
20–24	385	355	0·42	149
25–29	315	288	0·30	86
30–34	258	233	0·25	58
35–39	205	187	0·20	37
40–44	160	150	0·05	7
				412
			multiply by 5	2060
			divide by 2·06	1000

[a] Based on Guinea.

approximating most nearly to primitive conditions). In the last column of
the table we thus get the estimated births to each quinquennial age-group
of mothers. The results obtained must be multiplied by 5 to take account
of the fact that the representative woman spends five years in each age-
group (just as we had to multiply by 5 in order to obtain total fertility, from
figures of the specific fertility per annum in each of the age-groups). The
result thus obtained, of 2060 offspring per 1000 females born into each
generation, or 2·06 each, can be described as *net total fertility*. A total
fertility of 7 is the average number of children born to a woman who has
lived right to the end of the reproductive period, but the net number of
successors to each generation of women is only 2·06, when we take into
account the proportion of mothers and potential mothers who died before
reaching the end (or, for that matter, even the beginning) of the reproductive period.

To calculate whether or not the generation is replacing itself, we must
compare the numbers in the original generation with the numbers of their
female offspring. We have seen that the average ratio of male births to
female is 1·06. It appears therefore that this figure of 2·06 corresponds to
exactly 1·00 female offspring, or precise replacement of the previous
generation.

Total fertility divided by a factor of 2·06 (or slightly different factor if it
is deemed that another sex ratio at birth should be used) is described as
'gross reproduction rate'. Likewise, net total fertility divided by the same
factor is described as 'net reproduction rate'. In the case of the population

which we are considering, with a net reproduction rate of precisely 1·00, this means that each generation is expected precisely to replace its predecessor, and that over a long period no net increase in population is to be expected.

At one time, gross and net reproduction rates were widely used in analyzing trends of population in Europe and America. They were found, as will be seen in a subsequent chapter, to have seriously erroneous effects when used for such measurements. They may work reasonably well in communities where marriage is early and almost universal for women: but in European or American populations net and gross reproduction rates will be considerably affected, from year to year, by the changes in the rate of marriage (probability of conception being much higher in the first year of marriage than subsequently).

The figure for total fertility in the above example of 7·0 accords quite well with what evidence we have for total fertility in primitive and simple agricultural populations.[1] It is presumed that there is little permanent widowhood, and that nearly all women of reproductive age are married, possibly some polygamously. Total fertility for Formosa for quite a long period[2] until recently has been found to have been in the neighbourhood of 7. A recent study for mainland China[3] estimated the number of births for a number of decades into the past by calculating backwards, using the Scripps Foundation Survival Table, from age distributions shown in the 1953 Census, and also in sample studies in the 1930's. The estimated numbers of births between 1930 and 1950 appeared to be at least 20 per cent below those which would have been obtained by applying the Formosan specific fertility rates to the age structure of the mainland Chinese population, so far as it can be estimated. No reason for this discrepancy is known. This total fertility of approximately 6 only just sufficed, as far as can be ascertained, to keep the mainland Chinese population stable during the rather troubled conditions of the 1930's and 1940's. During previous decades, some growth of population had been taking place.

The significant decline in mortality, and improvement in the rate of population increase, which clearly began about 1750, was due to medical improvements, due to better knowledge and application of medical science (but also to one very important medical improvement which took place independently of human effort). Attempts by some historians to show that it was the industrialization of England (and other countries) which came first, and the increase in population in consequence, have been unsuccessful, and have been abandoned.

---

[1] Krzywicki, *Primitive Society and its Vital Statistics* (1934).
[2] Tuan, *Population Studies*, July, 1958.   [3] Clark, *Population*, June–July 1964.

A demographic model gives us fairly good grounds for believing that falling mortality accounted for the observed increase of the rate of population growth in England in the late eighteenth and early nineteenth centuries, without our needing to formulate any hypotheses about changes in age at marriage, or changes in marital fertility. In this model, the known Swedish mortality rates are assumed to be applicable to England and Wales, and the 1851 proportions married at given ages to be approximately applicable to the eighteenth century.

The model predicts very closely the observed rates of population growth (Table II.6).

TABLE II.6. DEMOGRAPHIC MODEL OF THE EIGHTEENTH AND EARLY NINETEENTH CENTURIES POPULATION GROWTH IN ENGLAND

Age-group	Female Survivors of 1000 Total Births Based on Swedish Mortality of		Expected[b] Percentage Married Not Widowed	Marital[c] Specific Fertility	Specific Fertility All Women[d]	Offspring Survival Rates of:	
	1757–63[a]	1816–40				1757–63	1816–40
15–19	1448	1731	2	0·43	0·01	14	17
20–24	1391	1683	30	0·43	0·13	181	219
25–29	1338	1627	60	0·41	0·25	334	406
30–34	1247	1558	70	0·37	0·26	324	405
35–39	1202	1487	75	0·30	0·22	265	327
40–44	1130	1400	70	0·15	0·10	113	140
45–49	1049	1308	65	0·02	0·01	10	13
Total Fertility					4·90		
Gross Reproduction Rate					2·38		
Net Reproduction Rate						1·241	1·527
Average Length of Generation Years						31·6	31·7
Average rate of Population Growth per cent per Year						0·7	1·4

[a] Only general survival rate given: ratios of female to general rate assumed the same as in 1816–40.

[b] Based on 1851 data for England and Wales, but raised slightly because of eighteenth-century rates of male emigration having probably been lower than nineteenth century.

[c] Henry's general estimate for eighteenth- and nineteenth-century Europe (15–19 added).

[d] Product of two previous columns.

Medical knowledge may have been advancing before the eighteenth century, but the pace was slow. In the seventeenth century the standard medical text was still the writings of Galen. The Great Plague which devastated London in 1665 was a bubonic plague similar to that which had caused the Black Death, and the repeated devastating epidemics which scourged Europe throughout the whole of the second half of the fourteenth century; or indeed to the Great Plague in Constantinople under Justinian, or the Plague of Athens recorded by Thucydides; and by the seventeenth century doctors still knew as little as before about its causes, and how it spread. It was not in fact until 1900 that the mechanism by which plague is disseminated was discovered[1] — largely as a result of some isolated outbreaks in Australia, a country normally free from plague, following the visits of ships from Asia; these unusual circumstances, together with some first-class medical detective work, made it possible to fix the blame upon rats as carriers. This however was only part of the story. It is not the rat itself, but one of the fleas on the rat, which carries the infection to human victims. Further research showed that, out of the numerous species of fleas carried by the rat, plague could only be carried by a single species, *Xenopsylla cheopis*. But the last and most extraordinary part of the story is that *Xenopsylla cheopis* is extremely particular about the species of rats which it will bite. It lives on the black rat and will bite humans; but literally, would rather die than try to bite a grey rat, of the kind now prevalent in Europe. Up to the end of the seventeenth century it was the black rat which had shared the houses and ships of our ancestors in Western Europe. The grey rat appears to have been indigenous to Norway and Northern Europe. In the eighteenth century, perhaps because it found the climate getting colder (which geographers tell us was the case), or perhaps by accident, it began securing passage on ships, and finding its way to England and other Western European countries.[2] It was a larger and fiercer animal than the black rat, whom it recognized and attacked as a competitor for food and shelter. In the fight between the two species, the black rat in Western Europe was quickly extirpated. It was this strictly exogenous zoological event which freed Western Europe from the plague and, in the long run, probably did more to determine the rise in Europe's population than any other single event.

Among our ancestors the other great killer, besides plague, was smallpox. The virtual extirpation of smallpox, or at any rate its reduction to a very mild form, was largely brought about by vaccination, first successfully practised by Jenner about 1795. But it is important not to neglect the fact that Jenner was only improving on techniques already practised, namely inoculation of patients with human material, by rather repulsive processes, apparently first discovered in the Middle East, and which spread to Europe during the course of the eighteenth century.

All eighteenth-century medicine indeed appears to us rather barbarous and disgusting. There is a Cambridge story of the early nineteenth century,

---

[1] The extraordinary story here recounted is told by Fabian Hirst, *The Conquest of Plague* (Oxford University Press, 1953).

[2] That the grey rat arrived about this time is confirmed by a curious fact, namely the popular jest of describing it as the 'Hanover Rat' (because it arrived at about the same time as the Dynasty of Hanover in 1714).

of a professor of medicine who boasted that he had a stock of medical stories so repulsive that any one of them was guaranteed to make his hearers puke on the spot. But we have to conclude that seventeenth-century medicine was probably more barbarous and disgusting still. The medieval doctor, still faithfully following the ancient writings, with the best intentions quite probably increased the mortality rate rather than reduced it. A firmly-held idea in medicine then was that patients should be bled. Many patients were not able to survive more than two or three visits from their doctors. Some medical historians have held that the gradual cessation of the practice of bleeding, which came about during the eighteenth century, itself saved many millions of lives.

The improvements in medicine taking place in the early nineteenth century, limited though they were, drew adverse comments from Malthus. The Census Commissioner for England and Wales, in his report on the Census of 1861, records Malthus as saying: 'I feel not the slightest doubt, that if the introduction of cowpox should extirpate the *smallpox*, and yet the NUMBER OF MARRIAGES CONTINUE THE SAME, we shall find a very perceptible difference in the *increased mortality of some other diseases*.' Disease, to Malthus, was something which obligingly played its part in fulfilling the 'Principles of Population', which he believed himself to have discovered.

As we see from the survival data, becoming more numerous and reliable as the nineteenth century advances, progress continued, but slowly. The discovery of anaesthetics in the 1840's probably saved many lives, as did antiseptics under Lister and others in the following decade (though they were to be replaced before the end of the century by asepsis). The reasons for the need for antisepsis or asepsis were not at the time understood. In the 1860's Pasteur, demonstrating the part played by micro-organisms in disease as well as in fermentation, was regarded as a dangerous crank by many medical men. It was not until the closing decades of the nineteenth century that the 'germ theory of disease', as it was then called, acquired general acceptance, and work on immunization could begin. Early methods of immunization sometimes had the opposite effect to that intended, as in Bernard Shaw's tragi-comedy 'The Doctor's Dilemma' (which presents a highly entertaining picture of the state of medicine at the turn of the century, and reads and acts as well today as it did then). None the less a distinct improvement in the rate of decline of mortality became visible at about that time. Immunization and preventive medicine were progressing; one of the most dramatic events of the period was the checking of yellow fever, previously a great killer in hot climates. But it was not until the 1930's that procedures for immunization against the major infectious diseases, particularly those which attacked children, were brought to the level of efficiency which we now take for granted.

The next general inflection in the curve of declining mortality appears in the 1930's. Over some forty years, immunization had practically accomplished its task. It was to be succeeded by chemo-therapy. In our excitement about antibiotics, which first became available in the 1940's, and whose use is now universal, we should not neglect the importance of this prior step. It was in 1935 that, for the first time, drugs were brought into use which, without harming the patient, could attack harmful micro-organisms within his body — the ultimate dream of the Victorian pioneers of micro-biological research, who in their own time, apart from some immunization, had been only able to assist the patient by comparatively ineffective external treatments. Chemo-therapy at one blow almost wiped out pneumonia and a number of other diseases which had been great killers up to that time. The curves of declining mortality take another and sharper inflection at this period.

By the subsequent decade antibiotics had been discovered and applied to the treatment of a great variety of diseases and injuries. Other medical improvements, too numerous to mention, have also been proceeding at a rapid pace. The results are visible in the recent accelerated decline in mortality, an acceleration even more marked than that of the 1930's.

This quick conspectus of medical history, in which experts will probably detect a number of errors, may seem to some trivial or irrelevant. But it is not. Here we find the underlying cause, for better or worse, of the increase in the rate of world population growth which has been going on, at an ever accelerating pace, since the middle of the eighteenth century.

We now return to our net reproduction model, which indicated no population increase at lowest survival rates and maximum fertility rates, and consider some other possible fertility rates in conjunction with various improvement on lowest survival rates. Table II.7 gives the specific fertilities in Formosa,[1] averaged for the generations of women born 1888–1917 (for the more recently born generations some fall has appeared), Ivory Coast[2] and Brazil in 1940.[3]

There are two interesting features about the figures for the Ivory Coast; 13 per cent of the women are polygamously married; and also specific fertility must have already started to fall by the time of inquiry — the total fertility shown by the women then over 40 was 6·55.

Although the Formosan figures show a total fertility of 7, as do the

[1] Tuan, Population Studies, July 1958.
[2] Gouvernement Général d'Afrique Occidentale Française, *Enquête Nutrition et Niveau de Vie*, 1955–6.
[3] Mortara, *Revista Brasiliera de Estadística*, 1947 and 1948.

TABLE II.7. HIGH SPECIFIC FERTILITIES

Age	Formosa Women born 1888–1917	Ivory Coast 1955	Brazil 1940
15–19	0·103	0·185	0·018
20–24	0·322	0·280	0·256
25–29	0·328	0·284	0·308
30–34	0·292	0·224	0·271
35–39	0·242	0·107	0·206
40–44	0·116	0·056	0·127
44–49	0·010	0·019	0·040
Total Fertility	7·03	5·77	6·45

Guinean, applying them to lowest survival rates indicates total births 6 per cent below the replacement rate; applying the Brazilian or Ivory Coast figures 18 per cent below replacement rate. The reason for this paradoxical result is that although the Formosan total fertility is the same as the Guinean, it is distributed differently through time, with an increased proportion of births at later ages. It appears therefore, that not only high total fertility, but also early marriage, is necessary to maintain the population under lowest survival conditions. The Ivory Coast figures also reach their maximum early, as do the Guinean, although at a lower level. The lower level of the Formosan figures at the earlier ages can probably be explained by some postponement of marriage. It is not known whether the higher level at later ages is due to greater biological fecundibility, or to other factors. Still more, we lack an explanation of the comparative high fertility at later ages shown by seventeenth- and eighteenth-century European populations (tables given in Chapter I).

In Table II.8 both Guinean and Formosan specific fertilities are applied to certain other low survival rates, namely those for Guinea and China already quoted. These however, are both approximate, and show respectively unusually low and unusually high ratios of female survival in relation to male. While accepting these data as indicative of the general rate of survival, the male/female ratios are estimated from Chinese data by a method given in Table II.10.

The net reproduction rate measures the extent to which the population replaces itself, or more than replaces itself, in the course of an average generation. The average length of a generation depends on the way in which specific fertilities are distributed among the age groups, i.e. it would be much lower in Guinea than in Formosa. In Brazil, for example, the average length of a generation is 26 years. Mortara computed a net reproduction rate of 1·80 for 1940. Taking the 1/26th power of this (by logarithms) we

TABLE II.8. NET REPRODUCTION ON VARIOUS ASSUMED FERTILITIES AND SURVIVALS

Age	Chinese Survival Rates Survivors from 1000 female births (mid point of age group)	Offspring at specific fertilities of Guinea	Formosa	Guinean Survival Rates ditto	ditto	ditto
15–19	486	88	49	558	100	56
20–24	449	188	139	503	211	156
25–29	414	124	137	459	138	151
30–34	380	95	110	419	105	121
35–39	345	69	86	386	77	96
40–44	311	16	37	349	17	42
45–49	278		3	314		3
Multiply by 5 (net total fertility)		580	561		648	625
		2·90	2·80		3·24	3·12
Divide by 2·06 (net reproduction rate)		1·41	1·36		1·57	1·51

obtain 1·023, or 2·3 per cent, as the annual rate of population increase corresponding to this net reproduction rate of 1·80. To take another example, for Egypt in the 1940's[1] (the figure would be higher now) a net reproduction rate of 1·4 was computed, with a mean length of generation of 28·4 years.

If we assume 25 years as the average length of a generation we obtain the correspondence shown in Table II.9 between net reproduction rates and per annum rates of population increase.

TABLE II.9. CORRESPONDENCE BETWEEN NET REPRODUCTION RATE AND ANNUAL INCREASES

Net Reproduction Rate	1·2	1·4	1·6	1·8	2·0	2·2	2·4
% per annum rate of population increase	0·7	1·4	1·9	2·3	2·8	3·2	3·5

Table II.9 indicates a wide range of rates of population growth, but no wider than is found in fact. The Boni and the Oayana, already mentioned, show respectively rates of population growth of 3·0 per cent and 0·6 per cent per year.

In Africa, the net reproduction rate computed for the Ivory Coast was

[1] El Badry, *Milbank Memorial Quarterly*, July 1955.

1·74. Myburgh[1] computed 1·5 for Ghana, 1·6 for Swaziland and 2·0 for Southern Rhodesia. In the Bakweri Tribe in the Cameroons,[2] where total fertility was only 4·5, net reproduction rate was calculated at only just about replacement level. In the Bonjonga villages, counts taken in 1903, 1928 and 1953 revealed a fairly steady rate of decline at the rate of ¾ per cent per year — subject however to a rise in the population on the plantations, which appeared to be going on at about the same rate.

Dandekar[3] obtained for a rural sample in Maharashtra a total fertility of only 5·04 and a net reproduction rate of 1·29. He also calculated the male net reproduction rate at 1·46 — a calculation from the specific fertilities of the males in each age-group, not often made, but important when it appears that population growth may be limited by a relative scarcity of males, which may be the case in a state near to Bombay, where a substantial number of men may be away from the villages for prolonged periods.

A calculation for primitive Indian tribes in the jungle[4] showed a total fertility of 6·3, subject to the important qualification that husband and wife both survived to the end of the reproductive age — (so that, measured in the usual manner, the total fertility figure would have been lower). In many of the tribes abortion was found to be quite frequent. One tribe practised polyandry, and was found to have a total fertility of only 5·2. For these tribes a net reproduction rate (again subject to the qualification that only families with husbands surviving to the end of the wife's reproductive period were included) was 1·8.

Net reproduction rates for a long period have also been calculated for Jamaica.[5] Between 1879 and 1923 they remained within the range of 1·– 1·55, rising to 1·85 by 1950–2.

Few demographic questions can be of greater interest for the present day world than that of the net reproduction rate and the rate of growth of the population of China. We have to work, however, in an almost complete lack of the necessary information. Indeed we probably know more about the level and rate of population growth in China in the distant past (see Chapter III) than in modern times. The available information has however been assembled[6] into a more or less consistent, though highly approximate demographic model.

From the mid-nineteenth century onwards estimates of Chinese population have been conflicting and uncertain, except that it is generally

[1] *Central African Journal of Medicine*, 1956.
[2] Ardener, *Plantation and Village in the Cameroons.*
[3] *A Demographic Survey of Six Rural Communities*, Gokhale Institute, 1959.
[4] Mujumdar, World Population Conference, 1954. The work was done by the Department of Anthropology, Lucknow University.
[5] Roberts, *The Population of Jamaica.*
[6] Clark, *Population*, June–July 1964, October–December 1966.

agreed that immense losses were suffered in the Taiping and Nien wars of the 1850's. A census was taken in 1953. Critics are divided among those such as United States Census Bureau, who believe that the Census understated population, and those who think that there was some overstatement.

Buck, conducting his large scale survey of Chinese agriculture[1] from Nanking in the early 1930's, made some estimates of total Chinese population at that time on varying hypotheses, some of which led him to estimate a figure as high as 600 millions. He was however persuaded by American demographers not to publish these results, so much out of line with contemporary estimates. It now appears however that he was fairly correct. The twenty years between his time and the Census of 1953, years of internal disorder, Japanese invasion and revolution, may have been expected to have been years of stationary or declining population.

The only satisfactory mortality table for China appears to be that prepared in 1933–4 by the Scripps Foundation, working in a sample area (already referred to). This area however, from the nature of the case, appears to have been one suffering less than the normal from war lords, epidemics, etc., and for China as a whole rather higher rates of mortality have to be assumed for most periods. Since 1953, with the establishment of political order, and some measures of public health, the proportion of non-survivors among young people is assumed to have fallen at a little less than 3 per cent per year (as compared with the 5–6 per cent per year observed in many other countries), with correspondingly lesser falls in the number of non-survivors to higher ages. This estimated decline in mortality, however, was assumed to have been violently interrupted in the five chaotic years of disorganization and food shortage which followed 'The Year of the Great Leap Forward' in 1958.

Age tables are available for the 1930's, and also in the Census of 1953 (though these latter bear a suspicious resemblance to the results of a few sample studies which were then available, and it is doubtful whether the ages of the whole population were recorded or tabulated). 'Jobbing back' from these age distributions by means of the assumed mortality tables leads us to some highly approximate conclusions about the numbers of births in the past. However, the independent calculations based on the 1930's and on 1953 agree with each other reasonably well. Both indicate that, after the mid-nineteenth-century disasters, population growth was resumed in the 1870's, but at a comparatively slow rate.

Accurate specific fertilities are available for many years for Formosa. One would have thought, on the face of it, that the mainland Chinese

[1] Published as *Land Utilisation in China*.

would show very similar specific fertilities. But it appears impossible to make this assumption fit the other data. We have to conclude that mainland Chinese fertility is at least 10 per cent lower than Formosan.

The general conclusion is that the Census of 1953 somewhat overstated population, which is estimated at about 560 million at that date; and that it had been at about the same level in 1930 and in 1915. The assumed specific fertilities, at the high rates of mortality then prevailing, kept the population about stationary, except for the worst period in the 1940's; the estimate for 1948 is about 540 million.

After 1953 population began increasing at 1·1 per cent per year — never at the 2 per cent per year rate which was then officially claimed. Between 1958 and 1963 the rate fell to 0·4 per cent per year, and since then is estimated to have risen again to about 1·1 per cent per year, to give a total of some 650 million in 1968. If there are no further disturbances, the rate of increase will quickly accelerate.

CHAPTER III

The History of Population Growth

IN Chapter II we calculated the interaction between various survival rates and specific fertilities, and the average rates of population growth ensuing. These results should now be compared with the available evidence (there is much less than might have been supposed) about actual observed rates of population growth, present or past, under conditions of high specific fertility and low survival.

Many people believe that it is a law of nature that all populations, at all times and places (unless deliberately checked) tend to go on expanding until they reach the 'limits of subsistence'; after which, they are kept in check by 'vice and misery'. This was the famous theory which was propounded in 1798 by the Rev. Thomas Robert Malthus in his *Principles of Population*. The majority of his contemporaries in Britain disagreed with him. If they had not, not only would most of us not be here, but also the world would have been a vastly different place in many other respects; the British Commonwealth would probably not have come into existence, most of what is now the United States would probably have been Spanish-speaking, and Britain would probably have remained an easy-going eighteenth-century type agrarian society. Malthus's ideas were however received in France, and played a major part in reducing France's influence in world affairs.

Malthus's ideas, we are told, played a considerable part in helping Darwin to formulate his theories.

Population, Malthus claimed, tended to increase in geometrical progression. The growth of the productivity of agriculture, on the other hand, he stated, could only be in arithmetical progression — no evidence was given for this statement. This being so, it was a mathematical certainty that any rate of population increase, however small, continued in geometric progression, must eventually overtake any conceivable food supply. Malthus, a Cambridge man, was fascinated by this piece of mathematical theorizing, simple though it was.

Malthus's theory in fact conflicts with a great deal of evidence, both geographical and historical — to say nothing of the calculation which we have made, showing that a population with the survival rates of a nomadic tribe, and specific fertilities of the kind now observed in Africa, even at their maximum, will only just succeed in maintaining itself.

In Malthus's defence however it must be said that both geographical and historical knowledge in 1798 were far more limited than they are now. It must also be said, in view of the many claims which have been made in his name with which he would certainly have disagreed, that he favoured limiting population growth only by some moderate deferment of marriage. Furthermore, very few of his disciples are aware of an important statement which he made in the 1817 edition of his book, namely that 'were it possible for men to limit the number of their children by a wish, the natural indolence of mankind would be greatly increased, and the population of many countries would never reach its proper or natural extent'. He was apparently aware, at any rate when he wrote this edition, that many parts of the world were still, from the point of economic and other requirements, underpopulated; and, more significantly, of the beneficial stimulus to economic development which population growth can exert.

Building therefore on this idea, originally developed by Malthus himself, we now reach a conclusion which is, in effect, a converse of Malthus's own original proposition, namely that, in a great many times and places, population is undesirably low, and may be increasing at a very low rate. The time comes, of course, when population growth does threaten to overtake the 'means of subsistence', as they are understood in that time and place; and then the consequence is that population growth itself provides the necessary stimulus, inducing the community to change its existing methods of producing or obtaining food for more productive methods, which will enable it to support a larger population. When Malthus wrote his first edition, the population of Britain was approaching 10 millions, and, judging by what he knew of contemporary agricultural methods, he did not see how an increased number could be fed. But Malthus is to blame for being apparently unaware, throughout quite a long lifetime, of the agricultural, commercial and industrial revolution going on all around him, which not only enabled Britain to produce manufactured exports to purchase food grown elsewhere, but also greatly to increase agricultural production within the country.

A virtual absence, or very low rates of population increase, are in fact generally observed by anthropologists among primitive peoples in the world now.[1] To take one interesting example, Australians often reproach themselves with the fact that the full-blooded aboriginal population, still living a nomadic hunting life, appears to be stationary in numbers. It is true that the evidence for this is not very accurate. For many years the

[1] See particularly, Krzywicki, *Primitive Society and its Vital Statistics.*

writer was State Statistician of Queensland, which has a substantial aboriginal population, and used to prepare reports showing that it was approximately stationary, based on the only available evidence, namely questionnaires sent to the police officers responsible for the very large semi-arid districts in which the aborigines lived. These police officers, in the course of their multifarious duties, nevertheless made quick estimates, which were probably the most accurate obtainable, which did in fact indicate a stationary population. But we do now have considerable other evidence to show that this is only what was to have been expected.

Much more valid and comprehensive, though indirect, evidence can be obtained by 'jobbing back'. At the present time we see world population growing at nearly 2 per cent per year, and in some countries at 3 per cent or 4 per cent per year. Nothing approaching these rates prevailed in the past.

In the perspective of the thousands of centuries of man's previous existence on earth, the modern era must appear as one of unusually prolonged and unusually rapid growth. In earlier epochs, there probably were also periods of growth, alternating with periods of stagnation or even decline, but it is highly improbable that there has ever been an era of sustained world-wide growth such as that of the past 300 years, or a period of such rapid growth as occurred during the past 50 years. For, had mankind's numbers been continuously increasing as rapidly as they did from 1900 to 1950, the whole present world population could have descended from one human couple in only 24 centuries. Nevertheless, it is known that human beings have peopled the earth for thousands of centuries before recorded history began.[1]

At the beginning of the Christian era the order of magnitude of the world's population was some 250 million, and in A.D. 1650 some 500 million. The average rate of increase over this period therefore can only have been something like 0·04 per cent per year, almost inappreciably low compared with the rates of population growth to which we are now accustomed. The figures admittedly are not of a high order of accuracy. Suppose, to make an extreme assumption, the whole population of the world at the first date was 40 per cent lower, at 150 million, and at the latter date was 20 per cent higher, at 600 million, this still only means that the average rate of increase over the period was 0·09 per cent per year.

At a rate of increase of 0·04 per cent per year, it takes more than 16 centuries for population to double itself. For the more distant past the average rate of increase must have been far lower again. So far as biologists

---

[1] Memorandum submitted to the World Population Conference, 1954, by the Population Division of the United Nations.

can judge, the human race has existed in this world for something like a million years (however, the evidence on which this statement is based seems to be very uncertain, and some biologists are so casual that one wonders whether they have even got the correct number of zeros). If the figure is correct, and the first available estimate of world population, at the beginning of the Christian era, stood at 250 millions, this implies an average rate of growth over the intervening aeons so infinitesimally slow that it took over 37,000 years for world population to double itself, or 500 years for it to increase by 1 per cent. These calculations are based on the human race having started from only two people, which Christians are bound to believe, though they are free to speculate on the date at which it happened. Those who prefer to hold the belief (which also has many difficulties) that the human race started from a large number of beings becoming human at the same time, and still adhering to the estimated duration of a million years, are bound to hypothecate a rate of growth much slower yet.

The slow average rate of population growth over historical time can be more closely analysed. Our information shows long periods of time, for many countries, in which there was not only an absence of population increase, but an actual decrease. These are to be explained by exceptional mortality, and not by declining reproductivities. 'Russia being mentioned as likely to become a great empire, by the rapid increase of population: — Johnson "Why, Sir, I see no prospect of their propagating more. They can have no more children than they can get". Boswell: "But have not nations been more populous at one period than another?" Johnson: "Yes, Sir: but that has been owing to the people being less thinned at one period than another, whether by emigrations, war or pestilence, not by their being more or less prolifick. Births at all times bear the same proportion to the same number of people."'[1] It is true that pestilences, wars, and periods of political anarchy, have effected disastrous reductions in population in the past. But Dr. Johnson was not entirely correct. Ancient populations may also have declined through the motives and methods which are familiar in the modern world. Cicero (in the *Pro Caelio*)[2] imagines the notorious Clodia being condemned by the spirit of her ancestor, asking whether he constructed an aqueduct to bring water to the city in order that she might use it for an infamous purpose: and we have also Villon's reference to the 'petits bains des filles amoureuses'. Riquet[3] also brings forward evidence of restrictions on conception in the seventh–ninth centuries A.D.;

Si la marque du progrès scientifique devait consister à savoir modifier la nature, suivant un plan déterminé, au gré de l'homme, les contemporains des

---

[1] Boswell's *Life of Johnson*, diary for 26 October 1769.
[2] Quoted by Landry, *Traité de Démographie*.   [3] *Population*, October–December 1949.

premiers chrétiens y avaient parfaitement réussi dans le domaine de la sexualité, sans attendre le siècle du télégraphe et du chemin de fer.

Les Pénitentiels (VII and IX siècles) fournissent un catalogue de toutes les formes steriles et dégradantes de l'assouvissement sexuel, en y joignant pour chaque cas une pénitence assortie. Cela permet de douter qu'à cette epoque, comme dans la précédente et les suivantes, les Chrétiens aient respecté la sainteté du marriage uniquement par incapacité d'imaginer autre chose.

It is quite true that most of the historic (still more the prehistoric) evidence on population has an extremely low degree of accuracy. When a pioneer is exploring unknown country, but confines his record to that which is accurately measurable, he may give a very misleading impression. If he sees faintly a range of mountains in the distance, he should record it on his chart, with the best estimate that he can make of its height and position, to be checked later when further information becomes available.

As we go further back in time and the accuracy of the information on population diminishes, its interest increases. On the subject of the numbers of our ancestors in the remote past archaeologists are able to make some interesting though very approximate estimates. From examination of burial grounds Nougier[1] estimated a population, in the Palaeolithic Period, of only 10,000 for the whole of France; but rising to millions in the Neolithic Period. To Palaeolithic Britain he attributes a population of only 'some hundreds or thousands' — only the Thames Valley being settled. Grahame Clark[2] also gives early Palaeolithic Britain a population measured only in hundreds, with some summer visitors from Europe. By the Mesolithic Period[3] he gives Britain a population of 3–4,000, 20,000 in the Neolithic Period, 30–40,000 in the Middle Bronze Age, mostly in England; early Bronze Age Scotland only carried 2,500 population.[4] Grahame Clark gives Iron Age Britain 400,000 population.

The population of the world before the introduction of agriculture has been estimated at 5–10 million.[5]

A summary of available information on world population up to 1800 is given in Table III.1, followed by detailed reviews of the information for each country. The following references are frequently quoted and are not further specified in detail:

Beloch, *Die Bevölkerung in Griechisch-Römisch Altertum*, Leipzig, 1886.
A. M. Carr-Sanders, *World Population — Past Growth and Present Trends*, 1922.
P. C. Putnam (of United States Atomic Energy Commission), *The Fu ure of Land-Based Nuclear Fuels* — and private communications.
M. K. Bennett, *The World's Food*, 1954 (particularly for the period 1000–1600).

[1] *Population*, April–June 1954.   [2] *Archaeology and Society*.
[3] This estimate was also made by Fleure, *Geographical Review*, October 194 .
[4] Childe, *What Happened in History*.
[5] Goran Ohlin, World Population Conference, 1965.

Willcox, *Studies in American Demography*, 1940.
Usher, *Geographical Review*, January 1930.
Taylor, *Canadian Journal of Economics and Political Science*, August 1950.
Russell, 'Late Ancient and Medieval Populations' (*Transactions of the American Philosophical Society*, 1958).
Cipolla, *Economic History of World Population*.
Durand, World Population Conference, 1965.
Reinhardt, *Histoire de la Population Mondiale*.

TABLE III.1. WORLD POPULATION TO 1800
(millions)

	A.D. 14	350	600	800	1000	1200	1340	1500	1600	1650	1700	1750	18cc
Egypt	7	4	2·7	3	3	2	3	2·5	2·5	2·5	2·5	2·5	2·5
Rest of North Africa	4·2	2	1·8	1	1	1·5	2	3·5					2·5
AFRICA TOTAL	23	30	37	43	50	61	70	85	95	100	100	100	100
U.S.A. and Canada								1	1	1	1	2	6
Other America								40	14	12	12	13	19
AMERICA TOTAL	3	5	7	10	13	23	29	41	15	13	13	15	25
China	73	60	54	55	60	123	62	100	150	100	150	207	315
India and Pakistan	70	75	75	75	70	75	75	79	100	150	200	200	190
Japan	2	3	6	8	10	12	14	16	18	22	26	26	26
Asia Minor, Syria, Cyprus	14	17	11	12	10	10	11	8	7	7	7	7	7
Other South West Asia	20	24	15	15	12	11	11	7	6	6	6	6	6
Asian U.S.S.R.	5	5	5	5	5	6	6	6	6	6	6	6	6
Other East Asia	5	6	7	8	10	11	13	15	16	20	25	32	40
ASIA TOTAL	189	190	173	178	177	248	192	231	303	311	420	484	590
England and Wales									4·6	5·2	5·8	6·1	9·1
Scotland									0·85	0·95	1·04	1·25	1·6
Ireland									1·2	1·6	2·5	3·1	5·2
British Isles	0·4	0·3	0·8	1·2	1·7	2·8	5·3	4·0					
Spain									6·6	7·8	9·3	10·4	15·9
Portugal	6	4	3·6	4	7	8	9·5 {7·0 {1·3	6·0 1·3	5·0 1·3	6·4 1·6	8·2 2·3	10·5 2·9
France									{20	20	21	28	
Belgium	6·6	5	3	5	7	12	30	16	16 {1·2	1·6	2·2	3·1	
Netherlands									0·9	1·2	1·6	2·1	
Italy	14	5	4	4	5	7·8	9·3	10	12	11	13	16	19
Greece	3	2	1·2	2}	5	4	{2} {2}	4·5	5·5	6	7	8	8·5
Rest of S.E. Europe	2	3	1·8	3}									
Scandinavia							{0·6	0·5	0·8	1·0	1·2	1·4	1·8
Germany (excl. Eastern Provinces) and Austria	3·5	3·5	2·1	4	4	8	{14	11	15	12	15·5	18	23
Russia in Europe (present boundaries)						{7·5	6	8	6	11	14·5	19·5	28 40
Poland, Czechoslovakia, etc.	4	4·8	2·8	6 {1·0	1·4	1·8	3·5	5	5	5·5	8		
Hungary				{1	1·5	2	4	3	2·5	2·5	3·5	5	
EUROPE	39·5	27·6	19·3	29·2	39·2	51·5	84·5	67·8	83·4	90·0	105·8	129·8	172·8
OCEANIA	1	1	1	1	1	1	2	2	2	2	2	2	2
WORLD	256	254	237	261	280	384	378	427	498	516	641	731	890

AFRICA

Egypt. For A.D. 14 Johnson's estimate[1] is preferred to Beloch's 5 million (though Russell also supports Beloch). Glotz[2] finds a population of 7 million in the fourth century B.C. at the time of Alexander. In the intervening Ptolemaic Period it is possible that the population stagnated, but it seems likely that it declined.

[1] *Economic Survey of the Roman Empire* (Tenney Frank, General Editor).
[2] *Ancient Greece at Work*.

Issawi[1] puts Egypt's population at 6–7 million in the Roman and early Arab period. By the fourteenth century he estimates that it had declined to 4 million or less. There then followed another long period of misrule under the Mamelukes and the Turks. We know fairly accurately the population of Egypt in 1800 because Napoleon, in the course of his invasion, took a census. At that time it was no more than 2½ million. In 1840 it was officially estimated at 3·2 million, but quite probably was still only 2·5 million.

There is indirect evidence of population decline in Roman Egypt. Documentary evidence is abundant, not only from the hieroglyphic inscriptions of ancient Egypt, but also for Roman Egypt, which wrote letters and kept accounts on papyrus, a form of paper obtained from a kind of large bulrush growing on the banks of the Nile. (This was much cheaper, though less durable, than the parchment or vellum which were the alternative writing materials of the ancient world, and Egypt exported considerable quantities.) In a humid climate it will not keep well, but in the rainless Egyptian air papyrus lasts for a very long period. About fifty years ago were discovered the Oxyrhynchus Papyri — the contents of a great rubbish heap into which thousands of old letters and papers had been dumped, up to late in the third century A.D., when it appears to have been covered over. We thus have more information about economic life in Roman Egypt than we have for any other province.

Information on rents and land values, which Johnson has extracted from these and other sources, yields, to an economist, strong indications of declining population. By the third century A.D. houses were so abundant that one could be rented for a year for 20 *drachmai*, i.e. not much more than five days' wages of a skilled worker. The evidence from land rents is even more conclusive. To allow for the steady rise in prices, they are re-expressed in the form of wheat, of which the average yield was 1·7 tons per hectare.[2] Economic theory and experience alike tell us that the proportion of the product expected to go to the landowner will be highest in a densely populated country, with no fresh land available for settlement, and with no substantial opportunities for emigration or industrial employment open to the rural population. In such cases the landlord can charge as rent the full marginal product of the land, which is approximately half the total crop. Something like this ratio has prevailed in the modern world (before recent changes) in China, India and Japan. In the Middle East it prevails in densely populated irrigated areas, but not in the more sparsely populated areas. A ratio of about 40 per cent has prevailed in modern Spain, and in

---

[1] *Egypt at Mid-Century* and *Egypt in Revolution*.
[2] Glotz, *Ancient Greece at Work*. Yields in Greece were much lower.

England from the seventeenth to the nineteenth centuries. In pre-Nasser Egypt the figure was 38 per cent,[1] and in the 1890's, when the pressure of population was less, appears to have been about 31 per cent.

In ancient Egypt, the proportion of the product taken in rent fell from 38 per cent in the first century A.D. to 26 per cent in the third — a clear indication that population was becoming less dense relative to land. Capital was becoming more abundant relative to population and rates of interest were falling; land could be purchased for 5¼ years' purchase of its rental in the first century, but required more than 7 years' purchase in the third century.

In the main table, the population in A.D. 350 is taken at 4 million in place of Russell's 3 million, but the other data to 1500 are Russell's. Population between 1500 and 1800 is assumed stationary.

Rest of North Africa. For A.D. 13, Beloch's data show 0·5 million for Cyrenaica and 6 million for the rest of North Africa. Russell's reduction of this total is accepted, also his subsequent figures. Of the total for 1500, 1 million were in Tunis. An estimate[2] based on Bonné is available for 1800.

Rest of Africa. Putnam's estimate for A.D. 14: other data (for Africa as a whole) from Bennett and, since 1650, from Carr-Saunders, who considers that slave raiding and tribal wars were reducing population during this period. Bennett estimates a rise at a slow uniform rate from 50 million in 1000 to 90 million in 1600. The latter figures are raised slightly to agree with Carr-Saunders. Willcox, however, estimates an unchanged 100 million for all Africa from 1650 to 1850. So also does Durand from 1750 to 1850, and this figure is adopted.

The prohibition of the slave trade and the establishment of political order should have enabled African population to increase during the nineteenth century. But this was offset by the devastating spread among Africans, on their first contact with Europeans, of epidemics of diseases such as measles, to which Europeans were immune, which proved fatal to them.

The population of Uganda, which was first brought into contact with Europeans about 1894, fell steadily from that date until about 1925. In this case the fall was mainly attributable to epidemics. 'It is doubtful whether even the dreadful ravages of the slave trade have accomplished more destruction than the epidemics of recent years', wrote Sir Albert Cook[3] in 1918. In Kenya[4] also there was a decline until about 1920. In Tanganyika

---

[1] Bresciani–Turroni, *Weltwirtschaftliches Archiv*, October 1933.
[2] *L'Egypte Contemporaire*, 1942.
[3] In his book, *Uganda Memories*.
[4] See Report of East African Royal Commission.

the evidence for depopulation is more definite still, and the turn did not come until the 1930's. In recent years the population of Uganda, in spite of an abnormally low fertility, has been increasing at 1–1½ per cent per year, of Kenya 1·6 per cent.

However, some anthropologists, led by Rivers, have attributed depopulation of primitive communities, after the first contact with Europeans (particularly in Polynesia) to a psychic illness, to a feeling of boredom and loss of all interest in life, once the routine of their tribal life has been interrupted.

AMERICA

For A.D. 14 an estimate by Putnam is used. Estimates for 1650 from Carr-Saunders. Willcox makes 'Other America' only 7 million in 1650, 10 million in 1750, followed by a very steep rise to 23 million in 1800. For the population of America at the time of the first arrival of European settlers in 1492 Vanzetti[1] estimates only 6–8 millions, including the 1 million in United States and Canada. His estimate of 18 million for 1800 is close to Carr-Saunders's. Cipolla's estimate of 15 million for the whole of America seems preferable to Carr-Saunders's 12 million: Carr-Saunders's figures are again used to 1800.

Another estimate for 1750 by Humboldt (quoted by Reinhardt) gave Latin America 16 million population, of whom 3 million were white, 7¼ million Indian, 5 million mixed race and 0·8 million Negro. Further support for the idea of substantial growth of Latin American population in the eighteenth century is given by Kingsley Davis,[2] by Reinhardt, who estimates a rise in the population of Brazil from 0·18 million in 1660 to 2·5 million in 1780 (2·2 per cent per year), and by Newling,[3] who also finds the population of Jamaica growing at 2·1 per cent per year, from 48,000 in 1703 to 283,000 in 1787.

In Jamaica, however, the increase was due to heavy additional importation of slaves from Africa. The slave population rose from 45,000 in 1703 to only 205,000 in 1775 in spite of the importation of 359,000 slaves during that period.[4] The slave population suffered high mortality and marriage was discouraged, and apart from new introductions it showed,[5] between 1722 and 1788, a median rate of fall of 2·3 per cent per year (varying between 1·5 per cent and 3·7 per cent for different periods). After 1787, slave trading was reduced, and prohibited in 1805; between 1787 and 1834,

[1] *Land and Man in Latin America* (Società Italiana di Sociologia Rurale, 1961).
[2] University of California, Institute of International Studies, Reprint 131.
[3] University of Pittsburgh, private communication.
[4] Gourou, Annuaire du Collège de France, 1964–5.
[5] Roberts, *The Population of Jamaica*.

Newling's figures show an overall rate of population growth of 0·6 per cent per year (to 371,000 in 1834).

It appears that there was a great reduction of the indigenous population of America after contact with the whites. Castro[1] estimated that the population of what is now El Salvador fell from 130,000 in 1524 to 60,000 in 1551, recovered to 77,000 in 1570, and after that rose slowly to 133,000 in 1770, 147,000 in 1778 and 171,000 in 1796. Vanzetti left open the possibility that his estimates for the beginning of the sixteenth century might be too low, but considered 20–30 million the maximum for the whole of America. Steward[2] made an estimate of 15½ million, including 1 million for U.S.A. and Canada, 4½ and 6 millions for the Aztec and Inca civilizations respectively, ¼ million for the West Indies and ¾ million for Central America. Rosenblat[3] prepared detailed estimates (distinguishing races) for 1650 and 1825 (Table III.2).

TABLE III.2. LATIN AMERICAN POPULATIONS

	1650	1825
	(millions)	
Mexico	3·8	6·8
Antilles	0·61	2·84
Rest Central America	0·65	1·6
Venezuela	0·37	0·8
Colombia	0·75	1·33
Guianas	0·10	0·26
Peru	1·60	1·4
Chile	0·55	1·1
Brazil	0·95	4·0
Other areas in S. America	2·0	2·9
Total Latin America	11·38	23·03

Recently however the pre-Conquest estimate for Mexico alone has been raised[4] to 25 million. The next available estimate, for 1810, is 6 million. War and enslavement played their part in reducing population; but here again the principal factor was probably epidemics[5] of European diseases, to which the Amerindians lacked any immunity. Bennett agrees in making

[1] *La Población de El Salvador*, Madrid, 1942.
[2] Quoted *Population Bulletin*, February 1962.
[3] *La Población Indigena de America*, Buenos Aires, 1945.
[4] Proceedings of the 34th International Conference of Americanists, Vienna, July 1962. This result is also agreed by the University of California, Institute of Ibero-American Studies (quoted Stanislawski, *Geographical Review*, April 1964, p. 272). Cook & Borah (*Historia Mexicana*, 1962–3) find evidence from Spanish records for the 25 million estimate for 1500, and for only 1–2 million less than a century later.
[5] Poole, *Geographical Journal*, March 1951.

the whole of America 41 million in 1500 and 15 million in 1600, and his estimates are entered in the table (with interpolations before 1000).

ASIA

Andaman Islands. While not large enough to be entered in the main table, it is interesting to record an example of depopulation which has been closely studied, namely that of the primitive inhabitants of the Andaman Islands in the Indian Ocean.[1] The number of tribesmen has fallen precipitously.

1858	3200
1900	625
1911	455
1921	309
1931	74

Among the Onge tribe, in the remotest part of the islands, the rate of decline was from 282 in 1911 to 99 in 1921. Cappieri believes that this illustrates a principle deduced mathematically by Livi; where marriage is confined to the members of one's own community, as it is in a tribe, the community should be of a minimum size of 500, if biologically dangerous inbreeding is to be avoided. The tribes of the Andaman Islands fell to well below this size. In addition, there have been numerous epidemics in the islands, widespread venereal disease and extremely high infant mortality. There is a marked male surplus, and the women are polyandrous.

China. No other country has such long records of population change as China, and although there are many difficulties in their interpretation, they certainly deserve the attention of all who are interested in population movements. The estimates which various writers have published are all based upon the periodic official registrations, made for tax and other purposes; the differences between them represent the varying opinions of Chinese scholars on the question of how comprehensive the registration was, the allowances to be made for children, for inhabitants of remote areas, for systematic evasion, etc.

Ta Chen[2] thought that the evidence showed Chinese population moving in discernible cycles, with maxima shown by the Census under the Western Han Dynasty in A.D. 2, the T'ang Dynasty in 754, the Sung Dynasty in 1100, and the Ming Dynasty in 1600.

The idea of cycles was carried further back by Taylor.[3] In 500 B.C., he estimates, the Chinese population stood at 15–18 million — occupying an

---

[1] Cappieri, World Population Conference, 1954.
[2] *American Journal of Sociology*, December 1946.
[3] *Canadian Journal of Economics and Political Science*, August 1950.

area constituting only about one-third of present-day China. We know little about the outer areas, which were probably only thinly inhabited by hunting peoples.

The state of civilization in China at that time was not entirely satisfactory. It is recorded in the biography of Confucius, who lived about 600 B.C., that when the sage, at one time in his career, was employed as a tax-collector by the Duke of Lu, he spoke reproachfully of the extravagance of his employer, who demanded one-fifth of the peasants' produce, whereas in the 'Golden Age' (already by that time in the remote past) the recognized maximum had been one-tenth.

The subsequent centuries were a period of mounting warfare and disorder, which came to an end with the establishment of centralized rule over the whole of China by the Chin Dynasty in 221 B.C. By this time, persistent wars had reduced the population to 7–9 millions.

Historians will long continue to debate the Toynbean principle, whether periods of newly established centralized Imperial rule, restoring peace after long centuries of warfare, lack creative energy. In China, in the two centuries after the establishment of the Chin Dynasty, the area of settlement was doubled, to about two-thirds of modern China, and a very large population increase took place, to an estimated 71 millions in A.D. 2. If we assume that the original population[1] of the outer territories absorbed into China during this period was two millions, we still conclude that the rate of population growth over this period averaged a steady 0·9 per cent per year.

The best estimates for Chinese population from the beginning of the Christian Era to 1953[2] have been shown on Diagram III.A. The scale (logarithmic) required to show the changing numbers over this very long period makes some of the slopes look very steep; in fact the highest estimated rate of growth, as is shown on the diagram, was only 1·2 per cent per year.[3] The Chinese population cycles are associated with the names of

---

[1] At a density of 1 person/sq. km. (i.e. for a population practising some domestication of animals, but not a settled agricultural population) we take the population of the two-thirds of the area of modern China not covered by the Chinese population data of B.C. 500 and B.C. 221 at 4 million (and of the one-third not covered in A.D. 2 at 2 million).

[2] The estimate of the U.S. Bureau of Census (*The Size Composition and Growth of the Population of Mainland China*, International Population Statistics Reports, Series P.90, No. 15) of 602 million for 1953 (i.e. suggesting an understatement of 3 per cent in the official Census), is entered on the diagram, though the model prepared in Chapter II suggests a lower figure.

[3] Data are obtained from Ping-Ti Ho, *Studies on the Population of China 1368–1953* (Harvard University Press, 1959), whose results are used from 1393 onwards; Durand, *Population Studies*, March 1960, whose work appears to give the best general account; and also some results by Usher, *Geographical Review*, January 1930, whose figures for 1260 and 1290 are used to supplement Durand. In the later period, the data for 1750 and 1812 are Durand's. Available alternative estimates, excluded from the diagram, are 60 million for A.D. 2 (Ta Chen, Taylor and Usher); for A.D. 156, Usher's 50 and Taylor's 60; for A.D. 606, Usher's 46; for A.D. 733, Usher's 45; for 754, Taylor's 65 and Usher's and Ta Chen's

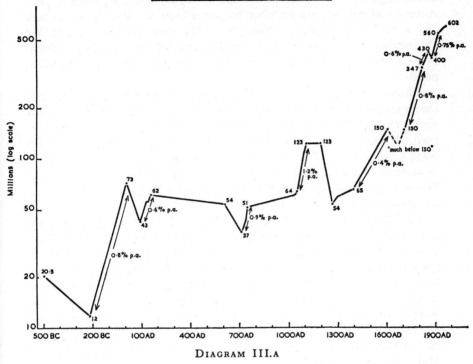

CHINESE POPULATION 500 B.C. - 1953 A.D.

DIAGRAM III.A

dynasties, which historians in fact appear to treat not only as dynasties, but as the essential political and cultural units in Chinese history. The population peak at the beginning of the Christian Era represented the high point of the Western Han Dynasty, followed by a rapid decline, and recovery under the Eastern Han Dynasty in the first two centuries of the Christian Era. This was followed by a decline under the Sui Dynasty, and

63; for 1080, two violently conflicting estimates of 100 by Taylor and 33 by Usher; and for 1100, Ta Chen's 43, which is almost certainly too low. For 1381, Durand and Usher give 60 million; for 1393 they give 61 million and 59 respectively. Ping-Ti Ho cannot be very definite about the rates of growth between 1393 and 1600, but it does not appear that he will agree with Usher's figure of 61 million for 1600, which appears too low. For 1650, which Ping-Ti Ho can only describe as 'much below 150 million', Carr-Saunders estimates 150 million, Willcox 113 million; and Usher and C. H. Chen (Proceedings of the International Statistical Institute, Vol. XXV) estimate 105 million for 1661. Chen gives 112 million for 1685 and Usher 101 for 1690, 116 for 1710. Chen's estimate is 141 for 1724. For 1750, Willcox's estimate is 199, and Usher's 177. Chen has 160 for 1753 and 182 for 1766. For 1781 Durand has 270 and Usher 277, and Durand 294 for 1791. Willcox makes a further estimate of 264 to 1800. For 1812 we have 360 from Usher and only 271 from Chen.

in the eighth century a rise under the T'ang Dynasty, a period of great
cultural and political vigour, when the capital city An Shan is said to have
had a million population. However 'at the very height of the T'ang
Dynasty's grandeur and influence' An Lu-Shan's Revolution (A.D. 756–66)
revealed grave popular discontent, and 'decimated more than 30 million
people'.[1]

A further period of rapid growth took place under the Sung Dynasty in
the eleventh century. Ping-Ti Ho draws attention to the importance of the
discovery and dissemination of a new quick-ripening rice after the year
1000. Population growth was checked in the twelfth century, under the
Sung-Chin Dynasty. The thirteenth century was rendered disastrous, even
more than in Eastern Europe, by the invasions and devastations of the
Mongols, and Chinese population appears to have been reduced to less than
half its former level in some fifty years.

The Ming Dynasty, another period of cultural achievement, between the
fourteenth and sixteenth centuries, was one of moderate population
growth. The first part of the seventeenth century was another period of
grave disorder and population decline. Ping-Ti Ho identifies the date of the
beginning of rapid population growth at about 1685. Throughout the
eighteenth century he finds real evidence, quite apart from the official
records, of population increase. China, from this date until the twentieth
century, was once again a strictly ordered and centralized state under the
rule of the Manchus, a dynasty originally of foreign rulers (as were the
Mogul emperors in India).

Chinese population movements during the last two centuries have
recently been reviewed in detail.[2] Durand, Usher, Ping-Ti Ho and a writer
in *Population* all agree in showing a point of inflection, some slowing down
in the rate of population growth, about the last decade of the eighteenth
century. The philosopher-Emperor Ch'ien Lung, ruling at that time, gave
way to a series of weaker successors, who were unable to maintain order.
The 'Opium War' with Britain in 1839–42, to compel China to trade with
western countries, and one of whose terms of peace was the cession of Hong
Kong, shook Chinese morale badly. However the real check to population
came in 1850, with the outbreak of the bloody Taiping Rebellion (started
by a religious leader, who preached a sort of parody of Christianity; the
name Taiping means, ironically, 'Heavenly Peace').

Ping-Ti Ho has shown that the five most densely populated provinces[3]
of central China, devastated in the Taiping War and the Nien War which

---

[1] Alltree, in the symposium *Toynbee and History*, p. 263.
[2] Clark, *Population*, June–July 1964.
[3] Anhwei, Chekiang, Hopei, Kiangsi and Kiangsu. Fukien also appears to have lost
population.

followed it, which had an estimated population of 171 million in 1850, even by 1953 had only recovered to 145 million.

Ping-Ti Ho agrees with Carr-Saunders in putting Chinese population at 430 million in 1850, and the same again in 1900, with 'a serious fall' between 1850 and 1870.

The best estimate appears to be that population increased at about 0·75 per cent per year, at almost as high a rate as in the eighteenth century, between 1870 and 1915. In the recurring disorders and foreign invasions from that date until the Census of 1953 however the rate of growth in the aggregate was very slow.

An interesting further study can be made in China of provincial rates of population increase.[1] In view of the extraordinary losses of population in certain provinces in the Taiping War, these are omitted in the comparison for the last century. For the dates reviewed, namely 1393, 1780 and 1842 (and also, of course, for the Census of 1953) the sum of the provincial data accorded reasonably well with the accepted national estimate. (See Diagram III.B.)

For the first period, the negative relationship between initial density and decadal rate of population growth is marked. For the 1780–1842 period, such a relationship appears to hold, but with considerably less precision. For the 1842–1953 period the relationship is again found to be close — and would have been even more marked had the data for the five declining provinces been included.

One possible explanation of the observed results is migration to the less densely populated areas. Migration might be expected to lead to a rate of population growth much greater than normal in the sparsely populated areas, without having any very marked effect on the population in the dense areas. It is also possible however that differential mortality prevailed, a true Malthusian situation, with life easier to maintain in the less densely populated areas. It is also possible that marriage was earlier in the less densely populated provinces.

For Manchuria, under Japanese control for part of the period, and the Western outer territories some estimates for 1910 and 1930 are available.[2] So far as they can be relied on, they show a strong attraction of population to the more sparsely settled areas (Table III.3).

The maximum population which can be fed in any region by agriculture of the Chinese type, and at Chinese standards of diet, as we shall see later, is perhaps about 600 persons/sq. km. (more of course if there are inter-regional imports of food). In 1842 the most densely populated province,

---

[1] Data from Usher, Putnam, Ping-Ti Ho and Chandrasekhar (*China's Population*).
[2] *Population Index*, April 1952. The data for 1787 and 1850 are Ping-Ti Ho's.

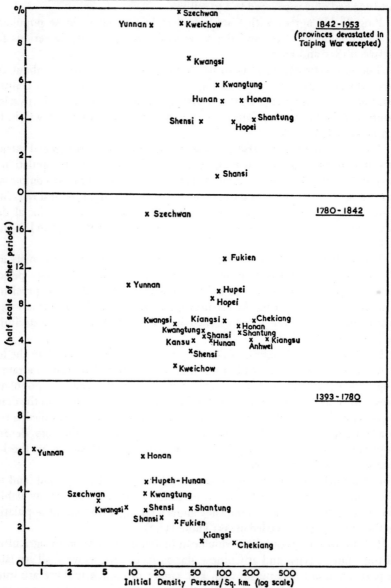

CHINA—DECADAL RATES OF POPULATION INCREASE BY PROVINCES

1842-1953
(provinces devastated in
Taiping War excepted)

x Szechwan
Yunnan x   x Kweichow

x Kwangsi

x Kwangtung
Hunan x   x Honan

Shensi x   x   x Shantung
            Hopei

x Shansi

1780-1842

x Szechwan

x Fukien

x Yunnan

x Hupei
x Hopei

Kwangsi   Kiangsi x   x Chekiang
    Kwangtung x   x Honan
    x Shansi   x Shantung
Kansu x   x Hunan   x   x Kiangsu
    x Shensi   Anhwei

x Kweichow

1393-1780

x Yunnan

x Honan

x Hupeh - Hunan

Szechwan   x Kwangtung
    x
    Kwangsi x   x Shensi   x Shantung
        Shansi x   x Fukien
                Kiangsi
                x   x Chekiang

(half scale of other periods)

Initial Density Persons/Sq. km. (log scale)

DIAGRAM III.b

TABLE III.3.   POPULATION GROWTH OF OUTER PROVINCES

		Initial density persons/sq. km.	Decadal rate of increase %
Manchuria and Jehol[a]	1787–1850	2·8	19·8
	1850–1910	8·7	29·5
	1910–1930	23·6	22·2
	1930–1953	35·3	17·2
Inner Mongolia	1910–1930	0·6	25·8
	1930–1953	3·9	13·0
Sinkiang	1910–1930	1·3	9·1
	1930–1953	1·5	33·9
Sikang	1930–1953	0·8	24·7
Chinghai	1930–1953	1·7	16·3

[a] To 1910, provinces of Liao Ning and Kirin only.

Kiangsu, which includes the large cities of Shanghai and Nanking, attained the density of 387 persons/sq. km. This cannot be described as the Malthusian limit, though it was approaching it. Nor can we categorize as an illustration of Malthusian theory the fact that the Taiping and Nien Wars, when they came, wrought their greatest devastation in the provinces already most densely populated.

Nevertheless, it may be permissible to generalize that very high population densities among an unwarlike people make them much more subject to devastation and massacre. 'The thicker the hay, the easier it is mown' was Alaric's grim remark before the sack of Rome.

India and Pakistan. India, like China, appears to have experienced long periods of stationary or declining population. The first estimate by Pran Nath[1] is for the time of the Emperor Asoka in the second century B.C., for which date he finds a population of 100–140 million. For the beginning of the Christian Era Usher estimates only 70 million; but it is quite possible that there had been serious losses in the disordered period after Asoka. Bennett estimates that a long period of virtual stagnation occurred before the checking of warfare by the establishment of the Mogul Empire in the sixteenth century.

Year	1000	1100	1200	1300	1400	1500	1600
Population (millions)	48	50	51	50	46	54	68

[1] *A Study of the Economic Conditions of Ancient India*, Proceedings of the Royal Asiatic Society, 1929.

Morland[1] estimated the population of early seventeenth-century India (including what is now Pakistan) at 100 million. This was one-third of what it was in the 1911 Census, about the time when he was writing. For the more densely populated southern region, he estimated for the early sixteenth century a population of 30 million, or half of what it was in 1911, i.e. growing much more slowly than the north in the subsequent centuries. Morland's figure was accepted by Radhakamal Mukerjee.[2] Bennett's figures are adjusted proportionately throughout to agree to 1600.

Indian historians agree that there was considerable depopulation in the wars and disorders of the late seventeenth and eighteenth centuries. The Mogul Empire had increasing difficulty in maintaining order, in face of disloyal generals, and their own family disputes. Serious disorders began after the death of the Emperor Aurungzeb in 1707, and were probably at their worst in the late eighteenth century, when the Mahrattas were raiding all over India. In the Punjab in the mid-eighteenth century 'people left the smaller villages, and population became concentrated in the larger ones more capable of defence against outside aggressors. Even in these larger villages, farmers had to plough with swords in their hands, bringing under cultivation only as much land as could be conveniently defended'.[3]

Population growth was resumed when order was restored. This occurred at different dates in different parts of the country, probably as early as 1770 in Bengal, not until about 1850 in the Punjab and Sind. All the available evidence seems compatible with the hypothesis of a decline in the eighteenth century. It also seems clear that there must have been periods of declining population in the earlier centuries.

Chandrasekhar[4] also accepts Morland's figure for 1600 and Shirras's 130 million for 1750. For the mid-nineteenth century Chandrasekhar quotes McCulloch's estimate of 133 million and Mukerjee's of 150 million. Durand points out that the results of the first Census in 1871, used by Carr-Saunders and Willcox, were understated, and that Kingsley Davis's figure of 255 million for that date should be used. From this he deduces a figure of 190 million for 1800, which is accepted here (but his figure for 1750 is not).

Japan. Our general historical review[5] begins with Sawada's estimate for the Nara Era, in the eighth century A.D., of 6–7 million (of whom a substantial proportion were serfs). The next estimate is for the late sixteenth

---

[1] *India at the Death of Akbar* (1920).   [2] *Economic History of India.*
[3] *Hissar District Gazeteer*, 1904. I am indebted to Mr. Rafiq Ahmad for this quotation.
[4] *Population Review* (U.S.A.), January 1958.
[5] *Population Problems of Japan*, No. 5 (Japanese National Committee for UNESCO, 1962).

century, of 13–18 million. Taeuber[1] quotes figures showing a higher rate of growth.

9th century	3·7 million
11th „	4·4 „
13th „	9·8 „
Late 16th „	18·0 „

Kotono[2] also estimates the population in 1600 at 18 million.

It was just at the beginning of the seventeenth century that Japan, after a long period of civil wars, started a new period of peace and order, albeit of economic and social stagnation, under the Tokugawa regime. Honjo, who has made a thorough study of the economic history of the period, estimated[3] that population was rising in the first part of the Tokugawa period. This period came to an abrupt end in 1868, when the Emperor, after centuries of nominal rule, resumed actual government.

For 1650 Landry[4] estimated 23 million population, while for 1700 Kotono estimates 26 million. It seems to be agreed that a population maximum was reached at about 1721, which Sale[5] estimates at 29 million at that date, the Japanese National Committee for UNESCO at 32 million.

The period from 1721 to 1868 is described by the Japanese National Committee for UNESCO as one of 'famines, epidemics, abortion, infanticide'; and throughout this period population only moved within the range of 30–32 million (29–30 million according to Sale). Lower estimates are made by Taeuber and Notestein,[6] as follows:

1750	25·9
1756	26·1
1804	25·6
1834	27·1
1852	27·2

Kotono makes the same estimate of 27 million for 1852. For 1872, at the time of the first official enumeration (not a full census) all authorities agree on a population of 34·8 million.

It is clear that the second half of the Tokugawa period was one of almost complete cessation of population growth. This was the subject of an extraordinary study by the great Victorian mathematical economist, Edgeworth,[7] in which he depicts a Japan which he must have thought up after seeing Ko-Ko in 'The Mikado', with the authorities encouraging civil

---

[1] *The Population of Japan*, Princeton, 1958.
[2] Of Hokkaido University, writing in *Melbourne University Science Review*, 1963.
[3] *Kyoto University Economic Review*, December 1927 and July 1928.
[4] *Traité de Démographie*.
[5] *Journal of the Royal Statistical Society*, 1908.
[6] *Population Studies*, June 1947.   [7] *Journal of the Royal Statistical Society*, 1895.

war, and as many executions as possible, with the object of keeping down the population, which they knew to be beyond the means of subsistence. This is most interesting as a piece of Edgeworthian writing, but it does not agree with the account given by Honjo. Tokugawa Japan was not a country in a state of primitive barbarism. Instead, it bore some remarkable resemblances to Baroque Europe. There was a considerable amount of trade, benevolently regulated by despotic public officials, though all intercourse with foreigners was forbidden. The country had become to a considerable degree urbanized. Taxation was excessive, and there were frequent famines. The Imperial power had become nominal, and the taxes went to support an elaborate hierarchy of the nobility and their *samurai*, an upper-class nominally consisting of soldiers, although, just as in contemporary France, there were some 'bourgeois gentilshommes' among them. As time went on, they became more and more idle, more and more numerous, and more and more impoverished. The drastic abolition of the old social order in 1868 must have been welcomed as a great relief.

In Tokugawa Japan both abortion and infanticide were widespread — whether due to excessive taxation, or to some deeper reason, it is difficult to say. Honjo quotes Baron Ro-Tzan, of the Sendai clan, reporting to the Shogun (the effective ruler of Japan) about 1810 to say that, up to two generations ago, 'a couple of farmers used to bring up five or six or even seven or eight children; but in recent years it has become the fashion among the farmers not to rear more than one or two children'. He attributed the difference largely to infanticide. So far from agreeing with Edgeworth's explanation, he complained that the lack of rural population growth, together with movement of population to the towns, was causing good agricultural land to lie waste.

Honjo also quotes the story of Baron Rakuo, who in 1784 ordered that a bale of rice should be awarded to any couple on his estate who 'in spite of their poverty' refrained from infanticide and brought up more than five children. The existence of such documents makes clear how widespread infanticide was.

The inexplicable part of the story is that, immediately after the revolution in 1868, the whole attitude of the Japanese people towards families changed. Infanticide and abortion practically disappeared, and for two generations the Japanese brought up some of the largest families in the world. In the 1920's, however, a reversal of trend again began.

MIDDLE EAST

Beloch's estimate of 19·5 million for Roman territory in Asia in A.D. 14 included 13 million in Asia Minor (of whom 6 million were in the

'Province of Asia'), 6 million in Syria, and 0·5 million in Cyprus. Russell's reduction to 14 million, and his subsequent estimates to 1500, are accepted. Usher estimates 20 million for non-Roman South West Asia (Persian Empire, including Iraq, and Arabia). For A.D. 600 Russell estimates 9·1 million in Iraq, 4·6 million in Persia, 1 million in Arabia, which appear consistent with Usher's figure.

For 1800 we have Bonné's estimates of 5·5 million for Anatolia, 1 million for Iraq, 0·8 for Syria and Lebanon, and 0·3 for Palestine, or an estimated 13 million for the whole of the Middle East. Between 1800 and 1900 Bonné shows the population of Iraq (1 million in 1800) and of Palestine (0·3 million) doubling, of Asia Minor (5·5 million) doubling, an average rate of increase of some 0·7 per cent per year. Syria and Lebanon (0·8 million in 1800) are shown as trebling, an average rate of increase of 1·1 per cent per year.

No estimates are available of the populations of Asia Minor and Syria during the first few centuries A.D. But the general indications are that they were at least maintained if not increased. Afterwards the general decline of population in the Middle East probably proceeded in about the same way as in Egypt.

'Population in the thirteenth-century Byzantine Empire cannot be ascertained but was certainly declining, through war and piracy.'[1] Bennett's estimates of a figure oscillating around 30 million between 1000 and 1600 appears too high.

In Cyprus, as late as 1881, the first Census revealed a population of only 186,000, as against Beloch's 500,000 in A.D. 14. A figure of 170,000 was estimated for 1491 and 1571.[2]

Even in Roman times, some of the Middle East may have been de-populated, in comparison with the great days of the Sumerian or Babylonian Empires.

Glotz estimated[3] that at the death of Alexander in the fourth century B.C. the population of 'Syria' (presumably including the whole of Alexander's Asian dominions) was 30 million.

Many of these striking cases of population decline have occurred in countries subject to malaria (Iraq, Italy, Ceylon, Greece). Some historians have speculated that malaria was the cause of population decline, though why it should have shown itself at one date and not at another they cannot explain. In fact, malaria spreads as a consequence, and not as a cause, of civil disorder and population decline. Once it has got hold, however, it

[1] Charanis, *Joshua Starr Memorial Volume*, Conference on Jewish Relations, New York, 1953.
[2] *Population Index*, January 1955.   [3] In *Ancient Greece at Work*.

tends to accelerate the population decline. Malaria can only be spread, as is known, by the *anopheles* and kindred species of mosquito, which breed only in stagnant water, not in running water. A settlement depending upon irrigation by running water, when in proper order, keeps its swamps drained and its ditches clear, and there is no danger of malaria. But sooner or later a time may come when these extensive works, the heritage from previous generations, are neglected through war, civil disorder, or perhaps through rural depopulation consequent upon the growth of an empire and of commercial cities, as in Iraq under the Caliphs. In the uncleared ditches and swamps the mosquitoes breed rapidly, and malaria gets a hold upon the people, which it is very difficult to break. Chronic malaria reduces reproductivity, and it clearly increases mortality. Furthermore, even after recovery, malaria sufferers are often left with their vitality so reduced that they become increasingly incapable of restoring their irrigation system to working order. Thus they become involved in a vicious circle of depopulation and disease. Much of the Romagna in Italy, for instance, which was fully populated in ancient times, was only restored to its ancient population and productivity by great efforts in the present century. The availability during the last twenty years of cheap and powerful insecticides has made it possible, for the first time, to exterminate the *anopheles* and kindred mosquitoes over wide areas, without the long labour of draining the swamps. This has already had a remarkable effect upon population trends in Ceylon and Greece, and probably elsewhere.

U.S.S.R. In Asia. Russell estimates that from the first to the ninth centuries 4·65 million people inhabited 3·8 million sq. km. of Soviet Asia and Mongolia (omitting 12·5 million sq. km. virtually uninhabited areas). Bennett makes this figure rise from 5 million in 1000 to 13 million in 1600. But the Census[1] of 1897 indicates only 7 million in Asian Russia; under-enumeration may have occurred, but should not be substantial. (Lorimer estimates only 3·4 million for 1858; but at that time the boundaries of Russia in Asia were not extended so far as they are now.) A comparatively stationary population before 1800 appears more probable.[2]

Other East Asia. The estimate for A.D. 14 is Putnam's.

Ceylon appears to have been another example of depopulation. Visual evidence of this remains in the fact that two-thirds of the country is still virtually uninhabited, but covered with remnants of buildings, irrigation works and other evidence of a dense population of civilized men in the past. The historical evidence is that this civilization, based on irrigation, was

---

[1] Quoted by Lorimer, *The Population of the Soviet Union* (League of Nations, 1946).

[2] United Nations Population Division (*Determination and Consequences of Population Trends*), from their adjustments to Willcox, imply a population of 3 million in 1650, 4 million in 1750, and 5 million in 1800.

destroyed by repeated invasions from India, leaving only a small population who were able to make a living, without elaborate irrigation works, in the high rainfall land in the west of the island. The report on the 1946 Census of Ceylon stated that when this civilization was at its height, about the eleventh century A.D., the country may have had a population of 10 million. The first Census taken by the British authorities in 1827 revealed a population of only 820,000.

For *Korea*[1] we have an estimate going back to 1404, when the population was given at 0·35 million, rising to 1·5 million by 1648, an average annual rate of increase of 0·6 per cent. From that date the rate of increase rose to 1·0 per cent per annum, giving a population of 7·6 million by 1807, and then decelerated again to 0·6 per cent per annum to give a population of 15·5 million in 1913. These movements are similar to those estimated for China.

The population of many of the remaining Asian countries has been only very imperfectly known even in the present century. Estimates for Indonesia[2] show a rate of growth of more than 2 per cent per year during the nineteenth century. Breman[3] estimates for Java and Madura (not the whole of Indonesia) 6 million in 1800 and 29·5 million in 1900, as against the previously accepted estimates of 4 and 28·5 respectively. Durand gives Indonesia 10 million in 1750, 14 million in 1800 and 22 million in 1850. Some who know the country well think that a rate of growth of 1 per cent annually is more plausible, and that the early population data were too low. There is some evidence[4] that the population of Java was stationary in the eighteenth century. The situation in Ceylon and the Philippines appears to be similar.

For the whole region, jobbing back from a population of 110 million in 1900, an estimate of 40 million is made for 1800. Carr-Saunders's figure is used to 1650. Remaining figures are interpolated.

Table III.4 gives the comparisons between the different Asian totals.

TABLE III.4. ESTIMATES OF POPULATION OF ASIA (EXCLUDING U.S.S.R.) (millions)

	1650	1750	1800
Cipolla		500	
Carr-Saunders	327	475	497
Willcox	257	437	595
Durand	—	480	630
As given in Table III.1.	311	484	590

[1] *Population Index*, October 1954.
[2] Keyfitz, *Economics and Finance in Indonesia*, October 1953.
[3] Quoted *Population*, October–December 1963, p. 794.
[4] Kidron, private communication.

EUROPE

Where not otherwise specified, Beloch's data have been used for A.D. 14, Taylor's for 300, Usher's for 1340, 1600 and 1700, Carr-Saunders's for 1650 and 1750, and those of *Statistisches Jahrbuch für das Deutsche Reich, Internationale Teil*, 1938, for 1800.

British Isles. The population of Britain is believed by some to have risen during the period of Roman rule in the first four centuries A.D., but Russell makes it fall. It seems to be agreed by all historians that in the subsequent period of extreme disorder and bloodshed the country was largely depopulated — Taylor thought that it was reduced by two-thirds. Depopulation had however probably already begun, judging by the evidence of shrunken and abandoned cities, during the later epoch of Roman Britain.

Russell's estimates are accepted. Nef[1] holds that a rapid population increase was taking place throughout Western Europe from the eleventh to fourteenth centuries. C. E. Stevens[2] holds that, after the first period of disorder at the time of the Saxon invasions, the population of Anglo-Saxon England was clearly rising (though there may have been another setback with the Danish invasions). From the eleventh century onward, beginning with the publication of Domesday Book, we have more information about the population of mediaeval England than we have about any other contemporary country.[3] Russell puts the population of England of 1086 at 1·1 million, Wales at 0·1, Ireland at 0·4 and Scotland at 0·12. Atsatt,[4] however, and most other writers, puts England in 1086 at 2 million. Russell raises his population to 2·6 million by 1260 and Atsatt hers to 2·88 million by 1164, both representing increases of a little over ½ per cent per annum. Just before the Black Death, the population of the British Isles had risen to over 5 million — a considerably reduced rate of increase on Atsatt's estimate, a steady rate of growth on Russell's. The Black Death is most often remembered as a single visitation in 1348; but in fact, as Russell conclusively shows, from a careful analysis of wills and other documents, it was really the first of a series of recurring pestilences which had brought the population of England by 1377 down to 2·3 million. Russell's figures for the different countries are given in Table III.5.

TABLE III.5. POPULATION OF THE BRITISH ISLES
(millions)

	1377	1545
England	2·3	3·25

[1] Private communication.   [2] Private communication.
[3] Josiah Cox Russell, *English Mediaeval Population.*
[4] Marjorie Atsatt, *Population Estimates for England and Wales from the 11th to 19th centuries.*

Wales	0·125	0·252
Scotland	0·35	0·69
Ireland	0·5	0·75

He gives the population of England, after succeeding outbreaks of plague, as follows (in millions):

1348	3·76
1350	3·13
1361	2·75
1369	2·45
1374	2·25

For 1377 we have some quite extensive records based on the collection of the poll tax in that year. If we are willing to assume that the percentage decline of population between 1348 and 1377 was the same in different regions, we can compare regional percentage rates of increase over the period of growth 1086–1348 (bearing in mind that they will be a little overstated if we agree that Russell made his base figure too low for 1086). From 0·3 per cent per annum for the growth rate of Southern England and East Anglia, which were already well populated in Norman times, we proceed to a figure of 0·5 per cent per annum for the Midlands, 0·6 per cent per annum for Northumbria and Cornwall, 0·8 per cent per annum for Lancashire and 0·9 per cent per annum for Yorkshire. These latter districts were much more lightly populated in Norman times, particularly Yorkshire, which was thoroughly devastated by William I.

It looks as if the figure of 0·3 per cent per annum measures the rate of natural increase of an agricultural community under mediaeval conditions, and that the higher figures for outlying counties (or for England as a whole in the first century after the Norman Conquest) may represent in parts the effects of immigration. The fifteenth century was one of foreign and civil wars, and it was estimated by Atsatt that the population of England and Wales in 1485 was still 2½ million, as it had been a century earlier.

Seventeenth-century England averaged a growth rate of only 0·25 per cent per annum. Data from 1701 onwards are from Deane and Cole,[1] and show a sudden acceleration after 1750. This acceleration of the rate of growth of population is of the greatest significance alike to demographers and economic historians.

Ireland. Until the last quarter of the eighteenth century, the British Parliament effectively prevented industrial and commercial development in Ireland, and compelled most of the population to live upon agriculture — as in Iceland (see below). But in Ireland the climate was more genial than

---

[1] *British Economic Growth.*

in Iceland and some natural fuel (peat) was available, though not in abundance. The really important difference however came from the introduction of the potato.[1] Many of the Irish potatoes are believed to be descended from the original garden plot of Sir Walter Raleigh, who certainly had little idea of providing a staple food, but thought of it only as a culinary curiosity. Potatoes will grow in Iceland for that matter, but nobody had then introduced them. As a result, in spite of the impeding of her industries, Ireland's population was able to grow, living at a simple but healthy level.

Irish population[2] was already increasing at the rate of 0·9 per cent per annum in the period 1687–1725. There was then a setback until the middle of the century, after which the rate again rose to 0·9 per cent between 1750 and 1780, and to 1·7 per cent between 1780 and 1820, even though substantial emigration had already begun by then. In the 1820's the net rate of increase was 1·4 per cent per annum, and in the 1830's, well before the famine, the net rate had fallen to 0·5 per cent per annum — emigration was already extremely high.

Spain. One of the most striking examples of depopulation in the Dark Ages was Spain, which suffered more continuous warfare and devastation than any part of Europe. Along the border of Christianity and Islam warfare raged continuously from the eighth to the fifteenth century. Not only destruction of the elaborate Roman irrigation system, which had been taken over by the Gothic and Moorish invaders, but also wholesale depopulation, were the natural consequences of so grim a history. The second century A.D. peak of 8 million was not regained until late in the thirteenth century, and 10 million by the end of the fifteenth century.[3]

Anuario Estadístico de España quotes some early Census records about 1600 and 1750. Cortes[4] estimates 7–9 million for 1500, Reinhardt 7 million. Cortes estimates 4 million for 1125, for Spanish territory of that date (much of the peninsula was still Moorish). Reinhardt quotes the population of Catalonia in 1378 at 450,000 (12 persons/sq. km.) and of Aragon in 1404

---

[1] English grumbling about the Irishman's willingness to live on potatoes has gone on for centuries and so we may confine ourselves to one of the earliest quotations on the subject, at a time when the idea was at any rate original. Sir William Petty, the first economist, wrote in 1691 — 'What need have they to work, who can content themselves with *Potato's*, whereof the labour of one man can feed forty'. His figure was about correct, and was confirmed by Arthur Young, so far as concerns growing the average Irishman's potato ration of those days (8 lbs. per head per day). But he forgets that milk and oatmeal also formed a substantial part of the diet.

[2] K. H. Connell, *The Population of Ireland.* Connell points out that the traditional Irish diet of that day, namely potatoes, milk and oatmeal, though dull, was nutritionally almost perfect; and has evidence to show that Irish mortality, by eighteenth-century standards, was then probably very low.

[3] Vandellos, *International Statistical Institute Bulletin,* 1934.

[4] *Economic Development and Cultural Change,* January 1961.

at 250,000 (5 persons/sq. km.). He makes population fall to 5 million by 1650, whence a further increase took place. Robertson's[1] estimate of population nearly doubling between 1500 and 1600 (4 million increase) appears improbable.

We have a number of estimates for the second half of the eighteenth century.[2] From 1700 to 1857 the rate of growth averaged a fairly steady 0·7 per cent per annum. The only recorded period in which it fell short of this was the 1790's.

France, Belgium, Netherlands. The population of France had probably risen to quite a high level by the third century A.D. There seems to be evidence (rather less than in Britain) of contraction of cities in the later part of the Roman epoch. It has been estimated by Levasseur[3] that population fell back to a minimum of 6–8 millions in the eighth century, remaining at that level until about 1050. (Levasseur also put the third century population at 8 million). Several historians would put the epoch of greatest confusion and destruction, and consequently of maximum depopulation, about the end of the ninth century. Nef[4] has stated that there is quite unmistakable evidence of a rapid growth in population in France between 1000 and 1300.

Helleiner[5] thinks that the general population increase throughout Western Europe, from the middle of the eleventh century to the outbreak of the Black Death in 1348, was threefold. (This represents an average rate of increase of 0·38 per cent per year). In fact, there appears to have been an accelerating rate of increase. D'Avenel[6] thinks that the population of France doubled between 1260 and 1340 (a rate of increase of 0·9 per cent per annum). He has abundant supporting evidence from the level of rents, which in the twelfth century took only 10 per cent of the product, but which rose rapidly after that date. He attributes the population increase to the great movement for the manumission of serfs which began in the thirteenth century.

Under French law at that time serfs could not leave property to their children. (For that matter, knights and their descendants in France were also the legal property of the manor, lay or ecclesiastic, and the consent of the Seigneur was even required for entering the monastic life.)

Lot's[7] high estimate of 23–24 million for the population of France before the Black Death has been raised still further by J. T. Krause[8] to 30 million. Russell's figures of 6 million for 1000, 10 million for 1200 and 19 million

[1] *South African Journal of Economics*, March 1950.
[2] *Population*, January–March 1956.
[3] *La Population Française* (1889). [4] Private communication.
[5] *Canadian Journal of Economics and Political Science*, August 1949 and *Europas Bevölkerung und Wirtschaft im Späteren Mittelalter*, Vienna, 1954.
[6] *La Fortune Privée à travers sept Siècles.*
[7] *L'État des Paroisses et des Feux en 1328.* [8] Private communication.

for 1340 are therefore raised. It is estimated that the Black Death in France caused an immediate loss of one-third of the population, with further losses later.

In France the effect of pestilences was accentuated by the devastation wrought by English armies in the Hundred Years' War, and the still more dreadful Civil War and social disorganization which followed from it. 'Mercenaries continued to live on the country after their disbandment, and turned many regions of France into deserts.'[1] In the graphic words of a contemporary writer, there were many parts of France in which you could travel for miles without hearing a cock crow. We can perhaps understand the devotion which French people pay to Saint Joan of Arc, who restored order and peace after the ghastly times through which France had been passing.

These estimates of the trend of population are fully confirmed by D'Avenel's data on rents, which passed through a minimum in the early decades of the fifteenth century. It was not until the eighteenth century that the fourteenth-century ratio of rent to product was restored — thereby closely confirming the estimates of population trend.

Brabant (now lying across the Belgo-Netherlands border) was estimated to have a population density of 35 persons/sq. km. in 1374: by 1437, according to Cuvelier, it had risen to 55 (450,000 population). This density however was no higher than the French average before the Black Death.

Russell's total for the Low Countries for 1500 includes 0·42 million in Flanders, 0·32 million in Brabant, 0·17 million in Holland, 0·12 million in Hainault and 0·06 in Luxemburg. Some interesting estimates, based on fairly good foundations, are available[2] for certain Netherlands provinces (Table III.6). Exceptionally rapid growth, by the standards of the time, was taking place during the sixteenth century in the maritime and commercial region of Holland, in spite of the Spanish War, and fairly rapid growth in Friesland, also a maritime region. Growth came later in the agricultural province of Overijssel, and in the sandy heaths and woodlands of Veluwe (so familiar to us from Dutch paintings). In Holland population growth ceased in the eighteenth century — and Holland's great age of maritime, commercial, political and cultural achievements ceased with it.

The French figure for 1650 is Sauvy's[3] and for 1700 Reinhardt's: Reinhardt estimates that by 1710, at the end of Louis XIV's wars, French population had fallen to 18 million. France was growing at the rate of nearly 0·5 per cent per year during the first half of the seventeenth century,

---

[1] Pirenne, *Economic and Social History of Mediaeval Europe.*
[2] Faber and others, Landbouwhogeschool, Wageningen, Bijdragen 12, 1965.
[3] *Richesse et Population.*

TABLE III.6. NETHERLANDS POPULATIONS

	Holland			Friesland			Overijssel			Veluwe	
Year	Population (000)	% per year rate of growth	Year	Population (000)	% per year rate of growth	Year	Population (000)	% per year rate of growth	Year	Population (000)	% per year rate of growth
1514	275		1511	75–80		800	12		1526	36	
1622	672	0·8	1650	145–155	0·5	1475	53	0·2	1650	41	0·1
1680	883	0·5	1744	135	–0·1	1675	71	0·1	1749	54	0·2
1750	783	–0·2	1815	173	0·3	1723	97	0·7	1795	66	0·4
1795	783	0				1748	122	0·9			
						1764	132	0·5			
						1795	134	0			

but during her period of greatest apparent magnificence in the late seventeenth century was a country of stationary population, due to the endless wars of *Le Grand Monarque*.

A study for Provence[1] shows nearly a 60 per cent loss of population in the Black Death. Being comparatively free from wars in the fifteenth century, the population of 1348 was however regained by 1540. From that date, growth was a little slower than in the rest of France.

Italy. For A.D. 14 Tenney Frank's estimation of 14 million (including 4 million slaves) is preferred to Beloch's (and Russell's) 6 million. Russell's figures are used from A.D. 800, with the intervening period interpolated.

A large decline in population may be possible, not only in a period of warfare and disorder as in the Dark Ages, but also, as in the case of Italy in the first three centuries of the Christian era, at a time of fully maintained political order, as the centre of a world empire. The conventional explanation of *latifundia perdidere Italiam* ('It was the great estates which destroyed Italy') cannot be accepted.[2] There may have been some decline in reproductivity or increase in mortality in Italy over this period, but an important, if not indeed the dominating factor, in its loss of population was probably emigration. Men of Italian birth and upbringing would have found unusual opportunities for advancement, whether as soldiers, civil servants, or traders, throughout a vast empire, and it is reasonable to estimate that they emigrated in very large numbers. In the early years of the Empire, Italy was the only area where every free inhabitant enjoyed full rights of citizenship; it was not until the beginning of the third century that Septimius Severus reduced Italy to the status of a province, and Caracalla made citizenship universal.

If the *latifundia* did play any part in driving the free population away, we must remember that they originated at the end of the third century B.C., after the long Punic Wars, which themselves had caused depopulation. No estimates are available of the population of Italy just before the Punic Wars; quite probably, in Central and Southern Italy at any rate, it was equal to, or higher than, that of the Augustan era.

Italian population since 1500 was reviewed by Beloch[3] and Cipolla.[4] A decline began in the early seventeenth century, for reasons which Cipolla[5] has analysed — monopolistic restrictions by guilds, excessive taxation, competition from northern countries, large areas relapsed to banditry and

[1] Baratier, *La Démographie Provençale du XIII au XVI Siècle*; and review by Biraben, *Population*, July–September 1962.
[2] 'It is doubtful whether Pliny's famous growl about *latifundia* can be taken seriously.' Tenney Frank, *Economic History of Ancient Rome*.
[3] *Bevölkerungsgeschichte Italiens*, Berlin, 1961.
[4] *Population in History*, London, 1965.   [5] *Economic History Review*, 1952.

malaria. From about 1660 however a slow but steady population recovery began.

Average persons/sq. km. in 1340 were 34, rising however to 85 in Tuscany. In this province depopulation appears to have been considerable, reducing it to near the Italian average of 33 in 1500. Romagna in 1378 after the plague had fallen to 30. In 1550 densities were 50 in Venetia and 100 in Liguria, and fairly uniform elsewhere except for Sardinia. Sardinia,[1] which had a population of 500,000 (density 21 persons/sq. km.) in Roman times, is said to have fallen through war, malaria and piracy very low by the sixteenth century, when it became part of the Spanish Empire. By 1700 its density was still only 13 persons/sq. km.

Greece. As with the depopulation of Italy under the Roman Empire, it is to be expected that there would have been a similar depopulation of Greece after the establishment, in the fourth century B.C., of the huge Alexandrine Empire, which stretched from the Sudan to Central Asia. Even though this empire almost immediately split up into separate kingdoms, they were nevertheless all governed by Greek-speaking rulers, and the opportunities for men of Greek speech and education, as officials and traders, must have been very great. In the case of Greece, we have some evidence, from Polybius and elsewhere, that reproductivity had fallen to a low level; but emigration probably played a more important part. We have fairly clear evidence both directly, and also by indirect reasoning from economic evidence, that the population of Greece, for one reason or another, fell substantially in the period after Alexander.

It seems that the early development of Greek civilization had been accompanied by a rapid increase in population. Hesiod, in the seventh century B.C., makes it clear that land and livelihood in his day were much harder to get than they had been in the free and easy days of the Homeric Age. For the fifth century B.C. we have the first definite estimates. Glotz[2] quotes estimates for Attica ranging from 215,000 to 350,000, of whom about one-third were slaves. For Laconia he estimates 400,000, including 25,000 *Spartiates* (military aristocracy), 100,000 *perioikoi* (traders and craftsmen), and 275,000 helots or serfs. The area of Attica is only of the order of 1000 sq. km.; it therefore had a population much larger than could be supported by their type of agriculture. Laconia, a much larger area, might have come near to supporting its whole population on subsistence agriculture, if it had not contained a good deal of mountainous area. The fact that one-quarter of the population were traders and craftsmen shows that there must have been, in spite of appearances to the contrary, some measure of urban life in Sparta.

[1] Dozier, *Geographical Review*, October 1957.   [2] In his book, *Ancient Greece at Work*.

At the time of Alexander, Greece proper, excluding Macedonia, is estimated by Glotz to have had a population of 2½ million, or about 35 persons/sq. km. over all. In view of the high proportion of mountainous area, this exceeded the country's agricultural capacity. Macedonia by that time had risen to a population of 3 or 4 million (15 to 20 persons/sq. km.).

Rising population, and a limited area of land, presented a problem which the Spartans solved by establishing a military despotism over adjacent areas and reducing the inhabitants to a miserable serfdom; the rest of Greece, by the creative achievement of transforming an agrarian community into one of traders and seamen, and by planting colonies along the entire length of the Mediterranean coast. These same men also created some of the finest art and literature which the world has known.

This period of population increase, however, was followed by a rapid decline in the third and subsequent centuries B.C. Moreau[1] estimated that the population of the city of Athens was 200,000 in 431 B.C. and the same in 300 B.C.; at the former date however, the numbers enjoying full rights of citizenship were 40,000, at the latter date only 31,000. This was also a period of declining political influence and cultural achievement. Were further evidence required, we have a highly circumstantial piece of economic evidence quoted by Michell.[2] He has obtained a record of the receipts from the letting of 15 farms (probably grape-growing) on the Island of Delos. The money values fluctuated considerably — there was a sharp but temporary rise in prices following upon Alexander's dissipation of the Persian treasure hoards — but we can express these rents in real terms by dividing by the current wages of labourers on the island. The average rent per farm fell from 8·0 man-years in 305 B.C., to 4·2 in 269 B.C., and 3·3 in 169 B.C. Michell remarks that at this time the export trade in wine to the Black Sea was less than it had been in earlier periods. Is not this all evidence of declining population, and decreasing need to import wheat from the Black Sea? In the fifth and fourth centuries B.C., the population of Greece had been dependent upon foodstuffs imported from areas far afield, for which wine, olive oil, silver and manufactured goods were sent in return.

By the time of Augustus, Beloch estimates that the combined population of Greece and Macedonia had fallen to 3 million, at which level it is believed to have remained stationary for some centuries.

Carr-Saunders believed that depopulation was occurring generally throughout the Roman Empire. Rostovtzeff[3] strongly resists this conten-

---

[1] *Population*, October–December 1949.
[2] *Canadian Journal of Economics and Political Science*, February 1946.
[3] *Social and Economic Survey of the Roman Empire*.

tion, and brings forward abundant evidence of the foundation of new cities and colonies to prove the contrary. Rostovtzeff seems to have proved his case in respect of Western Europe and the Western Provinces in North Africa, up to the third century A.D., though not beyond it.

Scandinavia. Precise population statistics began for Finland in 1761,[1] with some earlier[2] figures back to 1721. With some fluctuations between decades, the average rate of growth for the eighteenth century was nearly 1·4 per cent per annum, a little less in the first half of the nineteenth century. In the eighteenth century, Finland was a country of immigration. But even so, these figures are very high.

For the other Scandinavian countries we can make more precise comparisons from the figures given by Gille and Reinhardt. For Norway, the growth rate, which was 0·2 per cent before 1750, suddenly jumped to 0·8 per cent for the second half of the century. In Sweden, our first good estimate is for a population of 900,000 in 1635. Our next estimate is for 1.46 million in 1721. But it has been estimated[3] that there was no net increase in population over the period 1700–21, owing to the 'Great Northern War', and subsequent epidemics. By this reckoning the Swedish growth rate was already 0·7 per cent in the seventeenth century, and was higher still (1·1 per cent) in 1721–35, the recovery period after the wars; but from 1735–50 was only 0·2 per cent. For the second half of the eighteenth century it rose to 0·6 per cent. In Denmark the rate of growth remained at 0·2 per cent until 1775, then rose to 0·4 per cent for the last quarter of the century.

Few countries have had a stranger population history than Iceland. In eighteenth-century Iceland we get an example of population decline, not through family limitation, or war and disorder, or emigration, but simply as a result of economic oppression. The King of Denmark, as monarchs did in those days, declared all commerce with Iceland a monopoly, which he sold or gave to his friends. The monopolists rigidly restricted all commerce to themselves, and forbade any local commercial or manufacturing development. Iceland, then as now, had to import most of her food, fuel and timber, and the country's economic development was constricted within the narrow capacity of her fishery[4] and grazing resources. So the Icelandic civil and religious authorities working together devised an extraordinary system whereby no man was allowed to marry until he

[1] For a summary, see *Population Index*, January 1940.
[2] Quoted by Gille, *Population Studies*, June 1949.
[3] Montgomery, *The Rise of Modern Industry in Sweden.*
[4] We tend to get the wrong impression if we look at Iceland at the present day, where the resources of power-driven fishing vessels and refrigeration of the catch enable Icelandic fishing to pay for the import requirements of a much larger population. In the days of sailing boats and dried cod Iceland's opportunities were much more limited.

possessed a certain minimum area of grazing land (sometimes acquired by purchase, but generally by bequest). At least, the marriage ceremony was legally permitted to those who did not fulfil this qualification, but on the understanding that the children of such marriages — likewise illegitimate children — would be taken from the parents and brought up by the public authorities in a state of virtual serfdom. These provisions proved a sufficient deterrent. In the Census of 1703[1] the average age of marriage for men was shown to be in their forties, for women in their thirties. The population, which had been 50,000 in 1703, remained about the same or slightly less for the rest of the eighteenth century (some disastrous volcanic eruptions helped in the work of depopulation) but began to rise at about $\frac{1}{2}$ per cent per annum in the nineteenth century, when the monopolistic restrictions were relaxed.

Thorarinsson[2] estimates 500,000 for Sweden and 250,000 for Norway in 1100. An estimate[3] for Iceland at that date shows 77,000, not substantially changing in the subsequent two centuries.

In both Denmark and Sweden[4] population, and cultivation, began to decline about 1330, and not because of epidemics — indeed Scandinavia largely escaped the Great Plague. Emigration to Finland and Norrland may have been the explanation.

Germany, Austro–Hungarian Empire and Eastern Europe. Any review of the population of this area is made difficult by repeated boundary changes. For some parts of the area information is in any case more than usually incomplete, and some estimates have to be based on supposed densities per square kilometre.

We can define an area bounded on the East by the border of the Soviet Union as it has been since 1945 and examine estimates of past population of U.S.S.R. in its present boundaries.

A German estimate[5] for Russia in Europe, available decennially from 1800 (interpolated) agrees for 1815 with a recent Russian estimate[6] with a difference of 1 million, which is a plausible estimate for the Asian territory then forming part of the Russian Empire (only a small part of Russia in Asia as we now know it) i.e. 44 million and 45 million respectively. Biraben's estimate[7] for what is now the whole of U.S.S.R. in its post-1945 boundaries was 46 million for 1800, and if advanced to 1815 at the pre-1800 rate of

---

[1] Iceland was the first country to take a census in the modern sense of the word. The full tables showing age at marriage have only recently been discovered.

[2] *Geographical Review*, October 1961.

[3] *Geographical Review*, June 1958.

[4] Bolin, *Cambridge Economic History*, Vol. I, p. 473.

[5] *Handwörterbuch der Staatswissenschaft*, 4 Aufl. Bd. II, pages 688–9.

[6] Liashchenko, *Istoria Narodnayo Khoziaistvo U.S.S.R.*, 1956.

[7] *Population*, Numéro Spécial, June 1958.

growth[1] becomes 50 million, which is compatible with 44 million in European Russia plus 6 million in Asia, as previously estimated.

Biraben's estimate is used for 1750 of 34 million in all, or 28 million in Europe (Cipolla estimates 30 million in all for 1750), and extrapolated back at the same rate to 1700. (Extrapolating backwards at about the same rate gives a link with Russell's figure for 1500.) The early eighteenth-century estimates of Lorimer[2] (17·5 million for 1722 for Russia in Europe, 1921–39 boundaries) and of Liashchenko (14 million in 1722 for Peter the Great's territory, corresponding to 21 million for the whole of Russia in Europe on the 1815 ratio of populations in the old and the new territories) appear too low.

West of the post-1945 boundary of the Soviet Union therefore we have to consider the areas shown in Table III.7.

TABLE III.7. EAST EUROPEAN POPULATIONS

Area in 000 sq. km.

	1913	of which gained 1912–13	1921–37	Post-1945	Date of earliest 19th century Census or estimate[h]
Albania	29	29	29	29	None
Austria			84	84	
Austro–Hungarian Empire	652[c]				1830[c]
Bulgaria	112	13	103	111	1890
Czechoslovakia			128[a]	128	
Danzig			2		
Germany — Eastern and East Berlin	507[b, d]		464[d]	{108	1816
Western and West Berlin				{248	
Greece	122	57	130	133	1830
Hungary			93	93	1850
Montenegro	14	5			None
Poland	77[g]		213[e]	312	1852
Rumania	138	7	244[f]	237	1859
Serbia	87	39			1830
Turkey in Europe	24		24	24	None
Yugoslavia			248	256	
	1762		1762	1762	

[a] Excluding area ceded in 1945 to U.S.S.R. of 12000 sq. km.
[b] Omitting 20000 sq. km. ceded on the Western borders in 1919 (to France, Belgium and Denmark).
[c] Omitting 24000 sq. km. of Austro-Hungarian territory ceded to Italy in 1919.
[d] Omitting 14000 sq. km. ceded to U.S.S.R. in 1945.
[e] Omitting 17000 sq. km. ceded to U.S.S.R. in 1939–45.
[f] Omitting 50000 sq. km. ceded to U.S.S.R., 1944.
[g] Part of Russian Empire in 1913, not part of U.S.S.R. now.
[h] As published in *Statistisches Jahrbuch für das Deutsche Reich*, Internationaler Teil, 1934–38.
[i] 1850 for Hungary.

The whole of Albania, and large areas of Bulgaria, Greece and Serbia, as shown in 1913, had before 1912 been part of the Turkish Empire, for which no good data were available.

[1] A substantially higher growth rate was estimated by Biraben for the nineteenth century; but in view of probable large losses in the Napoleonic War of 1812–14, the lower estimate of growth is used.
[2] *The Population of the Soviet Union*, League of Nations, 1946.

A very comprehensive contemporary review was made about 1790 by Bötticher[1] of Konigsberg. Some other early estimates were given by Reinhardt and Vielrose.[2]

TABLE III.8.   EAST EUROPEAN DENSITIES IN PERSONS/ SQ. KM.

Austria		Bulgaria		Czechoslovakia			
1870	68	1910	45	1900	90		
1830	51	1890	35	1790[b]	72		
1790[a]	48						

Germany, 1816		Greece		Hungary		Poland	
Brandenburg	32	1910	37	1890	53	Before partition	
East Prussia	25	1880	23	1870	47	of 1772[d]	24
Mecklenburg	24	1870	20	1850	40	After partition	
Pomerania	23	1830	14	1790	20[c]	of 1772	20
Grenzmark Posen-						1791[e]	18
West Prussia	18						

Rumania		Serbia		Turkey in Europe	
1910	53	1910	62	1790	17
1890	37	1870	28		
1859	28	1830	14		
1790 Transylvania	29				
Bukovina	17				

[a] Whole of Austrian Empire, other than possessions in Italy and Netherlands, not specified elsewhere in this table.
[b] Bohemia and Moravia only. The Eastern part of the country is much less densely populated. For the whole country Reinhardt estimates 21 in 1804 and 14 in 1754.
[c] Reinhardt estimates 21 for 1804 and 20 for 1787. 'Illyria', now the coastal area of Yugoslavia, had, in Bötticher's estimate, a density of 18.
[d] Bötticher's estimates. For the Eastern part, ceded to Russia, estimated density was 19.
[e] Vielrose's estimate of population growth applied to Russell's estimates (excluding Silesia and Pomerania) for the fourteenth century.

Table III.8 gives available recorded or estimated densities for this area. These may be used to throw some light on the population of its less densely populated and less known parts.

The inhabitants of Turkey in Europe (including all the population of Albania, of Bulgaria, Greece, Rumania and Serbia, and of 51,000 sq. km. of Bosnia–Herzegovina, before the partial liberation of their territories in the early nineteenth century) had been living under the same misrule which had kept the population of Turkish South-West Asia approximately stationary over a very long period. The population of the whole of this area, totalling 577,000 sq. km. is therefore taken at 15 persons/sq. km. in

[1] Statistical Tables of Europe (English translation published in 1800 by Stockdale).
[2] Demografie (Prague): quoted Population, January–March 1961.

1800, rising gradually from Russell's figure for 1500. It also appears best to classify together Poland, Czechoslovakia, and 71,000 sq. km. in the four lowest-density German areas, i.e. 412,000 sq. km. in all (omitting all of what is now Soviet territory) at an average density of 20 in 1800. To this area (which escaped the Black Death) may be applied Russell's estimated density for the fourteenth century, and Vielrose's for 1000 and 1600.

Hungary, Illyria, Bukovina and Transylvania (239,000 sq. km., according to Bötticher) approximating to Hungary in its 1913 boundaries, were largely under Turkish rule in the sixteenth and seventeenth centuries, and suffered severe depopulation, making rapid recovery in the eighteenth century. Macartney[1] estimates fifteenth-century population at 4 million, and in 1700 at only 2½ million for a territory similar to that of 1913, or 325,000 sq. km., i.e. densities of 12 and 8 respectively. For 1700 Reinhardt estimates only 0·5 million in Transylvania and 1·5 million in the rest of Hungary, i.e. densities 5 and 7 respectively. Transylvania's density had risen to 10 by 1754 and 14 by 1787. (It was assumed that the density of 20 quoted above for 1787 was for all Hungary, including Transylvania.) Earlier years are extrapolated back in proportion to the data for Poland and Czechoslovakia.

Bötticher's estimates for Austria (as defined in Table III.7, i.e. excluding all areas now part of Poland or Czechoslovakia) show that for no province (except for the mountainous district of Upper Austria) did density fall below 40. The whole of Austria with its population of 4·3 million can therefore be classified with that of Western Germany (remaining 534,000 sq. km.). Excluding the four lowest-density areas, Germany in 1816 had a population of 19·9 million, or say 19 million in 1800 (population growth was probably slow during the Napoleonic Wars). This total of 23 million is carried back to 1200 by means of an estimate of Abel's,[2] which stands at 24 million (for a somewhat different area) for 1800. (The eighteenth-century growth rate for Prussia — then a comparatively sparsely populated area, probably attractive to immigrants — was much higher than in Germany as a whole. Reinhardt estimated that between 1748 and 1770, under Frederick II, and in spite of 0·5 million war losses, it rose from 3 to 6 million, or by 0·84 per cent per year.)

The Thirty Years' War, from 1618 to 1648, had fearful effects. An estimate of even a 40 per cent reduction of population was made by Franz.[3]

---

[1] In *Chambers's Encyclopaedia*, article on Hungarian History.
[2] *Jahrbuch für Nationalökonomie und Statistik*, 1935.
[3] *Der Dreissigjährige Krieg und das Deutsche Volk*, Berlin, 1938, quoted by Goran Ohlin, World Population Conference, 1965.

Data before 1200 are Russell's. An interesting new series of estimates for Saxony has recently become available.[1] This one-time frontier area, where a sparse, mainly Slavonic population living at 5–14 persons/sq. km. (with many areas uninhabited) in 1100 had grown to a mainly German population living at an average of 23 persons/sq. km. in 1300, represented a steadily increasing proportion of the estimate for Germany as a whole.

Saxony

Year	1100	1300	1550	1750	1830
Estimated population '000	40	400	550	1000	1857

Plague losses in the fourteenth century are not estimated, but mining development in the fifteenth century helped to restore population. The Thirty Years' War, and subsequent epidemics, are estimated to have halved Saxony's population. The urban proportion is put at one-fifth in 1300 and about one-third subsequently.

EUROPEAN TOTALS

Comparison may now be made (Table III.9) between the total so far obtained and various alternative estimates for Europe as a whole. Robertson[2] considers that in Europe by 1500 'pre-plague population was little more than re-established', and that population in France was definitely lower. He estimated a 20 per cent rise from 1500 to 1600. Helleiner[3] states that Western Europe trebled between 1050 and 1350, i.e. an average increase of 0·38 per cent per year — probably in fact accelerating in the latter part of the period: the data above show a rise from 24·7 million in 1000 to 69·3 million in 1340.

Helleiner dwells on the sustained check to the rate of growth of population which occurred after 1350. He thinks that the aggregate population of Western Europe in 1500 was only just about what it had been before the Black Death. He invokes the evidence of the change in the terms of trade, which Postan has recorded. They certainly turned heavily against agriculture during this period, owing to the low price elasticity of demand for food at a time of declining population, but also (this is a point made strongly by Pirenne[4]) to the increasing degree of monopoly among urban traders, subject now to less threat from the establishment of new towns. This check to population growth, Pirenne thinks, probably began to appear quite early in the fourteenth century. He contends that by the

[1] Blaschke, Economic History Conference, Munich, 1965.
[2] *South African Journal of Economics*, March 1950.
[3] *Canadian Journal of Economics and Political Science*, August 1949.
[4] *Economic and Social History of Medieval Europe.*

TABLE III.9. EUROPEAN TOTAL POPULATION
(millions)

	As given in Table III.1.	Bennett	Külischer[a]	Willcox[b]	Carr-Saunders[b]	Cipolla	Russell	Durand[e]
B.C. 400		23						
A.D. 14	40	37					33	
200		67						
350	28						27	
600	19						18	
700		27						
800	29						29	
1000	39	42					38	
1050		46						
1100		48						
1150		50						
1200	52	61					48	
1250		69						
1300		73	73					
1340[d]	85						70	
1350		51						
1400		45					37[e]	
1450		60						
1500	68	69					57	
1550		78						
1600	83	89	95					
1650	90	100		97	97			
1700	106	115		130				
1750	130	140		138	137	120		150
1800	173	188		188	187	186		200

[a] *Allgemeine Wirtschaftsgeschichte II*, p. 29. Beloch (*Zeitschrift für Sozialwissenschaft 1900*) makes the same estimate for the proportionate increase from 1300 to 1600.
[b] Excluding Asiatic Russia.
[c] Including Asian portion of U.S.S.R. (estimated above at 6 million).
[d] An independent estimate by Wagemann gave Europe in 1340 a population of 100 million, *Institut für Konjunkturforschung Wochenbericht*, 30 June 1938.
[e] Estimate made for Europe and Near East as a whole but not for individual countries.

middle of the fourteenth century population in France and the Low Countries had risen to a density which it was becoming difficult to support, with the then available transport and social organization. Land transport was still very difficult and costly, and any region lacking water transport was therefore primarily dependent upon its own resources. Bad weather in the years 1315–17 had already caused a number of local famines. We are not, however, entitled to speculate that, had the Black Death and subsequent epidemics never occurred, there would instead have been a famine crisis. The building of an adequate road system, or a great movement of colonization, might have served as alternatives.

It took Europe, as a whole, until 1500 to recover from the effects of the wars and pestilences of the fourteenth century — much longer in the case of France. In England it was probably not until fairly late in the sixteenth century that the population of 1348 was recovered. The sixteenth century was one of expansion; Robertson puts the European average growth at 20 per cent over the century.

In the seventeenth century the advance continued, except for Germany, which lost 20–40 per cent of her population in the Thirty Years' War, in

Italy, where there was also considerable war and disorder, and in Spain, where the loss was probably due to emigration to America. The Spanish figure for 1700 is uncertain, but it looks as if a considerable loss had occurred. The German recovery after 1650 was at the rate of about 0·5 per cent per year. France was growing at the rate of nearly 0·5 per cent per year during the first half of the seventeenth century, to lose again in the exhausting wars of the late seventeenth century. England's growth in the first half of the seventeenth century was slower, but Scotland by then probably had a high growth rate.

Seventeenth and earlier eighteenth-century England averaged a growth rate of only about 0·25 per cent per year.

Oceania's population is estimated by Putnam for the beginning of the Christian Era: Carr-Saunders and Willcox make it constant at 2 million from 1650 to 1850.

In Table III.10 are reviewed alternative estimates of world population totals:

TABLE III.10. WORLD POPULATION TOTALS
(millions)

		From Table III.1.	Bennett	Putnam	Cipolla	Willcox	Carr-Saunders
A.D.	14	256		235			
	1000	280	275				
	1100		306				
	1200	384	348				
	1300		384				
	1400		373				
	1500	427	446				
	1600	498	486				
	1650	516				470	545
	1700	641					
	1750	731			767	694	728
	1800	890				919	906

We now turn to a more detailed review (Table III.11 and III.12) of the available information of decadal percentage rates of increase of population, before 1800, including some already quoted, and then after 1800.

An acceleration in the middle of the eighteenth century is noticeable in a number of countries.

After 1800, of course, both the accuracy and the amount of information about population increase considerably. However to this day we lack accurate information about most of Africa, and a number of Asian and Latin American countries. We have good series for most European

TABLE III.11. DECADAL PERCENTAGE RATES OF
POPULATION GROWTH BEFORE 1800

AMERICA: *Puerto Rico*

1765–1812	34

United States

1620–30	128
1630–40	390
1640–50	86
1650–60	63
1660–70	35
1670–80	36
1680–90	36
1690–1700	29
1700–10	32
1710–20	41
1720–30	35
1730–40	44
1740–50	29
1750–60	36
1760–70	35
1770–80	29
1780–90	41
1790–1800	35

ASIA: *China* early periods
of growth (see Diagram
III.A) — 4–12

Korea

1700–1800	8
1648–1807	10

EUROPE: *Czechoslovakia*

1700–50	5
1750–1800	8

Denmark

1700–25	2
1725–50	2
1750–75	2
1775–1800	4

England and Wales

1700–10	2
1710–20	0
1720–30	–1
1730–40	0

1740–50	3
1750–60	7
1760–70	7
1770–80	7
1780–90	10
1790–1800	11

Finland

1700–21	14
1721–35	17
1735–50	11
1750–60	18
1760–70	15
1770–80	14
1780–90	12
1790–1800	14

France

1700–55	2
1755–62	4
1762–76	6
1776–1800	4

Iceland

1700–35	–4
1735–50	7
1750–75	0
1775–1800	–1

Ireland

1687–1712	11
1712–18	6
1718–32	3
1732–54	3
1754–67	7
1767–72	6
1772–81	15
1781–90	17
1790–1821	17

Italy

1700–70	4
1770–1820	4

Norway

1700–35	2

Norway (cont.)		*Spain*	
1735–50	2	1700–54	7
1750–75	8	1754–69	8
1775–1800	9	1769–87	7
		1787–97	2
Russia			
1722–62	8	*Sweden*	
1762–96	13	1635–1700	7
		1700–21	–1
Scotland		1721–35	13
1700–50	4	1735–50	4
1750–90	5	1750–75	6
1790–1800	7	1775–1800	6

SOURCES FOR TABLES III.11 AND III.12

If not otherwise stated: From 1900, U.N. *Demographic Year Books*, Tables 4 and 6.

Census data 1850–1900, U.N. *Demographic Year Book*, 1955, Table 4. Other data 1800–1900, *Statistisches Jahrbuch für das Deutsche Reich*, 1934, Internationale Teil, p. 17.

AFRICA: Egypt: Bonné, *Middle East Journal*, Winter 1951. Census of 1882, 1897 and subsequently decennially adjusted.

Kiser (*Milbank Memorial Quarterly*, October 1944) estimates 2·5 million for 1800, a slight decline to 1821, and a rise to 4·5 million by 1846. This latter implies a rise of nearly 30 per cent per decade, and is most improbable. From 4·5 million in 1846 to Bonné's 6·8 million in 1882 is a rise at the rate of 12 per cent per decade. If the rise from 1800 to 1846 was uniform, as appears more probable, this represents a rise at 13 per cent per decade.

AMERICA: Brazil: Mortara, World Population Conference, 1954. (1810 and 1867, Proceedings of the XXXIV International Conference of Americanists, Vienna, 1962.)

Mexico: from 1900, De La Pena, World Population Conference, 1954.

Puerto Rico: Rios, World Population Conference, 1954.

U.S.A.: *Historical Statistics of the United States* and Rossiter, *Population Growth* (U.S. Bureau of Census).

Argentine: *Una Nueva Argentina*, Buenos Aires, 1940.

ASIA: India: Jain, World Population Conference, 1954. Adjusting for extension of Census area and increasing completeness of enumeration.

Iraq: Hasan, *Bulletin of the Oxford Institute of Statistics*, November 1958.

Japan: Kotono, *Melbourne University Science Review*, 1963 for 1852.

Korea: *Population Index*, October 1944 before 1920. 1950–60, South Korea only.

Indonesia: Breman, quoted *Population*, October-December 1963, p. 794.

EUROPE: Austria: Old Boundaries until 1910.

Czechoslovakia: Reinhardt, *Histoire de la Population Mondiale*.

Denmark: Reinhardt and Gille, *Population Studies*, June 1949.

Finland: Reinhardt, Gille, and *Index*, January 1940.

France: Toutain, Cahiers de l'ISEA, Supplement 133 (adjusted for boundary changes).

Germany: *Statistisches Jahrbuch für das Deutsche Reich*, boundaries of 1921–37. 1950–60 data for West Germany and West Berlin.

Greece: *Population*, October 1960.

Hungary: old boundaries to 1910.

Iceland: (see Denmark.)

Ireland: K. H. Connell, *The Population of Ireland* (series begins 1687). Includes Northern Ireland till 1910.

Italy: Cipolla, *Population in History*, present territory.

Netherlands: Central Planbureau Overdrukken 33.

Norway: (see Denmark.)

Spain: *Population*, January-March 1956 and Usher, *Geographical Review*, January 1930.

Sweden: (see Denmark.)

United Kingdom: Deane and Cole, *British Economic Growth*.

U.S.S.R., 1800 to 1850: *Handwörterbuch der Staatswissenschaft*, 4 Aufl. Bd. II, p. 688.

The Real Productivity of Soviet Russia, U.S. Senate, Committee on the Judiciary, 1961 (for 1950).

Biraben, *Population*, Numéro Spécial, June 1958. See also table of populations before 1800.

Yugoslavia: Serbia to 1910.

countries — but here their value is qualified by repeated boundary changes. All available information about rates of growth of population, which after all is what should concern us most, is fully set out in Table III.12, with the effects of boundary changes eliminated. Table III.13 gives a summary of recent population totals for all but the smallest countries; Table III.14 gives the data published by *Statistisches Jahrbuch für das Deutsche Reich* in the 1930's, of principal available data between 1800 and 1930; Table III.15 gives a brief summary of world and continental aggregates, and figures for a few leading countries, since 1800.

As causes of these broad movements which we have observed, we have analysed the great changes in mortality, and referred to the wars. Changes in fertility will be considered in the next chapter.

It remains now to examine the part played in certain countries by migration, and also by war losses.

Emigration is generally from countries already well populated. It is rare — Ireland and Puerto Rico are outstanding exceptions — for the amount of emigration to be of an order of magnitude comparable with the natural increase of population. In newly developing countries, on the other hand, immigration may contribute the major proportion of the country's increase in population — by the nature of the case, it must provide nearly all in the case of a newly settled country.

TABLE III.12. DECADAL PERCENTAGE RATES OF INCREASE AFTER 1800

	1800–10	1810–20	1820–30	1830–40	1840–50	1850–60	1860–70	1870–80	1880–90	1890–1900	1900–10	1910–20	1920–30	1930–40	1940–50	1950–60	1960–66
AFRICA:																	
Algeria										14	17	4	13	18	16	23	22
Egypt			←13→							0	17	13	12	14	21	27	29
Mauritius							←12→		26		−1	2	9	3	11	37	31
Tunis								←14→	3			8	15	20	25	18	13
S. Africa (whites)																18	
S. Africa total population											22	16	25	21	20	27	26
AMERICA:																	
Argentine	←24→					29	←45→	46	49	35	34	21	34	19	21	19	17
Bahamas							10	11	9	12	8	−5	13	15	13	33	43
Bermuda						17	15		21	17	8	−6	38	0	15	19	24
Brazil		←13→											22	22		36	28
British Honduras	14				16	17		30	26			15		15	22	30	35
Canada		33	35	33	36		23				21	22	18	11	22	30	19
Chile						33		17	12	11	17	12	15	11	18	23	20
Colombia						23	14	18	14	10	25	12	22	24	29	25	30
Costa Rica													18	24	25	46	49
Cuba							←5→		8	−3	39	24			20	23	26
Ecuador													31	27	29	35	32
Greenland						11				13	13	7	20	19	30	43	44
Guadeloupe								←17→	−2	12	17	8	16	25	21	31	30
Guatemala									10	19			38	29	22	34	36
Guyana						16	31	30	7	←6→	−15	0	4	11	23	34	26
Martinique						5		8	15	19	11	29	16	19	30	25	40
Mexico												−5	−4	11	28	35	38
Nicaragua													16	19	30	39	38
Panama												37	22	27	28	40	29
Peru								←20→				16	15	21	33	27	22
Puerto Rico								←14→	9	16	16	16	19	17	21	22	36
Surinam													26	21	18	47	15
United States	←36→	33	35	33	36	35	30	30	26	21	15	15	16	7	15	18	11
Uruguay								22	40	32	21	27	28	15	12	17	33
Venezuela									12		21	30	18	20	34	48	
West Indies total		←6→							10	←14→	22	3	18	20	18	18	26
incl. Jamaica							14	15				10	4	18	16	14	34
incl. Trinidad															33	30	
ASIA:																	
Brunei											15		20	20	18	83	43
Burma											10	11	11	15	15	12	23
Cambodia													←22→			33	28
Ceylon									9	18	9	17	14	28	29	28	
China (Taiwan)										15	13	24	30	27	21	39	36
Cyprus												12	16	16	16	16	9
Federation of Malaya										41	24	30	30	25	16	33	36

Region / Country													
Hongkong	37	32	27	17	27							15	
India	28	20	13	14	11	37	7	1	11				
Pakistan	24	23	10	19	9	1	18	1		16			
Indonesia (Java)	25	23	8		16	13	18		14			13	
Iraq	36	34	45	54	42		13						
Israel	44	68		15			12		6				
Japan	10	12											
Jordan	36	34	25	22	14		10						
Korea	31	20	21	26									
Laos	28	36	36	26	52								
Philippines	39	35	24	20	25								
Singapore	30	60	21	19	14								
Syria	35	42	18	8									
Thailand	34	43	21										
Turkey	29	32	23										
Vietnam	38	34											
EUROPE:													
Albania	34	32	12	9	2	-2	9	9	8	8	7		14	18
Austria	6	2	3	0	7	0	11	10	10	9	8		19	
Belgium	7	6	14	4	19	0	16	13	10			10		6
Bulgaria	8	10		11	7	12	7	13	6		13	14	16	12
Czechoslovakia	7	9	12	5	9	5	12	12	12	13	11			
Denmark	8	7	5	7	6		11	14	15	12		4	13	6
England and Wales	8	6	8	1	0	5	26	1	1	3	7		7	12
Finland	14	11	1	7	6	-5								
France	14	9	1	7	6	5		15	11	7	9			
Germany	-2	11												
East Germany	6	-6	3	15	27	5	8	15	17	7	13		7	4
Greece	3	7	1	7	9	12	9	11	1	1	8	13		
Hungary	19	23	18	13	15	0	7	10	3	-6	-11	20	14	
Iceland	8	-5	0	1	-6	2	3	-3	9	6		8	7	
Ireland	11	6	6	9	6	7	15	7	6	12	8	7	13	
Italy	8	14	14	13	7	6	6	13	10	10		8		
Netherlands	7	20	10	6	18	12	18	11	4		4		6	
Norway	9	13	9	11	14	1	13	7	11	9				
Poland	8	8	8	4	14	9	12	8	7	2		3	11	12
Portugal	7	7	10	5	11	7	6	6	6	10	4	6	10	
Rumania	9	15	4	16	16	7	17	14	5	6	4	10	10	
Spain	7	2	5										12	12
Sweden	9	15	15	15	16	3	17	15	15	7	18			
Switzerland														
Scotland	22	1	2	-1	-1							5	16	16
U.S.S.R.	15	16	-5	5	14							10	11	11
Yugoslavia	13	14	3	15	16							18		8
OCEANIA:													
Australia	21	26	16	9	21	22	18	19	41	40			
Fiji	38	36	33	20	12	21	30	23	28		-17		-17	
Hawaii		24	16	9	20						-18			
New Zealand	24	35	30	35	28	33	24	71	44					
Western Samoa	22	35	18	15	44									

TABLE III.13. WORLD POPULATION BY COUNTRIES, 1920–66ᵃ (millions)

	1966	1950	1940	1930	1920		1966	1950	1940	1930	1920
AFRICA	318	207	176	157	140	**EUROPE (excl. U.S.S.R.)**	449	395	381	356	329
Algeria	12	9	8	6	6	Austria	7	7	7	7	6
Congo	16					Belgium	10	9	8	8	8
Morocco	13	9	8			Bulgaria	8	7	6	6	5
Nigeria	59					Czechoslovakia	14	12	15	14	13
South Africa	18	12	10	9	7	Denmark	5	4	4	4	3
Sudan	14					Finland	5	4	4	3	3
U.A.R. (Egypt)	30	20	17	15	13	France	49	42	40	41	39
						Germany, East	16	17}			
NORTH AMERICA	217	167	146	135	117	Germany, West	57	48}	70	65	62
Canada	20	14	12	10	9	Berlin (E. and W.)	3	3}			
U.S.A.	197	152	133	123	106	Greece	9	8	7	6	5
						Hungary	10	9	9	9	8
LATIN AMERICA AND						Ireland	3	3	3	3	3
CARIBBEAN	253	162	131	109	91	Italy	52	47	44	40	37
Argentine	23	17	14	12	9	Netherlands	12	10	9	8	7
Brazil	85	52	41	34	27	Norway	4	3	3	3	3
Chile	9	6	5	4	4	Poland	32	25	35	31	27
Colombia	19	11	9	7	6	Portugal	9	8	8	7	6
Cuba	8	6	5	4		Rumania	19	16	16	14	12
Mexico	44	26	20	17	14	Spain	32	28	26	23	21
Peru	12	9	7	6	5	Sweden	8	7	6	6	6
Venezuela	9	5	4	3	2	Switzerland	6	5	4	4	4
						United Kingdom	55	51	48	46	44
China	642	545	581	575	567	Yugoslavia	20	16	16	14	12
India	499	358	316	277	250	**U.S.S.R.**	233	181	192	176	158
Pakistan	105	75	69	58	54	**OCEANIA**	18	13	11	10	9
Indonesia	107	76	70	61	52	Australia	12	8	7	6	5
Japan	99	83	71	64	55	New Zealand	3	2	2	1	1
REST OF ASIA						**WORLD**	3288	2499	2340	2145	1968
(excl. U.S.S.R.)	348	237	196	167	146						
Afghanistan	16	12			6						
Burma	25	18	16	14	13						
Ceylon	12	8	6	5	4						
Iran	26	16	16								
Korea (N. and S.)	41	30	24	19	17						
Philippines	33	20	16	13							
Taiwan	13	8	6	5	4						
Thailand	32	18	15	12	9						
Turkey	32	21	18	15							
Vietnam (N. and S.)	20	24	22	17	15						

(A number of small countries are not shown above but are included in the continental and world totals)
(Contemporary boundaries, which have been much changed)

ᵃ U.N. *Demographic Year Books*, 1960 and 1966 (except for China).

The measurement of emigration presents considerable difficulties, even in countries where movements are wholly or predominantly across the sea, more so across land frontiers. It is difficult to distinguish permanent migrants from the ever-increasing numbers of temporary travellers, for business or pleasure; or those truthfully recorded as temporary travellers, who afterwards change their minds and stay; or those who evade frontier controls. Migration is only really accurately known for these countries where both the Census and the birth and death records are accurate enough to make it possible to compute net migration as the difference between recorded intercensal population change, and natural increase through excess of births over deaths. If we specify the additional requirements that two[1] censuses should have been taken comparatively recently, and that we should exclude very small countries with a total population under 100,000, we are left with rather a short list (Table III.16).

The amount by which the second column exceeds the first shows the net rate of immigration in per cent per year of existing population and the net rate of emigration where it falls short. In two of the traditional immigrant-receiving countries, Australia and Canada, net immigration is still proceeding at substantial rates; at lower rates in Latin America and New Zealand; and in United States at a rate of only 0·1 per cent per year. Some of the principal immigrant-receiving countries now are France, Germany, Netherlands and Switzerland in Europe, the two latter despite their already high population density; and this comment applies *a fortiori* to the immigration into Hong Kong and Singapore in Asia.

In United Kingdom, immigration and emigration, both substantial, are now about in balance. Substantial emigration is discernible from Italy, Portugal and Spain: extremely heavy emigration from Ireland continues. Jamaica loses half and Puerto Rico three-quarters of their respective natural increases: but Guyana retains its quickly growing population, and Trinidad has net immigration.

In reviewing emigration, we must bear in mind the difference, sometimes very great, between gross and net emigration (through returning emigrants). An extreme example was Puerto Rico in 1953,[2] with a gross emigration of 320,000 and a net emigration of only 69,000. Another striking example is Italy.[3] In 1921–5 (measurement is not possible for an earlier period) the rate of reflux was 83 per cent of gross emigration to *European* destinations. For migration to non-European destinations, where the reflux should be expected to be much less, it was still about half of gross emigration between 1901 and 1925. By the 1930's reflux was about equal to gross emigration, both for European and non-European destinations.

A useful approximate summary (Table III.17) of European migration to other continents in the period 1946–60 was prepared by Bouscaren.[4]

Certain data are available (Table III.18) for rates of *net* emigration in earlier periods.

It should be a matter of great importance to all who are concerned with population problems to study the maximum rates at which emigration can proceed, and under what circumstances. Except for Ireland, rates of

---

[1] In the case of Hong Kong, we depend upon the 1961 Census and an official estimate for 1958.
[2] Rios, World Population Conference, 1954.
[3] Cosmo, *Banca Nazionale del Lavoro*, January–June 1954.
[4] *Research Bulletin for European Migration Problems*, The Hague, June 1962.

TABLE III.14. POPULATIONS 1800–1930[a]

Pre-1914 and post-1914 boundaries shown separately if significantly different

	1800	1830	1870	1880	1890	1900	1910	1920	1930
N. AFRICA									
Algeria	2·5	4·5 (1846)		3·3	4·1	4·7	5·6	5·8	7·2 (1936)
Egypt			5·2	6·8		9·7	11·3	12·8	14·2
N. AMERICA									
Canada		0·58 (1820)	3·69	4·33	4·83	5·37	7·21	8·79	10·4
U.S.A.	5·3	12·9	38·6	50·2	62·9	76·0	92·0	105·7	122·8
LATIN AMERICA									
Argentina	0·31		1·74	2·54	3·79	5·11	7·88	8·7	11·2
Bolivia				1·19	2·02	1·75	2·26		2·97
Brazil	3·25		10·0		14·3	17·3	23·4	30·6	40·3
Chile		1·01	1·95	2·30	2·62	2·88	3·33	3·75	4·29
Colombia	2·0	1·5	3·0			4·5 (1905)	5·1	5·9	7·9
Mexico	6·5		9·2	9·9	11·4	13·6	15·2	14·3	16·6
Peru			2·7		4·6		4·5	5·5	6·2
Uruguay				0·51	0·71	0·94	1·13	1·50	1·90
Venezuela				2·1	2·3		2·7	2·4	3·2
ASIA									
Ceylon				2·76	3·01	3·57	4·11	4·51	5·31
India and Pakistan			206·0	254·0	287·0	294·0	315·0	319·0	353·0
Japan			33·1	35·8	39·6	43·8	49·6	56·7	63·9
Philippines	1·50	2·59	4·71	5·57	5·98	7·63	8·89	10·3	12·3
EUROPE									
Austria		15·6	20·4	22·1	24·0	26·2	28·6		
,,							6·65	6·54	6·72
Belgium	3·13 (1816)	3·83	5·13	5·56	6·11	6·75	7·48	7·47	8·09
Bulgaria				2·01	3·31	3·74			
,,							4·34	4·85	6·09
Czechoslovakia				11·1	11·7	12·7	13·6	13·6	14·7

	1800	1830	1870	1880	1890	1900	1910	1920	1930
Denmark	0·93	1·22	1·78	1·97	2·17	2·45	2·76	3·10	3·54
Finland	0·83	1·37	1·77	2·06	2·38	2·71	2·92	3·27	3·67
France	28·3	33·2	37·7	37·7	38·3	39·0	39·6	39·2	41·8
"			36·1						
Germany	24·8 (1816)	30·6	41·1	45·2	49·4	56·4	64·9		
"						50·6	58·4	59·9	66·0
Greece		0·75	1·46	1·68	2·19	2·50	2·63	5·53	6·20
Hungary		13·2 (1850)	15·5	15·7	17·5	19·3	20·9		
"						6·9	7·6	8·0	8·7
Italy	17·2	21·2	26·8	28·5	30·2	32·5	34·7	36·4	
"							36·3	38·0	41·2
Yugoslavia (Serbia)		0·68	1·31	1·90	2·16	2·49	2·91	12·0	13·9
Netherlands	2·10	2·61	3·58	4·01	4·51	5·10	5·86	6·86	7·94
Norway	0·88	1·26	1·74	1·92	2·00	2·24	2·39	2·65	2·81
Poland	9·0		16·9			25·6	29·0	26·6	31·3
Portugal			4·2	4·6	5·1	5·4	6·0	6·0	6·8
Roumania	2·9	3·7 (1841)	3·9 (1859)		5·0	6·0	7·2	16·3	18·1
Russia (excl. Asia)	39·0		72·0	90·0		103·0 (1897)	131·0	116·0 (1926)	
"			61·0	76·0		88·0 (1897)	112·0		
Spain	10·5	14·6	16·2	16·6	17·6	18·6	20·0	21·4	23·9
Sweden	2·35	2·89	4·17	4·57	4·78	5·14	5·52	5·90	6·14
Switzerland		2·19 (1837)	2·66	2·83	2·92	3·31	3·75	3·88	4·07
U.K. Great Britain	10·5	16·3	26·1	29·7	33·0	37·0	40·8	42·7	44·8
Ireland (N. and S.)	5·2	7·8	5·4	5·2	4·7	4·5	4·4	4·4	4·2
OCEANIA									
Australia	—	0·07	1·65	2·25	3·17	3·77	4·45	5·44	6·63
New Zealand	—	—	0·26	0·49	0·63	0·77	1·01	1·22	1·49

[a] *Statistiches Jahrbuch für das Deutsche Reich.*

TABLE III.15. SUMMARY OF WORLD POPULATION

SINCE 1800

	Population in millions			Rates of growth per cent per decade					
	1800	1900	1962	1800–50	1850–1900	1900–20	1920–50	1950–60	1960–62
Africa	100	122	269	0	4	7	14	24	26
U.S.A. and Canada	6	81	206	34	26	19	13	18	29
Latin American and Caribbean	19	63	224	12	14	22	20	32	32
China	315	500	620	6	3	7	0	10	4
India and Pakistan	190	283	546	4	4	4	12	20	24
Indonesia	6	38	98	15	26	17	13	22	30
Japan	26	44	95	1	10	12	15	12	10
Rest of Asia (excl. U.S.S.R.)	47	120	306						
Europe (excl. U.S.S.R.)	133	284	434	9	7	8	7	8	9
U.S.S.R.	46	127	221	9	13	10	6	15	17
Oceania	2	6	17	9	14	21	13	27	23
WORLD	890	1668	3036	6	7	9	9	18	18

TABLE III.16. CALCULATION OF NET MIGRATION RATES

Per cent per year of present population

Country	Intercensal period	Natural increase	Population change shown by Census	Net immigration
N. AMERICA				
Barbados	1946–60	1·87	1·3	− 0·6
Canada	1956–61	1·95	2·6	0·6
El Salvador	1950–61	3·36	2·8	− 0·6
Guadeloupe	1954–61	2·82	2·9	0·1
Jamaica	1953–60	2·69	1·3	− 1·4
Martinique	1954–61	2·96	2·8	− 0·2
Mexico	1950–60	3·14	3·1	0
Panama	1950–60	2·97	2·9	− 0·1
Puerto Rico	1950–60	2·71	0·6	− 2·1
Trinidad and Tobago	1946–60	2·77	2·9	0·1
U.S.A.	1950–60	1·50	1·6	0·1
S. AMERICA				
Argentine	1947–60	1·58	1·7	0·1
British Guiana	1946–60	2·95	2·9	0
Chile	1952–60	2·25	2·5	0·2
ASIA				
Hong Kong	1958–62	2·87	4·5	1·6
Japan	1955–60	1·04	0·9	− 0·1
Malaya	1947–57	2·91	2·5	− 0·4
Singapore	1947–57	3·41	4·5	1·1
EUROPE				
Austria	1951–61	0·36	0·2	− 0·2
Belgium	1947–61	0·47	0·5	0
Denmark	1955–60	0·77	0·6	− 0·2
Finland	1950–60	1·20	1·0	− 0·2
France	1954–62	0·66	1·0	0·3
Germany (West)	1956–61	0·61	1·2	0·6
Ireland	1956–61	0·93	− 0·6	− 1·5
Italy	1951–61	0·84	0·6	− 0·2
Netherlands	1947–60	1·46	1·7	0·2
Norway	1950–60	0·97	1·1	0·1
Portugal	1950–60	1·22	0·5	− 0·7
Spain	1950–60	1·20	0·8	− 0·4
Sweden	1950–60	0·54	0·6	0·1
Switzerland	1950–60	0·74	1·4	0·7
United Kingdom	1951–61	0·46	0·5	0
Yugoslavia	1953–61	1·35	1·1	− 0·2
OCEANIA				
Australia	1954–61	1·37	2·3	0·9
New Zealand	1956–61	1·74	2·1	0·4

TABLE III.17. SOURCES OF EUROPEAN EMIGRATION 1940-60

	000/year
United Kingdom	150
Italy	130[a]
West Germany	80
Netherlands	50
Spain	45
Portugal	30
Greece	20
Austria	16
Total *gross*	600
net	450

[a] Total to all destinations 285,000 gross, about half of that net.

emigration exceeding 1 per cent of population per annum are rare. To some extent, rates of emigration are a matter of definition — if we regard Puerto Rico as part of the United States, and Ireland as part of the United Kingdom, we deprive ourselves of two interesting examples of very high emigration rates, of 2·1 and 1·5 per cent per year respectively of the entire existing population, even when measured net. (The gross figure for Puerto Rico for 1953, quoted above, was no less than 12 per cent of the entire population; gross figures for Ireland are not available, as migrants to Britain are not distinguished from short period travellers.) Jamaica, with a net emigration rate of 1·4 per cent, also stands very high in the list. Community of language between the migrants' old and new home; political association between the countries, or at any rate absence of legal restrictions on migration; and comparatively short distance, should all be expected to contribute to a high rate of migration. But a Puerto Rican migrant is going to a country with a different language; and the distances are great for the Jamaican travelling to Britain, and also for the Puerto Rican travelling to New York. The forces making for migration may be powerful enough to overcome these obstacles. Italy's gross migration rate attained its maximum of 2·5 per cent of the population in 1913, of whom more than half were long-distance migrants to other continents. The European migrants had a short journey; but they were travelling to countries with different languages, and where some legal restrictions were placed upon them.

There are some unexpected features about emigration. It is a process which builds up cumulatively; people are much more likely to emigrate where they have relatives and friends who have emigrated already, who can supply them with reliable information about the country of their proposed

TABLE III.18. NET EMIGRATION. ANNUAL RATES PER THOUSAND POPULATION

(Asterisked figures represent net immigration)

Austria[a]			Ireland[j, k]	1780–1845	4·5	
(Excl. Hungary)	1869–80	3·2		1851–60	19·4	
	1880–90	6·9		1861–70	16·9	
Barbados[b]	1891–1921	10		1871–80	12·7	
Finland[c]	1751–90	0		1881–90	16·3	
	1791–1800	5		1891–1900	11·8	
	1801–10	15*		1901–10	8·2	
	1811–20	3*		1911–26	8·8	
	1821–30	1*		1926–36	5·6	
	1831–40	2*		1936–46	6·3	
	1841–50	2*		1946–51	8·4	
	1851–60	1*		1951–6	13·4	
	1861–70	2	Italy[g]	1876–81	1·3	
	1871–80	1*		1881–1900	3·6	
Germany	1816–50	1·3[e]		1901–10	4·5	
	1851–93	3·0[e]		1910–20	0·8	
	1880	2·4[d]		1921–30	3·0	
	1900	0·5[d]		1931–40	0·7	
	1913	0·4[d]	Netherlands[h]	1900–09	1·1	
	1920	0·2[d]		1910–19	1·8*	
	1925	1·0[d]		1920–29	0·1	
	1930	0·5[d]		1930–39	0·1*	
	1938	0·2[d]		1945–9	0	
Greece[f]	1890–4	0·7		1950–4	1·9	
	1895–9	2·8		1955–8	0·4	
	1900–4	5·1	Poland[i]	1895–1914	4·7	
	1905–9	6·0	Spain[d]	1900	4·2	
	1925–9	0·3		1913	10·1	
	1930–4	0·5*		1920	3·9	
	1935–9	0·3*		1925	2·8	
	1950–4	1·1		1930	1·4	
	1955–9	0·2				

[a] Meuriot, *Des grandes agglomérations urbaines.*
[b] Roberts, *The Population of Jamaica.*
[c] *Index*, January 1940.
[d] Sauvy, *Richesse et Population*, gross migration to non-European destinations.
[e] Mulhall, *Industries and Wealth of Nations.*
[f] *Population*, October 1960.
[g] Coppola d'Anna.
[h] Central Bureau of Statistics.
[i] *Population Index*, October 1939.
[j] Connell, *The Population of Ireland* and Brinley Thomas, *Scottish Journal of Political Economy*, November 1959.
[k] Territory as now constituted, except that the first three data are inclusive of Northern Ireland.

Table III.18—*contd.*

Sweden[a, b]

1751–60	0·7
1761–70	0·7
1771–80	0·4
1781–90	0·8
1791–1800	1·0
1801–10	0·6
1811–20	0·1*
1821–30	0
1831–40	0·4
1841–50	0·1
1851–60	0·7
1861–70	3·7
1871–80	3·2
1881–90	7·4
1891–1900	3·7
1901–10	3·6
1911–20	1·1
1921–30	1·5
1931–40	0·9*
1941–45	1·2*
1945–50	2·8*
1951–5	1·3*

Syria & Lebanon[c]

1860–1900	2
1900–29	6
1931–8	0·5

European to Asian Russia[c]   1900–14   1·6

U.S.S.R.[d]

1882–96	0·2
1897–1914	0·5
1917–22	2·4
1923–30	0·1
1931–4	0·5
1935–8	0·1
1939–40	1·7
1941–5	1·1
1946–8	1·8

United Kingdom[b]

	England	Scotland	Wales	N. Ireland
1851–60	1·6	10·1	2·8	
1861–70	0·7	4·4	4·7	
1871–80	0·5	2·8	3·5	11·9
1881–90	2·3	5·8	1·1	10·8
1891–1900	0·2	1·3	0·5	5·5
1901–10	1·9	5·7	4·5*	5·2
1911–20	1·6	5·0	2·1	4·7
1921–30	0·3*	8·0	10·2	8·2
1931–38	2·4*	0·8	7·2	0·5
1939–45		0·3	0·1*	2·3
1946–50	0·6*	9·2	1·8	6·3
1951–57	1·2*	5·3	1·9	7·0

Combined gross extra-European migration[f]

1816–50	4·0
1851–93	7·4
1880	4·7
1900	4·1
1913	8·1
1920	4·3
1925	3·2
1930	1·8
1938	0·7

[a] Montgomery, *The Rise of Modern Industry in Sweden*. The author thinks that deaths may have been understated, and emigration consequently over-estimated, in the earlier periods.
[b] Brinley Thomas, *Scottish Journal of Political Economy*, November 1959.
[c] Fish, *Geographical Review*, April 1944.
[d] Biraben, *Population*, Numéro Spéciale, June 1958.
[e] Carr-Saunders, *World Population*.
[f] Sauvy and Mulhall (see note to Germany) excluding Ireland.

destination, and possibly financial help with travelling as well. And it is not the poorest, most backward and most hungry communities which emigrate. 'In particularly poor isolated rural areas a hard lot is accepted as a matter of course for lack of knowledge of means of improving it — it is the rural areas in transition, areas in first contact with urban and commercial influences, that send out swarms of emigrants.'[1]

This principle was found to apply strongly in Finland.[2] Of the 356,000 Finnish emigrants between 1816 and 1930, no less than 45 per cent came from a small area in Ostrobothnia, containing only 13 per cent of Finland's population. It was not that they spoke the Swedish language, which might give them wider international contacts than Finnish; but that this part of the coast became commercialized, while the rest of Finland was still living by subsistence agriculture. It should also be pointed out (whether or not these factors have any bearing on migration) that in this region a greater degree of economic equality prevailed than in the rest of Finland, a greater measure of religious observance, and also a greater rate of homicide.

Soil and climate indeed are comparatively favourable, and wealth was accumulating, but for various reasons local manufacturing employment failed to grow. Such employment might have been found in the expanding industrial areas of Southern Finland. But the Ostrobothnians preferred to emigrate almost entirely to the United States, before the quota restrictions in 1924, later to Sweden, Canada and Australia.

Italian experience[3] however shows how greatly this situation of selective migration from certain provinces can change, even in the course of 30 years — and then change again in another generation.

The best method of measuring inequality in such phenomena as provincial emigration rates is by drawing what is sometimes called the Lorenz Diagram (though on this occasion at any rate we may use its alternative Italian name of Gini Diagram). The provinces are arranged in ascending order of emigration rates; on the horizontal scale are then shown the cumulated provincial populations as a proportion of all Italy and on the vertical scale the cumulated proportions of emigrants. If emigration rates were entirely equal, the diagram would take the form of a straight line running obliquely across it. The greater the departure of the actual line from this theoretical limit, the greater the degree of inequality.

In the 1880's (though the southern province of Basilicata already had a high emigration rate), emigration was mostly from the Northern provinces, wealthier, better educated, and also more in contact with the rest of Europe

[1] Kirk, *Europe's Population in the Inter-war Years.*
[2] Jutikkala, *International Population Conference, Vienna, 1959,* and *Economic History Conference, Munich,* 1965.
[3] Cosmo, *Banco Nazionale del Lavoro,* January–June 1954.

DIAGRAM III.c

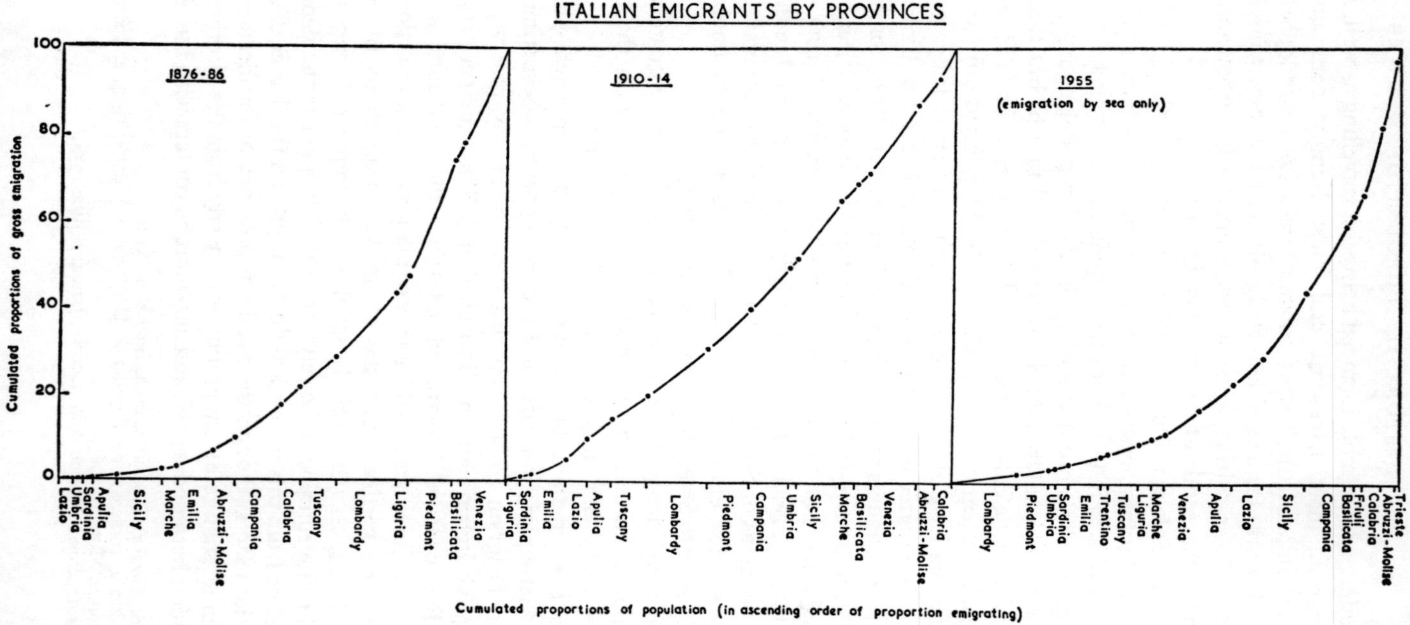

ITALIAN EMIGRANTS BY PROVINCES

Cumulated proportions of gross emigration

Cumulated proportions of population (in ascending order of proportion emigrating)

1955 (emigration by sea only)

Trieste
Abruzzi-Molise
Calabria
Friuli
Basilicata
Campania
Sicily
Lazio
Apulia
Venezia
Marche
Liguria
Tuscany
Trentino
Emilia
Sardinia
Umbria
Piedmont
Lombardy

1910-14

Calabria
Abruzzi-Molise
Venezia
Basilicata
Marche
Sicily
Umbria
Campania
Piedmont
Lombardy
Tuscany
Apulia
Lazio
Emilia
Sardinia
Liguria

1876-86

Venezia
Basilicata
Piedmont
Liguria
Lombardy
Tuscany
Calabria
Campania
Abruzzi-Molise
Emilia
Marche
Sicily
Apulia
Sardinia
Umbria
Lazio

than Central and Southern Italy. (Venetia and Lombardy had been part of the Austrian Empire within the memory of most people then living.)

By the 1910/14 period however a high degree of uniformity between the provinces had already been obtained. The southern provinces of Calabria, Campania and Sicily had moved into the high emigration category.

By the 1950's, a high degree of inequality had again arisen, but of a different kind. The principal sources of emigration now were the southern provinces, together with Trieste and Friuli, partly German speaking, and cut off from their old trading connections.

Before we examine statistics of gross and net immigration, we may consider the situation in Canada, predominantly a country of immigration, but with a substantial emigration. Britain is in the converse position.

Canadian migration to the United States became marked by the 1860's, and from that date to 1900 averaged over 8 per 1000 per year of the Canadian population.[1] Since then however it has fallen substantially, and for the last decade the figure has stood at 3.[2] On the grounds of short distance, identity of language, and complete absence of legal restrictions, one would expect this rate of migration to be high, if there were any substantial differences in real income level between the two countries.

TABLE III.19. NET IMMIGRATION 1946–60
(millions)

	Total	Of which of European origin
U.S.A.	$3\frac{1}{4}$	$2\frac{1}{2}$
Canada	2	1·7
Latin America	2	2 (net 1·6)
Israel	1	1

In Britain during the period 1946/60, while gross emigration to other continents averaged 150,000 annually, as shown in Table III.17, there was during this period[3] an average inflow of 8,000 from the white Commonwealth countries, of 15,000 from the coloured Commonwealth countries, and 25,000 from Ireland. The net inflow of coloured Commonwealth migrants, as is well known, accelerated rapidly to 58,000 in 1960, and is now subject to restriction. Bouscaren[4] also gives a summary (Table III.19) of the principal destinations of immigrants. To this should be added over $1\frac{1}{2}$ million (entirely European) to Australia and New Zealand.

Of the newly settled countries, some have relied much more than others

[1] *Bank of Nova Scotia Bulletin*, July 1947.
[2] U.S. Statistics, quoted in *Canada Yearbook*.
[3] These figures, which have to be obtained by a difficult indirect method, privately communicated by Prof. Brinley Thomas, University of Wales.
[4] *Research Bulletin for European Migration Problems*, The Hague, June 1962.

upon immigrants to people them, and some have changed their policy from time to time. But there seems to be a limit of about 10 per thousand[1] annually of existing population to the rate at which immigrants can come, probably because of the social and political pressures which arise when immigration is too rapid — except for the very earliest stages of settlement, about which we generally lack accurate information in any case.

The growth of population in the early United States, which was rapid, was mainly a natural increase[2] — the great days of immigration came later. Official migration records begin in 1819, but understate immigration, through false statements by shipmasters, but also by omitting entries through Canada (and also some illegal importation of slaves). Between 1790 and 1820 contemporary estimates show only 4–6,000 immigrants annually: Rubin estimates 500,000 for the whole period, averaging however only 2·7 per thousand annually per head of U.S. population, whose total growth rate was 30 per thousand annually.

Table III.20 gives the figures for subsequent decades, until the great reversal of U.S. immigration policy in the 1920's.

TABLE III.20.   U.S. ANNUAL NET IMMIGRATION[a] PER
THOUSAND EXISTING POPULATION

1820–29	1·3	1850–59	9·8	1880–89	8·0	1910–3	10·3
1830–39	4·0	1860–69	6·7	1890–99	3·7		
1840–49	8·2	1870–79	5·1	1900–09	6·3		

[a] Whelpton, *Social Forces*, March 1928; Brinley Thomas, *Scottish Journal of Political Economy*, November 1959.

During recent years the figure has been between 1 and 2 only.

Canadian statistics are considerably confused by immigrants who, after a shorter or longer stay, proceed to the United States. Births and deaths were not accurately recorded until 1921; but for the earlier decades some approximate estimates are given in Canada Year Book (Table III.21).

In recent years, as we saw in the Table III.16, the figure of net immigration has risen to 6. The decade 1901–11, in which it rose to 12, was one of quite exceptionally rapid development, which could hardly have been expected to last.

Immigration to Brazil[3] averaged nearly 5 per thousand between 1886 and 1913, but since then has been low, and subject to some restriction.

---

[1] Equivalent to 1 per cent — it is more convenient to classify per thousand.
[2] Rubin, *Research Bulletin for European Migration Problems*, The Hague, October 1959.
[3] Landry, *Traité de Démographie*.

TABLE III.21. CANADIAN POPULATION GROWTH RATES
PER THOUSAND PER YEAR

	1851–61	1861–71	1871–81	1881–91	1891–1901
Natural increase	23	19	18	16	14
Population increase			14	11	10
Net immigration	6[a]	–1[a]	–4	–5	–4

	1901–11	1911–21	1921–5	1926–30	1931–9
Natural increase	18	16			
Population increase	30	20			
Net immigration	12	4	–3·3[b]	4·0[b]	–1·5[b]

[a] Estimates of the Rowell–Sirois Commission on Dominion-Provincial Relations, 1938.
[b] *Population Index*, April 1954.

Argentine,[1] on the other hand, kept up a rate of *net* immigration of 8 per thousand or more from 1880 to 1929, with a record[2] of 22 for 1906–10.

Net immigration into Australia[3] shows considerable fluctuations (Table III.22). Apart from the Gold Rush of the 1850's, for which accurate figures are not available, high figures were attained during certain boom periods; but it appears that they could not be permanently sustained.

TABLE III.22. AUSTRALIAN NET IMMIGRATION PER
THOUSAND ANNUALLY OF EXISTING POPULATION

1860–69	13·1	1910–13	14·2
1870–79	9·6	1920–29	6·0
1880–89	14·9	1930–38	0
1890–99	0·2	1947–51	11·6
1900–09	0	1952–60	8·2

France[4] has been a country of net immigration since the 1870's, but at low rates, usually below 1 per thousand, but rising to 6 per thousand in 1921–6, then falling again rapidly.

Ceylon[5] is one of the few Asian countries with substantial immigration (from India), and also good estimates of the rate of natural increase (Table III.23).

For the peak periods of Australian immigration — in the 1860's, the 1880's, 1909–13, the 1920's and the 1950's an explanation may be sought in the relative movements of British and Australian real wages; for Australian immigration until recently has been almost entirely from

[1] Sauvy, *Richesse et Population.*   [2] Landry, *Traité de Démographie.*
[3] Commonwealth Statistician, *Demography Bulletins*, 1938 and 1962.
[4] Sauvy, *Richesse et Population.*   [5] Census of Ceylon, 1946.

TABLE III.23. NET IMMIGRATION TO CEYLON PER THOUSAND
RATES PER YEAR

Census Year	Population in millions	Increase on previous Census	Natural Increase	Net immigration
1827	0·89			
1871	2·40	22		
1881	2·76	14	4·7	9
1891	3·01	9	4·9	4
1901	3·57	17	7·0	10
1911	4·11	14	9·3	5
1921	4·50	9	7·5	2
1931	5·31	16	13·5	3
1946	6·66	21	14·2	7

Britain; and the contacts between the two countries are of very long standing, so that it should not be necessary to bring into consideration any time required to disseminate information. This explanation does not however give a good fit. Up to the 1880's, on what information we have, Australian real wages were 50 per cent or more above British. But it was in the 1880's, at the time of maximum immigration, that this ratio was falling, largely through quite a rapid rise in British real wages. It is true that during the 1890's, when migration came to a standstill, Australian real wages were only some 10–20 per cent above British. On the other hand, Australian real wages were only slightly higher than British at the time of the renewed migration boom in 1909/13; and also during the 1920's. During the 1950's also they were only some 15 per cent higher. The recent increase in immigration must be explained by greater efforts to attract migrants, including subsidized fares, from the 1920's onwards; and also by the migrants' estimate of prospects of employment. Irish and West Indian immigration to Britain in fact has been found to show a remarkable year-by-year sensitivity to changes in the employment situation. McQuade[1] analysed the data of European applications for migration into Canada in the January–March peak period of each year for 1953–64. The number of applications could be quite precisely foretold by the formula of 79,500 less (11,300 multiplied by the percentage rate of unemployment in Canada during the previous July). The rate of unemployment in Britain, on the other hand, had no significant effect upon the rates of emigration from Britain into Canada.

Brinley Thomas, the leading worker in the field of the economics of emigration[2] showed that emigration has swung in long cycles, with

[1] *Research Bulletin for European Migration Problems*, The Hague, 1964, No. 3.
[2] See particularly his contribution to *Essays in Honour of Åkerman*, Lund, 1961.

complementary movements in the countries of emigration and of immigration. For the latter, he worked mainly on data in the United States — Australia and Canada move more or less in phase, but not entirely so. There are four clearly distinguishable periods of major outflow both of population and of capital from Europe, namely in 1845–54, 1863–73, 1881–8, and 1903–13. These were periods of violent upward movements in all economic indicators in the United States. By ordinary methods of reckoning, they were periods of boom in Britain also; but one very important factor, only recently studied, namely the rate of construction, in fact fell in Britain during these periods; and rose markedly during the so-called 'depression periods' between them. Brinley Thomas advances the highly original theory that the rising demand for resources, mainly for construction, but also for certain other industries in Britain during these supposed depression periods (the rises in construction may have been largely due to falls in the rate of interest) directly checked the flow of migration abroad. The flow of labour from agriculture to urban employment within Britain should also be brought into this theory; this was found to be high during the so-called depression periods, and low during the periods of high net emigration abroad.

We may consider finally what statistical evidence we have (Table III.24) about the loss of lives in war. Landry[1] states that France lost 128,000 men and Germany 46,000 in the war of 1870–1; he cannot find adequate evidence on any earlier wars. He does however quote some interesting evidence to prove that in wars before the 1914–18 war (which in itself did much to improve immunization and other medical practice) the number of soldiers who died of disease exceeded the numbers killed in battle.

On earlier occasions (the experience of the British Army in the South African War of 1899–1901 told the same story), the bringing together of great bodies of men under campaigning conditions nearly always provided the predisposing conditions for the spread of epidemics, particularly

TABLE III.24. WAR LOSSES AS PERCENTAGE OF ALL MEN MOBILIZED

		Killed in battle	*Died of disease*
French Army, war of	1870–71	3·7	14·0
Russian Army, ,,	1876–77	6·0	15·5
Japanese Army, ,,	1894–5	1·5	5·0
French Army, ,,	1914–18	13·5	2·0
German Army, ,,	1914–18	13·7	1·0
Belgian Army ,,	1914–18	8·5	3·0
American Army ,,	1914–18	4·5	1·7

[1] *Traité de Démographie.*

dysentery and typhus, whose aetiology, even in 1900, was still not understood. Superior knowledge and stricter practice of hygiene by 1914 were able to save many millions of men from disease — in order that more might die in battle.

The military losses in the First World War were estimated at between 9 million[1] and 13 million[2] — less than one year's normal rate of increase of the world's natural rate of increase of population at that time. The 'deficit of births' has been estimated respectively by Lorimer and Notestein at 10 million for Russia and $12\frac{1}{2}$ million for Western Europe. But the principal elements in the slowing down of the growth of world population during this period were the influenza epidemic of 1918, which killed 10 million people in India alone, the typhus and other epidemics in Eastern Europe, and revolution, civil war and famine in Russia in 1917–21, which led to a further loss of some 10 million lives. The true cause of the influenza epidemic is still unknown — the typhus appears to have been an indirect consequence of the war.

In the Second World War (Table III.25) the deaths of combatants totalled again some 13 million.[3] But on this occasion the civilians killed in the war, through bombing, execution, famine and massacres, who totalled in all countries only 100,000 in the First World War,[4] now numbered millions. Non-combatant deaths directly due to the war have been tentatively estimated by Vincent at as high as 18 million. However, the Second World War was not, for various reasons, followed by epidemics and famines in the same manner as its predecessor. Even if we accept Vincent's figure in full, we get total war losses amounting to 1·3 per cent of the world's population, or only a little over one year's natural increase.

Birth deficits seem to have been on a very much smaller scale than in the First World War, even in Russia and Japan. This war seems to have led to a *postponement*[5] rather than to a permanent deficit of births. This has occurred because throughout the world so many married couples now have decided in advance how many children they want, and war postpones rather than prevents their conception: whereas under conditions of 1914, when children were conceived more nearly to the limit of natural

---

[1] Landry, *Traité de Démographie*.
[2] Willcox, *Journal of the American Statistical Association*, 1928. The principal difference between the two estimates is for Russia's losses which Willcox placed at 5 million and Landry at only 1·7 million.
[3] Generally similar figures are quoted in *League of Nations Monthly Bulletin of Statistics*, May 1946; *Metropolitan Life Insurance Bulletin*, January 1946; Vincent, *Population*, January–March 1947.
[4] *Metropolitan Life Insurance Bulletin*, December 1940.
[5] In many countries the war led to an acceleration of marriages which normally would not have occurred till later; so even this postponement of births was to a considerable extent counteracted.

TABLE III.25.

	1914–18 War Losses[a]		1939–45 War Losses		
	Military losses 000	Do. as percentage of men aged 15–49	Military losses 000[f]	Do. as percentage of men aged 15–49	Civilian deaths millions[g]
Australia	60[d]	5	29[l]	1·5	
Austria–Hungary	1200	10			
Belgium	40	2	7	0·3	0·1
Bulgaria	100[e]	10	insignificant		
Canada			39[l]	1·3	
China			250	0·2	
Finland			50	5·0	
France	1320	13	167	1·9	0·4[j]
Germany	2000	12	3250[k]	16·6	0·5
Greece	100	8	50	0·3	0·5
Hungary			75	3·0	
India			36	0·04	
Italy	700	9	175	1·5	
Japan			1500	8·4	
Netherlands			6	0·3	0·2
New Zealand			12	3·0	
Norway			1	0·1	
Poland	250	6	125	2·5	4·6
Portugal	8	½			
Roumania	250	14	100	3·0	
Turkey	500	15			
Union of S. Africa	7[d]	2	9	1·6	
U.S.S.R. (Russia)	5000[c]	16	over 3000[i]	over 8	10·0
United Kingdom	744	7[b]	298	2·4	0·1
United States	116	½	325	0·9	—
Yugoslavia (Serbia)	365	27	75[h]	2·0	1·4

[a] Willcox, *Journal of the American Statistical Association*, 1928.
[b] Proportion for Great Britain — proportion for Ireland was 2 per cent.
[c] Landry in *Traité de Démographie* estimates only 1·7 million. *Metropolitan Life Insurance Company Bulletin*, January 1946, agrees with Landry.
[d] Landry's data.
[e] Landry estimates only 33000.
[f] *Metropolitan Life Insurance Company Bulletin*, January 1946.
[g] Vincent, *Population*, January–March 1947.
[h] Guerrilla losses only. Vincent estimates total military deaths at 300,000.
[i] Vincent estimates 7 million. [j] Including 100,000 executed.
[k] Vincent estimates 2·8 million. [l] Over 1/3 of these were airmen.

capacity, a birth lost during the war could generally not be made up afterwards.

In the First World War the greatest losses, in proportion to population, were suffered by the Serbian Army. This was a classic tragedy of an army wiped out by typhus. Extremely severe losses were also suffered by Russia, Roumania and Turkey; here again epidemics played a large part.

In the Second World War military losses were for most countries less than they had been in the First World War, except for Germany, Russia, the United States and Japan. Losses were also however relatively heavy in some of the smaller combatant countries, Finland, Hungary, Roumania and New Zealand.

CHAPTER IV

Population and Food*

MOST people have some knowledge of the different components of food, and of their functions, firstly of providing calories, to maintain bodily activity and warmth (it is true that some people seek to reduce their calorie intake rather than to increase it; but there is no such thing as non-calorific food). The second function of food is to provide proteins, to do maintenance work on muscles and other body tissues. These supplies of fuel and maintenance materials must also be supplemented, as it were, by some lubricants, required in small quantities only, but whose absence may lead to serious harm — the vitamins and minerals. Cases of deficiency of these latter components have been known, sometimes with dramatically harmful results. The outstanding cases of vitamin deficiency, however, have been amongst sailors and explorers. Most other deficiency diseases have also arisen among peoples living, for one reason or another, upon stored rather than fresh food — such as the classic case of beri-beri among Asian coolies living on imported polished rice. A poor peasant community, growing its own food, may be in danger of calorie or protein shortage; but it is not likely to be in danger of being short of these small quantities of vitamins and minerals, obtainable from a variety of salads and other fresh foods.

The belief held at one time by some physiologists, that it was necessary for a substantial proportion of fat to be included in the diet, has now been discarded. Many physiologists now seem to regard fats (particularly margarine and butter fat) as potentially harmful, to be tolerated rather than encouraged; no physiologist seems to regard them as positively desirable, though all agree with the commonsense conclusion that, in small quantities, they make food more palatable.

It is the same with the belief about proteins from animal sources (meat, fish, eggs and milk). At one time it was held that we ought to obtain at least half our protein requirements from such sources. This theory has now also been abandoned. Physiologists now hold that so long as the supply of vegetable protein is adequate, the amount of animal protein required is very small indeed (the requirement in fact is probably not for the animal protein

---

* The first part of this chapter is condensed from *The Economics of Subsistence Agriculture* (1964), by the present author and M. R. Haswell. This book should be consulted if detailed references are required.

as such, but for a certain vitamin associated with it). Proteins are however ranged (in accordance with their measured effects upon the growth of rats — though some biologists question the validity of this method) according to 'biological quality'. In this test, animal proteins come highest. Of the cereal proteins, that from maize appears to have the lowest quality.

There should not be many people now who still believe the extraordinary mis-statement, originally made in 1950, and so widely circulated around the world, that 'a lifetime of malnutrition and actual hunger is the lot of at least two-thirds of mankind'. Why such an obviously erroneous statement should have received such widespread credence is a problem for the social psychologist; a great many people seem to have suspended their normal critical faculties because of the intensity of their belief that the world was over-populated, or needed a world revolution (or both, for some people).

However the World Food and Agriculture Organization (F.A.O.), once sardonically described by *The Economist*[1] as 'a permanent institution devoted to proving that there is not enough food in the world', while recognizing the untenability of the 'two-thirds of mankind' legend, nevertheless sought to harness it in its 'Freedom from Hunger Campaign'. In view of the findings of its Director of Statistics,[2] F.A.O. reduced the proportion of the world's population stated to be in actual hunger to 10–15 per cent, but there were another 35–40 per cent, making a total of half of the world 'malnourished'. F.A.O. apparently succeeded in persuading President Kennedy, Prince Philip, and many lesser dignitaries that half the world was malnourished and most informed opinion believes them. F.A.O. gave no evidence to support their statement, nor even defined 'malnourished' until much later, when they produced their *Third World Survey*. Here they stated (page 9) that people were malnourished unless they lived at the dietary standards of Western Europe, deriving at least 20 per cent of their total calorie intake from animal products, fruits and vegetables, and fats and oils. No evidence at all was given for this standard beyond the statement that 'it is generally agreed'. It was on this proposition, for which no physiological evidence at all was quoted, that half the world was stated to be malnourished. The available medical evidence in fact appears to indicate that most of the inhabitants of Western Europe, far from living at a standard which can be defined as the borderline of malnutrition, are in considerable danger of overnutrition. F.A.O., like many similar organizations, appears to waste enormous sums of money, and devotes much of its energies to political manoeuvres to secure its own perpetuation and aggrandisement. From this point of view, if F.A.O. were

[1] 23 August 1952.
[2] Sukhatme, *Journal of the Royal Statistical Society*, Series A, Part IV, 1961.

disbanded and a fraction of its revenue devoted to the universities and private institutes where real educational and research work is being done, the world would be better off.

Beginning in 1950, F.A.O. assembled a number of leading physiologists to prepare reports on the calorie requirements of different populations.[1] These reports were accepted as the best available information on the subject. Very serious doubt has been cast on them however, and on Sukhatme's use of them to prove that 10–15 per cent of the world's population was hungry, in a recent study by McArthur.[2] Other evidence recently brought to light also confirms McArthur's conclusions.

It appears that the F.A.O. scale of requirements for children was set much too high. Cullumbine's[3] survey of food consumption in Ceylon — one of the principal sources from which Sukhatme drew his conclusions — showed that a number of Ceylon Tamil boys aged from 8 to 15 were only consuming 50–55 per cent of F.A.O.'s supposed calorie requirements (their figure having been slightly adjusted to allow for Ceylon's average temperature of 25°C). The important point, which Sukhatme did not bring out, was that these were boys from 'upper and middle-class families'. Cullumbine has discounted the possibility that their food intake was limited by income or food shortage, and he was confident that the actual bulk of food consumed was quite satisfying. The food intakes also compare quite well with theoretical estimates of requirements, based on measurements of their basic metabolic rate, and estimates of the energy which they used in play.[4]

In Table IV.1, F.A.O.'s 'reference requirements' for children, and Sukhatme's adaptation[5] of them in his paper to an 'actual requirement scale' for India, are compared with some estimates by Fox[6] for Africans, who are living at about the same temperature, but substantially larger-bodied. Fox's estimates covered basal metabolism and also 'specific dynamic action', i.e. walking and other movements, except for agricultural work. In this community, adult males averaged 63 kilograms weight, females 55.

The most convincing evidence however comes from McArthur's analysis

[1] F.A.O., *Nutritional Studies on Calorie Requirements*, No. 5, 1950, No. 15, 1957.
[2] *Journal of the Royal Statistical Society*, Series A, Part III, 1964.
[3] Ceylon Journal of Medical Science, Vol. VI, p. 202 (1949) (quoted by McArthur).
[4] *Journal of Applied Physiology*, Vol. II, p. 640 (1950) (quoted by McArthur).
[5] How Sukhatme made the Indian figures come out higher than the general 'reference requirement scale' is not clear. He states in his paper that he has adjusted for average adult body weights of 55 kilograms and 45 kilograms for adult men and women respectively, and for an average temperature of 20°C. It appears that he has estimated average body weight too high and the average temperature too low, thus in both ways somewhat exaggerating food requirements.
[6] Ph.D. thesis, University of London, 1953.

TABLE IV.1. CHILDREN'S CALORIE REQUIREMENTS PER DAY

FAO Reference Scale			Sukhatme (India)			Fox (Africa)		
Age	Male	Female	Age	Male	Female	Age	Male	Female
0–1	1120		0–1	1288		0–2	700	600
1–3	1300		1–4	1288		3–5	808	751
4–6	1700		5–9	1843		6–10	1072	918
7–9	2100		10–14	2603		11–15	1262	1249
10–12	2500	2400	15–19	3012	2064	16–20	1526	1296
13–15	3100	2600						
16–19	3600	2400						

of the situation in Japan. Statistical surveys of the food intake of a large sample of the Japanese population had been made every year since 1946, which should have given time for the development of the most accurate possible techniques of measurement. The application of Sukhatme's method to the data leads to the conclusion that some 20 per cent of the population in 1962 were actually hungry in Japan, a comparatively high income country, without any exceptional inequalities in the distribution of income — 'a conclusion which, in the light of all the other evidence available, seems meaningless in any practical sense'.

Sukhatme (perhaps this was only to be expected) tended to minimize the extent of hunger in China — though at the time of his paper, in 1961, it was probably very severe. The Chinese, including the children, at many seasons of the year engage in arduous physical work for long hours; and many of them have a comparatively high body weight. If we assume an average body weight of 55 kilograms for men and 45 kilograms for women, in the climate of Northern China (average temperature 10°C) the F.A.O. scale indicates average calorie requirement, for the whole population, at 2365 calories/day. For Southern China, assuming 5 kilograms lower body weights, and temperatures 10° higher, we obtain a figure of 2209. The average for China, if the F.A.O. scales are true, must be 2250 at least, possibly over 2300. Table IV.2 shows estimates of calorie intakes per head of the Chinese population in recent years, compiled from the best available information, published in the *China Quarterly*, together with a privately communicated result estimated from accounts given by refugees entering Hong Kong from Kwangtung Province, which appears to have been particularly badly hit by food shortage.

Most people are aware that the food shortage in China has been bad; but it seems impossible that the national average should have been so far below minimum physiological requirements, even in comparatively good years such as 1958 and 1959. Here again therefore we have strong grounds for

TABLE IV.2. AVERAGE CALORIE INTAKES IN CHINA IN
RECENT YEARS
(per head of whole population)

	1958	1959	1960	1961	1962
'W.K.', *China Quarterly*, Apr.–June and July–Sept. 1961	Over 2200	2000	1900		
Alsop, *China Quarterly*, July–Sept. 1962		1800			1300–1600
Robertson, *China Quarterly*, Jan.–Mar. 1963					1600–1800
Kwangtung refugees to Hong Kong:					
Rural					1380
Urban					1650

thinking that the level of minimum physiological requirements must be substantially below the F.A.O. Reference Scale.

In the F.A.O. Calorie Reports it is indicated that, for children under 15, the Reference Scale is meant to apply all over the world, irrespective of the different body weights to which the children are expected to grow up as adults, except for small allowances for temperature. Both Cullumbine's and Fox's results indicate that the F.A.O. Reference Scale for children ought to be almost halved.

The calorie requirements of men performing specific agricultural and other tasks can be directly measured by means of apparatus which records the rate of exhalation of carbon dioxide (differences in temperature and body weights should also be taken into account if we wish to apply the results to others than the population among whom the results are obtained). Some experiments in Africa show that these requirements can be very high for certain types of work, 372 calories/hour for bush-clearing, and 504 for tree-felling. It is well known however that men engaged in such extremely arduous tasks cannot work continuously. The F.A.O. Calorie Report quotes (p. 59) an estimate by Lehmann to the effect that men doing such work, if their health is to be preserved, must rest intermittently to an extent which brings their long-run calorie requirement down to 300 calories/hour for Europeans, possibly 250 for Africans, with higher temperature and lower body weight. Experiments in India[1] showed that men in their 20's doing hard labouring work in a Southern Indian textile mill, of average body weight 47 kilograms, used energy at the rate of 203 calories/hour, averaged over an 8-hour shift. This is considerably harder work than is presumed for the F.A.O. 'Reference Man'. The total requirements of these Indian labourers, including basic metabolism and non-work activities,

[1] Banerjea and others, *Indian Journal of Medical Research*, 1959, Vol. 47, p. 657.

were put at 3050 calories/day. As against this, a Japanese farmer[1] weighing 52 kilos, and doing $7\frac{1}{2}$ hours farm work per day, has his needs put at only 2500. This figure, for a larger-bodied man in a colder climate, is so much lower than Banerjea's that one may conclude that it has been taken from the F.A.O. Reference Scale — which is based on a European Reference Man of somewhat sedentary habits, and is inadequate for men doing prolonged hard work. Fox's results (page 51) show only 165 calories/man hour equivalent[2] for farm work (including the walk to and from the plots).

Walking was found to require 145 calories/hour for men, 126 for women. Various farm tasks were analysed, and found to call for energy expenditure at rates between 95 and 315 calories/hour for men (less for women, in the body weight proportion).

Phillips's[3] and Trowell's[4] results give higher figures, for men averaging 55 kilograms weight, of 184 calories/hour for walking, and 213–504 for various farm tasks. Fox however points out that the performance of heavy farm tasks was interspersed by considerable periods of rest, or performance of light tasks.

The totals can now be assembled for the average per head requirements of whole populations, in those parts of the world where calorie shortages are likely to be in question.

As between different countries, calorie requirements per head vary not only with temperature and average body weight, but also with the different proportion of children found in a 'young' population with high birth and death rates. The age composition for such a population used in the F.A.O. Report is also used here.

Calorie requirements per head per day for the whole population are thus seen to range from a little over 2000 for larger bodied people, or in colder climates, working an average of 8 hours day throughout the year; falling to as low as 1625 for small bodied people in a hot climate working an average of 4 hours a day throughout the year.

These conclusions are certainly more compatible with the figures for China given in Table IV.2.

Contrary to general belief, it is quite possible (though nobody would say that it was desirable) for man to live almost entirely on cereals — that is to

---

[1] Watanabe, Shikoku, *Acta Medica*, Vol. 15 (in Japanese — quoted by McArthur).

[2] Averaged over the year, per head of the whole village population, 222 calories/day (plus 46 calories/day for remunerative work other than on their own farms). Expressed per head of the adult male equivalent of the working population (taking women as 55/63 of men, in accordance with their relative weights) this becomes 365 calories/day/man equivalent. The farm work done by the men, including the walk to and from the plots, was only 1·6 hours per day, averaged over the year; by the women 2·95 hours.

[3] *Journal of Tropical Medicine and Hygiene*, Vol. 57, 1954.

[4] *East African Medical Journal*, May 1955.

TABLE IV.3. CALORIE REQUIREMENTS PER DAY

	Assumed body weights of adults kg.	Average temp. C°	Requirements per man aged 20–29[a]		Requirements[c] per head of whole population					Total	
					Children[d]	Women	Men				
			Seden-tary	Net[b] addition each hour/day worked			Seden-tary	Net addition for each hour/day worked		Men working 4 hour day	Men working 8 hour day
Central Africa	57½	25	2026	172	400	526	646	55		1792	2012
India, SE-Asia	50	25	1829	155	400	447	582	49		1625	1821
Southern China	50	20	1880	159	411	459	599	51		1673	1877
Northern China	55	10	1967	167	433	528	626	53		1799	2011

[a] Based on Trowell-Phillips results, adjusted elsewhere for body weights and temperatures.
[b] i.e. 250 cals./hr. working, less 78 cals./hr. which would have been consumed in sedentary occupation.
[c] Different sections of the population weighted according to their relative numbers, so that the figures can be summed directly to give average requirements per head of whole population.
[d] FAO 'Reference Scale' reduced by 45 per cent. Requirements adjusted for temperature, not body weight.

say, cereals properly so-called, not root crops, which are nearly all very low in protein — and subject also to the qualification that the quality of the protein in maize is somewhat suspect. Cereals yield about 3·2 calories/gram; the minimum and maximum requirements of 1625 and 2012 calories/day shown in Table IV.3 can therefore be met by the consumption of 185–230 kilograms/person/year of cereals. The protein content of cereals is very variable, not only between different species, but in the same species in different years; the range is about 8–13 per cent. Subject to the qualification about maize however, the 60 grams/person/day or thereabouts contained in the above quantity of cereals should be well above the protein requirements of the average population.

It is convenient to measure agricultural production, in under-developed countries, in 'grain equivalents' i.e. valuing other agricultural products (grain generally constituting the largest part of the agricultural output) in accordance with their exchange value against grain in the local markets. Allowing for a small quantity of animal products, of green vegetables, and of textile fibres, the minimum agricultural requirements of a population can be put at somewhat below 250 kilograms/person/year of grain equivalent, or under a quarter of a ton.

Our most distant ancestors however, so far as we know, did not bother about grain. When the world was young, and there was plenty of space for everybody, they lived by hunting and fishing — and a very enjoyable life it probably was for able-bodied men, at any rate to judge by the amount which wealthy business men are now willing to spend in order to obtain a few days' hunting and fishing, living under some approximation to primitive conditions. The areas in which they hunted were probably abounding in game.

> 'No hunter of the Age of Fable
> Had need to buckle in his belt.
> More game than he was ever able
> To take ran wild upon the veldt:
> Each night with roast he stocked his table,
> Then procreated on the pelt,
> And that is how, of course, there came,
> At last to be more men than game.'[1]

The net rate of population increase among primitive men however as we have seen was very slow. There were not anywhere 'more men than game' from the beginning of the world until about 7000 B.C., the date of the first known agricultural settlement.[2] It was probably increasing population

---

[1] A. D. Hope (Australian National University), *Texas Quarterly*, Summer 1962. Reprinted by permission.
[2] Cipolla, *The Economic History of World Population*.

density, or alternatively, in some areas, a change of climate, drying up the grasslands, which compelled our ancestors to take what was probably for them the very disagreeable step of commencing to live by agriculture.

Nougier[1] estimated that the population of palaeolithic France had fifty-five sq. km./person to hunt over, which was abundant. The Australian aborigines, who lived entirely by hunting and fishing, in a much drier climate, before the coming of white settlers, averaged thirty sq. km./person; and it is generally agreed that they did not have much to spare. A most interesting account of New Zealand[2] shows that while the moa (large flightless birds, now extinct) were there for them to hunt, the early Moriori lived at a density of 10–15 sq. km./person; after both the moa and Moriori had been exterminated, their Maori successors only lived at a density of over 30 sq. km./person. It looks as if, even in a good-rainfall climate, 10 sq. km./person represents the upper limit of density for a hunting population.

It was sometime in the Mesolithic Period, so far as we can ascertain, that the population of England had risen to nearly fifteen thousand, beyond the safe limit. It was becoming clear that the country was overpopulated. We can imagine our ancestors having meetings about it, and saying that some birth restriction was necessary. There may have been some who advocated emigration to Scotland — this would have been ruled out as an altogether desperate expedient. Then there might have been some young man with a rather theoretical outlook, who suggested practising agriculture, something of which perhaps they had heard remotely, which was already established in Babylonia and Egypt. This obviously would have been ruled out as being quite impracticable in England. But agriculture eventually had to be adopted, with we can imagine how much reluctance, because increasing pressure of population simply left no alternative. For some generations, however — as in some parts of the world now — the men still regarded agricultural work as so degrading that it could only be performed by women.

The land which now constitutes the United States and Canada covers 17 million sq. km., or about 12 million if we deduct tundra and desert. By the time the first white settlers arrived, this area had a population of one million. At this density, population was pressing on the limits of subsistence for a hunting and fishing community. We know that the practice of maize growing was spreading northwards from Mexico. An interesting summary of travellers' accounts of the diets of American Indians in the seventeenth century[3] indicates that they were then obtaining two-thirds of their calories from grain.

[1] *Population*, April–June 1954.   [2] Cumberland, *Geographical Review*, April 1962.
[3] Bennett, *Journal of Political Economy*, October 1955.

Most of the world, in its natural state, was tree or scrub-covered; but there are areas of natural grassland, shading into tundra at one end of the climatic scale, and into desert at the other. The first form of agriculture adopted by dwellers in these grassland areas, when population pressure made it impossible for them to live any longer simply by hunting, was probably the herding of tame animals, usually still living nomadically (as some do to this day), travelling with their herds to find fresh pasture when they have grazed out what they are occupying.

Domestication of animals reduces land requirements considerably. Even reindeer on the tundra[1] require only 0·6–1 sq. km. each, and a tribe can live on a few reindeer per head, together with fishing. In the best natural grasslands, land requirements may fall to ½ sq. km./person.

But it is quite otherwise in forest or scrub country — or in the arid lands watered by springs or rivers, believed to have been the cradle of agriculture in the Middle East. Here domesticated animals cannot find food (and, in forest country, cannot be properly watched by shepherds), and actual cultivation is necessary. Dwellers in wooded country must first make implements to cut down the forest or scrub. (There is a Professor of Archaeology who gives actual demonstrations of cutting down a small tree with a flint hand-axe; it is a slow process.) After drying in the sun the felled scrub is burned, and seeds planted in the ash, which contains a certain amount of fertilizing minerals which the roots of the trees have brought up from the subsoil, and which is free of weeds. Danish archaeologists,[2] attempting to reproduce the conditions of primitive agriculture, found that their rate of scrub clearing was very slow in comparison with what an African can do now with a good steel axe. They also found how much the crop was damaged by birds, especially on an isolated cultivated plot surrounded by scrubland — the primitive farmer's family probably had to watch the crop day and night.

The beneficial effect of the burn in fertilizing the land, and destroying the weeds, works off after two or three years. The farmer then seeks another plot of scrubland to clear. This 'cut and burn' agriculture was once almost universal throughout the world, and is still practised over much the greater part of Africa between the Sahara and South Africa, and in many areas of Asia and Latin America too. On some of the poorer soils it appears that a cycle of nearly 20 years is necessary for the regrowth of sufficient scrub to fertilize the soil. On better soils, the cycle may be ten years or less. But in either case, there is still a population density limit beyond which 'cut and burn' agriculture becomes impossible, and people — again with obvious

---

[1] Andreev and Zavkina, *International Grassland Conference*, Reading, 1960.
[2] *National Museets Arbejdsmark*, 1953, p. 43.

reluctance — have to proceed to the next more productive stage of agriculture, in fixed settlements, and with the soil requiring to be conserved and fertilized.

In Zambia Allen[1] has estimated this maximum density at only 8 persons/sq. km. Grove[2] calculates a *minimum* density of 125 persons/sq. km. of land actually cultivated — any attempt to cultivate at lower densities i.e. to occupy plots exceeding 0·8 hectares/person, would be going beyond the limit capable of being cultivated by hand, with the shortness of the African rainy season, and also the abundant weed growth which it brings. But if we assume an average cycle of 20 years between cultivations, two years' cultivation in each cycle, and one-third of the land incultivable, then Allen's and Grove's figures are reconciled. At the same time Grove points out that, under conditions of African hand-tool agriculture, a population density of 27 persons/sq. km. or more is necessary if driving away of wild animals and recutting of scrub are to be sufficient to keep the tse-tse fly in check. Gourou[3] pointed out that in 'Black Africa' (i.e. the whole area between the Sahara and the South African Republic) the amount of land actually cultivated in any one year is still only about 1/30th of the whole. Its inhabitants mostly practise 'cut and burn', not because they are ignorant of more intensive forms of agriculture, but because they prefer it, as it enables them to feed themselves with less labour than is required for more intensive agriculture. There are a few areas in Africa, such as the island of Ukara in Lake Victoria, and some mountain areas, where tribes have been hemmed in by their enemies into a small space, where they have had no alternative but to practise intensive agriculture, which they do very successfully.

The whole process whereby increasing population density, whether in modern Africa or in the past history of Europe, compels the introduction of more labour — intensive but more productive forms of agriculture — has been reviewed by Ester Boserup in a book[4] of such importance that it is summarized (with the author's approval) at length below.

The analytical methods used by economists, which are useful for dealing with situations limited in time and space, usually treat agricultural methods and property relationships as given. This seems to induce in them a dangerous bias towards regarding as permanent those institutions and techniques which historians have shown to be subject to continuous change. Or, if they do admit the occurrence from time to time of technical and political innovations, which they treat as 'exogenous' for the purposes

[1] Rhodes–Livingstone Journal, 1945.
[2] Contribution to Symposium *Essays on African Population.*
[3] *The Tropical World*; and privately communicated.
[4] *The Conditions of Agricultural Growth.*

of economic analysis, they tend to take the simple Malthusian view that these technical or political changes lead to a population increase (or decrease, as the case may be) until a new equilibrium is reached. In the great majority of cases, however, it is population change which is the cause, and technical and political change the consequence. At any rate in the early stages of the development of agriculture, the need to support a larger population from a given area of land is going to call for an *increased* input of labour per unit of food produced — particularly when we take into account the labour which will have to be used for private investment, in the form of improvements of farms, and public investment in means of transport, irrigation, etc. Once this important principle has been demonstrated, common sense tells us that it is very unlikely that any people should, of their own initiative, institute changes in agricultural technique which would, for a considerable time at any rate, make them engage in more labour per unit of food produced. They would only initiate such changes when compelled to do so by increasing population pressure.

The earliest stages of agriculture call for little input of labour and none of capital, apart from the production or purchase of axes. The first stage of cultivation, described as 'forest fallow', burning a mature forest growth, leaves the cultivator a loose and friable forest soil covered with ashes, which he can plant with a simple digging stick. After repeated burning, however, of less mature growth, we enter the stage described as 'bush fallow', where a certain number of weed and grass roots survive the fire, and where the soil has become considerably more compact, so that it has to be cultivated with hoes, and more frequent weeding is necessary. In the final stage, the soil becomes full of grass roots, which the hoe cannot kill, and the cultivator has to proceed to a system of 'short fallow', using ploughs. Under this system the supply of fertilizing ashes has become much less abundant, and they have to be supplemented by collecting dung, refuse, pond mud, litter from surrounding land, etc. as manure.

Economic historians have generally described nomadic pastoral tribes as an earlier form of society, giving place to agricultural communities as population density grew. But we should consider the reverse possibility, of an increasing population living by bush fallow agriculture, unable or unwilling to plough, deliberately adopting the nomadic life (if grasslands were available).

These succeeding stages each call for more labour per unit of food produced. When draught animals have to be kept, it is rarely, if ever, possible to find natural grazing in sufficient abundance to keep them all the year round. They may be inadequately fed when they are idle, but when they are urgently needed for farm work, they have to be well fed, which calls for the growing of fodder crops, or else the reduction of cereal supplies available for human food. So agricultural productivity per man hour of labour input, if we measure it that way, appears to be falling. If the economy is developed to a point where there are wage workers, their real wages per hour will also fall. The relative difference between their wages in the harvest season, when labour is really urgently needed, and in the off season, will increase. There is abundant evidence of this having been the case throughout Europe in the period 1750 to 1850, when population was increasing much more rapidly than before, and this increase was compelling great changes in agricultural methods and tenure. Farm workers were being compelled to consume cheaper foods than those to which previous generations had been accustomed, and also they worked many more days in the year, and hours in the day.

But, although this was an unhappy period for farm workers, product per man hour, not only product per man year, eventually increased. In the first place, the mere habit of harder and more continuous work proved economically beneficial. Secondly agriculture began to enjoy large economies of specialization — more particularly as transport became more available. Population growth therefore, in the long run, holds out much better prospects of development than does a stationary, still less a declining population. 'The historian cannot show us any example of population stagnation or decline whose results have been happy' firmly declares Sauvy.[1]

These developments, it has already been said, call for a good deal of investment, both public and private; but these include certain important 'indivisibilities', and a rising population therefore considerably reduces the real burden per head. Indeed, it is not until a certain critical level of population density has been reached that the construction of towns becomes economically possible. It is only with a comparatively dense population that a system of regular transportation of food, without which the town cannot live, can be organized without absorbing an inordinate share of the labour force. A great deal of the potential labour force of the ancient Incas appears to have been absorbed by the requirements of head-load transport. The famines frequently recorded in mediaeval times are more likely to have been due to under-population of agricultural villages — through premature attempts at urbanization, requiring too many soldiers, servants, etc. — than to rural over-population, to which they are generally ascribed.

There was, of course, a grimmer alternative for economic development, and that was enslavement. African history has shown that any tribe which for some reason or other had enjoyed more rapid population growth than its neighbours need neither face a Malthusian increase in mortality, nor

[1] *Théorie Générale de la Population*, Vol. 2, p. 20.

cultivate its land more thoroughly, but might embark upon slave raiding, which would enable it to secure the economic advantages of dense population and permanent settlement, while avoiding the burden of doing additional agricultural work themselves. Once this process had started it became cumulative — the strong could concentrate their attention upon the arts of war and become stronger, while the weaker tribes became weaker still as their population density fell. The increased demand for slaves arising from the plantation owners of North and South America in the seventeenth and eighteenth centuries was responsible for depopulating large parts of Africa, and for degrading what had once been settled agricultural peoples back to long-fallow agriculture or nomadism. Great urban civilizations have been founded on a predominantly enslaved population, including Nineveh and Timbuktu. Slaves existed in ancient Greece, but in relatively small numbers, and in urban employments, with however the important exception of the Spartans, who enslaved the surrounding (*Helot*) agricultural populations, and devoted themselves entirely to war.

We have also a most interesting example[1] of this process in reverse in Africa. 'One reason for Peters's investigation[2] of Barotseland in 1949 was that its home production of food appeared to be steadily falling — Livingstone had written of the Central Plain as a place of abundance where hunger was not known. Peters was particularly impressed by the enormous areas of abandoned gardens on drained peat lands. The loss of these highly productive areas had started with the abolition of customary labour service and the freeing of the serfs — the tribal authorities voted money for the upkeep of the drains, but by this time labour migration was absorbing more than half the Lozi manpower'.

When agriculture develops, as is usually the case, without slavery, and as the real wages of agricultural workers fall with the adoption of more intensive methods, the agricultural worker, if free to move, may go to seek urban employment. If this movement is extensive, it may lead to an accumulation of unemployed in the towns on the one hand, and a rise in food prices through rural labour shortage on the other, thereby making the lot of the poor in the towns even harder. A country faced, or believing itself to be faced with this predicament, may adopt three courses. There may be an actual legal re-introduction of serfdom, as was applied in eastern Europe in the sixteenth century, to previously free agricultural communities. In this case, the demand was accentuated by the beginnings of foreign commerce, demonstrating to land owners that they could sell cereals, and that prices in Western Europe were rising rapidly.

---

[1] Allan, *The African Husbandman*, pp. 154–5.
[2] Rhodes–Livingstone Institute Communication No. 19.

The next alternative is to put legal restrictions on internal migration. This, for instance, was enacted by the Republican Government in Spain as recently as 1934. Some restrictions are, however, very difficult to enforce, without an omnipresent police.

Finally, in many countries, attempts have been made to attract men back to the villages voluntarily, or at least to encourage them to stay there, by agrarian reforms which convert rentpayers into freeholders, and give some opportunities to landless labourers.

The state of affairs which we are considering is, on the historian's time scale, transitory. In the very long run, the desire of labour to leave the villages will raise the price of food, and eventually raise the real wage which the farm worker receives. The important exception to this proposition, of course, is in the case of countries which import an increasing proportion of their food supplies. This applies not only to nineteenth-century Britain, but to some present-day African and Latin American countries as well.

We have noted the succeeding stages of technical improvement, from forest fallow through bush fallow to short fallow and the introduction of draught animals, to which increasing care and attention has to be paid. A later stage is the introduction of the three-course rotation, which appeared in Northern Europe about 800 A.D. This raised output per unit of land by shortening the total period of fallow. It also provided better distribution over the seasons of the demand for both human and animal labour. However, crop rotations and the introduction of legumes and root crops for fodder were not new technical discoveries of the eighteenth century, as many historians have supposed. Lucerne and turnips were known in the ancient world, went into disuse when European population densities were low, but reappeared later. Where density was particularly high, in Flanders, extensive cultivation of turnips reappeared as early as the thirteenth century.

At every stage along this line, such improvements in agricultural organization (comprehensively described in England as 'the enclosures') were opposed, understandably but harmfully, by those enjoying traditional rights of grazing. Grazing in stubbles was an important element in these rights, and every time any progressive cultivator wished to shorten fallow, he met the graziers' natural opposition. This is an important issue in India and other Asian countries (other than Japan) now. The double cropping, which is possible and desirable in many areas, is resisted by the large number of poor men owning grazing rights.

It is rapid population growth which is the principal motive force bringing about, at certain periods in history, extensive clearings of uncultivated land, drainage of swamps, introduction of improved crops and manures, and the like, which historians tend to describe as 'agricultural revolutions', generally failing, however, to trace their origin to population increase. Future historians may well describe the decades beginning about 1950 as India's Agricultural Revolution. It is not permissible to say that things now are different from what they were. Many of the essential economic and political issues in the developing countries are similar to those of past centuries in Europe. The only qualification is that fertilizers, technical assistance, etc., can be more readily obtained from other countries — so long as there is ability and willingness to use them.

Indian agricultural policy, however, both under British and Indian rulers, has in many ways hindered rather than helped the required economic developments. In many parts of India the early British rulers, with the most humane intentions, granted to tenant farmers security of tenure, which they could indeed bequeath to their sons. This had the effect of depriving the land owners of both the incentive and the means to invest in land improvement, especially when rents had been fixed in terms of the low prices prevailing in the early nineteenth century, and steadily shrank in real terms as prices rose. Not many historians have pointed out the grim truth that the great agricultural improvements of late eighteenth- and early nineteenth-century England were introduced at a time when tenant farmers enjoyed anything but secure tenure. In present day India, the policy of keeping food prices as low as possible, accepting food imports whenever signs of scarcity appear, and at the same time allowing the land tax to fall to an almost titular level in terms of present day prices, gives farmers little incentive to increase their output. It enables the land owners (who are not a minority, as in some countries, but probably a majority of the population, at any rate enjoying immense voting power) to evade their share of the economic charges imposed by increasing population, which therefore fall all the more heavily on the wage workers, whether agricultural or urban. It enables the farmers to enjoy a great deal of leisure, and also standards of consumption far above those of the landless labourers. In 1947, shortly before his assassination, Mahatma Gandhi, who had a well-informed and shrewd knowledge of economics, strongly criticized the policy of low food prices and rationing which the Indian Government was pursuing. Force of circumstances now is breaking this policy down, and although low prices and food rationing prevail in the cities, the price of food in rural India has had to be allowed to rise to nearly twice the world price level.

The problems of India, however, are not those of the whole developing world. In many Asian, African and Latin American countries it has been discovered during the past century that export crops may provide a much higher income or wage per man-hour than growing food crops for the local market. The development of these plantations of export crops, earning high profits and paying high wages in relation to those of the surrounding communities (but at the same time expecting far more regular hours of work) created great inequalities and political tensions. But they provided employment for the growing populations, in many cases (Ceylon is an outstanding example) enabling them to import a substantial proportion of their food requirements. These issues should be less acute in the future, as the relative price advantage of export crops over food crops for the local market is now much less than it used to be.

A substantial proportion of the world's population still consists of subsistence agriculturalists. Some still practise 'cut and burn', and some are settled; but what they have in common is that most of the agricultural production of these peoples is confined to producing their own families' requirements. Subsistence requirements, we have seen, amount to a little below a quarter ton/person/year of grain equivalent. To introduce a little variety into the diet, and to have some reserve, they will aim at producing about 300 kg./person/year grain equivalent. The work of producing this however does not occupy them for very long. Even after 'cut and burn' has had to be abandoned, when the work admittedly becomes more laborious, most of the cultivators in Africa are still only occupied for a fraction of what we would regard as a normal working year — two to four hours a day, on the average. Then why do they not produce more? The reason is that there are limits to the amount a subsistence cultivator wishes to, indeed is able to eat, and that if he has any more output he would have great difficulty in selling it, if he has to carry all his produce a long distance to market on his head. The first and most urgent step required to improve the position of the subsistence cultivator is the provision of transport. It is not until roads and vehicles are available, and also an adequate supply of industrial products at reasonable prices to exchange for his produce, that the farmer is willing to produce anything substantially above his own family's subsistence requirements.

It is useful to continue measuring in the same convenient unit[1] of kilograms/person/year of grain equivalent. We find that, in the first stages of development above the physiological minimum of 200–250 units, the additional supplies are mostly eaten by the farm family. But this stage does not last for long. By the time cultivators have raised production to 400 units, they will wish to trade a substantial amount. At about 500 units, they will be able to make the most important technical change in their methods of

[1] The use of this unit to measure the progress of Asian agriculture was first suggested by De Vries.

production, namely using draught animals, whereas hitherto they have relied upon hand tools. These animals, who obtain part of their food from grazing, straw, etc., but who make some demand on the grain output, because they have to be fed some if they are to work well in the busy season, cannot therefore be kept till grain production has reached a higher level. The possession of draught animals opens up the possibility of substantial further increases in production. A farm family relying entirely upon hand tools is limited in the area which it can cultivate, however hard it is willing to work, mainly because of the pressure of requirements for labour in the weeding season.

It is true there are some exceptions to this rule — the Japanese, with a comparatively productive agriculture, still continue to use mainly hand tools, principally because of the exceptionally small size of their holdings; while the Indians, at a considerably lower level of productivity, use draught oxen, not solely out of religious veneration, but also because the rainy season in India is so short that it is necessary to cultivate very quickly when it comes, and hand tool cultivation definitely would not give sufficient speed. With draught animals, production continues to develop until it reaches about 750 units, at which stage it becomes possible to spare some grain to feed poultry and pigs. Other meat animals live mainly on grass, but do not yield much meat, except in a few countries where grazing is abundant. It is the keeping of pigs and poultry which makes possible a substantial supply of animal protein and a more palatable diet.

From this point onwards there is a continuous development of productive capacities, without any sharp dividing lines, right up to the most advanced forms of agriculture.

If we apply the title 'Subsistence Unit' to a quarter ton of grain equivalent we see that, while an African subsistence farmer only produces a small margin beyond the requirements of himself and his children, one man working for a year by the most modern methods on the Canadian prairies, aided by substantial supplies of fertilizers, equipment, transport, etc. can produce a thousand subsistence units (the amounts of other agricultural products exchangeable for a unit of grain however are not the same in the more advanced and in the subsistence economies).

As we become richer, we do not eat more, measured in bulk or weight, than a subsistence cultivator living on grain — indeed it would hardly be physically possible for us to do so. The way in which we do eat more is to take only a moderately increased amount of calories and proteins, but to take them in what we find more palatable forms, meat, fruit, eggs, dairy products and the like, the cost of producing which, in terms of land, labour, feeding stuffs and other factors, and consequently their exchange value relative to grain, is much higher than that of grain, per unit of calorie or protein supplied. The consumption of agricultural products by the average North American or Western European is ten or eleven subsistence units (measured at the relative prices prevailing in the advanced countries — much less if we measure at the relative prices prevailing in the subsistence countries). This figure, it is true, includes our consumption of agriculturally produced textile fibres, and also of our 'narcotics' — tea, coffee, cocoa and tobacco — but it is still surprisingly high. The Japanese, who have almost as good a health record, consume agricultural products at the rate of not much more than two subsistence units per head. They are still mainly content with a diet of rice, vegetables and a small quantity of fish, not very different from that of their ancestors.

Suppose, however, we set ourselves the standard of providing people with food and other agricultural products at the U.S. level of consumption per head, undoubtedly high, indeed perhaps, in the opinion of medical men excessive.

TABLE IV.4.

Number of families[a] provided with food and all other agricultural requirements (at present-day U.S. consumption standards) by one man working in agriculture.

	1934–8	1950–1	1959–60	Rate of increase % per year
Germany		1·7	3·1	5·2
France	2·8	3·3	6·1	6·2
Denmark	3·8	5·9	9·0	5·3
U.K.	4·2	6·4	9·7	4·1
Canada	4·1	6·8	11·8	5·0
Australia	9·6	11·7	15·7	2·2
U.S.	5·5	10·1	17·6	5·6
New Zealand	16·7	21·2	28·2	4·2

[a] Families computed from U.S, average of dependents to labour force.

TABLE IV.5.

Indirect employment in agriculture (production of fertilizers, equipment, etc.) as percentage of direct.

	1934–8	1950–1	1959–60
Germany		13	22
U.K.		69	86
U.S.	14	33	43
Australia		59	60
New Zealand		89	103

Table IV.4 shows not only the extremely high level which productivity has reached in some countries, but the dizzy pace at which it is further advancing.

Agriculture in New Zealand, the country which has reached the highest productivity, is now so productive that one man working on the land in New Zealand in 1966 produced enough food to feed — or, it might be more accurate to say, to overfeed, to the highest American standards — 37 families; and even this high figure is steadily increasing at the rate of more than 4 per cent a year.

It is sometimes said that such productivity is only obtained through having behind every farmer a whole array of men supplying equipment, fertilizers, etc. This is not the case. Even in New Zealand, the numbers thus 'indirectly engaged' in agriculture are only about equal in number to those directly engaged (Table IV.5). An interesting study[1] by Dovring in the United States has shown that not only have there been great economies in the direct employment of labour in agriculture, but also in the indirect; the manufacture of equipment, fertilizers, etc. has also greatly increased in efficiency during the last forty years.

So much for the amount of labour required for providing our food and other agricultural requirements. With good modern methods, it appears that any community can be served by the labour of some 3 per cent of its labour force in farming, with about the same number engaged indirectly in supplying equipment and fertilizers. But even this proportion is likely to continue falling rapidly; and if it became customary to eat austerely, perhaps more in the Japanese style, requirements could undergo a drastic further reduction.

But what about land requirements? Does the area of the earth suffice to feed present and prospective world populations?

For this purpose we must make a general survey of the world's potential resources of agricultural land. The classification which follows is based entirely on climate, which can be fairly precisely defined. No exclusion is made for poor soils, the description of which is largely a matter of opinion, and which in any case can be improved by fertilization, if we really need their output. As for mountainous topography, the really mountainous regions will have been classified as cold climate in any case. Steeply sloping land at lower altitudes can be grazed, or in some cases cultivated, if sufficient skill and effort is devoted to it. (Much of New Zealand in fact is very steeply sloping.) Likewise it is assumed that swampy land can be drained if necessary.

It may indeed be objected that, with a somewhat greater effort, climatic

[1] University of Illinois, Agricultural Economic Research Report No. 62 (1963).

factors themselves can be altered, arid land irrigated, possibly with water obtained by ocean distillation, perhaps even the tundras artificially warmed by nuclear power. But none of these possibilities is here taken into account; nor is the amount of food which could be obtained from the sea and lakes.

The concept used is to define as 'standard land' the sort of farm land to which we are accustomed in the humid temperate countries, capable of producing one crop a year, or substantial quantities of grazing throughout the summer. Lands where production possibilities are limited by in-adequacies of rainfall are then expressed as various fractions of 'standard land'. The limiting factor is taken as moisture rather than temperature, which is in fact the case over most of the world. The high temperature, high rainfall tropics are however entered as the equivalent of two units of standard land, implying the possibility of growing two crops annually. The factor of one-thirtieth for semi-arid climates is based on experience in Australia, where they are used for grazing only. There are however many parts of the world, e.g. North Africa, where careful cultivation makes possible some crop yields and much greater production from semi-arid land.

The climatic classifications in Table IV.6 are those of Thornthwaite,[1] where A, B, - - - measure degrees of humidity, A', B' - - - degrees of temperature. This seems more applicable to our problem than are rival climatic classifications. A sub-division is required in what Thornthwaite calls the 'taiga' climates (cold coniferous forest areas). Here the possibilities of agricultural production are limited by temperature, not by moisture, which is always adequate. Careful research work (done mainly in Finland) has shown that this limitation can be quite accurately measured by the device of 'accumulated month degrees'. Crops and grasses (except for a few very hardy grasses) only begin to grow at temperatures above 5°C. 'Accumulated month degrees' are calculated by adding together, for each month in which the mean temperature exceeds 5°, the amount of such excess.[2] When this figure stands at or above 38, all the usual European crops can be grown, including winter wheat and sugar beet. These two latter crops, and peas, become impossible at 30, though spring wheat is still possible. At 23, the climate becomes too cold for turnips, not satisfactory for spring rye, and on the margin for oats, but still satisfactory for winter rye. At 18, it is still possible to grow Timothy hay and some of the new strains of barley, and potatoes perhaps in a colder climate still. The results are expressed in Table IV.7 and Diagrams IV.A and IV.B.

The standard of two crops annually in the high rainfall tropics should in fact be considered a minimum. There are indications that in growing grass

---

[1] *Geographical Review*, July 1933.
[2] *Fennia, a General Handbook on the Geography of Finland*, Helsinki, 1952.

TABLE IV.6. CLASSIFICATION OF WORLD CLIMATES

Thornthwaite Classification	*Description*	*Equivalents in 'standard land'*
AA'R, BA'r, CA'r	Tropical climates with rainfall capable of growing two crops a year	2
Rest of A and B	Wet or humid sub-tropical and temperate climates, tropical climates wet or humid, but with irregular rainfall	1
CB'r, CC'r	Sub-humid climates, rainfall distributed through all seasons	5/6
CA'w, CB'w, CB's, CC's	Sub-humid climates, rainfall deficient in winter (w) or summer (s)	2/3
CA'd, CB'd, CC'd	Sub-humid climates, rainfall deficient in all seasons	$\frac{1}{2}$
D	Semi-arid, suitable for sparse pasture, rainfall considered too uncertain for cropping	1/30
D' 'Taiga' (cold coniferous forest land)	Over 38 month-degrees — Standard land	1
	30–38 month-degrees — Spring wheat land	9/10
	23–30 month-degrees — Rye land	7/10
	18–23 month-degrees — Sub-arctic grassland	$\frac{1}{2}$
	Under 18 month degrees — Near-tundra	0
E	Arid	0
E' and F'	Tundra and perpetual frost	0

and fodder crops — and if we are to live largely on a diet of meat and dairy products, these will be some of the most important crops — the tropical grasslands, if properly fertilized, can produce five times as much as the best temperate grasslands (Diagram IV.c — references in *New Scientist* 25 Oct. 1962).

An appreciable proportion of the world's potential agricultural resources, it is seen, are in the cold climate areas of Soviet Russia and Canada, where little use has yet been made of them. Taking the tropical lands as equivalent to only 2 units of standard land, the world possesses the equivalent of 7·7 billion hectares of standard land. If we apply the maximum co-efficient of five to the tropical lands, this figure becomes 10·7 billion hectares (Table IV.7).

We now go back to specify the areas of land required to produce our subsistence unit, or requirements for American and West European style of consumption at ten times the subsistence minimum, as the case may be.

DIAGRAM IV.A (i)

MAPS OF THORNTHWAITE'S CLIMATIC REGIONS

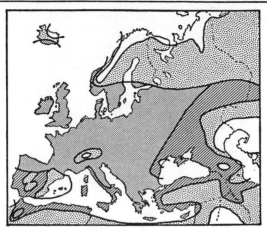

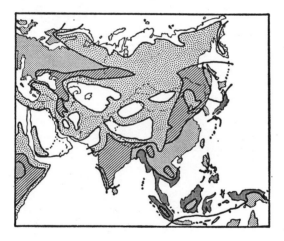

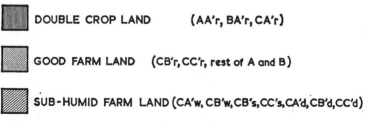

DOUBLE CROP LAND   (AA'r, BA'r, CA'r)

GOOD FARM LAND   (CB'r, CC'r, rest of A and B)

SUB-HUMID FARM LAND (CA'w, CB'w, CB's, CC's, CA'd, CB'd, CC'd)

SEMI-ARID GRAZING LAND
OR COLD FARM LAND   (D, D')

From K.L.W. Klages –"Ecological Crop Geography"

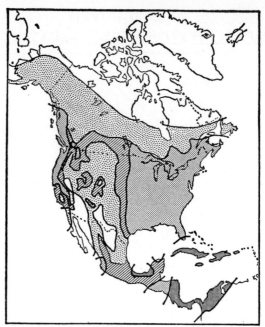

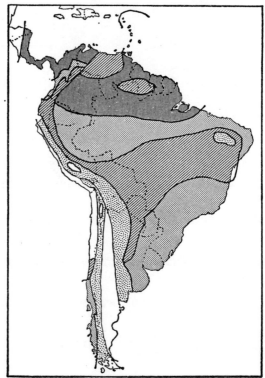

DIAGRAM IV.A (ii)

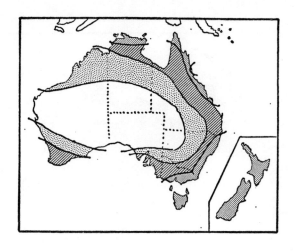

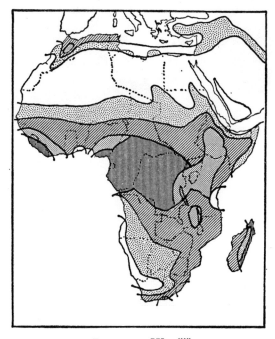

DIAGRAM IV.A (iii)

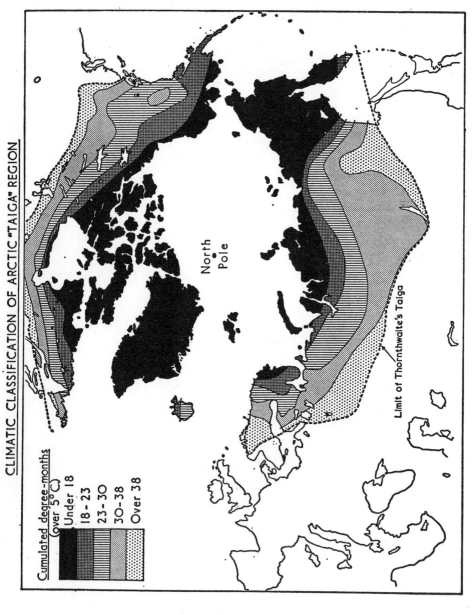

CLIMATIC CLASSIFICATION OF ARCTIC "TAIGA" REGION

Cumulated degree-months
(over 5°C)
Under 18
18 - 23
23 - 30
30 - 38
Over 38

North
Pole

Limit of Thornthwaite's Taiga

DIAGRAM IV.B

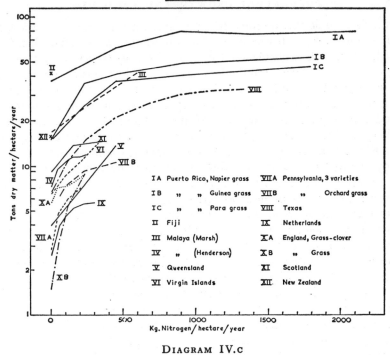

GRASS YIELDS

I A	Puerto Rico, Napier grass	VII A Pennsylvania, 3 varieties
I B	,, ,, Guinea grass	VII B ,, Orchard grass
I C	,, ,, Para grass	VIII Texas
II	Fiji	IX Netherlands
III	Malaya (Marsh)	X A England, Grass-clover
IV	,, (Henderson)	X B ,, Grass
V	Queensland	XI Scotland
VI	Virgin Islands	XII New Zealand

DIAGRAM IV.C

TABLE IV.7. POTENTIAL AGRICULTURAL AREA OF THE WORLD EXPRESSED IN TERMS OF EQUIVALENTS OF STANDARD FARM LAND (million hectares)

		of which	
	Total	*standard farm land equivalents of two crop tropical areas*	*standard farm land equivalents of cold climate areas*
U.S.A. and Canada	1006	4	367
Central and South America	1835	736	29
Europe (excl. U.S.S.R.)	403	—	47
U.S.S.R.	1109	—	539
Africa	1555	732	—
China	409	—	88
India and Pakistan	305	43	13
Rest of Asia	791	464	7
Oceania	268	60	—
WORLD	7680	2039	1090

But before we do this we must take into account man's need for wood, as well as for food and textile fibres. Consumption of wood (other than fuel wood, which will probably soon become obsolete) ranges from 2 cu. m. person/year round wood[1] in the United States and Canada to about 0·5 cu. m. in certain Western European countries which have to import nearly all their wood, and where prices are correspondingly high. The standards of wood consumption in a country like the Netherlands do not cause any serious deprivation, and can be taken as minimum requirements. Requirements in fact are falling. An F.A.O. and Economic Commission for Europe study[2] showed that, with increasing replacement by concrete and metal, the amount of wood required to build an average West European house fell from 9·1 to 7·6 cu. m. in the short period 1950–5.

The amount of wood pulp used in the United States clearly seems wasteful, whether we look at the bulk of the Sunday newspapers, or the unnecessary amount of wrappings. Those who are concerned about the conservation of future supplies of wood for pulping would do well to recommend the imposition of substantial tax on current use of fresh wood for pulping. This would have several beneficial consequences; it would encourage the collection of waste paper for repulping; it would hasten the search for other materials (e.g. dry fibre from sugar cane) suitable for pulping; it would conserve forests; and finally, it might reduce the amount of litter left in the streets and public places.

Wood consumption at the rate of ½ cu. m./person/year, which we have taken as our minimum, would amount in weight to about 250 kg./person/year dry matter, i.e. about the same weight as our minimum requirement of foodstuffs.

The land required, under continuous forest growth, to produce a given quantity of wood, is shown in Table IV.8.

The difference in rates of growth are enormous. Hot climates clearly have an advantage, though temperate climates with high humidity and careful forestry (e.g. Denmark and North California) can produce good yields of very high quality timber. The technical problems of using eucalyptus and bamboo for making wood pulp and paper, at one time made entirely from soft woods, have now been largely solved. Applying the economic Principle of Comparative Advantage, the comparative disadvantage of the cold climates for forestry is much greater than their comparative disadvantage for agriculture. In the long run therefore we may expect to see the world's supply of forest products increasingly derived from the

---

[1] i.e. measured as cut. For pulping, the whole log is used: when sawn wood is obtained, the volume is considerably below that of the round wood.
[2] *Trends in Utilization of Wood and its Products in Housing*, Geneva, 1957.

TABLE IV.8. FOREST GROWTH (MEASURED IN ROUND WOOD),
AVERAGE SUSTAINED YIELD

	Normal rate of growth cu. m./hectare/year
Queensland,[a] planted coniferous forests	58
Denmark, beech forest* [b]	47
East Africa[c]	35–40
California,[a] Redwood	21·5
Monterey Pine	15·9
Hemlock	17·6
Burma Bamboo,* [d]	20
Punjab,[e] irrigated eucalyptus	14·4
Union Bag and Paper, U.S.A.[f]	6·6
U.S. average[f]	2·2
Sweden[g] Highest region (Skaraborg)	5·1
Lowest region (Norrbotten)	1·2
U.S.S.R.[h] Ukraine	3·4
Total	1·1

[a] Director of Forests, Queensland, private communication. The Queensland claim is very high, but a figure of 52 has also been claimed for New Zealand (MacGregor).
[b] Champion, Forestry Department, University of Oxford, private communication.
[c] MacGregor, Forestry Department, University of Oxford, private communication.
[d] F.A.O., Timber Trends in Asia.
[e] Government of Irak Development Board — Report of Messrs. Binnie, Deacon and Gourley. Zuckerman (World Population Conference, 1954) claims that South Africa has reached a figure of 10 tons (20 cu. m.).
[f] Planned for 1975 (present yield 4·4). Yield with best soil and climate in Louisiana 17·6 (D. J. Hardenbrook, private communication).
[g] Statistisk Arsbok, 1956, p. 100.
[h] Paramonov Ukrainian Review No. 5 (Munich, 1957).
    * Original data in tons dry weight — one ton equated to 2 cu. m.

tropics and temperate zones, and the colder-climate lands devoted mainly to agriculture.

If we adopt the comparatively cautious growth figure of 20 cu. m./hectare/ year, then each person requires only 250 sq. m. continually under forest to supply his wood and pulp requirements. Even this figure appears to be capable of considerable improvement, as forest techniques improve; but, on the other hand, is clearly unattainable in cold climate forestry in countries such as Sweden.

It is possible to compute the amount of land required, under various circumstances, to produce the subsistence minimum of 250 kg./person/year grain equivalent. We are not of course expecting that the whole world on the average will have to live at the subsistence minimum. It may be better to estimate instead the amount of land required, using good farming techniques now known, to feed people at the standards now prevailing in the United States. Consumption of meat, fish and poultry is 83 kilograms/

person/year, of which about half is from pigs, poultry, etc. fattened on grain in a confined space and not needing grazing — this proportion however is increasing rapidly as grass-fed beef gives place to 'barley beef' (a kilogram of beef produced by this method is however considerably more demanding of cereals than a kilogram of pork or poultry meat). Each kilogram of pigmeat corresponds to 1·3 kilograms of live pig, requiring, in the hands of a good pig man, 5·3 kilograms of cereals to produce it; a kilogram of poultry meat (1·5 kilograms of live bird) only 3·7 kilograms feed, equivalent however to about 4 kilograms of cereals, if we take into account the agricultural value of protein and other supplements included in poultry feed. The pork and poultry half of such a meat ration could be produced from the cereals grown on 540 sq. m. To produce the remainder by grazing would require, on the methods already used by good English farmers, about 2,000 sq. m. But at the rates of fertilizing and stocking recommended by the British Grassland Research Station (and exemplified already by the yields obtained on many carefully managed grasslands of live weight yield of 1 ton/hectare/year) the figure of land required will fall o less than 1000 sq. m. Even this is still below the theoretical possibilities. The best temperate grasslands fully fertilized can yield grass at the rate of 15 tons dry weight/hectare/year, which should theoretically be capable of producing 2 tons live weight of beef.

The average North American or British cow yields 3 tons of milk per year. Fed entirely on grass, hay and silage (as they are by the more economically minded farmers — the feeding of expensive concentrated foods is nearly always uneconomic) the cow needs 5½ tons dry weight per year. To allow for the cost of breeding replacement stock (less a small credit for the meat from old cattle), we may raise this figure to 7½ tons, which can be produced on 5000 sq. m. (½ hectare) under the best conditions of temperate agriculture — yields can be far higher in the tropics.

Americans now consume milk (including the raw milk equivalent of all dairy products consumed) at the rate of 285 kilograms/person/year; and we may take 250 as our objective. This represents one-twelfth of the yield of a cow, and could be produced by the grass grown on a little over 400 sq. m.

There remain eggs, whose per head consumption in U.S. is now also declining, which are consumed at the rate of about 18 kilograms/person/year, corresponding to some 72 kilograms of cereal, or the produce of 200 sq. m.

Total requirements of space to produce an American type diet — which, we remember, stands at about eleven times subsistence level, in terms of agricultural costs — is given in Table IV.9.

TABLE IV.9. LAND REQUIRED PER PERSON TO PRODUCE
U.S. TYPE DIET

	sq. m./person
Cereals, sugar, etc.	500
42 kg. pig and poultry meat	500
42 kg. beef and mutton	400
250 kg. milk	400
18 kg. eggs	200
	2000

Each person's land requirements for American type food consumption are some 2000 sq. m., or one-fifth of a hectare (half an acre), or 2250 sq. m. including requirement of forest land. If we take world resources of agricultural land at 10·7 billion hectares of standard land equivalent, this could feed, at maximum standards, 47 billion people.

To estimate the amount of land required, on the other hand, to produce a subsistence diet consisting predominantly of cereals, and so the number of people whom the world's agricultural land could feed at this standard, it is not, however, permissible to multiply this figure by ten. The comparatively high exchange value of animal products against cereals represents to a considerable degree the labour and skill which have gone into their production, rather than their land requirements. To produce 250 kilograms of cereals (i.e. real minimum subsistence requirements) under the most productive conditions, as in Japan, requires 640 sq. m. To these requirements of agricultural land, of course, must be added the land required to produce wood, which we stated above as 250 sq. m./person required to produce the minimum Western European standards ($\frac{1}{2}$ cu. m./person/year round wood). If however we are considering real minimum standards, wood consumption per head in Asian countries, mainly bamboo, is only about one-third of this. For people living at Japanese standards of food consumption and Asian standards of timber requirements only 680 sq. m./person is required, and the world's potential agricultural and forest land could supply the needs of 157 billion people.

Recent calculations by a Russian scientist[1] are important in the first place in showing how greatly such calculations are affected by different price relatives, wheat being relatively high-priced in Russia. Malin took a standard diet, converting other foods into wheat equivalents, apparently after reducing meat, eggs and dairy products by that proportion of their

[1] Malin, World Population Conference, 1965.

value estimated to be represented by grain by-products consumed by livestock. He also omitted fibres, tobacco, etc. His results (Table IV.10) may be compared with U.S. actual per head consumption in 1961–2.

TABLE IV.10.   CONSUMPTION IN KG./PERSON/YEAR

	Malin's standards		U.S.A. 1961–2	
	Actual	Wheat equivalent (Russian relative prices)	Actual	Wheat equivalent (U.S. relative prices)
Grains	100	100	97	97
Meat and fish	50	200	83	625
Milk and dairy products	365	91	299	365
Potatoes	100	25	49	24
Sugar	30	31	49	93
Fruit and vegetables	300	45	184	228
Eggs	18	72	18	123
Fats and oils (not butter)	6	12	28	108
Coffee, tea and cocoa			7·6	85
Grains for brewing and distilling			16	9
Cotton			10	98
Wool (scoured)			1·0	31
Tobacco			3·4	60
Total		578		1946

Malin considers that on the methods of agriculture already prevailing in countries now making the most productive use of their land, such a standard diet could be produced on ½ hectare and 'with an adequate utilization of existing scientific data and modern equipment' on ¼ hectare. At present the world's agricultural area is 1·43 billion hectares of arable plus 2·58 billion hectares grazing land. He estimates the amount of land which could be intensively farmed on various assumptions (Table IV.11).

TABLE IV.11.   MALIN'S ESTIMATES OF CULTIVABLE LAND

	Billion Hectares
By extension of area on methods now used	2·67
With additional capital expenditure	5·49
With large additional capital expenditure and new methods	9·33

The latter figure approaches the 13·6 billion hectares of the earth's surface (excluding tundra and lands of perpetual frost). This estimate is even more optimistic than that given in Table IV.7.

Malin goes on to point out that solar energy is reaching the earth's surface at the rate of 1.08×10^{10} calories/hectare/year. On our present agricultural knowledge, the maximum proportion of this which we can capture in the form of plant growth (photosynthesis) he puts at 4 per cent (most scientists put it at only 2 per cent). However he considers that before long our chemical knowledge may improve to the point where we may be able to by-pass the process of photosynthesis altogether and tap a much higher proportion of solar energy in the form of food. The products of past photosynthesis stored in the earth in the form of coal and oil he estimates at 6.4×10^{15} tons of carbon, with a further 1.3×10^{16} tons of carbon in the form of carbonate rocks. However, our burning coal and oil have raised the carbon dioxide content of the atmosphere by 12 per cent in the last 150 years, and he thinks that a time may come when our descendants will have to rely entirely on solar and nuclear energy, and forbid any further burning of fossil fuels, in order to prevent further increases in the carbon dioxide and to conserve the oxygen in the atmosphere.

Putnam[1] also adverts on the rising carbon dioxide content of the atmosphere, though he gives a lower estimate of its rate of increase. He believes that this increase is having a differential effect on the climate, increasing the amount of arid land in U.S.A., but warming the tundra and making it more habitable in U.S.S.R.

We may conclude, if we are interested, with a sort of science-fiction picture of how agriculture might be conducted if we really were extremely short of space — possibly the problem which may face our descendants seeking to travel about the universe in large spaceships, or making their homes in air-locked domes on the surface of other planets, or on artificial satellites. Under these circumstances, of course, requirements for wood and fibre would first be cut to a minimum, perhaps completely replaced by chemical products capable of reconstitution after use. On the other hand, we must not be beguiled by the concept of some badly informed science-fiction writers, who substitute man's requirements of food by some form of pills or electrical charges. The 200–250 kg./person/year of cereals or similar food might be produced on much smaller areas than required now. But this does represent a physiological minimum, and cannot be obtained in any more concentrated form than cereals, fat and sugar. It might, however, be better economically, and probably more palatable also, under conditions of extreme shortage of space, to produce more succulent foods, so long as all the water could be completely recycled. In fact, it has been shown in laboratory experiments that the plants which take most advantage of the radiant energy which they receive and grow most quickly are those

[1] *The Future of Nuclear Fuels*, U.S. Atomic Energy Commission.

two old favourites of the amateur gardener, radish and broccoli. These plants, however, turn a considerable proportion of the energy which they receive into fibre — so, for that matter, do cereals and sugar cane. If stems, straw, etc. were not wanted for paper or wood pulp, they could be ploughed into the soil, as they are now, and would have a beneficial effect on subsequent crops. But a large part of the energy used to build up the fibres would be in such a case lost by oxidation, putting carbon dioxide back into the atmosphere, just as it is when the food is consumed by us.

To allow, therefore, not only for our own need for fibres, but also for the inevitable tendency of plants, whether we like it not, to put a substantial proportion of their energy intake into fibres, and also to allow ourselves something a little more interesting than the bare minimum diet, we can take requirements to be of the order of twice the food minimum, or 500 kilograms/person/year, i.e. 1370 grams/person/day, measured in terms of dry weight. The space required to produce this, under the conditions which we are contemplating, would depend upon the maximum rate at which plants could photosynthesize dry matter out of the radiant energy which they received from the sun; or, in the case of a remote spaceship, radiant energy for growing plants would have to be generated from a nuclear reactor carried in the spaceship.

With the temperature and humidity of an English July, and with the plants already having reached an advanced stage of growth, potato and sugar beet plants will photosynthesize at a rate of 30 grams/sq. m./day of dry matter. In the tropics, so long as heat and water are available, rates of 50 have been attained, on the one hand by agriculturally valuable plants such as sugar cane and elephant grass, on the other hand by the dangerous weed water-hyacinth. Solar radiation in the tropics is received over a wider range of frequencies and theoretically, therefore, should be capable of more photosynthesis in a given area. Experiments in the agricultural laboratory at Oxford have shown that with a suitable choice of plants rates of 40–45 can be maintained. Much has been written about the use of algae under these circumstances, which have the advantage of being able to use up sewage; but their rate of photosynthesis rarely exceeds 20. Some harmful weeds, under European conditions, have shown rates of 60. If we take a general rate of dry matter photosynthesized at 50 grams/sq. m./day — and it is to be expected that our descendants will be able to make improvements in agricultural methods and choice of plants which will greatly increase this figure, which is still only one-seventh of the theoretical equivalent of the total photosynthesis of which the incoming radiant energy might be capable — we then come to the interesting conclusion that the full support of one person requires the continuous cultivation of an area no larger than 27 sq. m.

> Full times are these could men but come awake
> And summon all their powers to overtake
> Marvels that science flings before their eyes.
> Could men but come awake — enchantments keep
> Their noblest faculties held fast in sleep
> And frightful dreams and real fears, alas!
> Before their soggy haunted vision pass
> Not least the Reverend Malthus with his trick
> Of killing conscience by arithmetic.[1]

[1] From *A Vision of Ceremony*, by Professor James MacAullay, University of Hobart (with author's permission).

CHAPTER V

The Measurement of Fertility

HAVING considered the full biological capacity of the human race to reproduce, we now proceed to the measurement and analysis of fertility in all those populations in which, for various reasons and by various methods, it is kept well below the biological maximum.

The simplest (and most unreliable) measure of reproductivity is the crude birth rate, or number of births per year per thousand of total population. Even this measure, of course, is only possible when we have accurate birth registrations, which in fact are available for far fewer countries and times than is commonly supposed.

Birth and death registration was originally a Scandinavian device. For Sweden it goes back to the mid-eighteenth century. The King of Sweden preferred to keep a detailed control over his subjects and their movements, for military as well as for other purposes. Similar registrations were later introduced into other European countries. Britain introduced birth and death registration in 1834.

While Europe, even including Russia, developed a fairly complete system of birth and death registration in the nineteenth century, this was not the case elsewhere. In the U.S. fairly good estimates were available from an early date, but precise registration was only introduced piecemeal by the laws of the different states. In this case however, estimates carefully prepared by indirect methods will suffice to fill the gap. In Canada, registration figures were extremely uncertain until a little over a generation ago. Registration on the other hand was near to complete from the start in Australia, a country which still bears the marks of having started its life under the rule of a military bureaucracy, when the Governor liked to know the precise numbers and whereabouts of all his subjects.

While a number of countries have recently begun registration, its accuracy is still very uncertain. The only Asian country with accurate vital statistics extending over a long period is Japan — and very interesting they are. Accurate statistics are now available for Ceylon, though for a shorter period. In Latin America, Brazil has uncertain registration, but an accurate census, designed by the Italian demographer Mortara in such a way as to yield a great deal of information about reproductivity. Otherwise, Latin

America is almost a statistical desert in this (and other) respects. In India, at any rate before 1951, we could not count upon the Census telling us much more than the total population. Its age tables were obviously inaccurate. The average Indian generally does not know his age, and in any case is not seriously interested in it. Demographic statistics for African populations are still in the most elementary stage.

It is now generally realized (although there are still a few people using them who ought to have known better) that crude birth rates cannot be expected to give an accurate measure of trends of fertility, and may indeed be expected, for years on end, to give a misleading one. There are a number of disturbing factors which cause the crude ratio between births and population not to mean what at first sight it might appear to mean. The complexity and subtlety of these factors has only been recognized by demographers by progressive stages. These factors are:

(*a*) Changes in the sex and age structure of populations;
(*b*) Recent changes in the number of marriages;
(*c*) Number of children already born into any given family.

That differences of sex and age structure could distort figures of crude birth rates was understood in the nineteenth century. To take a *reductio ad absurdum*, in a population with a great excess of males (as in some states of the American West in the early years of settlement), the ratio of births to population would still be low, even if every woman were having a child every year. The first improvement on crude birth rates therefore was the device of expressing the number of births as a ratio of the female population aged between 15 and 45. This simple measure, known as the 'Fertility Rate', was used by good demographers up to the 1920's — Bowley, using this simple instrument, made in 1925 his famous prediction that British population would rise to a maximum about 1941, and then begin to fall.

The next step forward in demographic technique was to take more detailed account of the age composition of the female population, instead of relating births to the crude total of the number of women between the ages of 15 and 45. Account may also be taken of the proportion of children who might be expected to survive and serve as replacements for the older generation, giving us Net Reproduction Rate (Chapter II). Gross and Net Reproduction Rates are generally associated with the name of Kuczynski,[1] who developed their use very widely. The outline of the method was

---

[1] Robert Kuczynski, Lecturer in Demography at the London School of Economics in the 1930's, not to be confused with Jürgen Kuczynski, a Marxist statistician, who has performed the statistical feat of proving that real wages have been declining everywhere except in Soviet Russia.

however originally discovered independently in the 1880's by Boeckh, an official of the Statistical Department of the City of Berlin.

To recapitulate the method, 'specific fertility rates' are calculated for women of each quinquennial age group. By adding together these 'specific fertility rates' for quinquennial age groups and multiplying the total by 5 (because the 'average woman' spends 5 years in each quinquennial age group) we obtain a measure of the 'total fertility' of an average woman. This measure is not affected by the varying age structure of the population at different times. We multiply this total by a coefficient, which may vary slightly (usually 0·485), of the expected ratio of female to total births. The result, the Gross Reproduction Rate, measures the number of female children to be expected from the average woman in the course of a lifetime.

If we then multiply the specific fertility of each quinquennial age-group by the survival ratio, giving the proportion of female children born who are expected to survive to their mother's age at the time they were born, and sum the results, we obtain the Net Reproduction Rate. This gives a measure of the extent to which each generation is replacing itself — a Net Reproduction Rate of one meaning that the surviving offspring will just suffice to replace their mothers.

Gross and Net Reproduction Rates became well-known in the 1930's, and by 1937 the League of Nations Yearbook was publishing them for many countries. Not every country at that time however classified births by age of mother, the basic information required for computing 'specific fertilities'. Where this information was not available, the roundabout device had to be adopted of assuming that relative fertilities at different ages in the country in question was the same as in some country generally similar in its economic and social attributes for which 'specific fertilities' were available. The specific fertilities of the second country were then applied to the age structure of the first country, to obtain a hypothetical figure of total births which could then be compared with actual births.

Britain was one of the last countries to obtain the necessary information, finally authorized by the Population Statistics Act of 1938. This Act was opposed in the House of Commons by Sir Alan Herbert, Member for Oxford University (the Universities had separate representation in Parliament in those days) in a famous speech delivered in verse, indicating that we already knew quite enough about the reasons for low fertility:

> They pulled down all the houses where the children used to crowd,
> And built expensive blocks of flats where children weren't allowed,
> And then when father got a job there wasn't anywhere to dwell,
> And the Minister still wonders why the population fell. etc.

Gross and Net Reproduction Rates however, almost as soon as

demographers had familiarized themselves with them, had to be discarded as obsolete. They may indeed give, under certain conditions, results which are even more misleading than the crude birth rate itself. To give them their due, they had done a good deal to illumine the darkness in the early stages of demographic research. But their unreliability appeared when they rose quite excessively in consequence of the acceleration of marriages with the beginning of the war in 1939 (a woman just married is more likely to have a child during the year than another woman of the same age not recently married), and war always brings a crop of additional marriages. The defects of Gross and Net Reproduction Rates were finally revealed in the early post-war years, when they suddenly rose to an enormous height, because of the temporary factor of returning soldiers resuming family life. Demographers came to realize that even in a population of unchanged age structure, a change in the numbers marrying in any year may completely upset their measurement.

This *contretemps* had the effect of turning demographers' attention away from the problem of adjusting for age of mother, to the problem of adjusting for duration of marriage. Pioneer work in this field in the 1930's was done by Burgdörfer in Germany and Depoid in France. Burgdörfer prepared tables, of great complexity, classifying each woman both by her age and the duration of her marriage, and estimating specific fertilities for each of his sub-classifications. Though this method was extremely cumbrous, it still sufficed to show that the popular impression of a rapid increase in German fertility in the 1930's, as shown by the Gross Reproduction Rate, which formed the subject matter of many of Hitler's speeches, was spurious. The gross reproduction rate had been artificially accelerated by a temporary increase in the number of marriages, and the true level of German reproductivity — 'Lebensbilanz' — was still in fact only just about at replacement rate. It is interesting and surprising that a German official in the 1930's was able to publish results so much in conflict with what his political superiors were saying.

Depoid devised a somewhat simpler system which contained the germ of more workable devices used by his successors. The real simplification of the problem came with the work done in Australia by Karmel.[1] His method can be applied in any country which records births by duration of marriage. The births in year n, from marriages of duration m, should relate to marriages contracted in the year $n-m$. (In practice, there may be a lot of awkward arithmetical interpolation, depending on the precise form in which the durations were recorded.) Subject to this qualification, we can however trace all the subsequent births which occur to marriages of any

[1] *Economic Record*, June 1944.

given year, and thus compute 'specific fertilities', specific for each year of marriage duration, rather than for age. This drastic simplification proved very fruitful.

Most births occur within the early years of marriage. The general movements of the fertility of a population can be estimated by summing these 'specific fertilities'. The low figures for the longer durations do not greatly affect the total. The great advantage of this method is that the result is quite independent of year by year fluctuations in the number of marriages.

The main reason why this method is so much simpler and more manageable than that of Burgdörfer and Depoid is that it just measures what it sets out to measure, namely the children born from each marriage, irrespective of whether the bearing or non-bearing of children was due to husband or wife having died, or their having been divorced.

Karmel however, over-simplified the problem. Dyne and Clark, also working on Australian statistics,[1] developed the Karmel method, and brought the age of mothers back into account. The duration of marriage is an important factor, but not the only factor, in determining the number of births. Those who marry younger on the average produce larger families than those who marry older. If we take any generation of women (i.e. those born within a particular year or quinquennium) it is possible to compute the proportion who die before reaching maturity, those who marry at various ages, and those who remained unmarried. From figures worked out from current statistics, we can show the expected 'total fertility' of those marrying at each age, combine them with their appropriate weights, and then deduce the total number of children born to this generation. This form of calculation gives us a true net rate. Those who die before marrying are excluded, and the effect of deaths after marriage is taken into account in Karmel's method of recording the births attributable to the marriages of each year.

When the British Royal Commission on Population reported in 1949, its statistical staff had made very detailed analyses of all the available figures by several different methods. But all the information before them was still greatly distorted by war and post-war conditions. While joining in discrediting the old Net Reproduction Rate, they went on to draw the sad conclusion that nothing was going to take its place as a general measure of reproductivity. The best that the demographer could do, they said, was to go on constructing tables and analyses of the reproductive experience of each generation from as many angles as he could, and not hope that any single figure or group of figures would tell him the whole story.

---

[1] *Economic Record*, June 1946.

'They order things differently in France', where immediately after the war, a generous governmental endowment was made available for establishing the Institut National des Études Démographiques under Sauvy's leadership. France had been the first country to embark upon population limitation, and it was appropriate that it should also be the first country to undertake large-scale research into its causes and consequences. For whatever reason, public opinion in France in 1945 was much more concerned with population than it was elsewhere.

While the facts and ideas of population in France were changing, research work on methods of measurement was proceeding too. In 1950 the Institute published an important new document[1] by Bourgeois-Pichat. For so important a document, it was written in very difficult French, full of mathematical symbols, never translated, and in any case almost immediately allowed to go out of print. What Bourgeois-Pichat did was to assemble the available evidence from all over the world showing specific fertilities as a function of both age and duration of marriage, including the work done in Germany, France and Australia already mentioned, some tables prepared by Quensel for Sweden in 1943 on a somewhat different basis, and an approximate tabulation which the English Registrar-General had prepared for the Royal Commission.

Bourgeois-Pichat succeeded in obviating the unmanageable cumbrousness of a complete age-duration table, through his important discovery that, for a given age at marriage, subsequent fertility could be treated as a parabolic function of duration. The large complete table could then be represented by two or three coefficients, only one of which showed any high degree of variability.

He found considerable differences between countries and times in the reproductivity of the first year of marriage, which is of course high, and which he treated as outside his series. There are also slight differences between countries in the upper age limit at which reproductivity falls to zero. But apart from these differences, all the births which may be expected to result, at varying dates in the future, from a given number of marriages, with a given age distribution, may be predicted by the use of a single coefficient, the 'μ coefficient', which gives a measure of comparative reproductivity between countries. For a country with average fertility for the first year of marriage, and average age of termination of fertility, the μ coefficient multiplied by 20 gives the order of magnitude of total fertility — free from distortions arising from changing age at marriage (Table V.1).

Bourgeois-Pichat's original technique required statistics of the marriage-age and duration of marriage of the mothers of all babies born in a given

[1] *Mesures de la Fécondité.*

TABLE V.1. APPLICATION OF BOURGEOIS-PICHAT FORMULA: TOTAL NUMBER OF CHILDREN BORN TO A WOMAN MARRYING AT AGE SPECIFIED FOR KNOWN VALUES OF μ

	Age at Marriage					Average — all ages of
Value of μ	15–19	20–24	25–29	30–34	35–39	marriage[a]
0·10	2·76	2·34	1·79	1·18	0·60	2·09
0·11	2·99	2·54	1·84	1·28	0·65	2·27
0·12	3·23	2·74	2·08	1·37	0·69	2·44
0·13	3·46	2·93	2·23	1·47	0·74	2·62
0·14	3·69	3·13	2·38	1·57	0·79	2·79
0·15	3·99	3·33	2·53	1·67	0·84	2·97
0·16	4·16	3·52	2·67	1·76	0·88	3·14
0·17	4·39	3·72	2·82	1·86	0·93	3·32
0·18	4·62	3·92	2·97	1·96	0·98	3·49
0·19	4·86	4·11	3·12	2·05	1·02	3·67
0·20	5·09	4·31	3·27	2·15	1·07	3·84
0·21	5·32	4·51	3·42	2·25	1·12	4·02

[a] Relative numbers of marriages of different ages weighted by Australian 1949 data.

year. Not many countries, however, record and publish these details.[1] So he has shown how the value of μ may be determined from simpler and more widely available statistics. For this simplified procedure, all that is required is the classification of marriages by age of bride for a series of 20 years preceding the required year n, and the total number of births in the year n. From the marriage statistics we can calculate the number of married women of each age surviving to the year n, i.e. the number of surviving married women cross-classified by age at marriage and duration of marriage. A much simpler alternative method, however, is to make no allowance for deaths subsequent to marriage. This was the technique proposed by Karmel in 1944. The cross-classification used in this case is then the number of marriages at each age in each of the preceding 20 years. No computation of the number of survivors is necessary. The technique has been used in the calculations leading to Table V.2.

[1] Germany is the only country which publishes official statistics in the form required by Bourgeois–Pichat, and those for 1933, 1934 and 1938 were used by him. For other countries figures were obtained from special articles and publications. These included the following: France 1913 and 1931: Pierre Depoid — Essai de détermination de la productivité des mariages suivant l'âge de l'épouse. *Bulletin de la statistique générale de la France et du service d'observation des Prix*, Tome XXIV. Fascicule III, avril–juin 1935, pp. 457 ff.
England and Wales, 1938: The Registrar-General's Statistical Review of England and Wales for the year 1938, Tables. Part II Civil, p. 204. Sweden 1933 and 1943: Carl Erik Quensel — Population movements in Sweden in recent years. *Population Studies*, Vol. 1, No. 1, June 1947, pp. 29–43. Queensland 1939 and 1943: Colin Clark and R. E. Dyne — Applications and extensions of the Karmel formula for reproductivity. *Economic Record*, June 1946, pp. 31–32.

The number of marriages at each age in the year $(n-1)$ is multiplied by the appropriate 'total effective duration' and then by the known or assumed value of the coefficient applicable to the country in question. This gives the total neo-nuptial births in the year n. When this is subtracted from the total number of births we get the number of births to marriages of durations of more than 1 year.

The number of marriages in each marriage-age-duration category (excluding durations of 1 year or less) is multiplied by the appropriate 'remaining effective duration'. The sum of all the products so obtained is divided into the number of births (excluding births from neo-nuptial conceptions). This gives the value of μ required.

If the values of μ for a series of years are known, a future value may be extrapolated and applied to the classification of married women to forecast births in the coming years.

TABLE V.2. 1949 VALUES OF μ IN VARIOUS COUNTRIES

Value of μ	Countries
0·10	England and Wales
0·11	Sweden, Denmark
0·12	Scotland
0·13	Australia
0·14	Norway, Switzerland, New Zealand, U.S.A.
0·15	France, Italy, South Africa (white population)
0·16	Finland, Netherlands
0·18	Spain, Canada
0·21	Portugal

An attempt was made[1] to extend the application of Bourgeois-Pichat's formula to as many countries as possible. Only a few countries publish statistics of marriages by age of brides, and even these statistics are not always available for long periods. In most instances, the series do not extend back past 1936, and in these cases the 1936 age proportions were used for earlier years (no serious error is thereby involved however: pre-1936 marriages only accounted for 7 per cent of Australian births in 1949). Where there were gaps in the published series, figures were interpolated. Re-marriages, which are usually included in figures for total marriages, were excluded on an arbitrary basis of an average rate per thousand marriages deduced from Australian data. As a result, the values of μ shown in Table V.2 were calculated.

Bourgeois-Pichat[2] also devised a still more simplified method for estimating μ for some countries (Table V.3), using the average age of

[1] Boulton, Economic News (Brisbane), 1951.
[2] Private communication, 21 November 1951.

TABLE V.3. μ COEFFICIENTS 1930–2

Austria	0·103
Germany	0·109
Sweden	0·113
France	0·121
England and Wales	0·125
Estonia	0·126
Czechoslovakia	0·128
Belgium	0·128
Denmark	0·130
Latvia	0·133
Luxembourg	0·136
Switzerland	0·138
Norway	0·148
Scotland	0·151
Bulgaria	0·174
Finland	0·175
Italy	0·214
Canada	0·215
Portugal	0·250
Greece	0·254

marriage, the proportion of women unmarried, and the 'classical' (Kuczynski) Gross Reproduction Rate.

This gives a far more accurate picture of conditions as they were about 1930–2 than does the Kuczynski Reproduction Rate, which was much affected by the temporary postponement of marriages due to the world economic depression. It will be seen that, in most of the countries which can be compared, the value of the coefficient in 1949 was lower than in 1930–2, except that we can say for France, for which we now have fuller information, that this was the result of a continued decline to 1935, followed by an increase.

But, important advance though Bourgeois-Pichat's method was, it was to be still further improved.

Inevitably, the methods of fertility analysis attempted in different countries are affected by the nature of the information available. Australia has had full figures since 1907 of births classified by age of mother, duration of marriage, and number of previous children. This abundant information, the fruit of the statistical statesmanship of Knibbs, has by no means yet been fully utilized; but it did at any rate serve to inspire some original work. In the United States, on the other hand, duration of marriage at time of birth was not, and is not, recorded. (Some question of national prestige is here involved; any country which publishes full statistics of birth by duration of marriage is liable to reveal some embarrassing figures, unless they adopt the saving device of showing 'under one year' as a single statistical entry.) The principal material which American demographers had to work on has been age of mothers, and sequence (number of previous children born). Whelpton developed the method of analysis which he called 'cohort fertility', i.e. taking a cohort of women born in any particular year or quinquennium, and tracing their subsequent history through succeeding census records and annual birth registrations. This analysis again is not nearly so simple as it sounds. It involves making certain adjustments for migration, and some very difficult interpolation problems. At the next stage, this analysis covers not only total number of children born, but also analyses them by sequence.

When, in the 1940's the 'net reproduction rates' then in use began to show such an extraordinary rise, most American demographers, if one may so put it, jumped on to the back of the high horse and then fell over on the other side. It is true that there are transitory elements in reproductivity at such a time; but they exaggerated their importance. Expressing themselves in financial language, they said that there was a 'post-war baby boom' in operation. Many of them began to predict how quickly and suddenly it would come to an end, and how much lower the number of births would be in the near future. These predictions were completely falsified. The main body of American demographers certainly got themselves a bad name. What was going on in the immediate post-war years was not merely a catching up of the war-time arrears of births but a basic change in the tendency of American reproductivity, which the demographers had still failed to detect several years after the war.

It is to the credit of Whelpton's method that in a paper presented by him to the World Statistical Conference at Washington in 1947, when the 'post-war baby boom' was at its height, his preliminary analysis of the number of births by sequence at any rate enabled him to take a cautious position, and to leave open the question of whether or not a permanent change in reproductivity had occurred, or whether the country was merely passing through a transitory baby boom.

The next move in the analysis of sequence came from Paris, in the work of Henry. French demographers have all the necessary data before them including age, duration and sequence. Henry, in a difficult piece of mathematical analysis, presented his results[1] in the form of 'probabilité d'agrandissement', i.e. the probability that a family which already has n children will obtain another during the course of one year. To use data for a single year to obtain a result of long-period significance calls for consider-

---

[1] *Fécondité des Mariages*, I.N.E.D., Cahier 16, 1953, and *Population*, April 1954.

able ingenuity. Let us put the problem this way. A family which is going to have, say, a fourth child, has only a limited number of years in which to do it; and must have the child, in fact, not too many years after the birth of the third child. Henry's ingenious method is to relate actual fourth births in the current year to certain data for past years representing what might be called all the potential parents of fourth children, i.e. all those who had a third child in various recent years. To get a fair comparison with the one year's record of fourth births, he takes, in effect, only one year's figure of third births, but it is a composite, weighted by durations of interval observed in the past. Thus fourth births in France are compared with a composite of 0·03 of the third births in the same year, 0·16 of third births in the previous year, 0·33 of those of two years earlier, 0·20 of the year before that . . . — adding up to 1 altogether. Data for such weighting were not in fact easy to obtain. For France, the results of a special inquiry in 1907 were available. Henry also discovered a Czechoslovak inquiry of the 1920's, with the results published separately for the four provinces of the country, in which very different family sizes prevailed (highest in the Sub-Carpathian province, now part of U.S.S.R.). Henry applies these somewhat different weighting systems according to the type of country whose fertility he is analysing. In 1961 the technique was improved[1] (though the results were hardly affected) by relating births of order n to actual births of order $(n-1)$ in previous years, instead of using the supposed weights derived from the 1907 inquiry.

Besides his own constructive efforts, Henry had to embark regretfully upon a criticism of the conclusions of his colleague, Bourgeois-Pichat. In a difficult and subtle piece of reasoning, with which it is hard to disagree, he shows that the Bourgeois-Pichat method is liable to introduce a certain amount of bias, if ages at marriage change.

In this way Henry was able to compute such 'probabilités d'agrandisse-ment', year by year, and found them subject to considerable change (Diagram V.A). Not all the changes are in the same direction. In modern France, there has been considerable increase in these probabilities up to third and fourth children, very much less in the case of higher sequences. But the extraordinary thing about his results for France is that the time-series of these probabilities, for all sequences, pass through a perfectly sharp turning point in the year 1935.

Henry then began to apply his method to other countries, including Australia,[2] (Diagram V.B) where he found, as in France, that for all birth orders except first births, which fell because of deferred marriages, an

---

[1] *Population*, July–September 1961, pp. 513–15.
[2] *United Nations Population Bulletin*, 1954.

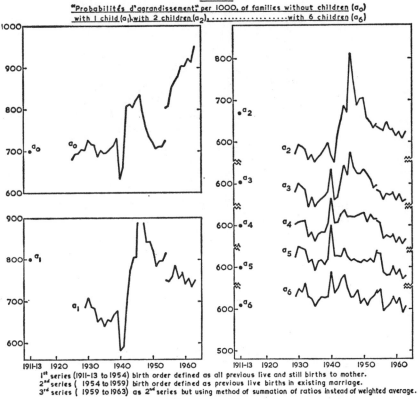

FRANCE

"Probabilités d'agrandissement" per 1000, of families without children (a_0)
with 1 child (a_1), with 2 children (a_2), ...with 6 children (a_6)

1st series (1911-13 to 1954) birth order defined as all previous live and still births to mother.
2nd series (1954 to 1959) birth order defined as previous live births in existing marriage.
3rd series (1959 to 1963) as 2nd series but using method of summation of ratios instead of weighted average.

DIAGRAM V.A

upward trend had come in the 1930's, unrecognizable at the time through the faulty demographic techniques then in use; and also Italy,[1] using data which can only begin in 1934. In Italy all the 'probabilités d'agrandissement' right up to the ninth child, were showing rapid increase in the years immediately before 1940. At this point, naturally, they were all checked by the war. They rose again to a post-war peak in 1946. But after that date they fell markedly (Table V.4 and Diagram V.c).

By multiplying and summing these probabilities we can obtain the expected total of children per marriage. For Italy these figures are given in Table V.5 (before 1934 using Gini's formula, based on summing fertilities specific for duration of marriage).

Henry also analysed the situation in U.S.A.[2] (Diagrams V.D and V.E).

[1] Henry and Pressat, *Population*, July–September 1955.
[2] *Population*, January–March 1961.

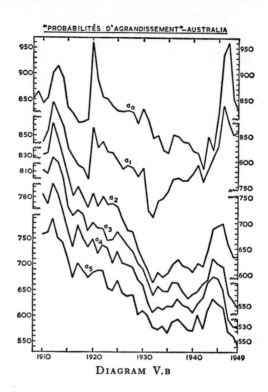

"PROBABILITÉS D'AGRANDISSEMENT"—AUSTRALIA

DIAGRAM V.B

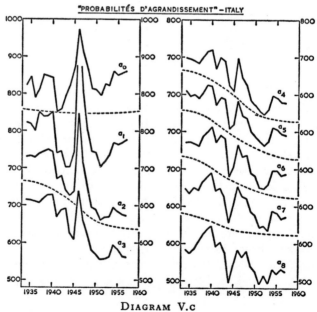

"PROBABILITÉS D'AGRANDISSEMENT" – ITALY

DIAGRAM V.C

TABLE V.4. ITALY 'PROBABILITIES OF ENLARGEMENT'
PER THOUSAND

Number of children born already

		0	1	2	3	4	5	6	7	8
Italy	1934–40	830	829	742	724	706	707	781	660	609
	1950–52	812	722	574	562	558	575	560	556	511
France	1911–13	760	730	675	600	590	590	600		
(for comparison)										

Here the rise in first births began somewhat earlier, but for other sequences the rise did not come until 1949, representing an even sharper change than that of France in 1935.

More recently Henry and Biraben have assembled summary data[1] for all the West European countries (Diagram V.F). With one or two exceptions, there is a strong tendency for the higher fertility countries to fall, and also for the lower fertility countries to rise, to the European average of 2·5.

Jacoby[2] applied Henry's method to New Zealand, computing 'probabilities of enlargement' (A_0, A_1, etc.) not year by year, but for marriages of given date (Table V.6). The first four probabilities appear to have been

TABLE V.5. ITALY — EXPECTED CHILDREN PER MARRIAGE

1903	4·26	1934	3·12
1915	4·22	1940	3·37
1921	3·94	1947	3·36
1925	3·56	1951	2·07
		1954	2·33

lowest for marriages of the 1920's (i.e. cohorts born about the decade 1900–10, as in U.S.A.) and risen subsequently: but the probability of the higher sequences continues to fall.

Wünsch[3] has applied Henry's method in Belgium, expressing his results *per marriage* and not for the whole cohort (Table V.7). Marriages of 1937 and earlier were calculated, from the Census of 1947, to show a total fertility of 2·46.

Henry's method, in effect, re-analyses reproductivity afresh each year. The ultimate size of the family, he implies, is a matter on which parents

[1] *Population*, June–July 1964, and Biraben, World Population Conference, 1965.
[2] *Population Studies*, July 1958.
[3] *Recherches Economiques de Louvain*, September 1964.

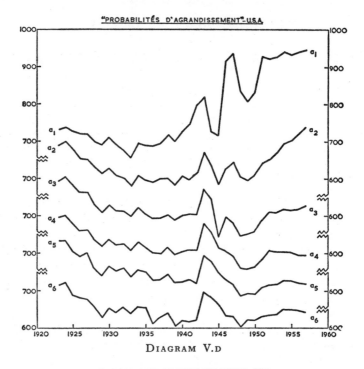

"PROBABILITÉS D'AGRANDISSEMENT"-U.S.A.

DIAGRAM V.D

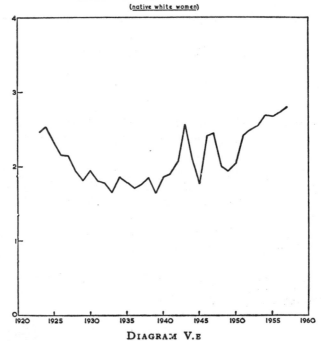

AVERAGE NUMBER OF BIRTHS PER MOTHER-U.S.A.

(native white women)

DIAGRAM V.E

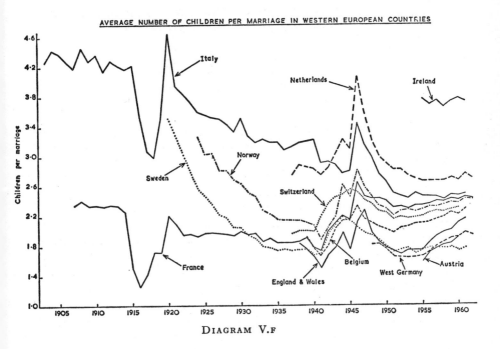

AVERAGE NUMBER OF CHILDREN PER MARRIAGE IN WESTERN EUROPEAN COUNTRIES

DIAGRAM V.F

TABLE V.6. NEW ZEALAND PROBABILITIES OF
ENLARGEMENT

	Marriages of				
	1913–14	1919–21	1924–6	1929–31	1934–6
Completed fertility	3·33	2·72	2·38	2·46	2·55
Do. per family with 1 or more children	3·72	3·17	2·96	3·00	3·16
A_0	894	859	803	820	809
A_1	826	798	748	768	803
A_2	799	689	673	667	710
A_3	674	614	585	564	600
A_4	638	574	579	601	533
A_5	607	572	535	552	542
A_6	607	575	594	561	512

TABLE V.7. BELGIAN TOTAL FERTILITY PER MARRIAGE
(COMPUTED BY HENRY'S METHOD)

1954	2·22	1959	2·44
1955	2·20	1960	2·30
1956	2·21	1961	2·45
1957	2·28	1962	2·36
1958	2·34		

may change their opinions, quite suddenly and drastically, within the course of a year or two — and he has evidence to support this presupposition.

The method of cohort fertility developed in the U.S.A. by Whelpton,[1] on the other hand, consisted of tracing the fortunes of a 'cohort' (those born in a particular year or quinquennium) of women, recording the first, second, and all subsequent births by sequence, and cumulating them. This analysis, which called for unusual skill as well as effort, had to be prepared without benefit of census data, depending entirely on registrations of births for the period 1920–58 inclusive. In the early part of the period registrations were only available for a limited number of states, and extrapolating devices had to be used. He recorded all births occurring at any age up to 47, and gave a few entries for cohorts born as far back as 1875, or as recently as 1933. As his birth statistics range over a period of 30 years only, he is able to give for no cohort an entirely complete table of reproductivity — though for most of the cohorts born in the first decade of this century his results are virtually complete.

If, however, we have to confine ourselves to ascertaining completed reproductivity up to the end of the woman's reproductive life in this way we shall make little progress. Some device for extrapolating the recorded cumulated total at a given age, to estimate total fertility by the end of the reproductive period, is very necessary. Such extrapolation can clearly be a good deal more precise for a cohort which has reached the age of say 35 than for one ten years younger. In fact, a formula has been found which, tested on past data, gives a good extrapolation for any cohort which has reached the age of 30.

The fact that births are recorded separately for the different sequences makes such extrapolation a good deal more precise than if we had merely dealt with births as a whole. Diagrams V.G and V.H show the nature of the information with which we have to deal. Many attempts have been made

---

[1] Whelpton, *Cohort Fertility of Native White Women in the United States*, and U.S. Department of Health Education and Welfare, *Vital Statistics, Special Reports*, Vol. 51, No. 1 (29 January 1960).

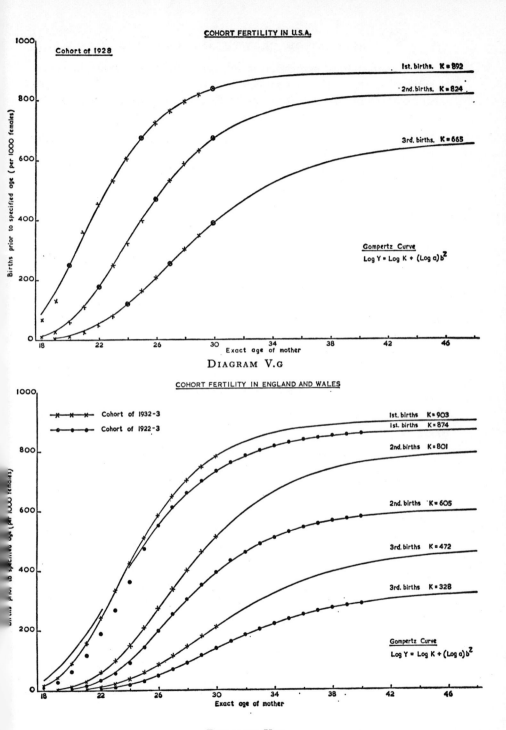

COHORT FERTILITY IN U.S.A.

Cohort of 1928

1st. births. K = 892

2nd. births. K = 824

3rd. births. K = 665

Births prior to specified age (per 1000 females)

Gompertz Curve

$$\text{Log } Y = \text{Log } K + (\text{Log } a) b^z$$

Exact age of mother

DIAGRAM V.G

COHORT FERTILITY IN ENGLAND AND WALES

×—×—× Cohort of 1932-3
●—●—● Cohort of 1922-3

1st. births K = 903
1st. births K = 874

2nd. births K = 801

2nd. births K = 605

3rd. births K = 472

3rd. births K = 328

Gompertz Curve

$$\text{Log } Y = \text{Log } K + (\text{Log } a) b^z$$

Exact age of mother

DIAGRAM V.H

to find a mathematical expression which would fit these curves, and serve to extrapolate them when incomplete — a very urgent task. The solution was discovered by Martin,[1] who showed that the Gompertz equation gives a close fit. The method of fitting is as follows:

X = Exact age of mother. X_0, X_1, X_2, are three selected values of X such that $X_2 - X_1 = X_1 - X_0$

Y = Cumulated number of births (per 1000 women) prior to specified age. Y_0, Y_1, Y_2 are the three values of Y corresponding to X_0, X_1, X_2

$Z = X - X_0$

$n = X_2 - X_1 = X_1 - X_0$

The Gompertz formula is: $Y = Ka^{b^Z}$ (where K is the asymptotic value of Y)

or
$$\text{Log } Y = \text{Log } K + (\text{Log } a)b^Z$$

where
$$b^n = \frac{\text{Log } Y_2 - \text{Log } Y_1}{\text{Log } Y_1 - \text{Log } Y_0}$$

$$\text{Log } a = \frac{\text{Log } Y_1 - \text{Log } Y_0}{b^n - 1}$$

$$\text{Log } K = \text{Log } Y_0 - \text{Log } a$$

Values of a, b and K obtained for Diagrams V.G and V.H were as follows:

	U.S.A. 1928 cohort			England and Wales 1922–3 cohort			England and Wales 1932–3 cohort		
	1st births	2nd births	3rd births	1st births	2nd births	3rd births	1st births	2nd births	3rd births
a	0·281	0·215	0·179	0·633	0·331	0·155	0·102	0·075	0·083
b	0·739	0·778	0·823	0·787	0·788	0·820	0·756	0·802	0·826
K	892	824	665	874	605	328	903	801	472

The deviation of the first births for a few years in both Britain and U.S.A. at the beginning of the period was 'the exception which proves the rule'. They refer to the years 1944–7, when many husbands or potential husbands had been absent. By 1948, it can be said, the 'intended' number of first births for the cohort had been caught up.

While there have been cases in which a cohort began to reproduce with one final objective in view and then in mid-career changed to a significantly different objective — the data are too complex and obscure for us yet to be

[1] *Population*, November–December 1967.

able to reach a final conclusion on this question — it definitely appears that the cohorts born in the first decade of this century in Britain and U.S.A. had low ultimate objectives throughout, and that those born later have rapidly raised their objectives. It is probable however that all cohorts for which we have data were however 'changing their minds' downwards (regarding third children) in the 1920's. But this fall was checked in the 1930's — and the check to the fall appeared first among the older, not the younger women. A new fall has appeared in U.S.A. recently.

When fertilities were rapidly declining, fear of war was often given as an explanation. Harrod pointed out the improbability of this theory — the 1920's were probably the only period in history when most people in fact (however inadequate their reasons) confidently expected that large scale war would never recur; and yet this was the period when fertility was falling most rapidly. There may indeed be a good deal in the opposite theory, that uncertain expectation of life may encourage parents to have children quickly.

To turn to more recent times, Freedman, Goldberg and Slesinger[1] record (Table V.8) how various cohorts were asked, at different dates, the total number of children they intended to have.

TABLE V.8. INTENDED FAMILIES IN U.S.A.

	1955	1960	1962
Cohort of 1926–30	3·1	3·3	3·1
1931–37	3·2	3·4	3·4
1936–42	3	3·1	3·2

There appear to be signs of an increase between 1955 and 1960.

An alternative mathematical function for precisely expressing (for children of given birth order) specific fertility by age of mother, measured by single years, was proposed by Mazur.[2] (This method refers to births by individual years of age, *not* to cumulated totals, as does Martin's formula. It can only be used for estimating cohort fertility for stable or quasi-stable populations.)

The necessary data were obtained from the registration statistics of the State of Washington, for 1945–9 and 1955–9. The fit is good.

Defining age in years as X,

Minimum and maximum ages of child bearing as W_1 and W_2, and age of maximum specific fertility as i.

---

[1] *Population Index*, October 1963, p. 373. Data for white and total population do not significantly differ. The 1936–42 data are for total population, others for white.
[2] *Journal of American Statistical Association*, September 1963.

Then births at age X as proportion of maximum are given by:

$$\left(\frac{X-W_1}{i-W_1}\right)^r \left(\frac{W_2-X}{W_2-i}\right)^{(W_2-i)/(i-W_1)}$$

where $\qquad r=\dfrac{W_2-W_1}{W_2-i}$ if $x>i$, $\dfrac{W_2-i}{W_2-W_1}$ if $x<i$

The results were:

		Order of Birth				
		1st	2nd	3rd	4th	5th & over
W_1	1945–9	14	16	17	18	20
	1955–9	15	16	17	17	19
W_2	1945–9	49	49	49	49	49
	1955–9	49	49	49	49	49
i	1945–9	20	23	25	26	32
	1955–9	19	22	24	26	30
Maximum specific		132	80	49	17	16
fertility		156	113	73	37	32

We can now survey the more abundant but less precise information which is available only in the form of gross reproduction rates (or better total fertilities, obtained where necessary, by multiplying gross reproduction rate by the factor of 2·05). 'Total fertility' may legitimately be described in simpler language as 'the average family', so long as the context makes it clear that we are referring to the average family expected to be produced by a woman who has survived to the age of 45, and also that we are describing the average produced per woman whether married or not. The 'average family per marriage' must necessarily be higher than this.

Although based on approximate data and methods,[1] we have some most interesting estimates (Diagram V.1) of the trend of total fertility in Europe since the beginning of birth registration (which began at different dates in different countries), earlier for France.

These results are extremely interesting. The decline in France began before the Revolution and continued steadily until the early 1850's (the accession of Napoleon III) after which it was checked for a time. It would be going too far to say that the Napoleonic regime deserves credit for this event; but the coincidence is certainly remarkable.

The decline in England began with dramatic suddenness in the late 1870's, and after that date continued unchecked. English writers have

[1] Depoid, *Reproduction Nette en Europe*, Statistique Générale de la France, 1941. Earlier data for France calculated by Bourgeois–Pichat, quoted by Toutain, Cahiers d'ISEA, Supplement 133, p. 38.

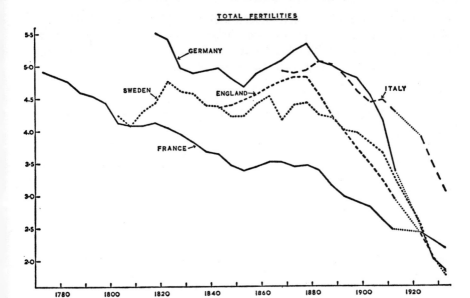

TOTAL FERTILITIES

DIAGRAM V.1

tended to attach considerable importance to the single event of the trial of Bradlaugh and Besant in 1877 for publishing a book advocating contraception, and all the publicity which it attracted; but there were probably more deep-seated factors at work, namely compulsory education and restrictions on child labour. In Germany and Sweden the downward turn also began in the 1870's, but at a more steady pace, until it was accelerated in the 1890's, by which date the downward movement in Italy had also begun.

Sauvy[1] gave (Table V.9) the following approximate dates for the beginning of general fall of fertilities in various countries:

TABLE V.9.   COMMENCEMENT OF FALL IN FERTILITIES

France	1760	England	1875
Sweden	1820	Germany	1880
Belgium	1840	U.S.A.	1885
Switzerland	1860	Italy	1885
Netherlands	1875	Hungary	1890

Besides the above, and the data for a number of countries believed to be of 'unrestricted fecundibility' already reviewed in Chapter I, we have some

[1] *Mercurio*, 15 January 1960.

further historical evidence on total fertilities, in most cases compiled by the Kuczynski method. For present day information, in most cases, better methods can be used. The historical information (not already shown in Diagram V.1) is arranged by continents and countries in Table V.10.

TABLE V.10. HISTORICAL DATA OF TOTAL FERTILITIES

| | | | Total fertility (childless women excluded) | % childless | | |
				Total	Negroes	Japanese
AMERICA:						
Brazil[a]	Women born 1870–79		7·54	21·0	23·3	18·4
	1880–89		7·43	18·9	22·3	10·4
	1890–99		7·31	17·1	21·0	7·3
Jamaica[b]	Total fertilities 1844–1923		5·4 (quoted in Chapter I.)			
	1943		4·26			
	1951		4·67			
United States[c]		1800	5·8			
		1870	5·1			
ASIA:						
Japan[d]	Total fertilities	1868	6·55–7·35	1937	4·59	1948–9 4·3
		1920	5·45	1938–9	3·9	1950 3·7
		1925	5·34	1940	4·29	1951 3·3
		1930	4·93	1943	4·46	1952 3·1
						1953 2·7
						1954–5 2·5
EUROPE:						
Austria[e]	Total fertilities	1895–9	5·09	1905–9	4·65	1925–9 1·99
		1900–4	4·90	1910–4	4·10	
Bulgaria[e]	„ „	1920–4	5·11	1925–9	4·65	
Denmark[e]	„ „	1875–84	4·56	1900–4	4·01	1915–19 3·13
		1885–94	4·40	1905–9	3·81	1920–4 2·84
		1895–99	4·20	1910–4	3·43	1925–9 2·41
Finland[e]	„ „	1870–4	4·92	1885–9	4·94	1910–9 3·54
		1875–9	4·98	1890–9	4·70	1920–9 2·88
		1880–4	4·85	1900–09	4·40	
Germany[f]	Total fertilities of marriages contracted					
	Before 1850		5·5	1920	2·31	1950 1·93
	1900		4·11	1930	2·18	1960 2·10
	1910		3·03	1940	1·83	

TABLE V.10. (*continued*)

					Cohorts born:[h]			
		1900–1910[g]	1910–1914[g]	1925–1929[g]	1900–1904	1905–1909	1910–1914	1915–1919
Hungary	Total fertilities	5·16	4·94	2·76	2·80	2·59	2·52	2·37
	Do. married women				3·06	2·78	2·74	

		1920–4	1925–9	1930–4
	Total fertilities	2·27	2·20	2·14

Norway	Total fertilities		Marriages of[i]	Total fertility	% childless
		1870–4　4·56	1880	6·52	4·1
		1880–4　4·53	1890	6·03	4·8
		1890–4　4·40	1900	5·49	4·6
		1895–	1910	4·39	6·9
		1904　4·24	1920	3·34	6·3
		1905–14　3·80	1925	2·75	10·1
		1915–19　3·42	1930	2·65	7·1
		1925–29　2·61	1935	2·65	

Cohort Fertilities[k] of Generations of Women Born:

1870	3·91	1900–4	2·07
1875–9	3·71	1905–9	2·04
1880–4	3·43	1910–4	(2·13)
1885–9	3·10	1915–19	(2·20)
1890–4	2·73	1920–24	(2·33)
1895–9	2·34		

Poland	Total fertility	1920–4[g]	4·32	1950[h]	3·68
		1930[h]	3·85	1955[h]	3·59
		1933–6[h]	3·05	1959[h]	3·18

Rumania[h]	,,	,,	1930	4·42	1957	2·73
			1948	2·89	1961	2·17

U.S.S.R.	,,	,,	1928[g] (Ukraine)	4·61	1957–8[h]	2·82
					1958–9[h]	2·81
			1929[g] (Ukraine)	4·08	1960–1[h]	2·81

United Kingdom[j]

Fertilities of marriages of	1861–9	6·16	1890–9	4·13	1930	2·09
	1871	5·94	1900–9	3·30	1935	2·04
	1876	5·62	1910–9	2·64	1940	2·00
	1881	5·27	1920	2·47	1945	2·18
	1886	4·81	1925	2·17	1950	2·21

OCEANIA:

Australia[g]	Total fertilities	1905–14	3·46
New Zealand	,,	,,	1910–14	3·17
		1915–19	2·96
		1920–29	2·71

[a] Mortara, *International Population Conference*, Vienna, 1959; from 1950 Census and *Revista Brasiliera de Estadística*, various issues, 1947–8. For 1940 total fertility (quoted in Chapter I) was 7·6 excluding childless, or 6·45 in all. Net reproduction rate was calculated at 1·80, with an average length of generation of 26 years, implying a 2·3 per cent per year population increase. Since then, of course, mortality has fallen faster than fertility.

[b] Roberts, *The Population of Jamaica.*

[c] Taeuber and Miller, World Population Conference, 1954; Grabill, *Fertility of American Women*, indicates remarkable geographical differences in the reproductivity of the cohort of white women born 1835–40, i.e. bearing children about the 1860's.

	Total fertility all women	Total fertility married women	% married women childless
New York and New England	3·8	4·5	13
Middle West and South	5·6	6·0	6
Oklahoma	6·4	6·5	5
Utah	7·4	7·5	2

[d] Taeuber, *Milbank Memorial Quarterly*, January 1947, and *The Population of Japan*. Taeuber and Notestein, *Population Studies*, June 1947.

[e] Kuczynski, *Economica*, May 1935.

[f] Schwartz, Bundesamt für Statistik, private communication. Prussia only to 1910. Based on Freedman's 'expectations' (*Population Studies*, 1959).

[g] Kuczynski, *Economica*, May 1935.

[h] Alsadi and Rosset, Ferenbac, Vostrikova, *Studies in Fertility and Social Mobility*, Akadamie Kiadö, Budapest, 1964.

[i] Jahn, *Population*, January–March 1958 (marriages at age 24–25). The mean age of marriage for women for the period 1856–65, as shown by the Census, was in fact 26·6 (for men it was 27·1 in the towns and 29·1 in rural areas, where they often had to wait to inherit land before they married).

[j] Census of 1951 (England and Wales only).

[k] Vogt, *Staatsøkonomisk Tidsskrift* 1964, Part 4 (last 3 data extrapolated).

NOTE

An important recent study (Szabady and others, *Population*, September–October 1966, p. 950) shows a rapid fall in fertility in Eastern Europe.

Total Fertilities

	1951	1956	1961
Bulgaria	—	2·2	2·2
Czechoslovakia	3·0	2·8	2·4
East Germany	—	2·3	2·4
Hungary	2·6	2·7	1·9
Poland	3·7	3·5	2·8
Rumania	—	3·0	2·4
U.S.S.R.	—	2·8	2·8
Yugoslavia	3·3	3·0	2·7

The U.S.S.R. showed a further fall to 2·6 by 1962–3.

Almost unbelievable however has been the effect of a decision made during the last months of 1966 by the Government of Rumania that abortions, hitherto very easily obtained, should henceforward be confined to mothers of more than 4 children, and to women over 45, with the penalty of lifetime deregistration for any doctor infringing the new law. By July–August 1967 the number of births had risen 2·7-fold in comparison with the same months in 1966 (Pressat, *Population*, November–December 1967).

CHAPTER VI

The Sociology of Reproduction

EVEN the most subtle and profound philosophers cannot fully explain the relationship between individual decisions and external circumstances. Nobody can deny, on the one hand, that decisions are made by individuals, nor, on the other hand, that external circumstances influence them. This is certainly the case in respect of decisions to beget children. Those of us who work with statistics find significant relationships between fertility and various external circumstances, which, in a sense, we can describe as causal. But we should never forget that every decision is ultimately an individual one.

Most people are aware that reproductivity may be affected by a family's income and wealth, the degree of education of the father or of the mother, the occupation of the head of the family, by whether their home is urban or rural, by their religious beliefs, and probably by many other factors. 'The rich get richer and the poor get children' was the Victorian epigram; and it was generally believed (on fairly good evidence) that larger families were statistically associated with poverty, unskilled occupation, lack of education, and rurality, with larger families also expected from Catholic than from Protestant parents, and from Protestant than from irreligious.

This group of generalizations was first challenged in 1930 by Arvin and Edin in Sweden, one of the countries where restriction of fertility had already proceeded furthest. Birth restriction, in Sweden as everywhere else, first appeared among the wealthier, more educated urban families, with the fathers in more skilled occupations. But, in time, this movement had run its course. Family restriction spread to the less wealthy, less educated, less skilled and rural families, in some cases to an even greater extent than among those who had first practised it, turning differential reproductivity in favour of the more educated.

This diffusion of ideas about family limitation in Sweden depended, of course, on the possibility of fairly abundant contacts between different social groups. In countries of more rigid social structure, as in Latin America,[1] this is generally impossible to this day. Tietze thought that this consideration should apply most of all in the case of the large Amerindian

---

[1] Tietze, *Human Fertility in Latin America.*

populations, who live almost entirely segregated from the rest of the community. But this plausible theory is open to question. In Peru,[1] the total fertility of the Indian population in 1940 was 5·45 as against 6·35 for the non-metropolitan Spanish-speaking population (urbanization had little effect on fertility, except in the capital city). It is believed that the situation is similar in Bolivia and in Ecuador.

Since the original Swedish study, more and more evidence, as we shall see below, has been accumulating which points in the same direction. Perhaps it will appear to our successors that the period of declining fertility, which began about 1780 in France, spread over all Western Europe and North America in the nineteenth century, and was reversed about the 1940's, was no more than a temporary period of transition, during which the normal differential reproductivities were reversed, while both before and after this period it was normal for the wealthier and better educated families to be more, not less, reproductive than their neighbours.

France being the country where the restriction of fertility had gone on for the longest time, and its political and economic consequences being most apparent, it is understandable that France should have devoted more thought, skill and resources to demographic research than any other country in this generation. But awareness of France's demographic stagnation, contrasting with the continuing increase in neighbouring countries, was already in the closing decade of the nineteenth century creating uncertainty in the minds of French statesmen, soldiers and scholars. It is to a Frenchman of this period, Arsène Dumont, that we owe the really pioneering researches into the sociology of reproduction. Like other pioneers, coming before his time, neglected and ridiculed by his contemporaries, Arsène Dumont was a strange character. Truth indeed is stranger than fiction. Had we encountered him in the pages of a Zola novel, we would have complained that he was ridiculously overdrawn. A caricature of the characteristic Frenchman of his times, unmarried, the possessor of a small inherited fortune, with a secure but lowly-paid position in the Civil Service, in which he was required to work hard, Dumont decided to retire from the Civil Service and to live on his capital while writing his great book on demography, which, however, attracted no attention at the time. The day came when his capital was exhausted, he could no longer pay his hotel bill, and he shot himself. Dumont was a fervent atheist, and a considerable part of his book is taken up with anti-religious arguments, and some rather puerile blasphemies. How tragic it was, he wrote, that good atheistic Frenchmen could not reproduce themselves, while believing countries all around them were still doing so;

[1] Stycos, *Population Studies*, March 1963; Heer, *Population Studies*, July 1964.

France's great need was to restore an interest in family life, 'in order to keep men out of the taverns and the girls out of the churches'.

But, wrapped up in these unexpected coverings, was the really important idea of 'la capillarité sociale'. It is a well-known phenomenon in physics — a consequence of surface tension — that if a small tube is inserted vertically in a liquid, then the surface of the liquid in the tube will rise above its surrounding level; and the narrower the tube, the greater the rise. It was this phenomenon which gave Dumont his analogy for the sociology of reproduction — the family's desire to rise socially and economically, and the greater possibilities of such a rise for a smaller family. Among property-owning families, the issue was simple; the fewer the children, the greater each one's expected inheritance, and the better therefore his prospects of succeeding in business. For civil servants and professional men, such as Dumont himself, the relationship was more subtle; promotion and professional success, he said, came to those who were seen at the right social gatherings, participation in which was much more difficult, both physically and financially, for those encumbered with a large family. Dumont assembled a number of important facts in support of his theory, including a much larger average family size among the non-French speaking minorities in France (Breton, Basque, Italian and German speakers), who, he reckoned, had little prospect of social advancement anyway.

This state of affairs was accentuated in France by the intense desire of French professional and business men to live in Paris rather than in the provinces, both for the sake of economic opportunities and of cultural contacts. Limited housing and high rents in Paris made the raising of a family still more difficult. Also among farmers, and to a considerable extent among other social groups in nineteenth-century France, it was then considered necessary (it is still the case in Ireland) for a father to provide dowries if he wished his daughters to make good marriages — another factor strongly limiting reproductivity.

Sauvy[1] carries this method of analysis back into the past — though what he has to say is still applicable to many peasant communities as they are now. 'Would the size of family in the Middle Ages still have been high', he asks, 'if each peasant had been able to cherish a hope of some day becoming a *seigneur*, or of his son becoming one, if he were able to concentrate all his efforts on giving one son a good education?'

Peasant families not only lacked a negative inducement against children, but felt a positive inducement for them. The mediaeval peasant, according to Sauvy, reckoned that a child who had reached the age of seven or eight contributed to the family farm work a value outweighing the cost of his or

[1] *Richesse et Population.*

her keep. So bearing a child and rearing it to this age, apart from all other considerations, was a good economic investment. This was a generally understood economic fact of the time, and frequently led, Sauvy records, to thefts or even to sales of children. It is not until public opinion begins to frown upon heavy use of child labour, or indeed imposes a legal obligation to send children to school, that this economic incentive to reproduction disappears — and these changes only came comparatively recently.

As late as the seventeenth century, so it appears from a recent biography, Judge Jeffreys (that unduly maligned character) fell foul of the merchants of Bristol, a city which had had a bad record for slave trading all through the Middle Ages, for their continuing practice of stealing children and selling them into slavery.

Sauvy believed that his estimate of the net economic value of children was valid even in the early nineteenth century. It was also apparently true in a community much richer than France.

'Even at six years of age the services of children become valuable, and with many of the lower classes of settlers this might operate against their wish to send them to school.'[1]

Nor is the case invalidated in such countries as India and the Middle East countries where, to outward appearance, the farmers and their families are unoccupied for a great part of the year. A difficult pattern of work is imposed on them by the climate, with long periods of idleness during the dry weather, but very concentrated activity during the limited period in which cultivation is possible. During these months, the farm economy is acutely pressed by labour shortage, and the labour of every child of seven and upwards can be very valuable.

Probably the really fundamental distinction is between peoples, on the one hand, who live in the 'nuclear families' of the advanced countries, where all or nearly all the responsibility for children falls on the parents, with grandparents, uncles, etc., usually absent, or at any rate sharing little of the responsibility and those who live in 'extended families', of which the fullest form is tribal life, but also found, for instance, throughout India,[2] and, in a modified form, in peasant and poorer industrial

---

[1] Report of the Select Committee on Transportation to Australia (House of Commons 14 July 1837), evidence of Sir Edward Kerry.

[2] There may be however certain qualifications to this principle in India. Results collected in West Bengal by Uma Datta (quoted by Moni Nag, World Population Conference, 1965), though not abundant enough to establish statistically significant differences, suggest that there may be fewer children in 'extended' families because of substantially less frequency of coitus, due to (i) lack of privacy; (ii) stricter enforcement of the religious bans on coitus on certain days, including up to 100 holy days a year in the Hindu calendar, as well as the days immediately following menstruation; (iii) the Hindu custom which makes older women consider it degrading to conceive once their daughters-in-law (who live with them) have begun to conceive.

communities. In the 'nuclear' family, the upbringing of an additional child is felt as a much greater burden than in the 'extended' family, even though, objectively, the nuclear family's economic resources may be much higher than the other's.

Having seen the essential background to the problem, we can now examine the most significant evidence of the effects upon fertility of income, occupation, education, rurality, and religion, followed by a closer analysis of the extent and mechanism of social mobility between the generations. As is usually the case in demographic analyses, the numerous variables are highly inter-correlated, and we must take exceptional care to see that we are not attributing to one variable what is in fact due to another. We must also bear in mind that these sociological factors may influence both age at marriage, and fertility within marriage; and we must analyse these effects separately so far as we can.

A method purporting to measure income differentials, in use until comparatively recently, was to compare sizes of families in the richer and poorer quarters of cities, between which wide differences were found. It took some time for demographers to understand how biased their method was — of two families of a given income, one childless and one with a large number of children, the former are much more likely to obtain a residence in an expensive, and the latter in an inexpensive quarter of the city.

Income is the factor selected first for analysis because it is the one on which fewest data are available. After all, incomes are generally only ascertained with any precision by tax officials (and not always by them), and tax officials are usually much too busy to co-ordinate their information with demographic statistics, even if this could be done without infringing the secrecy concerning individual incomes which is required of them. Still fewer are the cases in which information about incomes has been properly cross-classified against information about occupations, education, etc. Without such cross-classification, we are quite likely to be imputing to incomes the causation of differences which have really arisen because of other variables associated with income.

In the Scandinavian countries, however, the preservation of the secrecy of individual income tax returns is not regarded as so binding a duty on public authorities. (In Norway, believe it or not, it is customary for the tax assessments on leading citizens to be published in the local papers.) In Sweden, where considerable interest had been aroused, not only by the low level of reproductivity reached in the 1930's, but also by the Arvin–Edin results showing that the old trends of differential reproductivity might be changing, a special census was taken, at considerable trouble and expense, in 1935, with a view to collecting enough data to make possible all the cross-classifications required to show separately the effects on reproductivity of income, occupation and education.

To cross-classify for so many variables, together with age of wife and duration of marriage, would require a greater body of information than could be collected by any conceivable private inquiry, and a census was the only possible method. The results, though carefully analysed, nevertheless presented such a confused picture that other countries have been discouraged from following Sweden's example. However, this census did lead to a clear conclusion that, occupation and education being held constant, there was a strong negative relationship between income and reproductivity in the generation marrying 1901–15, which relationship had already largely disappeared in the generation marrying 1921–25 (generations marrying later had not yet come near enough to the end of their reproductive period by 1935 to make analysis worth while). In the younger generation, the negative relationship with income was found to persist, although in a modified form, among manual workers. Among salary earners, farmers and business proprietors however, the negative relationship had disappeared and there was some indication that it was by that date beginning to be replaced by a positive relationship.

Table VI.1 summarizes what appears to be the most significant information out of a very large quantity of figures.

An earlier result for Stockholm for the period 1919–22[1] showed even at that date quite a marked positive relationship between reproductivity and

TABLE VI.1. INCOME-REPRODUCTIVITY RELATIONSHIPS IN
SWEDEN, 1935

Marriages of	Urban			Rural		
	1901–15	1921–5	1931–5	1901–15	1921–5	1931–5
Farmers				X	X	X
Farm workers				n	n	N
Other employees	N	X	N	N	n	n
Salaried workers	X	X	n	N	X	X
Industrial workers	N	N	N	N	N	N
Other manual workers	N	N	N	N	N	N

X No clear relationship
N Definite negative relationship
n Slight negative relationship

[1] Quoted Notestein, *Annals of the American Academy of Political and Social Science*, November 1936.

income for all the non-manual occupations studied, and only a slight negative relationship for manual workers.

New Zealand also included a question about income in the Census of 1936, and, relating this simply to the number of offspring, found a positive relationship.

We have also some evidence for pre-nineteenth-century families.

'Historical studies made in the old records of the Kingdom of the Two Sicilies for some south Italian centres brought to light the fact that in the seventeenth and eighteenth centuries the largest families were not those of the poorest people, but that the number of children was largest in those families whose economic conditions were less unfavourable. Similar results are given by data collected to the present day in several parts of China, India and Siam.'[1]

De Meo's[2] results for the Kingdom of Naples in 1620 and 1753 are not quite what Gini says. With increasing property or income from property, the number of children per marriage (of a given duration) certainly increases; but so does the proportion of men remaining unmarried — up to 60 or 70 per cent of all the men aged 18–59 in the highest propertied groups. As a result, the net rate of increase per generation is highest for the men in the lowest property-owning category, with the propertyless men coming second.

Data for China, collected by Buck,[3] are given in Table VI.2.

TABLE VI.2. COMPLETED CHINESE FAMILIES (TOTAL CHILDREN BORN TO MARRIED WOMEN OVER 45) ABOUT 1930

Farms arranged by size	Average productivity of farm (tons grain equivalent/man equivalent/year)	Size of family
1st Quintile	0·83	5·03
2nd Quintile	1·17	5·06
3rd Quintile	1·46	5·28
4th Quintile	1·69	5·35
5th Quintile	2·07	5·51
Total	1·39	5·28

A thorough study was also carried out by Jain in Punjab in 1934–5 (Table VI.3). To avoid distortion due to different ages at marriage, the tabulation is confined to families with a marriage duration of ten years or more, in which the husbands were married at ages 15–25, the wives at ages

[1] Gini, *Statistical and Social Enquiry Society of Ireland*, Centenary Meeting, 1947.
[2] *Genus*, May 1938.
[3] *Land Utilisation in China*.

TABLE VI.3. DIFFERENTIAL FERTILITY IN PUNJAB, 1934–5

| Income Rupees/year | *Agriculturalists* | | *Non-agriculturalists* | |
	Children born	Children surviving	Children born	Children surviving
Below 200	4·87	3·24	4·82	3·08
200–400	5·04	3·48	5·12	3·39
Over 400	5·29	3·70	5·27	3·72

12–20.[1] The income-fertility relationship was clearly positive. Among the non-agriculturalists (but not among the agriculturalists) the differences in fertility were accentuated by differential rates of survival.

What appears to be much the most thorough study of any peasant community was that made by Styś for Poland.[2] Styś found that in the eighteenth century villages with more land per head of population had *higher* fertility, but that by 1931 these inter-village differences (with the average amount of land per person then rather low and uniform) had disappeared. Within any given village, however, he found a strongly marked positive relationship between income (as measured by the amount of land held) and fertility. He also obtained the most interesting result that this relationship was substantially modified by the proximity of a large industrial town, which both raised the fertility of the poor and lowered the fertility of the rich families. It also lowered mortality, presumably due to better access to medical treatment, and thus raised the net rate of population growth in the village. The results shown in Table VI.4 were obtained by an analysis of the records for twenty villages in 1948. Styś points out that the landless often had regular wage work and in fact might have higher incomes than the poorest owners of land. 'Births per year of fertile marriage' are determined, in case of the older women, by the number of births up to the actual date of the last recorded birth, i.e. it is assumed that births continued at a fairly uniform rate until fecundibility had ceased.

The rates of birth per year of fertile marriage were almost as high as the maxima estimated in Chapter I. It appears that there was little restriction of fertility in marriage, though very considerable restriction in the form of deferment of marriage in the poorer families. Though total fertility has now been considerably reduced, these differences have persisted into the present generation.

Another interesting example of positive association between earnings

[1] *Relation between Fertility and Economic Status in Punjab*, Punjab Board of Economic Enquiry, Publication No. 64, 1939.
[2] *Population Studies*, November 1957, and *Proceedings of the Society of Science and Letters of Wroclaw*, Series A. No. 62 (in Polish).

TABLE VI.4. PEASANT FAMILIES IN POLAND

Average land holdings in hectares	Age at marriage			Births per year of fertile marriage			Total Fertility	
	Year of birth of mother							
	1855–1902	1903–1914	1915–1929	1855–1902	1903–1914	1915–1929	Present generation	Previous generation
Landless	28	27	23	0·34		0·63	3·1	5·2
0–½	25	25	21	0·34	0·34	0·48	3·1	4·9
½–1	26	24	22	0·34	0·35	0·43	3·0	5·2
1–2	25	24	21	0·35	0·34	0·44	3·1	5·8
2–3	24	23	21	0·37	0·34	0·42	3·7	6·2
3–4	22	22	21	0·36	0·34	0·42	4·2	6·6
4–5	22	21	20	0·38	0·33	0·42	4·6	6·8
5–7	21	20	20	0·38	0·32	0·43	4·7	7·0
7–10	20	19	19	0·40	0·37		5·9	7·7
10–15	20	20	18	0·42			6·1	7·9
Over 15	18	20	23					8·6
Total	24	23	21	0·36	0·34	0·44	3·5	6·4

and number of children was found by Prokopovicz,[1] the well-known writer on the economics and economic history of the Soviet Union, in an early study in St. Petersburg. Among industrial workers, earning on an average 472 roubles/year, 90 per cent of those earning below 400 roubles lived alone, and only those earning over 600 roubles tended to have families with children.

A not very precise Japanese study[2] carried out in the 1950's, but relating to births in earlier decades, divided farmers qualitatively into 'upper, middle and lower' classes (it was stated that the former had obtained their larger holdings mainly through inheritance). Total fertilities were found to be 6·3, 5·3 and 5·0 respectively, with both men and women in the 'lower class' marrying about one year later than the other two classes.

An interesting study of Filipino farmers in 1952[3] showed what might be interpreted as a curved relationship (Table VI.5).

An urban study of Lucknow and Kanpur in India,[4] from abundant data obtained at the time of the issue of food ration books, segregated marriages of 11 to 20 years duration. Up to that marriage duration, four income groups, ranging from family incomes below 100 to over 500 rupees/month, showed no significant difference in reproductivity. The median age of the

[1] *Velikaia Reforma*, Vol. 6, Moscow, 1911 (quoted Gliksman, Rand Publication, P. 1336).
[2] Pamphlet No. 6, Population Problems Research Council (Mainichi Newspapers, Tokyo).
[3] Hawley, *American Sociological Review*, January 1955.
[4] Sinha, Delhi Session International Statistical Institute, 1951.

women at marriage was 15·0 for the lowest income group and 17·9 for the others. But the mean interval between marriage and first birth was 3·1 years for girls marrying at 13–15 (it was 1·7 years for mature marriages); and total fertility was probably not affected by early marriage. In the case of these very early marriages, custom among both Hindus and Moslems calls for a deferment of consummation.

TABLE VI.5. TOTAL FERTILITY (AGE 45 OR OVER) OF FILIPINO FARMERS' WIVES

Size of holding in hectares	Total fertility
Under 1	5·1
1–2	6·8
2–3	7·6
3–4	9·3
Over 4	7·9

Turning now to the high-income communities, we can begin with the study (Table VI.6) of French Government employees in 1906, which gave Henry the basic reference material for his method of analysing reproductivity.[1]

TABLE VI.6. OFFSPRING OF FRENCH GOVERNMENT EMPLOYEES MARRIED OVER 25 YEARS, 1906

Income francs/year	Non-manual workers	Manual workers
Under 500	2·51	2·71
501–1000	2·23	2·72
1001–1500	2·22	2·59
1501–2500	2·02	2·36
2501–4000	1·98	2·19
4001–6000	2·00	1·65
6001–10000	2·10	
Over 10000	2·44	

For manual workers there was a clear negative relationship between income and fertility. For non-manual workers, even at that time, there was an interesting curvature in the results, with a minimum fertility in the 2500–4000 franc income group, rising again with incomes above that.

The first really large scale detailed enquiry into American fertility (apart from Census studies) was made in Indianapolis in the 1930's — confined to white Protestant families, as a comparative homogeneous group. This

[1] Results quoted in Landry, *Traité de Démographie*.

study, whose results were published in many periodicals over a long period of years, was at first thought[1] to show the expected strong negative association between fertility and family income. But this generalization was shaken by the discovery[2] that 'couples planning number and spacing of children' (relatively numerous among the high incomes and relatively few among the low) showed a strongly positive relationship between income and fertility. The paradox was cleared up by Goldberg.[3] It is another story of association between variables leading to spurious conclusions. On this occasion, however, it is not the sort of association between variables which one would expect to have to watch for while analysing the reproductivity of an urban population; but the more subtle variable revealed by isolating 'first generation farm migrants' who constituted, Goldberg calculates, about one-third of the entire American urban population at the time of the survey. It was only among these that there was a really pronounced negative relationship between income and fertility. At the same time, their general level of fertility was higher than the average, and also they were disproportionately concentrated in the lower income groups, thus biasing the whole sample.

Recently, American demographers appear to have concluded that thorough interviewing and analysis of a small sample (including often questions about the family's ultimate expectations, though these answers should be used carefully) will give better results than an attempt at a larger sample less thoroughly treated. A small group interviewed[4] in 1955 showed the number of children said to be ultimately desired by families to be positively correlated with income — but also the interesting result that size of family ultimately desired was more strongly correlated with recent increases in income. Freedman[5] introduced a new dimension by computing the husband's 'relative income' in relation to the average income which might have been expected for him from his occupation, age, etc. He obtained the curious result that the statistical relation of fertility to actual income was negative, but that it was very strongly positive in relation to 'relative income'. As was only to be expected, fertility also showed a negative relationship with the number of years worked by the wife since marriage. The wife's ability to earn at the rate of $2000 per year or more was also shown to have a strong negative effect on the average size of the family (a reduction of 0·51 on an average family size of 2·61). In each of the above

[1] Karpinos and Kiser, *Milbank Memorial Fund Quarterly*, October 1939.
[2] *Population Index*, July 1947; Kiser and Whelpton, *Milbank Memorial Fund Quarterly*, April 1949.
[3] *Milbank Memorial Fund Quarterly*, January 1960.
[4] Notestein and others, Proceedings of International Statistical Institute, Stockholm Conference, 1957.
[5] *American Economic Review*, June 1963.

analyses, the effect of single variables has been isolated, and the cross-effects of the other variables eliminated. Farm families, and those of low fecundibility, have been excluded (Table VI.7).

TABLE VI.7. EXPECTED ULTIMATE FAMILY SIZE IN U.S.A., 1962

Expected 1962

Family income	Wives aged 18–29	Wives aged 30–39	Increase 1955–62
Under $4000	3·1	3·1	–0·1
$4–6000	3·2	3·3	0·3
$6–7500	3·4	3·1	0·4
Over $7500	3·2	3·0	0·3

Another study of expected ultimate size of family,[1] although not cross-analysed, suggests some interesting results. The wives under 30 appeared to have higher expectations than those over 30; and comparison with the previous survey of 1955 showed substantial increases for all but the lowest income group.

Among the few measures of reproductivity by income, properly cross-classified by age, was a survey carried out in 1939 in Melbourne by Prest.[2] Women over 40 had an average family of 3·0 in families earning less than £5 per week (predominantly unskilled workers); in the other income ranges, the size of family declined gradually from 2·3 at the £5–£7 income range to 2·1 for families with income of £9. The data for the younger wives indicated that they would probably not show significant differences by the time they reached the end of the reproductive period.

Finally, we have a thorough study (Table VI.8) made in the German Census of 1962. For the rural population (i.e. living in places with less than 3000 inhabitants) there is no significant association between income and fertility for a *given* age at marriage and marriage duration; but a positive association is found in the *actual* figures, i.e. a positive association is created by country people with higher incomes marrying earlier (as in Poland). There is no significant relation for the self-employed; but a definite positive relation between fertility and income in the other social groups, wage workers, private salaried workers, and Government salaried workers — particularly the latter.

The low figures shown in Table VI.8 do not represent, it must be remembered, total fertilities, but only the actual number of offspring achieved by families at the date of the Census (in the first columns). The second column has been standardized, to show what the offspring of the

[1] Freedman, Goldberg and Slesinger, *Population Index*, October 1963.
[2] *Social Survey of Melbourne*, 1942.

TABLE VI.8. FAMILY SIZE IN GERMANY, 1962

Income DM/month	By size of town						By social group							
	Under 3,000 inhabitants		3–50,000 inhabitants		Over 50,000 inhabitants		Self-employed		Government officials		Privately employed salaried workers		Manual workers	
	A	S	A	S	A	S	A	S	A	S	A	S	A	S
Under 600	1·84	1·95	1·60	1·70	1·32	1·38	1·78	1·70	1·37	1·54	1·26	1·40	1·62	1·71
600–800	1·96	1·96	1·78	1·77	1·50	1·49	1·65	1·62	1·74	1·68	1·44	1·47	1·86	1·83
800–1200	1·91	1·86	1·82	1·80	1·57	1·55	1·71	1·68	1·89	1·82	1·56	1·57	2·08	1·90
Over 1200	2·02	1·94	1·95	1·88	1·68	1·63	1·83	1·75	2·25	2·20	1·62	1·61		

A Actual.
S Standardized to national average age at marriage and marriage duration.

group would have been if it had had the national average age at marriage and marriage duration, insofar as some social or income groups may contain more or less than the national average of more recent or higher-age marriages. On the whole, the second column is better for making comparisons between social groups. It is defective insofar as unusually late or unusually early marriage in any social group may be expected to have a *permanent* effect upon the size of family — a consideration of less importance now than it once was, but still of some significance.

Reading Table VI.8 horizontally, with the effect of income analysed out, probably gives us the best available comparison of fertility between occupations in modern Germany. At all income levels, the lowest fertility is that of the privately employed salaried worker. It cannot be said that he is living in greater economic insecurity than the manual worker. On the other hand, he has relatively more to lose, and perhaps therefore has a greater fear of a period of unemployment. At higher income levels, the greater security of the government official, in comparison with the self-employed, appears to have some effect on fertility.

A somewhat more detailed comparison between occupations, and between 1962 and 1939, is given in the Census in respect of marriages of some 16 years' duration for the latter Census, 14 years for the former. It is true that this difference of marriage duration slightly biases upwards the 1962 figures in the comparison; but not to any serious extent, because in most marriages, above the fifteenth year, further additions to the family are small.

In addition, figures are available (Table VI.9) for the completed, or nearly completed fertility of various marriage cohorts in 1939; and also in 1962 (no doubt somewhat disturbed by war conditions) of marriages of 1940–5.

For the most recent marriages, fertility appears still to be declining for agricultural workers, to be stationary for other manual workers, and to be distinctly rising in the other categories. The trend for the different cohorts of marriages reveals clearly what is also found in other countries, namely a great reduction, though by no means the complete disappearance, of the large differentials between social groups which prevailed at the beginning of this century.

Besides these German figures, which we have examined first because they were associated with an incomes table, there is a considerable amount of material to be examined regarding occupational differences in fertility. The best procedure seems to be to examine first the information for the less developed countries, then to proceed in historical order to examine the information for the developed countries.

TABLE VI.9. AVERAGE OFFSPRING OF MARRIAGES BY
OCCUPATIONS, GERMANY

| Date of Marriage | Complete (or nearly complete) fertilities | | | | | Recorded 1962 | Marriages up to 14–16 years' duration | |
| | Recorded 1939 | | | | | | | |
	Before 1905	1905– 09	1910– 14	1915– 19	1920– 24	1940–45	1939	1962
Self employed:								
Farmers	5·34	4·50	3·96	3·39	3·01	2·59	1·95	2·07
Others	3·92	3·02	2·54	2·10	1·85	1·86	1·21	1·41
Salaried:								
Government	3·41	2·83	2·43	2·08	1·77	2·05	1·16	1·43
Private employment	3·29	2·58	2·19	1·85	1·30	1·83	0·99	1·19
Manual Workers:								
Agriculture	4·53	3·71	3·17	2·68	2·32	2·02	2·05	1·85
Other	4·53	3·57	3·04	2·55	2·20	1·98	1·42	1·41

For the Indian study already quoted, which shows a strong relationship between fertility and income both for farmers and non-farmers in a Punjab village, the fertility differences between occupations nevertheless are slight. Besides the general designations of farmers and non-farmers, separate records were obtained for manual workers (carpenters, barbers, blacksmiths) with an average family of 5·00, or comparable with a middle-income farmer; and for non-manual workers (teachers, priests and officials) the average family was 4·82, or the same as low-income non-agricultural workers. But all the occupational differences were slight.

In an urban study Sovani[1] reached universally negative conclusions, namely that it was impossible to relate fertility significantly to income, to occupation either of the father or mother, or to caste.

A very interesting occupational analysis of Buck's data for China in the 1930's (Table VI.10) was made by Ta Chen.[2] He found it necessary to analyse *surviving* children, as data for total offspring were not available, and, as in India, occupational differences may have been accentuated by differential mortality. He was however able to standardize each social group to the average age composition of the whole married female population (standardization for age at marriage would not be important in China, where all marriages were early). It is interesting to see that public officials again lead, as in modern Germany. The last five groups are presumably the lowest paid. Apart from them there is a considerable degree of uniformity.

The rural survey in the Philippines in 1952, already mentioned, showed average total fertilities of 7·7 for farmers and farm labourers, 6·9 for non-farm manual workers, and 5·5 for clerical and professional workers.

We now turn to historical information for occupational differentials in

[1] *Social Survey of Kolhapur City*, Gokhale Institute, Poona.
[2] *American Journal of Sociology*, July 1946.

TABLE VI.10.   SURVIVING CHILDREN, CHINA, ABOUT 1930

Public service	1·90
Cultivator part owner	1·88
Cultivator owner	1·73
Factory skilled worker	1·70
Merchant and entrepreneur	1·70
Landlord	1·67
Small merchant, workshop	1·66
Liberal professions	1·65
Farm tenant	1·59
Salesman, pedlar	1·57
Teacher	1·47
Labourer	1·30
Servant	1·28
Handicraftsman	1·25
Pauper	0·53

Europe. No study appears so thorough as that (Table VI.11) by Krause[1] for a Protestant village in Saxony over the whole period 1597–1799, during which no significant change in family size was observable.

TABLE VI.11.   OFFSPRING OF MARRIAGES CONTRACTED AND TERMINATED BY DEATH IN THE VILLAGE OF REINHARDTSGRIMMA, SAXONY, 1597–1799

Peasants	3·6
Small peasants, or with inadequate work as craftsmen	3·9
Cottagers	3·5
Servants	3·3

The occupational differences are not great, and may be due, as in Styś's data for Poland, to varying age at marriage.

A Census in Denmark in 1787[2] showed very late marriage (Table VI.12)

TABLE VI.12.   MARITAL STATUS OF MALES AGED 20–29 IN DENMARK, 1787

	Total '000	% married or widowed
Farmers	17·6	36
Men servants	28·1	2
Soldiers and sailors	5·8	17
Other occupations	17·9	31

[1] *Unterschiedliche Fortpflanzung in 17 and 18 Jahrhunderts.*
[2] Quoted Rubin, *Journal of the Royal Statistical Society*, December 1900.

among men servants (presumably mostly working on farms) who constituted a large proportion of the young male population; this must have
led to differences in total fertility.

The world's most astonishing record of late marriage (Table VI.13) was

TABLE VI.13. PERCENTAGE DISTRIBUTION OF AGE GROUPS OF
POPULATION OF ICELAND BY STATUS AND MARITAL CONDITION,
1703

	Men				Women
Age	Heads of households	Of whom married or widowed	Not heads of households	Of whom married or widowed	Married or widowed
20–24	3	1	96	0	5
25–29	18	12	82	1	21
30–34	45	34	55	1	41
35–39	67	57	33	1	52

provided by the Census of Iceland of 1703, which incidentally was the first
Census, as we now understand the word, to be taken in Europe.[1] The
median age for marriage was in the late 30's. It was virtually impossible for
men to marry until they were heads of 'households', which meant in effect
owning farms, because of the King of Denmark's monopoly which had
prevented all industrial and commercial development.

TABLE VI.14. TOTAL FERTILITY OF FAMILIES OF
FRENCH ARISTOCRATS

	Women marrying below age 20	Women marrying at ages 20–29
Marriages of 1650–99	6·37	5·97
1700–49	3·30	4·57
1750–99	2·38	2·13

From France comes the clearest indication[2] that family limitation, which
was taking place generally from 1780 onwards, had begun among the
aristocracy nearly a century earlier. Table VI.14 shows their total fertilities.
That the decline should at first have shown itself more strongly among
women who married below rather than above the age of 20 is surprising.
The data also suffice to show quite clearly that specific fertility per year of
marriage was declining at the higher durations.

[1] Republished 1960, with English sub-headings, by the Statistical Bureau of Iceland.
[2] Levy and Henry, *Population*, October 1960, p. 815 (total fertilities calculated from
age-specific fertilities).

Similar results have been found[1] for Denmark. Male gross reproduction rates for proprietors of manors were only 1·06 for men born about 1700. For those who were also soldiers, long absent from home, the figure was only 0·52. At these rates, of course, the aristocracy was quickly dying out, and was being replaced by newcomers, who however also only had a rate of 0·91. These figures are mainly explained by very late marriage. There is also interesting evidence that mortality among the Danish aristocracy increased in the eighteenth century.

The Census of England and Wales for 1911 included a fertility study (not repeated until 1951), from which could be deduced the comparative reproductivities of different social groups (Table VI.15), classified by date of marriage.[2] The figures are of course somewhat biased by the exclusion of unmarried women; the highest age groups are considerably biased in another respect. Mortality in the late 70's is so high that of those who married before 1851, surviving to 1911, those who married at 17 will be much more abundantly represented than those who married at 22: hence the apparent extremely high fertility of the pre-1851 marriages. In order to complete the table, the numbers in the three most recently married groups have been arbitrarily raised to give something like expected total fertility.

It is interesting to see how during this period the extent of occupational differentiation was increasing. It existed among those marrying in the 1850's, but with only about a 20 per cent difference between the highest and the lowest fertilities. The fall in family size began in business, professional and clerical families, quite strongly, among those marrying in the 1870's. Before long it had spread to other social groups, but to a relatively less extent, so that among those marrying in 1901–6 there was a more than 40 per cent difference in family size.

Stevenson also calculated standardized rates, which did not differ much from the actual rates given in Table VI.15. There were differences in the average age of marriage of men in the different social groups, but only of the order of a year or so. Average age of marriage in Victorian England tended to be higher all round than it is now. The English Registrar General's Report for 1886 gives an interesting tabulation of the average age of women marrying for the first time according to the occupations of their husbands. The figure was at its lowest, namely 22·5 years for miners, 23·7 years for 'labourers and artisans', 24·4 years for professional men and proprietors, and at its highest, 26·9 years, for farmers.

The results for 1951 (Table VI.16) were calculated in the Census, standardized for marriage duration. The results are available with or

---

[1] S. A. Hansen, Economic History Conference, Munich, 1965.
[2] Stevenson, *Journal of the Royal Statistical Society*, May 1920.

TABLE VI.15. TOTAL FERTILITIES IN ENGLAND AND WALES, 1911

	Before 1851	1851–61	1861–71	1871–81	1881–86	1886–91	1891–96	1896–1901	1901–06
Miners	9·13	8·23	8·27	7·76	7·23	6·55	5·61	5·06	4·26
Agricultural workers	8·19	7·94	7·28	6·70	6·17	5·45	4·69	4·27	3·79
Unskilled labourers	7·90	7·81	7·37	6·72	6·14	5·58	4·82	4·45	3·82
Semi-skilled manual workers	7·96	7·44	7·00	6·24	5·57	4·96	4·20	3·90	3·40
Skilled manual workers	7·37	7·58	7·11	6·29	5·56	4·91	4·16	3·83	3·31
Textile workers	7·22	7·36	6·71	5·84	5·10	4·41	3·64	3·26	2·83
Small business and clerical workers	7·79	7·31	6·63	5·58	4·68	4·09	3·50	3·30	2·96
Business and professional	6·65	6·42	5·92	4·80	3·96	3·40	2·90	2·76	2·52

*Date of marriage**

* Data for three most recent marriage groups shown arbitrarily raised by 1, 20 and 55 per cent respectively.

without standardization for varying ages at marriage. For example, farmers tend to show a higher reproductivity in marriage but a later age of marriage (first column showing higher figure than second), and members of the Forces early marriage.

The non-manual workers all show a tendency towards later marriage; but among them the higher paid administrative, professional and managerial workers seem to be somewhat more fertile than the lower paid.

TABLE VI.16. CENSUS OF GREAT BRITAIN, 1951
(All women married once only and enumerated with husbands)

Relative number of offspring (national average = 100)
for given duration of marriage —

Wives of:	Varying ages of marriage for different occupations not taken into account	Do. taken into account
Unskilled labourers	123	125
Agricultural workers	114	115
Semi-skilled manual workers	110	113
Soldiers, sailors and airmen	106	111
Farmers	114	110
Skilled manual workers	99	101
Personal service workers	99	97
Foremen	92	92
Shop assistants	88	87
Higher administrative, professional and managerial	91	85
Shopkeepers, small employers	84	82
Intermediate administrative, professional and managerial	85	81
Clerical	81	78

The United States also took a Fertility Census in 1910, from which it was possible to calculate back to obtain some differential fertilities for earlier generations[1] (Table VI.17). In this study very considerable geographical differences were found to prevail, and the occupational data were therefore standardized to a given geographical distribution.

TABLE VI.17. TOTAL FERTILITIES IN U.S.A., 1910

	Before 1840	1840–44	1845–49	1850–54	1855–59	1860–64	1865–69
Unskilled manual workers			4·37				3·34
Farm workers	4·98	4·84	4·63	4·47	4·25	4·03	3·74
Skilled manual workers		3·97	3·92	3·77	3·53	3·12	2·78
Business men		3·58	3·26	3·14	2·78	2·54	2·22
Professional men		3·69	3·01	3·00	2·64	2·50	2·10

Here the decline also began among those who were marrying about the 1870's (i.e. born in the 1840's and 1850's), but it affected professional and business men much more rapidly than farmers, so that the differential had become very wide for those born in the 1860's.

A small study[2] for a rural county in New York State in 1865 showed that total fertility was 5·6 both for farm owners and unskilled workers, if foreign-born; native-born farm owners had a lower total fertility of 4·5, and unskilled workers of 5·4.

Some hitherto unpublished data from the 1900 Census were analysed by Kiser[3] (Table VI.18). The farm data related to rural areas, and the others to towns of 50,000–125,000 population, in the East North Central States. In the course of only ten years, strong falls were shown by all groups except farmers.

TABLE VI.18. TOTAL FERTILITIES IN EAST NORTH CENTRAL U.S.A.

	Census of 1900 (women born 1855–9)	Census of 1910 (women born 1865–9)
Farm labourers	—	5·19
Farm owners	3·75	3·65
Farm renters	4·47	4·59
Unskilled labourers	4·22	3·63
Skilled manual workers	3·23	2·99
Business men	2·58	2·31
Professional men	2·45	2·00

[1] Notestein and others, *American Journal of Sociology*, November 1932 and *Milbank Memorial Quarterly*, October 1931.
[2] *Milbank Memorial Quarterly*, April 1955.
[3] *Journal of the American Statistical Society*, December 1932 and *Human Biology*, May 1933.

Differential fertility in U.S. was probably at its maximum about 1910. Comparison (Table VI.19) with later Census results[1] shows how much the differentials have since been reduced. (It must be borne in mind that these figures refer to marriage durations of 10–14 years, and are somewhat below total fertilities.)

TABLE VI.19. U.S. DIFFERENTIAL FERTILITY

Children born to white women married once only, enumerated with husbands, marriage duration 10–14 years

	1910	1940	1950
Agricultural labourers	3·78	2·83	2·66
Industrial operatives	3·43	2·80	2·56
Craftsmen	3·08	2·33	2·30
Clerical	2·92	2·10	2·16
Managerial	2·50	1·71	1·96
Professional	2·24	1·65	1·94
Other salaried workers	2·29	1·64	1·87
All	3·13	2·18	2·20

With a rather different classification, and taking the age-group 35–39, which should give results rather higher than in Table VI.19, these results can be brought up to date to 1960[2] (Table VI.20). The lower groups had mostly risen to 2·5.

TABLE VI.20. NUMBER OF CHILDREN EVER BORN PER WHITE WIFE AGED 35–39, BY OCCUPATION GROUP OF HUSBAND, 1940, 1950 AND 1960 CENSUSES

	1940	1950	1960
Farm Labourers and Foremen	3·6	3·7	4·0
Farmers and Farm Managers	3·5	3·3	3·2
Labourers, except Farm and Mine	3·0	2·9	3·0
Operatives, etc.	2·6	2·5	2·8
Craftsmen, Foremen, etc.	2·4	2·2	2·7
Service Workers, including Private Household	2·1	2·0	2·5
Clerical, Sales, etc.	1·7	1·8	2·4
Managers, Officials and Proprietors, excluding Farm	1·9	2·0	2·5
Professional and Technical	1·7	1·8	2·5

The inquiry into intended size of family made in 1955, already referred to, had shown 3·7 for farmers and 2·9 for others.[3] Apart from farmers and farm workers, occupational differentials have now become very small.

[1] Tietze and Grabill, *Eugenics Quarterly*, March 1957.
[2] *Population Bulletin*, September 1964.
[3] Campbell, Milbank Annual Conference, 1958.

In France, the inquiry into government employees in 1906, already referred to, showed completed families averaging 2·65 for manual workers, and 2·13 for non-manual. The number of *surviving* children per family was ascertained in the 1911 Census,[1] but had apparently not been adjusted for infant mortality, or for age distribution of fathers. A detailed sample study of several thousand families in 1950[2] (which also gave some very interesting sociological results, to which reference will be made later) tabulated (Table VI.21) the offspring (incomplete, but standardized to a uniform age

TABLE VI.21. SAMPLE OF FRENCH FAMILIES IN 1950

	Average size of family standardized by father's age	
	Present generation	Previous generation
Peasants	2·15	2·74
Rural wage workers	2·13	3·66
Proprietors, professional, executives	1·87	2·49
Urban manual workers	1·84	2·57
Retailers and artisans	1·68	2·46
Clerical	1·65	2·33
National average	1·87	2·64

distribution of fathers) found in different social groups in 1950, as compared with the same families a generation earlier. The totals were obtained by weighting the groups in proportion to their relative importance in the whole population of France.

These results indicate a continuing fall between the generation beginning to have children about 1910, and its successor (though the figures for the earlier generation are somewhat biased upwards by this method — the larger families of that generation had a greater chance of leaving a successor and thus getting into the sample). Apart from the very high figure for rural workers in the previous generation, among other occupations the differentials seem to have changed comparatively little, in face of a general fall in reproductivity.

A more recent study[3] (Table VI.22) compares the inter-war generation (median date of marriage about 1927) and the post-war generation, of women married in 1944, slightly adjusted to bring the results up to estimated total fertility. In this period the rise has been on the whole uniform,

---

[1] Tabulated by Landry, *Traité de Démographie*.
[2] Bresard, *Population*, July–September 1950.
[3] *Population*, September–December 1959, p. 732.

TABLE VI.22. AVERAGE SIZE OF COMPLETED FAMILY IN FRANCE
BY HUSBAND'S OCCUPATION
(women married below age 30)

	Inter-war	Post-war
Employers and Independents		
Farm owner-occupiers	2·73	3·18
Farm tenants	3·47	3·64
Manufacturers and artisans	2·20	2·64
Traders	1·96	2·45
Professional men	2·38	3·26
Salaried Workers		
Higher administrative	2·12	2·94
Lower administrative	1·89	2·69
Clerical, government	2·06	2·79
Clerical, private	1·70	2·64
Wage Workers		
Farm workers	3·43	4·10
Foremen	1·99	2·76
Skilled men	2·31	3·15
Technicians	2·69	3·46
Miners	3·23	3·83
Unskilled	3·11	3·99
Forces and police	2·34	2·97
All Occupations	2·49	3·12

approximately preserving the differentials which prevailed in the 1920's, though with a considerably more than average rise for professional men. These now stand above the national average; and the lowest position is now occupied by small traders, not clerical and administrative workers.

Swedish data, some going back to the period about 1920, have already been discussed under income differentials. Generally speaking, if we confine ourselves to men who have received primary education only, and at a given income level, the manual worker tends to have a larger family than the salaried or business man, where incomes are low. But the manual worker shows a negative income-fertility relationship. The highly-paid manual worker in Sweden tends to have a smaller family than the salaried or businessman with the same income. However these occupational differences, like income differences, seem to be tending to disappear.

Other comparisons (Tables VI.23 and VI.24) between generations were made in the 1947 Census of the Netherlands[1] and the 1950 Census of Norway.[2]

In Ireland religion has a great effect upon fertility. The Census however

[1] De Woolf and Meerdink, *Population*, April 1957.
[2] Jahn, *Population*, January–March 1958.

TABLE VI.23. DIFFERENTIAL TOTAL FERTILITIES IN
NETHERLANDS, 1947

	Proprietors of Businesses	Salaried Workers (not Government)	Manual Workers
Marriages before 1914	4·75	3·12	5·06
Marriages 1924–28	3·37	2·32	3·40

makes a separate tabulation for Catholics (Table VI.25), constituting 94 per cent of the population. Ireland is also known as a country of very late marriages. The tables refer to women aged between 20 and 34 at the time of their marriage. The last column in Table VI.25 shows total fertility for women aged 20–24 at the time of marriage. The difference between this and the preceding column therefore gives an idea of the effects of late marriage, which seems to be most marked among agricultural and other manual workers, and workers on own account.

TABLE VI.24. DIFFERENTIAL TOTAL FERTILITIES IN
NORWAY, 1950
Marriages over 18 years' duration
(women aged 20–29 at marriage)

	Married before 1912	Married 1913–32		Married before 1912	Married 1913–32
Farmers	5·87	4·50	Employers	4·35	3·28
Farmworkers	6·16	4·23	Small businesses	4·95	3·35
Fishermen	6·05	4·58	Salaried working in		
Artisans	5·55	3·67	business	4·43	2·90
Factory workers	5·47	3·32			
Building workers	5·84	3·94	Professions and		
Ships Officers	4·45	2·97	public service:		
Sailors	5·12	3·53	Proprietors and		
			administrators	3·51	3·06
			Salaried workers	4·82	3·39
			Manual workers	5·19	2·99

A considerable general decline took place in the course of 20 years, being most marked among the formerly highest groups, farmers, agricultural workers and workers on own account.

In Japan in the 1950's, the study already referred to concerning income differentials showed total fertility of farmers ranging from 5·0 to 6·3 according to their economic class, and 4·7 for rural non-farm families. An official survey by Okasaki[1] showed, for women marrying at ages 20–24, a total fertility of 5·0 for farmers, 4·4 for small traders and craftsmen, 4·3 for industrial workers and 3·9 for salaried workers.

[1] *Population*, October–December 1953.

TABLE VI.25. CATHOLIC FERTILITIES IN IRELAND, 1946

	Women aged 20–34 at time of marriage		Women aged 20–24 at time of marriage married 1921–26
	Married 1901–06	Married 1921–26	
Farmers and farm managers	6·32	5·07	6·04
Agricultural workers	6·06	4·88	6·15
Higher professional workers	5·04	3·91	4·50
Lower professional workers	5·10	4·48	5·27
Employers and managers	5·39	4·14	4·83
Workers on own account	6·06	4·45	5·54
Salaried workers	5·45	4·40	5·34
Non-manual wage workers	5·15	4·35	5·25
Skilled manual workers	5·89	4·70	5·89
Semi-skilled manual workers	5·94	5·19	6·30
General labourers	5·71	5·16	6·32

More abundant information is now available from the Census.[1] The continuing rapid decline in general fertility has been accompanied by a great reduction in differentials (Table VI.26).

TABLE VI.26. ESTIMATED TOTAL FERTILITIES BY OCCUPATIONS IN JAPAN

	1955	1960
Professional and technical men	2·2	2·2
Managers and officials	1·4	1·7
Clerks	3·4	2·7
Salesmen	2·3	2·1
Farmers and fishermen	4·2	3·0
Miners	3·3	2·3
Transport and communication workers	2·6	2·1
Service workers	2·0	1·8
TOTAL	3·0	2·3

In the course of a study of religious and linguistic differences in fertility in Switzerland, Nixon[2] estimated the specific fertility of married women of standard age structure (i.e. not the full gross reproduction rate) for the period 1947–55 (Table VI.27).

In Brazil, a study (Table VI.28) in differential fertility has been prepared for São Paulo, the most economically advanced province.[3] For any given occupation, fertility was substantially lower in the capital city than in the rest of the state (these figures will be discussed later).

[1] Quoted Kimura, World Population Conference, 1965.
[2] Review of the International Institute of Statistics, 1961.
[3] Revista Brasiliera de Estadística, July–September 1955.

TABLE VI.27. SWITZERLAND, STANDARDIZED NUMBER OF
CHILDREN PER 1,000 PROTESTANT MARRIED WOMEN

Farm Workers	219
Farmers	192
Professions	160
Technicians	140
Clerical Workers	121
Shopkeepers	123
Craftsmen	130
Semi-skilled	126

TABLE VI.28. TOTAL FERTILITIES BY OCCUPATION IN
SÃO PAULO, BRAZIL, OUTSIDE THE CAPITAL CITY, MEN
AGED 50–59

Agriculture	7·62
Mining	6·19
Manufacture	6·16
Commerce	5·70
Defence	5·67
Transport	5·55
Service industries	5·48
Social service	5·47
Public administration	5·42
Finance	4·52
Professions	4·10

In Chile in 1960[1] the difference was very marked. Urban women aged 45–49 showed an average total fertility of 3·08 live births (27 per cent childless), rural women 5·13 (19 per cent childless). The proportions childless are high.

For the Soviet Union, we have one figure for the 1920's, when academic research was still comparatively free, of male reproduction rates in Leningrad in 1926–7.[2] By this date the transition to lower fertilities in the Soviet Union had already begun, certainly in the urban areas. Total fertility for manual workers was found to be 4·67, for salaried workers 2·10, for professional men 1·83, and for proprietors of small businesses, of whom a number were still permitted at that time, 1·42.

In 1958–9[3] married women members of collective farms were found to have a total fertility of 3·42, women wage and salary workers 2·29, and non-farm women able to remain at home 3·27. In Hungary,[4] where general

[1] Goiburu, World Population Conference, 1965.
[2] Novoselskiy, quoted in 'Population Trends in Eastern Europe, U.S.S.R. and China', *Proceedings of the Milbank Memorial Fund Conference*, 1959.
[3] Vostrikova, World Population Conference, 1965.
[4] Klinger, International Union for the Scientific Study of Population, 1961 Conference.

fertility is now well below replacement level, the differential has been reversed. The ratio of agricultural to non-agricultural fertility, which was 1·3–1·4 before 1914, and in the period 1920–39 rose to 1·5–1·6, was 0·9 in 1959.

Within the non-agricultural sector the ratio of the fertility of manual to that of non-manual workers is now below 1·5.

Occupational differences in fertility only seem to become substantial in advanced industrial societies. In Egypt,[1] in rural areas (Table VI.29),

TABLE VI.29. TOTAL MARITAL FERTILITIES, EGYPT, 1960

	Large Cities	Rest of Egypt
Professional	5·17	8·37
Executive and Managerial	6·55	8·63
Clerical and Sales	7·33	7·48
Farming and Fishing	7·39	6·53
Industrial workers	7·39	7·06
Service workers	7·35	7·47

farmers seem indeed to be less fertile than men in other occupations, though a difference is beginning to appear in the large cities. In Morocco,[2] the occupational averages for total fertility in urban areas are all in the 5–6 range.

On educational differentials we have substantially less information. What we have is largely for the United States. Special reports on differential fertility prepared from the 1940 Census showed that, when other variables were controlled, the education of the father might make a 20 per cent difference to fertility; but that the education of the mother might make a difference to almost double the extent.

This difference, like the occupational difference, was rapidly declining during the 1940's, through rising fertility among those who had previously been lowest (and who were constituting an increasing proportion of the whole population).[3]

The 1960 data[4] show (Table VI.30) a further narrowing of the educational differentials among white women; but the differentials among coloured women are about as wide as they had been among white women in 1940. This should give sociologists matter for reflection.

[1] Zikry, World Population Conference, 1965.
[2] Berrada, World Population Conference, 1965.
[3] Tietze and Grabill, Eugenics Quarterly, March 1957.
[4] Estimates by Scripps Foundation for Research in Population Problems, published in Population Bulletin, September 1964.

TABLE VI.30. U.S.A. CHILDREN BORN TO WOMEN MARRIED
ONCE ONLY, ENUMERATED WITH HUSBANDS, MARRIAGE
DURATION 10–14 YEARS (EXPECTED COMPLETED FAMILIES
FOR 1960) CLASSIFIED BY EDUCATION

				1960	
		1940	1950	*White*	*Coloured*
Classified by education of mother					
College	1 or more years	1·63	1·94	3·05	2·4
High School	4 ,, ,, ,,	1·77	2·03	3·0	2·9
	1–3 years	2·11	2·22	3·3	3·7
Primary School	7–8 years	2·42	2·43⎱	3·7	4·7
	less than 7 years	3·11	2·93⎰		

Part of these differential fertilities arose out of later marriage by educated
women; but even after this variable had been eliminated, the differences
remained high. A cross-tabulation[1] in the U.S. Census of 1960 of size of
families according to both husband's and wife's education gave highly
significant regression coefficients, indicating that the average family, when
both husband and wife had received the minimum education was 2·64 for
women aged 45–54 in 1960, and 3·05 for those aged 35–44, less 0·082 for
each extra year of education received by the wife, and 0·042 for each extra
year received by the husband.

The 1955 survey in the United States regarding intentions, already
referred to, showed a further **decline** in this relationship. The younger
wives 'are no longer showing the historical association between low
educational attainment and high fertility'.[2] Notestein[3] found that the total
number of children said to be desired had a negative correlation coefficient
of 0·12 with the wife's education, 0·06 with the husband's. By the 1962
inquiry[4] the differences had practically disappeared.

In Puerto Rico in 1960 differentials were still wide[5] (Table VI.31).

Information is also available (Table VI.32) for Egypt.[6]

Okasaki's study in Japan[7] showed a rather small difference, with women
who had had ten years' education or more about 20 per cent below the
fertility of less educated women, for any given age of marriage.

[1] Dinkel, World Population Conference, 1965. I am grateful to Mr. A. G. Antill for
performing the analysis of variance of the data.
[2] Campbell, Milbank Memorial Fund Conference, 1958.
[3] Internal Statistical Institute Proceedings, 1957.
[4] Freedman and others, *Population Index*, October 1963.
[5] Stycos, World Population Conference, 1965.
[6] Zikry, World Population Conference, 1965.
[7] *Population*, October–December, 1953.

TABLE VI.31. TOTAL FERTILITY BY EDUCATION
(WOMEN OVER 45)

Schooling of Women:	San Juan	Other Urban	Rural
None	6·94	6·45	7·83
Primary 1–4 years	5·96	5·86	7·63
5–6 ,,	5·08	4·94	6·89
7–8 ,,	3·92	4·11	5·27
Secondary 1–3 years	3·03	3·30	4·45
4 ,,	2·39	2·52	2·65
College 1 or more years	1·91	1·94	1·93

TABLE VI.32. TOTAL MARITAL FERTILITIES BY
EDUCATION, EGYPT, 1960

Education of Father:	Large Towns	Rest of Egypt
Illiterate	7·95	7·22
Elementary	6·10	6·55
Primary	5·31	5·94
Secondary	3·34	3·70
College	2·67	2·73

TABLE VI.33. WOMEN'S EDUCATION AND FERTILITY IN
FORMOSA

	Total fertility to age 35–39	Total children said to be desired by wives
No education	5·7	4·4
Primary education incomplete	5·2	4·2
,, ,, complete	5·3	4·2
Secondary education incomplete	4·5	3·6
,, ,, complete	3·6	3·3

A slightly wider range was found in Formosa[1] (Table VI.33).
For mainland China in the 1930's[2] there were however signs of positive association between education and size of family (Table VI.34). The figures had been standardized to the normal Chinese age composition of the married female population; but it was necessary to use figures of survivors rather than of total children born. Infant mortality was probably much

[1] Freedman and others, *American Journal of Sociology*, July 1964.
[2] Ta Chen, *American Journal of Sociology*, July 1946.

greater among the poorer and less educated groups, and a comparison of total fertilities measured by the number of children born might have shown less difference.

It has been supposed that Indian data show that there is an association between age at marriage and the interval between births. This interval however has been found[1] in fact to be correlated with education, among Bengal Hindu families holding life insurance, better educated and wealthier than the average. Judging from Sovani's results, this factor may however be of little importance among the population as a whole.

For Sweden, the data were classified by the education of the husband, not of the wife. For a given income and duration of marriage, education was found to be negatively associated with fertility for most groups. Among professional men and civil servants, the association had become zero in the middle income range, and positive in the higher income ranges. Among the highest-income businessmen, a slight positive relationship was found in the special Census of 1935 for recent marriages, but a negative relationship for pre-1911 marriages.

Differing ages at marriage probably played an important part here. A pioneering study which first drew attention to the change which was taking place[2] of the live births in the first ten years of marriage of couples married in 1917–20, and both still living in Stockholm in 1930, tabulating number of children according to education, with both family income and age of wife at marriage controlled by cross-classification, showed that, for a given duration and age at marriage, fertility was nearly always *positively* associated with education. In reply to general criticism made at the time, Hutchinson pointed out that these conclusions were not affected by illegitimacy rates varying between the different educational groups.

TABLE VI.34. SURVIVING CHILDREN (STANDARDIZED FOR WIVES' AGES), CLASSIFIED BY HUSBAND'S EDUCATION, CHINA

	Percentage of population	Average Family
Illiterate	54·0	1·57
Privately schooled	11·6	1·80
Public Primary schools	25·9	1·68
Public Middle schools	5·4	1·75
Teachers' Training College	0·8	1·77
Professional and Technical Education	0·4	1·96
University Education	1·5	1·79

[1] Nag, International Statistical Institute, Delhi Session, 1951.
[2] Edin and Hutchinson, *Stockholm Economic Studies No. 4*, quoted by Hutchinson, *Milbank Memorial Quarterly*, July 1936.

Another Swedish study[1] of three cohorts of men, born about 1890, about 1900 and about 1910 respectively, distinguished those who were and were not educated up to university entrance standard (which is very high in Sweden). Sweden has long been a comparatively late-marrying country, and the pattern did not significantly change over this period for the country in general. The highly educated men undoubtedly married much later than the average. Thus throughout the period only 2 per cent of them were married at the age of 24, as against 14 per cent of Swedish men in general. The differences progressively disappeared with age. The educated men had caught up with the national average proportion married only at the age of 35 in the generation born about 1890, at the age of 30 for the generation born about 1910. This, however, represented a postponement rather than a prevention of reproduction. In the end, the total fertilities of the educated and uneducated proved to be practically the same (about 10 per cent below replacement rate) for the generation born about 1890; slightly higher for the educated, in the generation born about 1900; and high again for the educated in the next generation.

We now turn our attention to urban/rural differences, so far as these can be isolated from the effects of occupation, income, education, etc.

English writers in the seventeenth century had an idea that the larger towns were not only failing to contribute to the national increase of population, but might actually be reducing it. If Graunt's pioneer life table had been true (things were not quite as bad as that) London would have been suffering a large natural decrease, and would only have been able to maintain itself by high immigration from rural areas. Gregory King, like other writers, was concerned that population was failing to increase, in fact might actually be decreasing, with the recurring wars of the 1690's, and with the rate of emigration to America already substantial. It was he who first pointed out that, besides differential mortality, the offspring born to each marriage in London were below the national average, which he attributed to five factors (1) from the more frequent fornications and adulteries (2) from a greater luxury and intemperance (3) from a greater intentness to business (4) from the unhealthfulness of the coal smoke (5) from a greater inequality of age between the husbands and wives.

The outstanding fact seems to have been the extremely high infant mortality in cities, much above that of rural areas, due mainly to infectious diseases for which our ancestors had little or no treatment, whose spread was facilitated by lack of hygiene and extreme overcrowding. As late as the mid-nineteenth century in Britain infant mortality, i.e. deaths in the first year of life as a proportion of births, stood at about 20 per cent for the

[1] Moberg, *Population Studies*, June 1950.

urban population, and less than 10 for the rural population. The longest series of accurate records appear to be those for Stockholm, which show a figure as high as 35 per cent mortality in the first year of life for the first decade of the nineteenth century, and still at 32 per cent in the 1850's. Rural mortality was also high in Sweden, but only about half the Stockholm figures.

A valuable review of early data of urban/rural differences in fertility is given by Jaffé.[1] His method was to count the number of children under five recorded by the Census in comparison with the number of women of reproductive age. Where urban infant mortality was very much higher than rural however this may gravely bias the results. Thus for Stockholm in 1760 the relative fertility was only 47 per cent of that of the rest of Sweden if ascertained by the 'surviving children under five' method; but in this case information is also available which suffices to calculate true total fertilities (gross reproduction rates), on which calculation the Stockholm figure appeared at 91 per cent of that of the rest of Sweden.

As with the occupational, income and education differentials, the rural/urban differential appears to have been something which had been absent in the eighteenth and developed during the nineteenth century, judging by the Swedish figures, the only ones available continuously over this period (Table VI.35).

TABLE VI.35.   TOTAL FERTILITY IN STOCKHOLM AS PERCENTAGE
OF THAT OF REST OF SWEDEN

1760	91	1880	72
1820	76	1890	73
1840	70	1900	65
1850	74	1910	67
1860	73	1920	55
1870	81	1930	50

That this differential might develop comparatively late was also expected by Charles.[2] 'The manufacturing city passes through several stages. The early phase, characterized by extreme congestion, squalor and low wages, and exemplified by the Scottish Clyde and Trois Rivières (in Canada) may show families nearly as large as in surrounding rural parts. It is not until standards of living rise and professional and commercial occupations become more numerous that the characteristic small urban family pattern appears.'

However, she may have oversimplified the problem. In the cases which she mentions, religious differences may also have played a part.

[1] *American Journal of Sociology*, July 1942.
[2] *Trends in Canadian Family Size*, Census of Canada, 1941.

The large bias introduced into the figures by differential infant mortality can only be allowed for in the very broadest manner. Most of Jaffé's figures for low-income countries suggest that the urban-rural differences ascertained by the 'number of children under five' method are probably no more, indeed may be less, than would be expected from this bias. We may however draw some conclusions from his figures for more advanced countries, where infant mortality is comparatively low, and therefore less capable of biasing the results. In London since 1851 differential fertility, in comparison with the rest of England and Wales, appears to have been only 10–20 per cent lower. In the United States, however, the difference is much greater, perhaps due to the high proportion of first generation ex-farm families in the city, whose significant effect upon the urban totals was recently discovered by Freedman (see above). Throughout the period from 1800 to 1940 Jaffé found a differential generally exceeding 40 per cent; so did Kingsley Davis,[1] the differential not apparently varying with the size of city.

We may now review more modern information about rural/urban differentials in low income countries. There appears to be no significant differential in Egypt.[2] Kiser also analysed the Egyptian census of 1937, and found that the *net* reproduction rate was 1·39 in Cairo and Alexandria, as against 1·44 for the whole of Egypt. Zikry[3] found total marital fertility of Moslems in 1960 to be 6·67 in large cities and 6·46 in the rest of Egypt, the urban total however being brought down by the significantly lower figure for the Coptic Christian minority (who are largely engaged in commerce and the professions) — 4·09 urban and 6·12 rural.

For Africa, where the results, if they existed, would be of the greatest interest, demographic studies are still almost entirely lacking. The French sample study in Guinea[4] shows a most interesting pattern for Conakry, the principal city (Table VI.36). On the face of it, it appears that the older inhabitants may have preserved a previous fertility pattern, which changed rapidly with the increasing proportion of men in commercial and administrative occupations. It may perhaps be changing again for the younger generation.

In Latin America,[5] using the 'children under five' method, differentials have been found much larger than can be explained by differences in infant mortality. About 1940, fertility in the cities with population over 100,000

[1] *Milbank Memorial Quarterly*, July 1944.
[2] El Badry, *Milbank Memorial Quarterly*, June 1956.
[3] World Population Conference, 1965.
[4] *Population*, July–September, 1956.
[5] Casis and Davis, *Milbank Memorial Quarterly*, July 1946, and Lynn Smith, *Population Studies*, July 1958.

TABLE VI.36. FERTILITY IN CONAKRY AS PERCENTAGE
OF RURAL GUINEA

Age	
15–19	74
20–24	81
25–29	63
30–34	48
35–39	61
40–44	130

was only about 40 per cent of the rural (30 per cent in Cuba); and in most cases the figures showed an orderly descent with ascending size of city. A substantial part of this is however explainable in terms of a phenomenon which one would have thought was to be found only in the capital cities of the advanced countries, namely a surplus of females over males. By the 1940's the cities over 100,000 population in Latin America had attracted a surplus female population of the order of 25 per cent over the male. However, the more recent studies show that the urban/rural differentials were apparently greatly reduced by 1950.

The studies for the São Paulo province of Brazil (already quoted) were particularly valuable because they were standardized by age (offspring of men aged 50–59) and cross-classified by occupation. For a given occupation, the fertility differential between the capital city (the largest industrial city in Brazil) and the rest of the province was about 30 per cent for non-manual and about 22 per cent for manual occupations. The Brazilian Census for 1950 showed that, over the age range 20–39, there was a female surplus of 13 per cent in the cities, and a female deficiency of 2 per cent in the rural areas. (However it appears that there was in Brazil, as elsewhere, a certain amount of understatement of age by women in their forties, and the supposed 13 per cent figure for the surplus in the 20's and 30's may be too high; but the urban/rural difference probably really did exist.)

Asia does not show large differentials. The Census of Ceylon of 1946 (results not standardized for age, but this does not matter very much where all women marry young) showed that the average married woman or widow had 4·4 children in rural areas, 3·8 in urban. About half of this difference was explained by differential mortality; rural infant mortality being above urban, the surviving children were 3·2 and 2·9 respectively.

While most of the analysis of the Census of 1941 in India had to be abandoned because of war-time needs, Kashmir, at that time a 'Princely State', published an excellent State Report, analysing fertility by age of married women and religion for Jammu City and for the remainder of

Jammu Province. Here the Hindus, who were somewhat in the majority over the Moslems, showed a total fertility of about 5, and only a 5 per cent urban/rural differential. Moslems showed a total fertility of 3·1, with the urban fertility 22 per cent above the rural. The Census of India of 1951 measured total fertilities in some specimen areas, which were found to be of the order of 6 (very similar to those of 1931); and they showed no serious rural/urban difference.

Bengal Hindu families holding life insurance, i.e. much wealthier and better educated than the average,[1] with a generally lower total fertility, i.e. only 5·2, in an analysis confined to married women whose husbands were still living (and therefore with fertility above the general average) showed only a 3 per cent rural/urban differential.

In Japan the differences (Table VI.37) are moderate.[2] Here, as in Ceylon, the improvement in health services has made urban infant mortality lower

TABLE VI.37. URBAN-RURAL DIFFERENCES IN JAPAN

	1920	1925	1930	1935	1940
Gross reproduction rates:					
Tokyo	1·93	1·85	1·57	1·70	1·57
Other 5 largest cities	2·07	2·03	1·84	1·74	1·66
Other cities over 100,000	2·28	2·12	1·92	1·81	—
Cities 50–100,000	2·19	2·09	1·93	1·81	—
Cities under 50,000	2·09	2·14	1·86	1·84	—
All urban	2·07	2·02	1·82	1·75	—
Rural	2·86	2·76	2·56	2·49	—
Net reproduction rates:					
Urban	1·2	1·3	1·2	1·2	1·0
Rural	1·8	1·9	1·8	1·9	1·5

than rural; and so the differences of net reproduction rate are a little less than those of gross reproduction rate.

The decline was remarkably uniform. By 1950 the difference had narrowed further.[3] Total fertility was 3·86 in the metropolitan area, 4·35 in other industrial cities, 4·56 in 'transitional' and 4·93 in agricultural areas. An exception must be made for Hokkaido, the remotest part of the country, and one in which agricultural settlement is still proceeding, where the figure stood at 5·77 (perhaps Japan's only 'open space' is attractive to fathers of large families).

A more detailed study[4] also reports the number of children 'considered

[1] Nag, International Statistical Institute, Delhi Session, 1951.
[2] Taeuber and Beal, *Milbank Memorial Quarterly*, July 1944; Taeuber and Notestein, *Population Studies*, 1947, and *Milbank Memorial Quarterly*, January 1947.
[3] Taeuber, *Milbank Memorial Quarterly*, April 1956.
[4] Population Problems Research Council (Mainichi Shimbun, publishers), Bulletins No. 2 and No. 6.

TABLE VI.38. ACTUAL AND DESIRED FAMILY SIZES IN
JAPAN

District	Characteristics of sampled area	Families of women aged 45–60		
		Total born	Survivors	'Considered ideal'
Iwato	Mountain village (with some feudal tenures surviving)	6·1	4·6	4·6
Yamagata	Single crop rice culture	5·4	4·0	3·6
Shikoku	Double crop rice culture	5·1	3·9	3·3
Aichi	Near factory town	4·7	3·8	3·3

ideal' in certain areas (Table VI.38). In any given village, the rural non-farm desired fertility is generally about 20 per cent below that of farm families.

In Korea in 1935,[1] with a total fertility of 7, that of Seoul was about 30 per cent lower than the national average. Net reproduction rate was lower in about the same proportion, indicating no significant differences of infant mortality between town and country.

The Philippines in 1952[2] showed a total fertility of 7·2 per married woman (the figure for all women would have been somewhat lower) in rural areas, with urban fertility 25 per cent lower.

The nature of the decreasing differentiation is shown in a most interesting manner by the maps (Diagram VI.A) prepared by Roberts for Jamaica, a country where incomes have now risen substantially above those of subsistence agriculture. The area of somewhat reduced fertility (though still generally high) can be seen spreading outwards from the capital city. This phenomenon was associated with education. In the 1943 census, Kingston was found to be 89 per cent literate, the parishes within 25 miles averaged 70 per cent literacy, and the remainder of the country 62 per cent.

Turning now to Europe, it appears that some urban/rural differential may be of very ancient origin. The English Poll tax records of 1377[3] show that there was a female surplus of about 5 per cent in the towns, where only about 60 per cent of the population over 14 was married, as against 70 per cent in the rural areas. Modern Europe shows some very large differences, particularly in countries in the early stages of industrialization. Thus Spain in 1930[4] shows gross reproduction rates of only 1·06 in

[1] *Population Index*, October 1944.
[2] Hawley, *American Sociological Review*, January 1955.
[3] Russell, *English Mediaeval Population*.
[4] Almansa and Jimeno, quoted by Glass, *Eugenics Review*, July 1945.

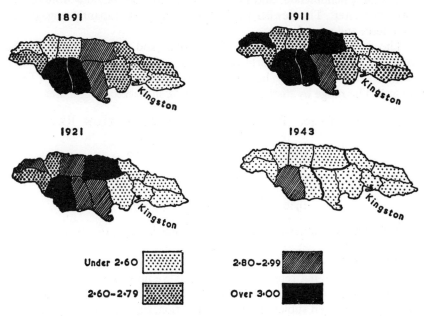

JOINT GROSS REPRODUCTION RATES BY PARISH, JAMAICA 1891-1943

1891   1911

1921   1943

Under 2·60

2·60-2·79

2·80-2·99

Over 3·00

Note: the heavy line in 1943 separates the island into regions of comparatively high and comparatively low fertility

DIAGRAM VI.A

Catalonia, 1·35 in the Valencia–Murcia area and 1·60 in the industrial Biscay coast, as against 2·09 in Andalusia and Estremadura, and 2·25 in the Meseta of Central Spain. These were partially offset by mortality differences; net reproduction rate was 20 per cent below gross in Catalonia but 30 per cent lower in the high fertility areas. Analysing the full provincial data, it was found that gross reproduction rate showed a correlation of 0·52 with the percentage of population dependent upon agriculture. Equally wide differences were found in Poland[1] (Table VI.39).

TABLE VI.39. POLISH NET REPRODUCTION RATES, 1927–30

	Jews	Christians
Rural	1·3	1·6
Towns under 20,000	1·1	1·2
,, 20–150,000	0·9	0·9
,, over 150,000	0·8	0·6
TOTAL	1·0	1·4

[1] Carpentier, *Population*, January–April 1949.

The different behaviour of the Jewish population should be considered as a social phenomenon, and not classified with the religious differentials discussed later. The Jewish population were predominantly engaged in commerce and manufacture.

The very large difference between urban and rural fertilities in the 1930's was reduced in the early 1950's by a slight fall in rural fertility and a rise in urban.[1] Recently however it has begun to widen again (Table VI.40). The range by districts was from 5·64 in Szczecin rural area (taken

TABLE VI.40. POLISH GROSS REPRODUCTION RATES

	Urban	Rural
1931–2	1·05	2·00
1950	1·56	1·95
1955	1·55	1·94
1958	1·38	1·87
1960	1·19	1·74

from Germany and newly settled by the Poles) in 1950, to 1·64 for Warsaw in 1960.

It was in European cities in the 1930's that differences were greatest. Measurement by net reproduction rates, as we now know, is treacherous; and the figures can be unduly affected by deferment or acceleration of marriage. But even subject to this qualification, figures for European cities (Table VI.41) in the early 1930's were exceptionally low.[2]

TABLE VI.41. NET REPRODUCTION RATES IN THE EARLY 1930'S

Vienna	0·25
Berlin	0·37
Hamburg	0·48
Copenhagen	0·61
Oslo	0·36
Stockholm	0·40
Riga	0·47
Paris	0·63
London	0·68

Kirk also found that Moscow and Leningrad were then not replacing themselves, and that births in Prague, Budapest, Belgrade and Warsaw were 'far below replacement level'. Carr-Saunders writing in 1933[3] also

---

[1] Rosset, *Studies in Fertility and Social Mobility*, Akademie Kiadö, Budapest, 1964, and Vielrose, World Population Conference, 1965.

[2] Kirk, *Europe's Population in the Interwar Years*. Landry (*Traité de Démographie*) gives a gross reproduction rate of 0·40 for Geneva in 1933 and only 0·57 for Paris in 1936.

[3] *World Population, Past Growth and Present Trends*.

pointed out that the net reproduction rate in Moscow had fallen below replacement level by 1929, and added 'It is almost certain that fertility will fall heavily in Russia, and it may fall with very great rapidity'. The Soviet census of 1939 showed that the ratio of children aged 0 to 3 per woman aged 20–39, which for Soviet Russia as a whole had stood at 0·80 both in 1926 and in 1939, in the latter year was 0·91 for rural areas and only 0·48 for urban. The crude birth rates for the leading urban areas for 1938 are available, and average 29 per thousand.

In France, after a long period of restricted fertility, some interesting geographical differences have appeared; but they are regional differences rather than simple urban-rural differences[1] (Diagrams VI.B, VI.C, VI.D). In France, we see that, apart from Paris, the areas of low fertility, even in the nineteenth century, were not the industrial and urban areas, but the

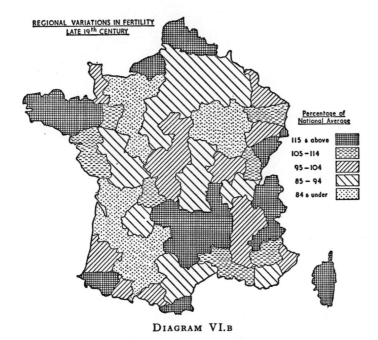

REGIONAL VARIATIONS IN FERTILITY
LATE 19th CENTURY

Percentage of
National Average

115 & above
105 – 114
95 – 104
85 – 94
84 & under

DIAGRAM VI.B

rural south-west. There were, in the nineteenth century, other rural areas of low fertility, which are now of comparatively high fertility, as they have become industrialized; the industrial north-east is a now comparatively high fertility area. In the nineteenth-century map, we can to some extent

[1] Chasteland and Henry, *Population*, October–December 1956.

see Dumont's theories in operation, with high fertility in Brittany, in the Basque-speaking areas along the Pyrenees, in the partially Italian-speaking areas in Savoy, as well as in the remote mountain regions in south-central France. Some of these now, however, have become low fertility areas. In France, the urban-rural differential has almost disappeared, in spite of the fact that one of the factors which is supposed to cause this differential is operating strongly in France, as in other urbanized countries, namely a disparity between the sexes, arising out of the tendency of males to remain in the rural areas, and an excess of females to arise in the larger towns. This

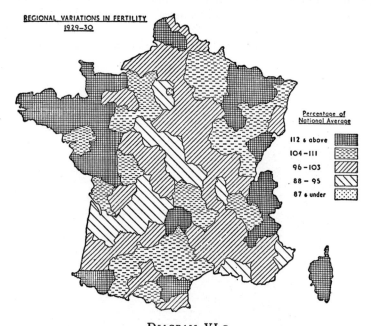

DIAGRAM VI.c

results in a much lower proportion of women at any given age being married in the large cities than in the country — though the hope of good matrimonial prospects was often what brought the young women to the cities (Table VI.42).

In a comparison of fertility between large towns in 1946,[1] the highest was found in the industrial town of Roubaix in the north-east, closely followed by Le Havre, Reims, Rouen and Lille. Fertility in Paris and Nice was only about two-thirds of this. For Germany, on the other hand,

[1] *Statistique Générale*, October–December 1950.

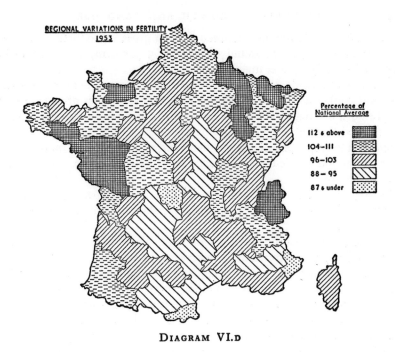

Percentage of
National Average

112 & above
104–111
96–103
88–95
87 & under

DIAGRAM VI.D

fertility in the larger towns is substantially below that of the rural areas, as we have already seen from Table VI.8 (with the income variable controlled). Tabulation with a larger number of town size groups shows a perfectly regular gradation. But the German census figures show that the urban/rural difference, which was only about 20 per cent (towns over 100,000 population compared with villages below 2000) for marriages of the late nineteenth century, enlarged rapidly up to marriages of the early 1920's, since which date there has been a gradual reduction of the difference.

TABLE VI.42.   MALE/FEMALE RATIO IN FRANCE 1946

	Male/Female ratio			% Women Married		
Age	France	Rural areas	Towns over 100,000 population	France	Rural areas	Towns over 100,000 population
15–19	0·982	1·063	0·881	5·5	5·6	5·2
20–24	0·911	0·963	0·850	41·5	41·7	38·0
25–29	0·973	1·043	0·880	69·3	71·2	64·1
30–34	0·969	1·025	0·896	79·1	81·7	73·5
35–39	0·988	1·066	0·890	80·3	83·1	74·7
40–44	0·996	1·075	0·893	78·6	81·6	72·8

In Ireland[1] the difference between Dublin gross reproduction rate and the national average was found to be only 5 per cent, which could be explained entirely by later marriage.

In the Netherlands on the other hand[2] the difference between Amsterdam and Netherlands as a whole was wider for marriages of 1924–8 than for pre-1914 marriages. This interesting study distinguished social groups, and showed that the urban-rural differences were least for office workers, as opposed to employers on the one hand and manual workers on the other. Over the period studied the difference was found to widen, however, for all three groups.

Norwegian data,[3] controlled for varying age of marriage by being confined to women married at ages 24–25, showed a difference between rural areas and Oslo of only 9 per cent for marriages of 1880, widening rapidly to 46 per cent for marriages of 1925. There were only slight signs of reduction of this difference for marriages of 1930.

From a regional study of England and Wales in the 1930's,[4] it was possible to make analyses by a method more refined than simple gross reproduction rates, taking into account the varying ages at marriage (Table VI.43). Some factors believed to be associated with relatively high or relatively low regional productivity are also tabulated. By 1951, however, there had been a great reduction in these regional differences. The Registrar General's report shows Greater London at 85 per cent of the national average, with the highest fertilities in Merseyside and the northern region (Northumberland and Durham), 18 and 14 per cent respectively above national average. Apart from these, all the regions were within the range 98 to 106.

Early data from the United States[5] show that both in 1800 and in 1870 agricultural fertility was about one-third higher than industrial. The data from the census of 1900[6] show about this difference between Chicago and adjacent rural areas, though the ratio was larger for manual workers than for professional and business men. By 1930, in the East North Central states,[7] if we compare cities over 250,000 population with the rural non-farm population (farm families have a higher fertility than their non-farm rural neighbours), we find rural fertility 33 per cent higher for native-born whites, 22 per cent higher for foreign-born whites, and 42 per cent higher for Negroes. These differences should be the subject of further sociological research.

[1] Geary, *Journal of the Statistical and Social Enquiry Society of Ireland*, 1941.
[2] De Woolf and Meerdink, *Population*, April 1947.
[3] Jahn, *Population*, January–March 1958.   [4] Clark, *Population Studies*, March 1949.
[5] Taeuber and Miller, World Population Conference, 1954.
[6] Kiser, *Journal of the American Statistical Association*, December 1932.
[7] Notestein, *Milbank Memorial Quarterly*, April 1938.

TABLE VI.43. REGIONAL FERTILITIES IN ENGLAND AND WALES, 1939

| | Net Reproductivity | | Percentage excess of female over male population (ages 20–39) | Percentage occupied among females 14 and over | Percentage occupied males engaged in agriculture |
	At Northumberland and Durham age of marriage	Lost by later marriage			
Greater London	0·642	0·081	17·0	38·8	1·1
Rest of South-East	0·702	0·072	8·8	30·2	11·7
Northumberland and Durham	0·800	—	5·8	24·1	4·1
Northern rural	0·768	0·053	3·0	27·5	16·2
West Riding	0·705	0·023	11·3	35·3	3·8
Lancashire and Cheshire	0·759	0·128	14·0	41·9	3·8
West Midlands	0·792	0·056	8·9	36·0	7·7
East Midlands	0·713	0·009	7·5	35·0	7·3
East	0·729	0·037	2·8	26·3	29·3
South-West	0·662	0·055	7·5	27·6	19·2
South Wales	0·745	0·002 (increase)	3·0	19·5	5·7
Rest of Wales	0·808	0·118	1·9	24·9	26·7

Many of these differences, however, disappear when we control the tabulation for income,[1] though for a full analysis other variables also, particularly the proportion of ex-farm families, should be taken into account. At a given income level, the ratios between large and small towns are substantially reduced.

Rural residence is still a factor, it was concluded from the 1955 study of family intentions,[2] though its significance is declining. The Puerto Rican urban-rural differences cross-classified by education quoted above (Table VI.31) are of considerable interest. The rural/urban difference is greatest in the middle ranges of education, less for the uneducated, with no difference for the college-educated.

Some interesting analyses were made by Charles in the 1941 Census of Canada.[3] To test the hypothesis that there was a differential attraction of the physiologically infecundible to the cities, she tabulated the proportions of women marrying at various ages who were apparently permanently childless in rural areas and in small and large towns. No significant differences were found. As with the United States data, she concluded that the urban-rural differences arose mostly among cultural groups of high fertility, and were slight among cultural groups where fertility was already low. After standardizing for all cultural differences, she obtained family sizes shown in Table VI.44.

TABLE VI.44. RURAL-URBAN FAMILY SIZE DIFFERENCES IN CANADA, 1941

	Rural	Urban
Maritime Provinces	4·9	3·7
Prairie Provinces	4·8	3·1
Quebec	4·6	3·0
Ontario	4·2	3·0
British Columbia	3·6	2·5

Relative differences were least in the Maritime Provinces, where 'smaller primary cultural differences at a high level of fertility are associated with lower money incomes and the absence of a metropolitan city. Though Halifax and St. John are large cities, they are rather different from the streamlined cities of the west, and perhaps less effective as centres of ostentatious expenditure'. She made a special study of the smallest and most isolated of the Maritime Provinces, Prince Edward Island, which at that time had the distinction of being the only white community in the world whose fertility had not fallen appreciably over the past fifty years;

---

[1] Karpinos and Kiser, *Milbank Memorial Quarterly*, October 1939.
[2] Campbell, *Milbank Memorial Quarterly*, Annual Conference, 1958.
[3] Charles, *Trends in Canadian Family Size*.

and sought to find the attributes which had brought this about. Apart from 44 per cent of the population being Catholic, of Scottish, Irish and French descent, unemployment was much lower than in the rest of Canada, there were no large differences of income, and subsistence was comparatively easy — 'there were few families without a cow and chickens . . . abundant fish and wild fruit'. Families made extensive use of child labour, and school attendance was comparatively poor; but university attendance was above the Canadian average.

Finally we turn to examine the effect of religion on fertility. Like the other factors, this also shows considerable inter-correlation with the other variables, and so it is desirable to have cross-tabulations with the other variables controlled. International comparisons clearly do not help here, because so many other variables also are involved in them. We can only use data where followers of different religions are living side by side in one country under fairly similar conditions. This consideration alone greatly limits the amount of possible information.

TABLE VI.45. RELIGIOUS DIFFERENTIALS OF CHILDREN
AGED 0–4 PER WOMAN AGED 15–39, INDIA, 1911–13

Parsi	0·388
Jain	0·624
Hindu	0·678
Buddhist	0·698
Christian	0·741
Moslem	0·770
Tribal	0·808
Sikh	0·841
All India	0·705

For India, a general review of census information[1] shows that religious differences are not great (Table VI.45) except for the Parsis, sometimes called 'the Jews of Asia' (though this simile is only applicable to those countries in which the Jews form a small, highly educated, and wealthy minority, as the Parsis do in India). The entry 'tribal' refers to certain primitive non-Hindu communities surviving in some of the remoter mountain districts of India. The Sikhs are a religious minority, but a powerful and aggressive one, considering themselves Hindus, but incorporating in their faith what appear to be Moslem characteristics.

The 1934–5 inquiry in the Punjab already referred to gave a religious classification (Table VI.46). The data had been standardized for age at marriage and duration of marriage, although the samples were small.

[1] Kingsley Davis, *American Journal of Sociology*, November 1946.

TABLE VI.46. AVERAGE SIZES OF FAMILY BY RELIGION AND CASTE IN INDIA

| | Punjab 1934-5 | | Mysore 1941 | Travancore 1941 | | Bengal 1941 | Lucknow and Kanpur 1951 | Banares Tehsil (rural) 1956 |
	Farmers	Non Farmers		Urban	Rural			
Hindus:								
Brahmins			6·4	5·7	6·3	6·0		5·9
Intermediate castes						5·8		7·3
Low and outcastes			7·2			5·6	5·5	7·0
All Hindus	4·8	4·9						
Moslems	5·1	5·0	7·1	6·0	7·2	6·4	6·1	7·4
Sikhs	5·0	4·9						
Christians	6·0	5·7		7·1	7·1		4·5	

Apparently there were no significant differences between Hindus, Moslems and Sikhs, but considerably higher fertility among the small Christian minority.

The columns may be read only vertically and not horizontally, because the durations of marriage, etc., were differently defined in different cases.[1]

A number of sociological theorists, following Dumont, have expected that religious minorities would show higher fertility than those around them. The evidence for higher fertility of the Moslem and Christian minorities in India however is slight and uncertain. Evidence already quoted for Egypt shows the fertility of Moslems to be substantially higher than that of Christians, particularly in the cities.

It has been said that political differences in France are essentially concerned with religion. Sauvy[2] boldly takes two groups of political parties whom he regards as essentially supported by the religious and irreligious respectively, and measures the relative numbers of votes which they obtained in the elections of the 1930's. There is no doubt that the religio-political differences between the Départements were deep — in many Départements the voting was more than 2:1 in favour of one group of

[1] *Punjab*, Jain, Punjab Board of Economic Enquiry, Publication No. 64, 1939. Refers to husbands married between the ages of 15 and 25 and wives married between 12 and 20, average of all marriages of duration of over 10 years.

Mysore, State Census: total fertility of married women aged 45, childless women excluded.

Travancore, State Census: the total fertility of all women.

West Bengal, a sample of 1941 Census, returns extracted by Indian Statistical Institute, Delhi Conference, 1951. Numbers in the sample inadequate for higher ages in some groups, and figures for lower ages therefore extrapolated on basis of the largest group ('intermediate castes'). Data refer to total fertility per married woman. The sample headings which have been equated to the first three lines of the table, were, 'literate Hindus', 'illiterate Caste Hindus', and 'Scheduled Caste Hindus'.

Lucknow and Kanpur, Sinha, International Statistical Institute Conference, 1951. Refers to all marriages of 11–20 years duration for wives aged 16–18 at time of marriage.

Banares Tehsil, Rele, *Milbank Memorial Quarterly*, April 1963. Brahmins included Kshatryas, the next highest caste.

[2] *Richesse et Population*.

parties or the other. The religio-political map (Diagram VI.E) which Sauvy prepared certainly bears some interesting resemblances to the comparative fertility map. Still more striking is the fact that these political differences apparently persisted largely unchanged (Diagram VI.F) in the 1965 Presidential Elections (Williams, *The Guardian* 25 Dec. 1965).

In Germany some very thorough studies of religious differentials of fertility have been made[1] (Table VI.47).

Even for marriages of the late nineteenth century, the Catholic/Protestant difference was on the average less than 20 per cent, and was more marked among farmers than among industrial workers. The difference everywhere seemed to reach a maximum with the generation married in the early 1920's (it was also in this generation that urban/rural differences were most pronounced). Since then the difference has rapidly declined, and in the larger towns has disappeared.

In Ireland on the other hand the Census of 1946 shows that the religious difference is comparatively low — of the order of one-third — among farmers and agricultural workers, but may reach 100 per cent or more (Catholic fertility double Protestant) in some of the urban occupations. (These results had been standardized for duration of marriage and age of

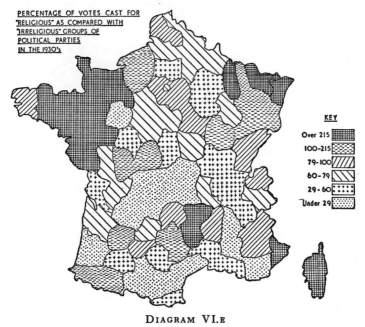

PERCENTAGE OF VOTES CAST FOR
"RELIGIOUS" AS COMPARED WITH
"IRRELIGIOUS" GROUPS OF
POLITICAL PARTIES
IN THE 1930's

KEY
Over 215
100-215
79-100
60-79
29-60
Under 29

DIAGRAM VI.E

[1] *Wirtschaft und Statistik*, 1943, pp. 117–31; and Census of 1950.

wife at marriage.) This quite different situation arises out of a Catholic fertility which is fairly uniformly high (though with a maximum for farmers, agricultural workers and the unskilled, and a minimum for professional men and managers) comparing with Protestant fertilities varying over a much wider range, but again at their highest among farmers and agricultural workers.

In the Netherlands the situation is complicated by the existence of a strict Calvinist Church and a 'Reformed' Protestant Church[1] (Table VI.48).

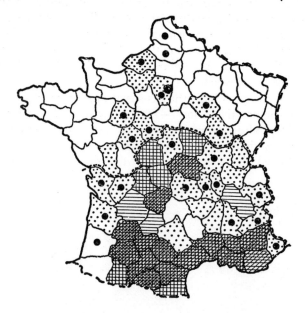

THE FRANCE THAT REJECTED DE GAULLE ·

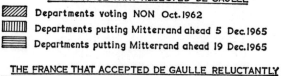

Departments voting NON Oct.1962

Departments putting Mitterrand ahead 5 Dec.1965

Departments putting Mitterrand ahead 19 Dec.1965

THE FRANCE THAT ACCEPTED DE GAULLE RELUCTANTLY

Departments giving him less than 43·7% 5 Dec.1965

Departments giving him less than 54·5% 19 Dec.1965

THE FRANCE THAT REMAINED LOYAL TO DE GAULLE

Departments giving him more than his national share of the votes in both rounds

DIAGRAM VI.F

[1] De Wolff and Meerdink, *Population*, April 1957.

TABLE VI.47. AVERAGE GERMAN PROTESTANT FAMILY AND PERCENTAGE EXCESS OF CATHOLIC OVER PROTESTANT (BRACKETED)

Sample areas -- total fertilities

	Black Forest		Upper Rhine	
Date of Marriage	Farmers	Industrial Workers	Farmers	Industrial Workers
1880–1900	5·96 (21)	5·30 (15)	4·55 (22)	5·02 (15)
1900–1918	4·64 (26)	3·75 (13)	3·59 (20)	3·52 (6)
1919–23	3·16 (29)	2·14 (19)	2·30 (25)	2·37 (13)

ALL W. GERMANY (FERTILITY OF RECENT MARRIAGES INCOMPLETE) IN 1950

	Rural Communes	Towns	Towns
Date of Marriage	(below 2,000 population)	2–100,000 population	over 100,000 population
1920 and earlier	2·92 (29)	2·49 (24)	2·12 (15)
1921–24	2·44 (29)	2·06 (26)	1·59 (19)
1925–28	2·45 (24)	2·10 (18)	1·75 (0)
1929–32	2·48 (17)	2·10 (12)	1·82 (4)
1933–36	2·27 (17)	2·00 (10)	1·69 (3)
1937–40	1·93 (9)	1·70 (5)	1·46 (0)

Fertility among Catholics and strict Calvinists appears very similar. In the generation married in the 1920's the differences were wider than the generation married before 1914. The ingenious method of analysis used indicates that in the Netherlands, unlike Germany, these differences still appear to be wide.

In Switzerland we find Protestant and Catholic populations side by side

TABLE VI.48. RELIGIOUS DIFFERENTIALS IN AMSTERDAM. AVERAGE DURATION IN YEARS FROM MARRIAGE TO BIRTH OF SPECIFIED CHILD

		Catholics	Calvinists	Reformed Church	No Religion
Manual workers	First child	1·9	1·8	2·2	2·1
	Second child	4·4	4·5	4·9	5·1
	Third child	6·2	—	6·8	6·9
Lower salaried workers	First child	2·0	2·8	2·2	2·5
	Second child	4·9	4·1	5·0	5·1
	Third child	5·8	—	6·7	6·7

TABLE VI.49. RELIGIOUS DIFFERENTIALS IN LEGITIMATE
CHILDREN PER MARRIED WOMAN 15-45, SWITZERLAND, 1930

Percentage of Population in Agriculture	Predominantly Catholic Districts	Predominantly Protestant Districts
Over 60	2·90	1·86
40–45	2·84	1·77
20–39	2·14	1·52
Under 20	1·51	1·08
All Areas	1·85	1·30
Do. 1900	2·25	2·23

under fairly similar conditions. The Census of 1930 did not lend itself to demographic analysis of fertility or religion; but it is possible to isolate (Table VI.49) predominantly Catholic and predominantly Protestant districts.[1]

Here the religious difference seems to have developed since 1900 and to be widespread everywhere, but most marked in the predominantly agricultural districts.

A very thorough study was made of marriages and births in Switzerland over the 1947–55 period, and also of some data from the Census of 1941.[2] Total fertility of farmers' wives was found to be 30 per cent higher for Catholics than for Protestants both among German and French speakers but only 18 per cent for Italian speakers (among whom were found both higher Protestant and lower Catholic fertility); and 45 per cent for the small isolated group of Romansch speakers.

Turning to data for the whole population, we must remember that the Catholic population of Switzerland consists to a very substantial degree of immigrant Italians, largely concentrated in the lower paid manual employments. At any given age level both male and female Catholics show a substantially *lower* fertility than Protestants (because of both a later average age of Catholics at marriage, and a large number of Protestant divorces). An analysis of age-specific fertility rates for married women shows that the relative excess of Catholic over Protestant fertility increases rapidly with age, the difference being over 60 per cent for women in their late 30's. Computed total fertility per Catholic marriage is about 10 per cent higher. An occupational analysis of specific fertilities for married women with age structure standardized indicates a 47 per cent difference amongst farmers and small traders, 28 per cent among craftsmen, 22 per cent among semi-

[1] Luvini, *Genus*, December 1942.
[2] Nixon, *Review of the International Institute of Statistics*, 1951.

skilled, and slight among professional and technical workers, and also among farm labourers.

Day's study[1] of the data from the 1954 Census of Australia however (Table VI.50) shows no change in the religious differential by age: but within the Catholic population shows large differentials as between the principal cities, the smaller towns, and rural areas.

TABLE VI.50. TOTAL FERTILITIES OF AUSTRALIAN WOMEN BY RELIGION 1954

| | | | Included in Catholic Total | | |
| | | | Six Principal | Other | |
Age	Non-Catholic	Catholic	Cities	Towns	Rural
40–44	2·1	2·5	2·1	2·8	3·3
45–49	2·1	2·5	2·2	2·9	3·6
50–54	2·2	2·7	2·3	3·0	3·6
55–59	2·4	3·0	2·5	3·5	4·1
60–64	2·8	3·4	3·2	4·0	5·0
65–69	3·3	3·9	3·5	4·3	5·0
70–74	3·8	4·2	3·4	4·8	5·2

In analysing total fertility of Canadian women in 1941, Charles[2] devised an additive system, taking as base the women with all the low-fertility characteristics — Protestant, English-speaking, urban, 13 or more years' education — who showed a minimum total fertility of 0·84 (a high proportion were unmarried). To this she added 1·31 for being French-speaking, and 0·26 for having any other European mother tongue. For foreign-born women she at first added 1·81, the largest of all her differential components — later however she found that this factor disappeared after standardization for religion, education, duration of marriage, etc. For those whose education was only 9–12 years' duration she added 0·85; for those with only a primary education she added 1·98. Finally, she considered that she could isolate the religious factor, representing an addition of as much as 1·28. However (as is sometimes the case when applying fertilizers in farming) the simultaneous application of several fertility factors produces a greater effect than the sum of their estimated separate effects. Where we get a combination of farm-born, French-speaking and Catholic we have to add a further factor of 1·00.

The first large-scale inquiry into differential fertility by religion in the United States, and in some ways still the most thorough, was that made in Wisconsin by Stouffer,[3] who cross-analysed by religion and by no less than

[1] *Milbank Memorial Quarterly*, April 1964. Approximate results read from diagrams.
[2] *Cultural Differences in Family Size*, 1941 Census.
[3] *American Journal of Sociology*, 1935–6, p. 143.

five other variables — duration of marriage, age at marriage, size of city, occupation, and date of marriage. The duration analysis was confined to the first three and a half and the second three and a half years of marriage. No significant change in the religious differential was observable over this period; though we have seen from other data that the differential probably becomes wider at a considerably later stage of the marriage. Also no significant differences appeared between Milwaukee and the smaller cities of the State of Wisconsin. The effects of age at marriage were clearly significant — the religious differential was substantially greater among the women marrying at the age of 21–25 than among those marrying below 21. (Other sociological researches have shown that Catholics in America generally marry later than Protestants, particularly Catholics of Irish descent, even though they are several generations removed from their ancestral country). Stouffer compared marriages of 1919–20, 1925–6, and of 1929–30, and found strong evidence that the relative size of the religious differential was declining over this period, as in Europe. Finally, the effects of occupation on the religious differential were also clear. Combining the data for the three dates of marriage, the average size of the religious differential was 19 per cent among unskilled and semi-skilled manual workers, 29 per cent among skilled manual workers, and 36 per cent among non-manual workers — both for Catholics and non-Catholics fertility decreased as we come up this occupational scale, but it decreased less rapidly for Catholics.

Another interesting study in the 1930's by Kiser[1] for the three cities of Brooklyn, Syracuse and Columbus showed that the age at which women married was related to their fathers' occupation and education. With a standardized age structure, the proportions of women aged 15–40 married rose from 48 per cent for professional men's daughters to 54 per cent for business men's daughters, 59 per cent for skilled manual workers' daughters, and 62 per cent for unskilled manual workers' daughters. The father's education seemed to have even more effect (the daughters of highly educated men marrying later). Kiser also found a strong religious differential which appeared to apply uniformly to all occupations and educational classes. Data for Indianapolis in 1941[2] of women aged 40–44 at that date (differentials have probably fallen since) who had been married only once, and who were not widowed or divorced, showed a differential of about 40 per cent applicable to all ages of marriages except those under 20. They also pointed out that higher education reduced Protestant fertility largely through delaying marriage.

[1] International Population Congress, 1937.
[2] Kiser and Frobden, *Milbank Memorial Quarterly*, January 1944.

A recent American study[1] showed that the religious differential, standardized for age, between Catholics and Protestants was 18 per cent, with Jewish fertility at 25 per cent below Protestant. Mixed marriages, however, whether with Catholic wife and Protestant husband or vice versa, showed a fertility 10 per cent below that of Protestant marriages. Fairly similar religious differentials were found at all levels of incomes and education, the only qualification to this rule being that Protestants showed a greater variance of fertility with income. The most recent study,[2] on current fertility expectations in 1963, brings out the points that within the Catholic community the relationship between education and fertility, negative elsewhere, disappears for women over 30, and actually becomes positive for women under 30.

The disappearance of any income-fertility relationship, alike among Catholics and non-Catholics, is again confirmed.

Goldberg[3] took account of the important facts already discovered regarding first-generation migrants from farms, their comparatively high general average of fertility, combined with their strong negative relationship between fertility and income. Among women aged over 40 in Detroit in the period 1952–8, with the data confined to second generation urban families, he first sought whether there was any effect upon fertility arising simply out of difference in occupation between the present-day parent and his own father, e.g. non-manual working sons of manual working fathers, but found no significant relation. Among the first-generation farm migrants, as we have already seen, fertility had a strong negative relationship with income, and also with occupation; both these relationships however had disappeared by the second generation. Educational and religious differentials did persist in the second generation, but in reduced form (Table VI.51).

TABLE VI.51. SIZES OF COMPLETED FAMILIES IN DETROIT, 1952–8

	First Generation Farm Migrants	Second Generation Urban
Catholic	3·40	2·37
Protestant	2·49	2·00
Wife's education:		
Primary	3·07	2·33
High School 1–3 years	2·38	2·21
" " 4 years	2·18	2·09
College	2·28	1·76

[1] *Milbank Memorial Quarterly*, July 1958.
[2] Freedman, Goldberg and Bumpass, *Population Index*, January 1965.
[3] *Population Studies*, March 1959.

Goldberg's results in Detroit, using a simple manual — non-manual classification of occupations, showed no significant effect of inter-generation change in occupation, or 'social mobility' as it is generally called, upon fertility. A very interesting study however within the Catholic population,[1] using a set of graded 'status positions', for parents married 1937–48, showed an average family of 3·00 for those who were in the same 'status position' as their fathers, but 2·92 for those who had gone down two or more 'positions', and 3·18 for those who had gone up two or more. This interesting result was followed by an inconclusive discussion as to whether the associated variables, movements between towns of different size, regularity of religious practice, and others, would suffice to explain the observed differences.

So far, most theorists of the sociology of reproduction have followed Dumont in seeing the desire for social mobility (in an upward direction) as the principal factor inducing parents to limit the size of their families — though there are a number of interesting signs that these relationships may be changing. We may now look at some of the information about the extent of social mobility in different countries before going on to consider some very interesting results about the relation between social mobility and family size obtained in France.

The simplest approach to the problem of defining and measuring social mobility is to say, for example, here we have a rural labourer; what chance have his sons of reaching skilled manual, clerical, administrative or professional occupations? But now we suppose that he is from a country such as Italy or Japan, where an unusually rapid transfer from the rural to the urban sectors of the economy is taking place. In such countries therefore every rural labourer and peasant has a better chance of seeing his sons move into the occupations which he considers of a higher order than in a country where such transfers between economic sectors are taking place at a much lower rate. What we really need, if we are to examine the relationship between social mobility and size of family, is some measure of *relative* social mobility, i.e. what proportion of peasants' sons become office workers in comparison with the proportion of all young men of their generation becoming office workers?

Considering the importance of the subject, little research has yet been done on social mobility.[2] The preparation of social mobility tables of any size calls for great effort and expense. The work is most expensive when it has to be done by individual interviewing, although a large number of

[1] Brooks and Henry, *Milbank Memorial Quarterly*, July 1958.
[2] A world-wide account of available information is given by Lipset and Bendix, *Social Mobility in an Industrial Society*.

related factors can be analysed in this way; such as the changes which a man may make in his occupation in the course of his career; or the interesting fact that greater social mobility is found among men leaving their home towns than among men staying there;[1] or, which concerns us most now, any indications whether the size of family affects the social mobility of the children.

Failing this slow and costly process of individual interviews, more statistically reliable information about much larger numbers of men can sometimes be obtained from public registers, such as father's occupation registered on a man's birth or marriage certificate. This method of course only records the occupation of both son and father at a particular moment of time; both of them may be subject to change.

An example of a fairly extensive study by personal interview, covering 3023 men, and using a fairly simple classification, is that prepared by Bresard for France[2] (Table VI.52).

The diagonal figures running obliquely across the table show the percentage of sons remaining in the same occupation group as their fathers. There is, it will be seen, quite a strong tendency to do this, being most marked in peasant families, least marked for civil servants. Even in a sample of this size (and the difficulties would clearly be greater in a smaller sample) the first two lines are based on small numbers, and many percentage figures obtained from them are hardly significant statistically. For what they are worth, however, they show that being the son of a business proprietor or professional man gives you a probability of becoming a business proprietor or professional man of 40 per cent, ten times that of the average of your generation of 4 per cent.

In France, in the generation preceding 1950, population had been almost stationary, and economic growth comparatively slow, so the opportunities for social mobility could have been expected to be less than they would be in many countries. But they were not absent. In this sample the previous generation consisted of 34 per cent peasants, 12 per cent clerical workers and only 3 per cent of each of the two highest categories. A comparatively slowly developing society of this sort gives us an opportunity for observing the number of 'down-starts' (as Bernard Shaw used to call them, in contrast with 'upstarts') or sons following worse paid and less distinguished occupations than their fathers. This is a social phenomenon which only comes to light in such analyses; in casual observation, one's attention tends to be drawn towards those who have succeeded, and diverted away from those who have failed.

---

[1] Sculler and Anderson, *American Journal of Sociology*, June 1954.
[2] *Population*, July–September 1950.

TABLE VI.52. SOCIAL MOBILITY IN FRANCE
(PERCENTAGE DISTRIBUTION OF SONS BY OCCUPATION)

	Numbers of Sons	(1) Business Proprietors and Professional Men	(2) Civil Service Administrative Grade, Teachers, Business Salaried Employees	(3) Retailers and Independent Craftsmen	(4) Peasants	(5) Clerks (Civil Service and Business)	(6) Manual Workers Urban	(7) Manual Workers Rural
All sons	3023	4	5	15	26	17	23	10
Sons of (headings as at top of table)								
(1)	94	40	18	18	9	10	5	0
(2)	95	14	25	11	14	23	12	1
(3)	540	5	6	46	8	17	16	2
(4)	1033	1	1	6	63	7	11	11
(5)	379	5	10	10	3	42	26	4
(6)	625	2	2	10	3	21	55	7
(7)	256	0	2	7	14	9	25	43
Standard deviation of differences from mean		14·3	9·5	13·0	22·3	11·3	15·5	14·0
Do. as multiple of mean		3·6	1·9	0·9	0·9	0·7	0·7	1·4

For comparison of different countries and times, the presentation of a long series of such tables would be laborious and space-consuming; and comparison would still be almost impossible, because no two analysts so far have used precisely the same social classification. A new technique of comparison is therefore proposed as follows. Reading down the columns in a table such as Table VI.52 giving the results for France, it is possible to compute the standard deviation from the mean. This standard deviation is then shown as a multiple of the mean (e.g. in the first column we measure the deviations from 4 and obtain the root of the mean of their squares at 14·3, which result we then divide by 4). The standard deviation expressed as a multiple of the mean is found to be lowest in the case of clerical and urban manual workers (i.e. these occupations tend to receive men of a wide distribution of parentage, without great differentiation) and on the other hand highest in the professional and business occupations, mainly because of the strong tendency for these occupations to recruit the sons of men themselves engaged in these occupations. But a high figure is also found for rural manual workers, themselves principally the sons of rural manual workers.

We can apply this technique first to a particularly interesting series from Denmark which compares succeeding generations (Table VI.53). (Some very small categories, which would clearly yield non-significant figures, have been combined.)

This long series of data shows a general fall in the SD/Mean coefficients, i.e. increasing social mobility, with each occupation drawing its recruits from a wider field, particularly for clerks, who apparently were a small hereditarily privileged group in the mid-nineteenth century. But it is interesting to see that the standard deviation has risen substantially for professions, no doubt due to the much greater expense of training required by modern standards. It has risen to a lesser extent for business men.

We now proceed to a general view of information capable of being classified in this manner (Table VI.54).

Almost everywhere is seen the tendency for the standard deviation for the professions to be high. This, of course, is due to the time and expense required for training for them, which makes entry difficult, quite apart from any tendency for sons to follow their fathers. In some cases, but by no means in all, high standard deviations are found in business occupations. This may be expected to be the case in comparatively slowly developing sectors of the economy, where custom (or sometimes even legal restrictions) can make business positions hereditary. At the other end of the social scale (although here again not always) fairly high standard deviations are found for rural and unskilled labourers — not through any difficulty in entering

TABLE VI.53. SOCIAL MOBILITY OF SUCCEEDING GENERATIONS IN AARHUS' (DENMARK)

	Men born 1919–28 (No. of cases 5443)			Men born 1909–18 (No. of cases 6258)			Men born 1899–1908 (No. of cases 5300)			Men born 1889–98 (No. of cases 3895)			Men born 1879–88 (No. of cases 2334)			Men born 1849–78 (No. of cases 903)		
	Distri-bution	SD	Mean	Distri-bution	SD	Mean	Distri-bution	SD	Mean	Distri-bution	SD	Mean	Distri-bution	SD	Mean	Distri-bution	SD	Mean
Business men	6	0·6	2·5	17	0·4	2·0	22	0·3	1·9	23	0·3	1·8	27	0·3	2·2	44	0·4	1·0
Professions	7			7			6			6			7			9		
Technicians and Salaried	4	0·8		7	0·5		8	0·5		7	0·4		5	0·6		5	0·7	
Salesmen	10	0·5		9	0·5		8	0·8		7	1·0		5	1·9		6	0·9	
Clerks	14	0·4		12	0·4		8	0·7		13	0·4		11	0·6		4	1·9	
Skilled manual workers	35	0·4		26	0·4		23	0·4		22	0·4		26	0·5		22	0·6	
Unskilled manual workers	24	0·6		22	0·6		25	0·5		22	0·6		19	0·5		10	0·9	

Geiger, *Soziale Umschichtungen in einen Danische Mittelstadt Aarhus*, 1951. The first entry refers mainly to small businesses not employing labour. 'Professions' includes teachers and higher Government officials.

these occupations, but through reluctance to enter them, and the tendency to leave them to the sons of fathers who followed them.

Where we have observations extending over more than one generation, we should expect to find a general fall in standard deviations i.e. for social mobility to increase. This is generally true; but there are interesting exceptions.

The rise in social mobility in the course of a generation is particularly marked in India, where the caste system, and the whole national tradition hitherto, would have led us to expect a strongly familial and hereditary structure of occupations. Indeed it is interesting to see that some of the present generation figures are as low as they are, and also that in Hubli, a comparatively remote and unknown country town, they are generally lower than they are in Poona. Some of the previous generation figures for Poona have a very high standard deviation. Fathers in that generation, in some cases, put 70 or 80 per cent of all their sons into their own occupation.

The figures for Japan are exceptionally interesting, because they were compiled on the same basis for the three sectors of the community, namely the six main cities, other urban areas, and rural. In every case (except for a small minority of farmers on the outskirts of big cities) social mobility increases as size of town increases. In the six main cities of Japan, indeed, social mobility appears to be considerably higher than in Western Europe and North America. The high mobility in the professional and managerial occupations in the big cities is striking. (It must be remembered that this figure does not necessarily mean that there are a number of opportunities in this field; this in fact is true, but the number of opportunities has been eliminated in the calculation of the standard deviation, which measures, in effect, for whatever opportunities there are, whether the sons of poorer families have a relatively good opportunity of obtaining them, in comparison with the sons of richer families.) In rural Japan, on the other hand, not only professional and managerial positions, but also skilled manual work, seemed to retain a considerable hereditary element in 1955, though less than in India. Some data were also obtained for the previous generation. In every case, social mobility had increased in the course of a generation.

In Britain, a strong hereditary tendency is found among farmers, and, to a less extent, among agricultural workers and small businesses. Otherwise, social mobility is comparatively high.

The figures for the United States show a strong increase in social mobility in the course of a generation in San José, a Californian city. (The high proportion of proprietors shown in the previous generation does no more than indicate that a high proportion of them were farmers.) In Indianapolis, the movement is less marked, and there are some signs of a rising standard deviation at the two extreme ends of the scale. The coloured population was practically confined to manual occupations; between the different types of manual occupation it showed fairly high social mobility.

Another method of analysis for the United States, which can be carried back to the eighteenth century, is to classify the parentage of business leaders (Table VI.55).

The nature of the families from which business leaders are drawn is changing, but very slowly. Sons of business men had about ten times the national average probability of becoming business leaders in 1928, a little over seven times the national average in 1955.

Anyone making a detailed analysis of this problem must, however, bear in mind that a social mobility table only observes occupations at a specified time, and that men may have changed occupation in the course of their careers.

In France, for instance (Table VI.56), a substantial proportion of business and professional men began their careers as clerks and salesmen; and small business men and clerks began their careers as manual workers. Farmers and manual workers, however, mostly remained in the career in which they began.

A much more mobile pattern is revealed, however, by a study in California[1] (Table VI.57). (It is possible that figures for the Eastern United States would show lower mobility.)

We have from Lipset and Bendix a number of other interesting results (Table VI.58) to show that only those engaged in professional occupations had spent the greater part of their time in one occupation. The authors also give detailed tables classifying the nature of changes of occupation recorded in a specified period, and also, for those now engaged in a given occupational group, the proportion who had at any time worked in other specified occupational groups. Again it appears that social mobility in Japan is very high; also that social mobility in California has increased considerably since the 1930's.

In the Californian study of the 1930's[2] each man's full occupational career was recorded. Men aged between 20 and 34 were found to have followed on an average 3·05 occupations, men over 35 more than 4.

Census classifications of occupational changes of the whole population are available for Sweden[3] for the periods 1930-6 and 1940-5, and for Canada for the period 1931-41. All these periods, unfortunately, were rather abnormal economically; but they yield some interesting results. An

---

[1] Lipset and Bendix, *Social Mobility in an Industrial Society*.
[2] Anderson and Davidson, *Occupational Mobility in an American Community*.
[3] Anderson, *Acta Sociologica*, Copenhagen, 1956.

TABLE VI.55. PARENTAGE OF BUSINESS LEADERS IN U.S.A.

	Parentage[a] of business leaders born:				
	1771–1800	1801–1830	1831–1860	1861–1890	1891–1920
Business	40	52	66	70	69
Gentry farmer	25	11	3	3	5
Small enterprise	9	4	3	1	0
Professions	3	12	11	12	11
Government officials	4	7	3	3	3
Clerks and foremen	7	2	2	3	6
Farmers	12	11	10	6	4
Manual workers	0	2	1	2	3

	Parentage of directors		Proportion of whole labour force in previous generation[d]	
	1928[b]	1955[c]	1890	1920
Owner large business	14	8		
Major executive	17	15		
Owner small business	20	18	6	7
Minor executive	7	11		
Professions	13	14	3	5
Farmers	12	9	24	15
Clerks and salesmen	5	8	5	14
Skilled manual workers	9	10	9	14
Other manual workers	3	7	53	45

[a] Lipset and Bendix, Social Mobility in an Industrial Society.
[b] Taussig and Joslyn, American Business Leaders, 1932.
[c] Warner and Abegglen, Big Business Leaders in America.
[d] Census of 1940, Comparative Occupation Statistics 1870–1940.

TABLE VI.56. PERCENTAGE DISTRIBUTION BY FIRST EMPLOYMENTS, FRANCE, 1953 (INSEE)

First employment

Present employment	Business and professional	Farmers	Small business	Clerks and salesmen	Manual workers (urban)	Manual workers (rural)
Business and professional	51	3	5	29	12	0
Farmers	0	82	1	1	4	12
Small business	1	7	47	9	30	6
Clerks and salesmen	1	7	4	56	25	7
Manual workers (urban)	0	7	3	5	73	12
Manual workers (rural)	0	14	1	3	14	68

TABLE VI.57. CHANGES IN EMPLOYMENT OF MEN OVER 30 IN OAKLAND, CALIFORNIA

Proportion of total career spent in present occupation

Present occupation:	80% and over	50–79%	Under 50%
Professional	70	9	22
Semi-professional	47	32	21
Own business	11	31	57
Clerical: Upper salaried	14	21	65
Lower salaried	18	33	49
Salesmen	26	24	50
Skilled manual workers	22	35	43
Semi-skilled workers	22	29	49
Unskilled	18	21	61

TABLE VI.58. PERCENTAGE OF MEN WHOSE FIRST OCCUPATION WAS THE SAME AS THEIR PRESENT

Present occupation:	England and Wales 1949	Japan (excl. farmers) 1950	Oakland 1949	San José 1934	France 1953
Professional	80	65	61	78	
Clerical	34	54	27	37	56
Skilled manual	53	57	53	47 ⎫	
Semi-skilled manual	51	33	25	34 ⎬	73
Unskilled manual	26	47	17	42 ⎭	

interesting direct comparison[1] of social mobility between Japan and the United States, regarding the prospect of a man of given parentage becoming a business leader is shown in Table VI.59. In respect of business leaders, though not perhaps of other social groups, Japanese social mobility is still substantially less than that of U.S.A.

[1] Abbeglen, *Economic Development and Cultural Change*, October 1960.

TABLE VI.59. U.S.–JAPANESE SOCIAL MOBILITY
COMPARISON

	Relative proportions in the population 1920 Japan U.S.A.		Relative proportions in the parentage of business leaders of the 1950's Japan U.S.A.		Ratio between preceding columns Japan U.S.A.	
Large businesses and government officials	1·7	4	42	30	24·6	7·5
Professional	2·8	4	5	16	1·8	4·0
Small Businesses	13·6	5	19	20	1·4	4·0
Clerical and Sales	6·6	12	9	16	1·4	1·3
Farmers	48·8	28	25	9	0·5	0·3
Manual Workers	26·5	47	0	9	0	0·2

If this discussion had been held forty or fifty years ago, when eugenic ideas were prevalent, there would have been many who would have urged that the differences between social groups were due to genetic factors. Now we know how difficult it is accurately to isolate genetic factors in human achievement. At one time it was thought that the quotient measured by intelligent tests (I.Q.) indicated innate rather than acquired ability — it was certainly designed to do so. It was found however in the Netherlands[1] that while 10 per cent of the population as a whole showed an I.Q. over 122, no less than 47 per cent of the children of teachers exceeded this figure. While this fact does not formally disprove the proposition that I.Q. may represent innate inherited factors, it certainly gives a strong presumption for believing that home environment and parental encouragement play a part in determining it. In the Netherlands, one third of all the sons of primary teachers reached university; male primary teachers, representing one per cent of the occupied population, fathered 7 per cent of male university students (and 15 per cent of the Deputies in the Dutch Parliament).

Regarding the prospects of young men entering the professions, it is clear that much depends on their parents' willingness and ability to get them into universities or other training centres — and to encourage them to stay there.

A good deal of scattered information is available analysing the parentage of students in universities and other places of higher study. These figures also indicate changes in the direction of greater social mobility; but again with remarkable slowness (Table VI.60).

[1] Idenburg, Director of Statistics, private communication.

TABLE VI.60. PARENTAGE OF STUDENTS

	FRANCE					SWEDEN			ENGLAND			
	Technical and professional schools 1959–60	Lycées 1942–46	Lycées 1959–60	Universities 1939	Universities 1959	Students passing matriculation examination (age 18–20) 1910	1930	1943	School entry selections Group I	School academic Record A	University admission from non-fee paying schools	All university admissions
Independent means and unoccupied	⎫ 3	3	—	16·6	14·0							
Professions	⎬	7	18	18·8	12·8	⎫ 34	36	33	⎫ 33·5	52·6	63·5	74·0
Large business proprietors and managers (not farm)	⎭	⎰ * ⎱		16·0	6·3	⎭			⎭			
Farmers	11	9	8	4·0	4·9							
Salaried workers: private	17	18	20	12·6	17·4	49	42	45				
Salaried workers: government	11	26	16	25·7	28·3							
Handicraftsmen and retailers	16	25	16	3·8	12·5							
Urban manual workers: skilled	⎫ 39	12	21	⎱ 1·6 ⎰	⎱ 3·0 ⎰	17	22	22	45·3	38·8	30·3	21·7
semi-skilled	⎬								16·3	7·1	4·9	3·4
unskilled	⎭								4·9	1·6	1·3	0·9
Rural manual workers	3		1	0·9	0·8							

* Included in 'handicraftsmen and retailers'.

France First and third columns, Girard and Bastide, Mercurio, 1962–3, (unknowns distributed). 'Lycées' give classical or modern humane studies as opposed to technical. Private schools excluded. Second column from *Population*, Jan.–Mar. 1951. Universities from Ministry of Education, quoted *Population*, October 1960.

Sweden Moberg, *Population Studies*, June 1950 (unknowns distributed). Second groups specified, apart from farmers, men with post primary education.

England (excl. Wales & Scotland) *Applications for Admission to Universities* (Committee of University Principals and Vice Chancellors, entrants of 1955).

In France the high and indeed increasing proportion of university places taken by the sons of civil servants is noticeable. The sons of handicraftsmen and retailers have also secured a greatly increased number of university places.

For England it is possible to make a most interesting study through a special inquiry into university entrants in 1955, read in conjunction with the *Early Leaving Report* of the Ministry of Education. It is seen that the proportion of children of manual working families becomes progressively lower as we mount the successive stages of the educational ladder. Much of this is believed to be due to the discouragement, or at any rate, the lack of encouragement which they receive at home.

A study in Belgium[1] showed the proportion of sons of manual workers among the students at Louvain University to be substantially higher than in France or England. The analysis of parentage was also made separately for the students in different faculties, without showing any very significant results except that in the study of *notariat* (solicitors' qualifications, as opposed to *droit*, or barristers') 53 per cent of the students were found to be themselves the children of *notaires*. In the medical faculty only 11 per cent of the students were the children of doctors. Finally, the analyst sought to relate success in examinations to parentage. Here again no significant results were found, apart from the fact that the children of university professors scored on the average 34 per cent above normal. It again remains to be decided whether the factors at work were hereditary or environmental.

We have, unfortunately, little information on the amount of education required for any given occupation; but it appears to be increasing (Tables VI. 61 and 62).

Finally we come back to the question which is critical for our present study, namely to what extent size of family does in fact impede the social advancement of the offspring.

Outstanding in this field is the remarkable work done in France by Bresard[2] (Table VI.63).

We obtain the remarkable result that the larger business proprietors and professional men, if they have families of four or more, tend to give their sons *more* education than the average, even though, no doubt, they give them less money. The combined effect of this better education, and perhaps also of the greater stimulus to succeed under which children of large families should be working, means that here a higher proportion of the sons of large families enter the first two occupational grades than of the sons of small

---

[1] Leplae, *Bulletin of the Institution of Economic and Social Research*, University of Louvain, December 1946.
[2] *Population*, July–September 1950.

I

TABLE VI.61. AVERAGE NUMBER OF YEARS' EDUCATION BY OCCUPATIONS

	Professional and semi-professional	Farmers	Other proprietors managers and officials	Clerical sales and kindred workers	Craftsmen and foremen	Operatives	Personal service workers	Farm labourers	Other labourers
U.S.A. native born white									
Males:									
Born 1875–84	16·0	7·2	8·5	10·3	7·6	7·2	7·5	6·5	7·0
1895–1904	16·0	7·5	11·5	11·5	8·2	7·8	8·1	7·2	7·4
1910–1914	16·0	8·1	12·0	12·1	10·3	9·0	10·3	7·7	8·0
France	14·6	7·4	13·0	10·4	8·5	7·6		6·4	6·6

U.S.A.: Census of 1940.
FRANCE: Bresard, *Cahiers Français d'Information*, 15 January and 1 February 1952.

TABLE VI.62. EDUCATION OF U.S. BUSINESS LEADERS

Date of Birth	1771–1800	1801–30	1831–60	1861–90	1891–1920
College graduate	22	8	15	39	67
Do. not graduated	10	8	13	18	17
High school (inc. private)	51	51	46	26	11
Grammar school or less	17	33	26	17	5

Lipset & Bendix, *Social Mobility in an Industrial Society.*

families. In all other social groups, however, and particularly among the lower paid salary workers, a larger family means that each child receives, on the average, less education, and has a lesser chance of entering the higher social groups. The sons of farmers and small business men, as was to be expected, have considerably less chance of entering their fathers' occupations when they are born into large families, and correspondingly more probability of becoming wage workers.

Lehner's study for Rome[1] (Table VI.64) shows a relative disadvantage for the larger families in all the occupations, including professional men and business proprietors. But while this relative disadvantage undoubtedly exists, it is much smaller than expected. It is at its most marked among salaried workers.

Moberg analyses the same problem for Sweden[2] in a different manner (Table VI.65).

Among manual workers, and men with primary education only, it was generally only those with less than average size families who were willing or able to educate their sons up to a high matriculation standard; and then these men so educated in their turn became fathers of comparatively small families. But it is interesting to notice that, even over the short interval of ten years covered by this study, this difference was much reduced, and probably by now has disappeared. Though their families are smaller than their fathers', and although they tend to marry late, the present generation of educated Swedes have substantially larger families than their less educated countrymen.

Bresard[3] isolated from his sample 1035 Frenchmen whose fathers had been farmers, recording the numbers of children fathered by them. The average family size of nearly four shown by this method is of course biased upwards (because the fathers of the larger families have a greater chance of getting their sons into the sample). It is nevertheless a very interesting sample for measuring the association between size of family in the generation of the fathers of present-day Frenchmen, and of their grandparents.

[1] World Population Conference, 1954.
[2] *Population Studies*, June 1950.　　[3] *Population*, July–September 1950.

TABLE VI.63. PROPORTION OF SONS FOUND IN OCCUPATIONS SPECIFIED ACCORDING TO SIZE OF FAMILY

Occupation of Father	Av. No. of years schooling received by sons, all sizes of family	Av. No. of years schooling received by sons, families of 4 or more	Sons in families of 1 or 2 children							Sons in families of 3 or more children						
			Larger business proprietors, professional men	Administrative Civil servants, business executives	Retailers and small business men	Farmers	Clerical workers, business and Civil servants	Urban wage-workers	Rural wage-workers	Larger business proprietors, professional men	Administrative Civil servants, business executives	Retailers and small business men	Farmers	Clerical workers, business and Civil servants	Urban wage-workers	Rural wage-workers
Larger business proprietors, professional men	13·0	14·0	35	16	19	9	16	5	··	45	20	18	8	4	6	··
Administrative Civil servants, business executives	13·1	12·8	13	38	11	11	16	11	··	14	17	12	15	28	12	2
Retailers and small business men	9·1	8·5	4	7	48	9	18	13	1	6	4	43	8	17	20	3
Farmers	7·5	7·3	1	2	6	70	8	6	7	··	1	6	59	7	13	14
Clerical workers, business and Civil servants	10·4	9·5	6	12	10	3	46	21	3	5	8	10	3	38	31	5
Urban wage-workers	8·0	7·3	2	3	11	2	25	54	4	2	2	8	4	18	55	9
Rural wage-workers	7·0	6·8	··	1	16	10	11	24	37	··	2	4	16	8	25	45

TABLE VI.64. PERCENTAGE DISTRIBUTION OF SONS'
OCCUPATIONS ACCORDING TO SIZE OF FAMILY, ROME

Son's occupation

Father's Occupation	Sons in families of less than 4					Sons in families of 4 or more				
	P	H	R	P	U	P	H	R	P	U
	(as for side headings)					(as for side headings)				
Professional men, business proprietors, higher Civil Servants	53	21	24	2	0	45	16	32	6	1
Higher salaried workers	19	44	29	8	0	27	27	34	12	0
Routine salaried workers, small businesses	7	14	56	22	1	7	10	49	32	2
Peasants, artisans, craftsmen	2	4	25	64	5	0	1	21	70	8
Unskilled workers	0	0	13	56	31	1	0	4	62	33

TABLE VI.65. FAMILY SIZES IN SWEDEN

Occupation or Education of Student's Father

	Larger Business Proprietors or Higher Officials, Graduates	Farmers, Men with some Post-Primary Education	Manual Workers, Men with Primary Education only
Men matriculating about 1910:			
Average size of family into which they were born	3·41	3·41	3·11
Average number of children they had themselves	2·36	2·31	1·84
Men matriculating about 1920:			
Do.	3·32	3·11	2·56
Do.	2·34	2·28	2·14

A strong association with both the maternal and paternal grandparents' family size is found.

In contrast with the French and Swedish results, however, a British study[1] of the size of families of teachers married before 1945 shows no association between the number of their children and the number of children in the family into which they were born.

[1] Scott, *Population Studies*, March 1958.

TABLE VI.66. AVERAGE SIZE OF FAMILY INTO WHICH BORN

| Social mobility | By occupation of father | | | | By date of marriage (all occupations of fathers) | | | |
	Professional and managerial	Other non manual	Skilled manual	Semi-skilled and unskilled manual	Before 1910	1910– 19	1920– 24	1925– 29
Upwards	—	2·05	1·98	3·19	3·50	2·40	2·38	1·62
Static	1·74	2·14	2·67	3·68	3·82	2·89	2·49	2·18
Downwards	1·87	2·66	3·69	—	too few to analyse			
	1·81	2·38	2·81	3·44	3·77	2·80	2·50	2·04

Finally we have a study[1] (Table VI.66) of a large sample of the population of England and Wales in 1949 classifying men according to whether their social mobility, in relation to their fathers' occupation, had been upwards, static or downwards, in relation to the size of the family into which they were born.

Here again we get the result that larger than average families are associated with downward social mobility, only to a slight degree for professional men and managers, to a much greater degree for other occupations. The classification by date of marriage however shows some signs that this discrepancy is increasing.

[1] Berent, *Population Studies*, March 1952.

CHAPTER VII

The Economics and Politics of Population Growth

IN an agricultural economy, increasing inputs of labour with the amount of land given, methods of cultivation and inputs of all other resources remaining unchanged — the assumption which the economist must necessarily make for the purposes of preliminary analysis, but which he all too readily comes to treat as permanent — lead to reduced returns per unit of labour input — 'The Law of Diminishing Returns' described by Victorian economists. In historical fact, however, the rigid retention of an unchanged system of cultivation is a rarity, and population increases, as we have seen, usually lead to changes both in methods of cultivation and in social and economic relationships, which are capable of greatly raising the return per unit of labour input.

In the whole non-agricultural sector of the economy, on the other hand — which includes not only manufacture, but also construction, transport, communications, commerce, services and government — it has long been understood that the opposite state of affairs may prevail. The operation of any of these sectors of the economy on a larger scale should lead (almost immediately, and without having to wait for a long period of social and technical readjustment, as may be the case in agriculture) to *increasing* returns per unit of labour input — though the possibilities of such increases may be much greater in sectors such as manufacture and transport than in construction or services. By the end of the nineteenth century economists were beginning to state this principle as 'The Law of Increasing Returns', in contrast to 'The Law of Diminishing Returns'. The phrase 'Increasing Returns' however went out of use in the 1930's, to be replaced by the phrase 'economies of scale'. The modern phrase is indeed more precise in concentrating attention upon economies purely due to the increasing scale on which business is conducted, as distinguished from economies arising from technical, social and other changes, which could have taken place without the scale of production having increased.

There was some comprehension of the principle of increasing returns, of the idea that the product of two men working together would be more than twice what they would have produced working independently, as long ago as the fourteenth century, in the works of the first of all writers on economics, the Arab philosopher-historian Ibn Khaldun.

'The individual cannot satisfy his wants independently but must co-operate with his fellow men; the foodstuff is not produced by one's efforts nor does each one produce his own consumption; in its production co-operate six or ten, blacksmith, carpenter, labourer, etc. Now when all these co-operate, they produce together a quantity of foodstuffs by far exceeding their wants.'

The growth of population, he goes on to say, is ultimately checked, not by scarcity of food, but by the decadence of civilization.

'When civilization reaches the stage of excesses and luxury with its accompanying vices, limits are automatically set on population. There happen then devastating famines. Famines are not the result of the land's incapacity to cope with the increasing demand but are the result of the political chaos and physical oppression which invade the state in its decline.'

But finally a note of hope.

'The pre-Islamic Arab feared that famine would exert its pressure and endanger his family's honour, so he used to kill his female offspring. The Koran utterly prohibited this infamous act by affirming that God who makes fathers subsist will also provide for the subsistence of their progeny.'[1]

A pioneer of economic thought better known to us was Sir William Petty. Writing in 1691, he made a more acute analysis of this problem, bringing out some points which apparently have not yet been understood by many modern economists. Petty was concerned, as were most of his contemporaries, at the economic and naval strength of the Dutch, estimated then to number 2·2 million people, living at what was then considered an exceptionally high population density, on only 8 million acres of land, much of which was heath land or swamp (as contemporary Dutch paintings show). Yet this small nation was then the world's greatest commercial, naval and colonizing power, founding New York, Cape Town and Jakarta within a few years of each other, able not only to defeat the English fleet, but even to stand up against an Anglo-French alliance (though it is true that this combined pressure did cause them to abandon New York).

Petty analysed a number of economic advantages in having such a high population density. In the first place, there was the provision of clergymen, lawyers and other professional men, then (as now) expensive to train. The sparsity of population in rural England itself led to much greater per head

---

[1] *Ibn Khaldun, Pioneer Economist*, by Mohammed Ali Nashat, Cairo.

expenditure on these services than in the case of the Dutch. Next, he pointed to many trading and manufacturing activities which could not have arisen at all in a country with poorer communications. The communications which he had in mind were mainly harbours and canals, not natural features, but man-made, only possible in a country with a population both abundant and hard-working. He then turned to consider the relatively low expenditure which the Dutch had to make on defence, not only because of their naval supremacy and their water-barriers against land invaders, but also from their practice of filling their army with hired foreign soldiers at sixpence a day, whereas Dutchmen earned three shillings a day (English farm labourers were working for eightpence a day at that time). High earnings in Dutch commerce and manufacture had attracted labour away from agriculture, 'wherefor there is little Ploughing and Sowing of Corn in *Holland* and *Zeeland*, or breeding of young cattle'. The Netherlands by this time consumed principally imported food, and of the farmed land, a considerable proportion was worked by immigrants from Denmark and Poland.

Petty finally made the points that the Dutch harbours were constructed in a way which made possible much more economical operation than other harbours. More important, the size of their merchant fleet and their long experience of maritime commerce (records from the Baltic show that the Dutch had predominated in the carrying trade since the beginning of the sixteenth century) enabled them to design specialized ships for different types of cargo, which in turn enabled them to quote lower freights than their competitors with their general-purpose ships.

Increasing returns, or economies of scale, to a considerable extent, arise out of the existence of 'indivisibilities' consisting not only of large pieces of capital construction or equipment, such as harbours and transport systems, which need to be constructed in any case, and are costly to operate, per unit of product, on a small scale, but become much more economical to operate as population and production increase. 'Indivisibilities' also occur with supplies of skilled or professional labour, of certain large-scale organizations, and of other scarce and costly economic resources. For small scale production, the presence of many indivisibilities may be necessary, only partially utilized; production on a larger scale will utilize them more fully, at little additional expense. This idea was discussed by Marshall, though not pressed by him to a conclusion.

The next step forward in the theory of increasing returns was in a classical paper by Allyn Young.[1] Economists and politicians during the

[1] 'Increasing Returns and Economic Progress', *Economic Journal*, December 1928. The present writer was Young's research assistant, working on this problem, from October 1928 to his death in February 1929.

1920's were interested in the economies of scale, but believed that these were to be best obtained by almost indefinite enlargement of the individual firm. The methods of Henry Ford in motor manufacture (well publicized) had captured the imagination of the world during the 1920's — large scale production, conveyor belts, high pace of working, high wages, extremely detailed specialization of each man's function, and, finally, attempting to manufacture every possible component within the firm. This latter idea has since largely been abandoned (except in Soviet Russia, where it still appears to prevail). Young pointed out what is now generally accepted, but which was a novel idea then, that the economies of scale were often not 'internal' but 'external', namely the progressive specialization and sub-division of processes between firms, so that the economies of large-scale production could often be compatible with the existence of small firms. Though Young wrote little, and left many of his ideas to be disseminated by oral tradition, he followed this matter up to its logical conclusion, and contended that an industrial country would directly benefit economically from an enlargement of population. What British industry needed, he said, coming from Harvard to teach in London, was an internal market of 100 million population.

The next important development of theory on this subject was a paper by Everett Hagen (unfortunately not subsequently reprinted) at the meeting of the International Association for Research in Income and Wealth in 1953. Inter-country comparisons of capital stock and of capital requirements in relation to national product were then still in a highly confused state (they were reduced to a substantial degree of order at the 1957 meeting of the International Association). Analysing the still very imperfect comparative information available, Hagen was however able to deduce that, other things being equal, densely populated countries required considerably less capital per unit of product than did sparsely populated. (So also did countries with exceptionally valuable mineral or forest resources, which from an economic point of view constituted 'capital-substitutes'.) A denser population could make more economical use not only of the whole transport system — railways, roads, harbours — but also of public buildings, and of various specialized types of factories, and other forms of capital 'indivisibilities'. And not only population density, Hagen pointed out, but also the rate of population increase, could play an important part in reducing capital requirements. One reason which he gave for this was, to use his curious phrase, that rapid population increase 'absolves' a country from many of the consequences of the errors in investment decisions, both public and private, which are bound to occur. An erroneously-judged investment, in a rapidly growing economy, stands a good chance of being able to be put to some alternative use; in a more nearly stationary economy it is much more likely to become a dead loss.

While no advocate of population growth for its own sake, Hagen nevertheless thus concluded that it had beneficial economic effects. Likewise Hirschman, in a subtle and original study[1] contended that in developing countries the critical factor limiting growth was not the scarcity of capital as such, but of 'enterprise' — of men possessing at the same time the means, the ability and the willingness to initiate investments. He classified population growth with some adventitious changes as factors which might have the effect of generating 'windfall profits', and thereby creating incentives to enterprise.

A similar line of thought was further developed by Streeten,[2] who urged the need for 'unbalanced growth'. 'Balanced growth', that catch phrase enjoying so much popularity among, but receiving so little real analysis from economists who advise governments, if it were in fact attainable, would probably be economically undesirable, because it would fail to provide the necessary stimulus to enterprise.

Another line of reasoning, at a point where economics borders on social psychology, was developed by Sauvy.[3] Analysing the French Budget of 1939, he found that only 20 per cent of all government expenditure was variable with changes in population. The other 80 per cent consisted of expenses which had to be met, irrespective, within wide limits, of whether population rose or fell. Thus a stationary or declining population finds itself faced with considerably increased per head 'overhead expenses' for government. But this is by no means all. There are private pension schemes, the burden on families of supporting the old and infirm, and a whole host of private as well as public overhead costs whose per head burden may become very heavy for a stationary population. It is at this point, Sauvy suggests, and he is probably right, that politicians make a more or less conscious decision, following a public opinion which perhaps moves by some unconscious process of social psychology, in favour of rising prices, or a falling value of money, for the purpose of obviating some of these burdens. 'The devaluation of money', Sauvy wrote, 'appears to be a reaction, may I say (*voire*) a revolt, of the younger and more active elements in the population against having too large a part of their product taken away from them. ... Throughout the nineteenth century it was only the *increase* in population which ensured the *stability* of the value of money.' Harrod has reached similar conclusions.

[1] *The Strategy of Economic Development.*
[2] *Oxford Economic Papers*, June 1959.
[3] *Richesse et Population.*

So far we have approached this problem theoretically. We shall now look at the available facts.

We now have abundant data measuring the rate of growth of real national product per head of population, or per man year or per man hour of labour input, in industrial countries. These rates of growth do not show any discernible correlation, positive or negative, with rates of population growth. This was pointed out when the data were brought together by Kuznetz,[1] who also made the same point in a recent address to the Asian Population Conference.

It is possible to analyse this situation more deeply, though still obtaining a similar result. The growth of real national product per man year of labour can be analysed into three elements, (i) the growth of productivity in the agricultural sector, (ii) the growth of productivity in the non-agricultural sector (iii) the rate at which labour is being transferred from the agricultural to the non-agricultural sector, which in nearly every case enables each worker to make a greater contribution to national product (the only exceptions being countries with a highly productive commercial agriculture, such as Australia, New Zealand and Denmark).

Data are available on the growth of national product in a number of countries for long periods, which it is possible to analyse in this manner. The results are shown in Diagram VII.a. The general rates of growth are widely scattered around a median of a little below two per cent per year (of real product per man year; if we expressed the result per man hour, taking account of the gradual shortening of hours, we should get a figure of a little above 2 per cent annually). These results show no discernible correlation with the rate of growth of the labour force.

In Chapter IV we saw the high rates at which agricultural productivity has been growing since 1940 in most of the economically advanced countries. A high rate of withdrawal of labour from agriculture may on the one hand help to stimulate further increases in agricultural productivity, and also when, as is generally the case, agricultural productivity per worker still remains well below industrial, the transfer of the labour itself will increase average national productivity. But can a country raise its average per head productivity as rapidly as it pleases simply by increasing the rate at which it transfers labour from agriculture to industry? There must be some *reductio ad absurdum*. We may put the question this way — is there some limit, whether we are considering transfers of labour from agriculture, or general population increase, to the absorptive capacity, within a limited period, of the non-agricultural sector of employment?

Information on this question, so far as it is available, is analysed in

[1] *Economic Development and Cultural Change*, Chicago, October 1956.

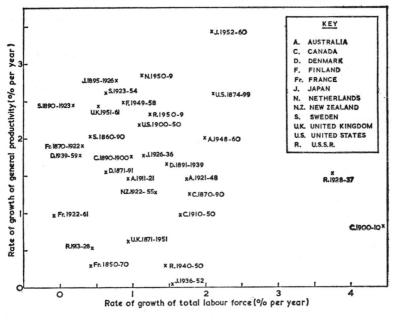

DIAGRAM VII.A

Diagram VII.B. The only evidence we have of adverse consequences from an exceptionally high rate of addition to the non-agricultural labour force is derived from Soviet Russia for the period 1928–37, when Stalin was attempting a phenomenally rapid industrialization; and from Canada for the period 1900–10, when there was a record rate of immigration. It would be interesting if we could obtain data about what happened in China in 'The Year of the Great Leap Forward' in 1958, when labour was withdrawn from agriculture on an immense and damaging scale, without making anything like a proportionate contribution to industrial production, the consequences of which the Chinese government has been trying to offset ever since. Attempts to raise non-agricultural labour force at rates as high as 5 per cent per year or more are likely to result in low or even negative rates of growth of industrial productivity. On the other hand, increases at any rate up to 3 per cent per annum (or even 4 per cent per annum, if we can judge from recent Japanese experience), are without discernible adverse effect on the rate of growth of productivity in this sector.

It does, however, appear that, in wealthy countries, the rates of productivity growth might be much higher than they are, were it not for the fact

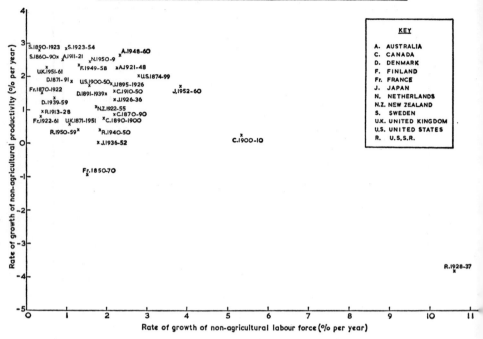

DIAGRAM VII.B

that so much of the additional demand at high income levels is turned towards services, both governmental and private, which, at any rate according to nearly all our experience so far, can only be supplied under conditions of productivity increase much slower than in manufacture or transport. Productivity increase in the building and construction sector is also slow.

If we confine our attention to the manufacturing sector, we get much clearer evidence of 'increasing returns', or of rising productivity brought about simply by the enlargement of the market. Verdoorn[1] made the simple generalization that productivity (i.e. product per man hour of labour input) tended to grow at the square root of the rate of growth of total product — re-expressed mathematically, the logarithm of productivity should be a linear function of the logarithm of product, with a slope of 0·5. This method of analysis is used in Diagram VII.c, where something approaching Verdoorn's relationship is found to prevail in an Anglo-American inter-

[1] First published in *L'Industria*, 1949.

industry comparison. A lower coefficient is found however in a general international comparison over a long period (Table VII.1). Verdoorn's interesting theorem appears to have been an overstatement, though it has been used by the Dutch Planning Bureau in both their long period and short period economic models. It is, of course, always difficult to analyse out the true effect of a change of scale of production, as distinguished from technical changes, or from the institutional and external factors which affect different industries or different countries. Table VII.1 shows, in comparable units throughout, measures of production and real product of man hour per labour in the manufacturing sector, for a number of countries at various dates going back to 1913.

Each figure of real product per man hour may be considered capable of being analysed into three elements (i) the conditions particular to the country, (ii) the conditions particular to the time when the observation was made, a general upward trend through time being expected, (iii) the consequences of the scale of production as such. These three elements are separated by analysis of variance.

The basis of the information is the figures for 'gross domestic product from manufacture at current market price'. In the past, it has been customary to measure 'value added' in manufacture, i.e. debiting only materials and fuel. The measure now used however debits all purchases from other sectors of the economy, including services. No debit, however, is made for depreciation. The year 1950 is taken as base for price conversions, because this was the year originally used by Gilbert and Kravis in the comprehensive international price comparisons which they made for the Organization for European Co-operation and Development. A uniform measure is obtained by converting all other currencies to dollars of 1950 purchasing power, assuming where necessary that coefficients designed for the national product as a whole are also applicable to manufacturing product. Production and productivity figures for earlier years are carried back on data given in *Conditions of Economic Progress*. They are carried forward, not by general index numbers of industrial production, but by figures from national accounts of real product from manufacture at given prices. This latter method allows for any change in the debits for inputs from other sectors, which a simple production index does not. Changes in manufacturing employment and in average hours worked in manufacture are from International Labour Office indexes with product and productivity both converted to logarithms. Analysis of variance gave a coefficient of 0·18. That is to say, for any increase in the scale of manufacture, all other things being equal, productivity tends to rise by a factor of the one-sixth power of the increase, not the square root.

TABLE VII.1. ECONOMIES OF SCALE IN MANUFACTURE[p]

	Gross domestic product from manufacturer at current market price[a] 1950	Purchasing power[o] of currency in 1950 $50	Manufacturing employment 000 [k] 1950
Argentine b p	14·58	0·198	1380
Australia[b] m £A	674·0	4·386	997
Austria[c] b sch	19·9	0·0870	840
Belgium b fr	88·7[d]	0·0259	1256
Canada b $	5·56	0·935	1271
Denmark b kr	6·26[e]	0·187	539
Finland b fm	151·8[f]	0·00538	411
France b fr	2945·0[g]	0·00335	4890
Germany b DM	36·15[h]	0·314	6806
Italy b lire	2755·0	0·001825	4682
Japan b y	978·0[i]	0·00621	5600
Netherlands b g	6·09	0·3655	1112
New Zealand m £ NZ	145·6[j]	5·03	175
Norway m kr	3720·0[l]	0·2025	358
South Africa[m] m £	257·0[i]	4·525	474
Sweden b kr	8·90[n]	0·274	978
U.K. b £	5·00	4·09	8220
U.S.A. b $	81·1	1·00	16113

NOTES:

a From U.N. Year Books of National Accounts Statistics, except where otherwise stated. Where 1950 data are given at factor cost, raised to market prices by the factor cost/market price ratio for the whole national product.

b For years 1949–50, 1952–3, etc. Base datum for 1949–50 from Australian National Accounts, raised to current market price.

c Original data inclusive of mining reduced by 4 per cent.

d From Cahiers Économiques DULBEA, raised to convert to market price.

e Factor cost, defined gross of maintenance Urban taxes, converted to market prices.

f Gas, water and electricity and mining included in original, which is reduced by 5·3 per cent.

g Original datum for 1952 reduced by 6·5 per cent to exclude mining and converted to 1950 by industrial production index and price index for whole gross national product.

h Original datum reduced by 10·3 per cent to exclude mining.

i Net product at factor cost converted to gross product at market price.

j For 1950–1, from Monthly Abstract of Statistics, July 1953.

k From nearest population census, extrapolated to 1950 on industrial employment index. Allowing for sickness, unemployment, holidays etc., this figure is multiplied by 49 times average weekly hours to give man-hours of labour input.

l As in Note *g* (but no exclusion of mining).

m Years 1950–1, 1952–3. Deduction of 11·2 per cent from original data to exclude construction. Data from 'Industrial Origin of Net Domestic Product' deflated by 'Home Goods' price index.

n O.E.C.D. estimate for 'value added' (Paretti and Bloch, Banca Nazionale del Lavoro, Der 1956, p. 225) reduced by 15 per cent for purchases of services.

o Argentine, Australia, Finland, New Zealand, South Africa, from Conditions of Economic Progress, extrapolated to 1950. Austria, Canada, Sweden, Wirtschaft und Statistik, 1954, p. 519. Japan, 1955 data from Kumano, Journal of Economic Behaviour, October 1961, extrapolated back to 1950. Rest from Paretti and Bloch, Banca Nazionale del Lavoro, December 1956, p. 225, who isolated manufactured goods from the Gilbert-Kravis O.E.C.D. study. For other countries general purchasing powers were used.

p I am much indebted to Mr. G. H. Peters for this analysis.

TABLE VII.1—*continued*

PRODUCTION

	in $ million of 1950 purchasing power					
	1910–13	1925–9	1935	1950	1952–4	1960–2
Argentine	1024	1239	1635	2887	2794	3465
Australia	742	1219	1744	2956	3654	5868
Austria	3896	1027	1084	1731	2123	3228
Belgium	1657	2171	2020	2297	2523	3556
Canada	1167	1841	2057	5199	6012	7480
Denmark	448	597	875	1171	1195	1713
Finland	161	320	489	817	988	1746
France	6965	10269	9339	9866	11306	18760
Germany	11975	12534	16420	11351	15983	31212
Italy	2140	3601	3879	5028	6753	13478
Japan	1444	4508	8338	6073	11116	37446
Netherlands	595	962	1430	2226	2555	4068
New Zealand	246	406	550	732	843	1308
Norway	199	268	366	753	859	1264
South Africa	63	289	428	1163	1158	1733
Sweden	609	845	1406	2439	2537	3628
U.K.	7985	11440	14812	20450	21759	28671
U.S.A.	20012	35736	35676	81100	92700	117800

REAL PRODUCT PER MAN HOUR

	$ of 1950 purchasing power					
	1913	1925–9	1935–8	1950	1952–4	1960–2
Argentine	1·02	1·02	1·10	1·01	1·04	1·59
Australia	0·88	1·09	1·39	1·44	1·75	2·41
Austria	0·55	0·79	0·86	0·96	1·16	1·52
Belgium	0·70	0·75	0·94	0·88	0·94	1·27
Canada	0·57	1·09	1·31	1·97	2·15	2·69
Denmark	0·60	0·82	1·04	0·92	0·98	1·25
Finland	0·44	0·67	0·86	0·92	1·15	1·83
France	0·57	0·74	0·96	0·93	1·05	1·62
Germany	0·58	0·61	0·74	0·71	0·84	1·43
Italy	0·23	0·39	0·43	0·46	0·60	1·01
Japan	0·27	0·46	0·56	0·46	0·73	1·55
Netherlands	0·42	0·56	0·94	0·84	0·94	1·33
New Zealand	1·72	1·76	2·11	2·14	2·36	2·91
Norway	0·52	0·92	0·99	0·97	1·07	1·59
South Africa	0·46	0·76	0·71	1·08	0·98	1·26
Sweden	0·53	0·68	0·94	1·23	1·34	1·89
U.K.	0·51	0·84	0·93	1·11	1·13	1·34
U.S.A.	0·81	1·37	1·86	2·54	2·72	3·83

Another analysis which can be made using these figures, together with figures of imports of manufactures, is to test the theorem of Carré.[1] Small countries, he suggested, must at first sight necessarily be expected to show the low productivity arising from the application of the theorem of economies of scale. An offsetting factor arises, however, from the fact of their importing a substantial proportion of their requirements of manufactured goods. In this way they can (assuming that they have sufficient manufactured or primary exports, or borrowings, to pay for the imports) employ 'phantom armies' of workers elsewhere, and in this way secure many of the economies of scale in an indirect manner. This idea, unfortunately, proved too good to be true. Each country's imports of manufactured goods, introduced into the analysis of variance as a possible further variable explaining productivity, were found to be non-significant.

Another method of analysis, however, does give results approximately confirming Verdoorn's square root law which may indeed be true for individual industries, with the more discouraging result above for manufacture as a whole — indicating the value to a nation of specialisation in a limited number of industries. Paige and Bombach,[2] improving on some pioneer work by Rostas, took U.S. and British data for 1950, and reduced them to comparable definitions of industries. They also obtained price conversion coefficients to express both outputs in common units of value. Measured in this way, the volume of output of the U.S. vehicle industry was about ten times that of Britain, while in textiles U.S. output was only a little over three times that of Britain. U.S. productivity exceeded British in all the industrial groups examined. But its relative superiority was found to be greatest where the comparative volume of production was also greatest. (See Diagram VII.c.) Assembled are the data, not only for the Paige–Bombach U.S./U.K. comparison for 1950, but also a comparison of U.K. industries in 1950 with their own record thirteen years later; and, again taking U.K. in 1950 as a base, with the U.S. figures for 1963. Crudely measured, we can fit all three sets of data by a line running diagonally across the diagram, with a slope of rather more than 0·5, indicating that the function by which productivity rises in response to increases in production is a little more than Verdoorn's square root law. However we must not take the result precisely as it stands. Between 1950 and 1963 in U.K. for instance, productivity rose in all sectors, including those — textiles, shipbuilding and leather — where total production had

---

[1] *Econometrica*, January 1958.
[2] *A Comparison of National Output and Productivity of U.K. and U.S.A.*, O.E.C.D., 1959.

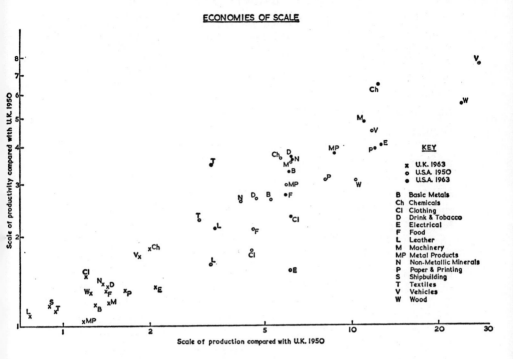

DIAGRAM VII.c

fallen. In all comparisons between different years we must allow for this general upward tendency of productivity.

If we draw a line through the U.S. data and carry it back to the point 1 on the horizontal scale, that is to say, so far as we can theorise on this subject, asking ourselves what the productivity of an American industry would be if it had to work on a scale no greater than that of a British industry, we find that the productivity is measured at more than 1 on the vertical scale. American industry, even when working for a limited British-sized market, would still be more efficient than British to the extent of some 25 per cent.

Even after allowing, as far as we can, for these disturbing factors, it still appears that the slope in the diagonal across the diagram might be in the neighbourhood of 0·5. Verdoorn suggested a theoretical explanation of many economies of scale in the 'learning curve', familiar to industrial psychologists — efficiency in doing a job depends on the number of times you have done it already. There must be a great many detailed studies in this field, but it is surprisingly difficult to collect general information. One remarkable result was published by Hirsch.[1] He analysed costs in an engineering plant which was turning out a great variety of products, some of which obtained numerous repeat orders, and some did not. The cost of each order was found to bear a fairly close proportionality to the reciprocal of the cube root of its serial number (i.e. the number of times the same article had been made before). This result does not relate productivity to the rate at which production is proceeding at the present time, but to cumulated production in all past periods.

Population growth not only reduces requirements of capital per unit of product, but increases its supply.

Keynesian theory, in its raw form, made the proportion of income saved always increase with rising income. The application of this crude theory quickly leads to a doctrine of secular stagnation, as it did in the hands of some of its over-zealous advocates in the United States in the 1930's. Most economists were left to conclude rather uneasily that there was a good deal in Keynes's explanation of the determination of short-period saving, but that it could hardly apply in the same way over the long period. In the 1950's Duesenberry (making considerable use of empirical work by Brady and Friedman) advanced a quite different theory of saving, namely that one's savings depended on one's relative position in the income scale, as compared with one's neighbour's. One interesting example of this theory was shown by Negroes in the U.S.A. saving more than whites at a given income level, because they stood at a relatively higher level on the income scale among their neighbours. But Duesenberry's theory in turn provoked a powerful counter-attack, led by Tobin, on behalf of what had by then come to be called 'old-fashioned Keynesianism', to restore the doctrine that savings were, on the whole, a function of absolute and not relative real income. (The higher savings of Negroes than of whites at a given income level could be explained, Tobin suggested, by the greater difficulties placed in the way of Negroes who seek to obtain bank loans or residential mortgages.)

Kuznetz then entered the debate with historical evidence, now refined to a high level of accuracy, showing that in the United States throughout the period since the end of the Civil War, with a great and sustained rise of real income per head, the long period measure of the proportion of income saved, with temporary fluctuations eliminated, had shown little change.

It seems clear that, while the level of real income per head is an important factor in savings, it is by no means the sole determinant. A study was set on

---

[1] *Review of Economics and Statistics*, May 1952.

foot, using long period data from all countries for which they were available, to throw light on certain other factors.

Our object is to obtain a long period analysis, and to exclude all short period and cyclical influences. For this reason, wherever possible, the years are grouped for periods as long as possible, preferably by decades; and where data are available for several decades in succession, alternate decades are generally omitted.

Information about savings in many cases took the form of net additions to fixed capital over the period, together with net inflow or outflow of capital from or to other countries. In some cases approximate estimates had to be made of capital accumulation in the form of inventories (which, in the long run, is always of a considerably lower order of magnitude than the formation of capital in the form of fixed assets). Occasionally also only the gross value of capital formation was available, in which case estimates were necessary of the amount of depreciation.

In a number of consumption studies, it has been found that the best fits can be obtained by relating absolute per head consumption to the logarithm of per head real income. This method is also used for measuring the relation between per head real income and saving.

Population growth, other things being equal, is found to have a positive effect upon savings. This indeed is to be expected, on the grounds, amongst others, that a slow growing population will have a higher proportion of old people, who tend to consume rather than to save capital; that parents of larger families may make more effort to save for them; and, perhaps most important, that with larger families younger men expect less inheritance, and therefore have to make greater efforts to accumulate for themselves.

Real incomes were expressed in dollars of 1950 purchasing power for all countries and times (not by the United Nations method, which converts at current exchange rates, but on the best possible valuation of the actual purchasing power of the different currencies).

A distinct relationship was found between capital outflow or inflow and savings (savings lower when capital inflow was higher, and vice versa). It is of course possible that we have got the causation the wrong way round, and that capital inflow is a *consequence* of low savings, and outflow of high; but a close study of Australia, a country with high and variable capital inflow, suggests that the causation is as indicated.

Finally we must take into account some beneficial economic change which appeared to come over the whole world at the beginning of the 1950's — principally the full employment of economic resources and, equally important, an expectation of its continuance, though other factors may have been at work too. All post-1955 data showed a substantially greater amount of saving, all other things being equal, than earlier periods (measured by fitting a dummy variable).

Another factor affecting savings was substantial war damage, which created an incentive, persisting for many years even after 1955, to save for purposes of reconstruction.

The following relation was obtained ($R^2 = 0.56$):

$$S = -4.40 + 2.10 \log_e Y + 0.58\,C + 0.10\,P + 5.08\,W + 3.15\,D$$
$$\quad\quad\quad (0.76) \quad\quad (0.13) \quad (0.04) \quad\quad\quad (1.06)$$

where S = Net savings expressed as a percentage of net national product at factor cost

Y = Real income per head of population expressed in dollars of 1950 purchasing power

C = Net capital outflow expressed as a percentage of net national product at factor cost

P = *Decadal* rate of population growth

W = War damage expressed as a multiple of 1938 net national product at factor cost

D = Dummy variable taking a value 0 for pre-1955 data, 1 for post-1955 data

Thus a 20 per cent rise in real income per head ($\log_e 1.2 = 0.1826$) raises the percentage of national income saved by 0.38. A 20 per cent per decade population growth raises the percentage saved by 2. The general change in the world economic climate since 1950 has raised the percentage saved by 3.15.

The population factor was tested to see whether population growth by immigration had any significantly different effects from natural growth; no significant difference was found.

Table VII.2 shows the countries covered and the data. Those not satisfied with the above equation (and the value of R^2 is not high) may develop further fruitful ideas from a scrutiny of the residuals unexplained by the equation. In particular, explanation should be sought for the persistently low figures for United Kingdom. Also Kuznetz's paradox has not been explained — the United States residuals show a very marked trend. Germany, except during the 1920's, saves considerably more than expected.

In assessing the effect of increasing rates of population growth on the rate of savings, we should bear in mind that, for low income countries, the capital-output ratio is usually of the order of magnitude of 2 or less; and therefore the effect of the increased savings upon the capital stock will also be significant.

TABLE VII.2. NET SAVING PERCENTAGES AND RESIDUALS

Country	Period	Net Savings Percentage of net National Product at Factor Cost	Residual not Explained by Equation
Argentine	1955–61	13·5	0·5
Australia	1861–70	8·4	−0·9
,,	1881–90	9·2	2·7
,,	1900/1–1909/10	14·6	2·9
,,	1920/1–1929/30	10·8	2·9
,,	1955/6–1961/2	18·7	4·4
Austria	1955–61	20·8	5·8
Belgium	1938	8·6	−2·1
,,	1955–60	13·1	−0·2
Brazil	1955–60	12·1	−1·6
Canada	1901–10	10·1	4·1
,,	1926–30	10·1	−0·6
,,	1955–61	12·0	−2·3
Chile	1936–40	−5·1	−0·1
,,	1955–60	1·0	−0·1
China (Taiwan)	1955–61	13·3	0·7
Colombia	1955–60	11·4	−1·5
Costa Rica	1955–61	11·6	−1·5
Denmark	1880–9	3·4	−4·3
,,	1900–9	6·7	−1·2
,,	1921–9	6·2	−3·9
,,	1955–61	14·8	0·1
Finland	1955–61	24·9	6·5
France	1845	16·7	8·1
,,	1885	8·9	−0·7
,,	1903–11	10·6	−0·5
,,	1928–30	8·1	−2·7
,,	1955–61	13·5	−8·8
Germany	1881–5	13·6	3·3
,,	1896–1900	17·5	6·4
,,	1911–13	17·0	5·4
,,	1925–28	6·9	0·4
(W. Germany)	1955–61	24·1	1·5
Greece	1955–61	12·4	−6·0
India	1954/5–1958/9	8·7	−1·3
Ireland	1926	9·0	3·8
,,	1953–61	10·2	−1·2
Italy	1862–70	7·4	0·6
,,	1881–90	6·4	−0·5
,,	1901–10	4·0	−3·8
,,	1921–30	8·2	0·9

TABLE VII.2.—*Continued*

Country	Period	Net Savings Percentage of net National Product at Factor Cost	Residual not Explained by Equation
Italy	1955–61	17·8	0·9
Jamaica	1950–3	6·2	−2·2
”	1957–61	11·5	4·2
Japan	1890–9	4·0	−1·6
”	1905–14	4·8	−1·7
”	1920–29	8·1	0·1
”	1955–61	29·1	7·2
Netherlands	1925–9	12·9	0·2
”	1955–61	22·2	1·9
New Zealand	1928–9	8·6	−3·5
”	1938–9	11·6	2·1
”	1955–61	16·8	2·0
Norway	1865–74	9·0	0·0
”	1885–94	5·3	−2·1
”	1905–14	7·3	−0·3
”	1920–29	5·1	−1·5
”	1955–61	19·5	1·3
Portugal	1955–61	8·3	−0·2
Puerto Rico	1955–61	4·9	−0·4
South Africa	1919–28	10·2	2·4
”	1929–38	11·6	2·2
”	1955–61	17·2	2·4
Spain	1955–60	13·5	1·7
Sweden	1896–1900	8·2	1·1
”	1911–15	13·6	2·9
”	1926–30	12·7	2·2
”	1955–61	16·7	2·6
Switzerland	1925–30	10·2	−0·1
”	1955–9	20·1	4·4
United Kingdom	1855–64	8·3	−3·2
”	1880–89	10·3	−3·2
”	1905–14	12·9	−2·7
”	1927–29	6·0	−5·6
”	1955–61	10·8	−5·4
U.S.A.	1869–73	13·1	4·4
”	1882–91	12·5	1·8
”	1902–11	12·7	0·9
”	1922–26	11·0	−1·4
”	1955–61	10·4	−5·5

SOURCES FOR TABLE VII.2

1. Savings

U.N. *Year Book of National Accounts Statistics* 1962 for 1955–61 data, and *Conditions of Economic Progress* for earlier data, if not otherwise specified.

AUSTRALIA: *Australian National Accounts* 1948–9 to 1961–2. Butlin, *Australian Domestic Product*, etc. 1861–1938/9.

AUSTRIA: Gross, *Weltwirtschaftliches Archiv*, July 1931.

BELGIUM: *Economist*, 24 June 1939.

CANADA: K. A. H. Buckley, unpublished thesis, quoted in *Capital Formation and Economic Growth*, National Bureau of Economic Research, 1956.

CHILE: Coers, *Estadística*, March 1944.

DENMARK: Bjerke and Ussing, *Studien over Denmarks National Produkt 1870–1950*.

FRANCE: Mayer, International Association for Research in Income and Wealth, Series III.

White, *The French International Accounts* (in preference to Mayer's data for income from abroad and capital outflow in 1885).

Pupin, quoted Goldenberg, *Quarterly Journal of Economics*, November 1946.

Marschak and Lederer, *Kapitalbildung*, London, 1936.

GERMANY: Hoffman, International Association for Research in Income and Wealth, 1959 Conference. *Vierteljahrshefte zur Konjunkturforschung* Sonderheft 22 (1931).

INDIA: Vakil and Brahmananda, International Economic Association, Gamagori Conference.

IRELAND: Kiernan, *Journal of Statistical and Social Inquiry of Ireland*, June 1933.

ITALY: Barberi, International Association for Research in Income and Wealth, 1955 Conference.

JAMAICA: U.N. *Year Book of National Accounts Statistics* 1957.

JAPAN: Rosovsky, *Capital Formation in Japan* (Producers' durable goods production and imports, plus construction, less military).

Ohkawa, *The Growth Rate of the Japanese Economy since 1878*.

NETHERLANDS: Wijnmaalen, Centraal Planbureau Overdrukken No. 26, 1953.

NEW ZEALAND: *Reserve Bank Bulletin*, November 1951, p. 167.

Monthly Abstract of Statistics, July 1953, Special Supplement.

NORWAY: Juul Bjerke, International Association for Research in Income and Wealth, 1959 Conference *Nasjonalregnskap*, 1900–29.

Bjerke's 'Net Domestic Product' (Table VI.3) is assumed to be at market prices and indirect taxes (Table VII.1) deducted.

SOUTH AFRICA: Franszen and Willers, International Association for Research in Income and Wealth, 1957 Conference.

SWEDEN: Lindahl and others, *The National Income of Sweden 1861–1930*, Vol. I, p. 255 (gross internal investment, excluding consumer durables); Vol. I, p. 268 (balance of payments); Vol. I, p. 172 (maintenance and depreciation of structures); Vol. I, pp. 140, 196; Vol. II, pp. 140, 408 (other maintenance and depreciation); Vol. I, pp. 224, 237 (net income excluding imputed services from consumer's durables other than houses).

SWITZERLAND: Marschak and Lederer, *Kapitalbildung*, London, 1936.
UNITED KINGDOM: Imlah, *Economic Elements in the Pax Britannica* and *Board of Trade Journal* (balance of payments).
Abstract of British Historical Statistics.
Feinstein, *Economic Journal*, June 1961.
UNITED STATES: Kuznetz, *Capital in the American Economy* (*Historical Statistics of the United States*, Series F).

2. War-time Damage

Conditions of Economic Progress, p. 608, also
BELGIUM: De Visscher, *International Affairs*, January 1946.
GERMANY: Gruenig, International Association for Research in Income and Wealth Conference, 1957.
ITALY: *Congiuntura Economica*, March 1946.
JAPAN: Yoshiue, International Association for Research in Income and Wealth Conference, 1957.
NETHERLANDS: Derksen, National Institute of Economic and Social Research (London), Occasional Paper X.
NORWAY: *Nasjonalintekten i Norge*.
UNITED KINGDOM: Brown, *American Economic Review*, September 1946 (not including external assets).

Since these calculations were made, some fresh evidence[1] from India shows a really rapidly rising rate of savings at a time of accelerating increase of population (Table VII.3).

TABLE VII.3. NET SAVINGS AS PERCENTAGE OF NET
NATIONAL PRODUCT, INDIA

| 1950–1 to 1952–3 | 5·0 | 1956–7 to 1958–9 | 7·9 |
| 1953–4 to 1955–6 | 7·7 | 1959–60 to 1962–3 | 9·3 |

These beneficial economic changes provoked by population growth are only one part of much wider changes in the nature of society, in its cultural and political as well as its economic aspects, which population growth evokes. In a previous chapter we have analysed this process for agricultural communities, showing how population growth compels them to change their methods of cultivation, and to economize in the use of land, albeit requiring them to work harder, but eventually producing a much more productive economy, capable later of sustaining an urban civilization. To study the developments of urban societies under the influence of population pressure calls for a width of information and a length of time span only to be expected of historians, whose work may bring to light qualifications or

---

[1] Reserve Bank of India Bulletin, March 1965, p. 14.

contrary cases to the examples set out below. But we do have historical evidence of a number of cases of the beneficial effect of substantial population growth in communities with a limited area of agricultural land, namely ancient Greece about the sixth century B.C., Holland in the sixteenth century A.D., Britain in the latter part of the eighteenth century, Japan at the end of the nineteenth and the beginning of the present century — and we may now be witnessing a similar sequence of events in India, beginning at the middle of the twentieth century. The cases have a number of features in common. The first is economic and commercial expansion, in which the development of foreign trade and shipping plays an important part, transforming the old-fashioned agrarian community into something quite different, with the greater part of its labour force occupied in commerce and industry. Accompanying this is a phenomenon sometimes associated with foreign commerce, namely the establishment of colonies — in the true sense of the word, of settlements of migrants from the mother country. (The word 'colony' is now often used as a derogatory term, in cases where the words 'territory' or 'dependency' would have been more appropriate.) In many of these cases colonial settlement, in the genuine sense, was also accompanied by imperialism, the establishment of political control over less advanced communities.

In many respects also these were periods of great cultural achievement. The world still marvels at the achievement of the Greeks from the sixth to the fourth centuries B.C., alike in architecture, in literature and in philosophy. Their achievements in painting and music may have been very great too, but have been lost. Subsequently they also achieved much in science and mathematics. The seventeenth-century Dutch enjoyed not only commercial and naval predominance, but also produced some of the world's greatest painting, with substantial scientific achievements also to their credit. Turning to Victorian England, regarding its performance in the visual arts, perhaps the less said the better; but this should not divert our attention from the very great achievements of the Victorians both as poets and as scientists. Japan has made substantial contribution to science, though it seems to be agreed that her great artistic achievements of earlier centuries have not been repeated.

In the political field, we find many annexations and aggressive wars. But, on the other side, we have many indications of population growth leading to a freer and more mobile society, both politically and economically.

The United States has enjoyed almost uninterrupted population growth for three centuries; and every American has come to take it for granted. It is easy to see that the economic, political, and cultural state of the country would be utterly different if this population growth had not taken place.

The establishment of markets, economic freedom, and competition, are generally desirable objects. Those who advocate them, however, are nearly always themselves members of advanced and well populated communities, and tend to take their own conditions for granted. It does not occur to them that the free market economy, which can be very beneficial under certain circumstances, only becomes possible if an important range of conditions is fulfilled; and that throughout most of mankind's history, and in a large part of the world at the present time, these conditions are not fulfilled. The successful operation of a competitive free market economy demands in the first place an ordered economy, enjoying (at any rate subject only to occasional lapses) peace and the rule of law; an educated community, capable of understanding the circumstances of their business, and of drawing up rational contracts with each other; a wide network of good and cheap communications and transport, so that both buyers and sellers are aware and capable of taking advantage of alternative opportunities — without this we get a world of petty monopolies or oligopolies (where the market is shared by a very limited number of competitors), or their counterparts, monopsonies or oligopsonies, where a limited number of buyers are in a position to exploit sellers. These necessary conditions for a free market usually cannot be attained in sparsely populated countries. Nor can they usually be attained in communities substantially isolated from commerce with their neighbours, whether through living on remote islands, or, as in some cases, isolated through their own policies. The present condition of such communities does not permit, but an increased population might render possible, sufficient sub-division of economic functions and intensity of competition for the successful operation of the free market.

Demands for state regulation of enterprise and of prices arise most strongly, and with some justification, either in sparsely populated countries, or in small and isolated island communities. It was in a similar manner, and for similar reasons, that the regulation of production and commerce by public authorities or by guilds prevailed in the urban communities of the past, effectively isolated from each other by high transport costs as well as by political barriers.

We have evidence of stationary or declining population leading to reduced freedom and mobility, in some cases to the most drastic degree. We have seen that the ancient world, at the time of the break-up of Roman civilization was losing, or at any rate failing to gain population. The costs of government became more burdensome, taxation increased, and (perhaps for the reasons which Sauvy indicated) political and social forces were set in motion which inflated the currency to a point where it became almost valueless. This inflation did not mitigate, indeed may have accentuated, the underlying fact, that there was a shortage of labour to perform all the tasks which society required. Barbarians were encouraged to settle, in very large numbers, on the vacant lands in the Empire, with a consequent lowering of economic and cultural standards, and at the same time, accentuating dangerous tendencies towards political and military anarchy. These barbarian settlements, however, were far from curing the labour shortage. By the third century A.D., long before the establishment of mediaeval serfdom as it has hitherto been understood, men were losing their economic freedom, were being compelled to remain *adscripti glebae*, as cultivators not free to leave their villages, or bound to remain in hereditary guilds following their father's occupation as sailors or craftsmen, or in other forms of labour for which the need was particularly urgent.

The hold of serfdom weakened from the eleventh century onwards, in the time of renewed population increase. Land owners and rulers were finding it easier to secure tenants and men to perform essential duties under freely negotiated contracts, which induced them to work much harder than serfs working under compulsion.

With the population decline of the late fourteenth and fifteenth centuries there came, according to Pirenne,[1] an increased rigidity in economic life. In most of Europe, this was swept away in the renewed population increases later. But describing the situation in fourteenth-century Flanders, Pirenne writes 'Between the master craftsmen and the apprentices or journeymen whom they employed, good will had lasted so long as it was easy for the latter to rise to the position of masters. But from the moment that population ceased to grow, and the crafts were faced with the necessity of stabilizing production, the acquisition of mastership had become more and more difficult . . . long terms of apprenticeship . . . raising of fees . . . each corporation of artisans was gradually transformed into a selfish clique of employers determined to bequeath to their sons or sons-in-law the fixed clientèle of their small workshops'.

The economic history of bondage, or serfdom, must not be oversimplified however. In much of Eastern Europe, outside the Turkish Empire, what had previously been a free peasantry was reduced to serfdom about the sixteenth century. The proximate causes may have been the rising prices of grain in Western Europe, largely due to the inflow of American silver and gold, and the opening up of sea communications, which gave the East European nobility the idea that they might earn cash from grain surpluses, which had previously been unsaleable. They were however also confronted by a sparse and mobile population ready and able

[1] *Economic and Social History of Medieval Europe.*

to migrate elsewhere if not legally restrained. Even in Denmark, bondage was actually reintroduced in 1740;[1] though this reinstated serfdom only lasted until 1780. With the growth of population and the extension of commerce, serfdom quickly disappeared, not so much on humanitarian grounds, but that it was found to be economically inappropriate, with sparsely-populated Russia coming last in 1861 (unless we take account of certain forms of near-serfdom still prevailing in some parts of Latin America, also a sparsely populated area).

But, it may be asked, would not many of the effects attributed to population increase have taken place without it? History unfortunately never provides us with evidence abundant enough for us to select proper samples and treat them statistically. However Dutch predominance in various spheres, as was mentioned in Chapter III, came to an end when population growth slowed down. And we do have one other very important case from which we can learn a great deal, namely France, which began to restrict the growth of population well before the end of the eighteenth century, while that of neighbouring countries went on increasing. And a number of French historians are now blaming the lack of population pressure for the comparatively slow progress achieved by French agriculture and industry in the nineteenth century. If population limitation were the key to economic progress, Sauvy stated unanswerably at the 1954 World Population Conference, then France would be the richest country in the world by now, for she has certainly practised it longest. It is true that since about 1870, when we begin to get some information about growth of national product, the rate of growth of productivity in France appears to have been as good as, or a little better, than that of her industrial neighbours. But this does not compensate for her late start. We have some direct evidence indicating a poor rate of growth of French productivity in the early nineteenth century.

It is a strange coincidence that in the year 1798, when Malthus was writing his book on the principles of population, and Jenner had just perfected vaccination, which was probably to do more than any other discovery to ensure population growth in Western Europe, Napoleon was successfully invading Egypt, and France, politically, came near to dominating the world. Malthus's own countrymen did not follow him, at any rate until much later, but the French did, and every Frenchman now is bitterly conscious that the decline of his country's influence in the world has been mainly due to its relatively lower rate of population growth. The English however have been slow in reaching a similar conclusion.

---

[1] Dovring, *Studies in Contemporary Society and History*, April 1965, p. 315.

The French historian, Combe, invented the interesting phrase 'le malthusianisme économique'. This was taken up in the recent Rueff-Armand Report, which has had a great influence on French economic policy. It describes that state of mind which prefers to restrict rather than to expand, which seeks protection, cartels, agreements to divide markets, rather than face the risks of expansion and competition.

This state of mind was spelt out more explicitly in Britain by Stamp, probably the leading formulator of economic policy in the 1930's, in a statement which he made as President of the British Association for the Advancement of Science in 1936, thereby attracting the maximum of attention. There was a logical connection, he stated, between 'planned population' and a restricted economy. 'Birth control for people demands ultimately birth control for their impedimenta.' So long as population is rising the products of new inventions and of new investments can readily be absorbed. But with a more or less stationary population the effects of new products and processes in displacing the old are likely to be much more keenly felt, and fiercely resisted by both capital and labour in the declining industries. So he went on to make, in all seriousness, the proposal that the introduction of all new processes should be deliberately slowed down so as to ensure that, in the older industries or processes which were to be displaced, there would be time for all the men to retire, and all the capital to be physically worn out. The cartellization of industry would favour such an arrangement. But in addition a special tax should be levied on all new industries which turned out to be successful, the proceeds being used to relieve the consequences of the displacement of labour and the technical obsolescence of capital. This, from the President of the largest of the railway companies of those days (already with much obsolescing equipment on its hands), and a Director of the Bank of England, had a considerable effect on British thought.

Keynes entertained similar ideas. But, in his own inimitable fashion, he proved himself able in due course to reverse his conclusions. In his younger days he had been a fervent Malthusian. In the 1920's he believed, on the evidence then available, that population growth in the industrial countries was finally and permanently coming to an end. A stationary population, he contended, would render private investment and the free market almost unworkable. This is one of the principal reasons he gave in his early work *The End of Laissez-Faire* (the central text of which took shape as a lecture delivered in Berlin, of all places). Keeping the free economy and expanding population logically linked in his mind, he nevertheless reversed his proposals in his Galton Lecture to the Eugenics Society in 1937. He preferred to see a free economy and abundant private investment, he said, and for this reason he advocated a rising population which would provide the best conditions for ensuring this.

Perhaps the last word on the politics of population was said[1] long ago by Ardeshir the First, King of Persia — 'There is no kingdom without soldiers, no soldiers without money, no money without population, no population without justice'.

[1] Quoted by Burckhardt.

CHAPTER VIII

Location of Industries and Population

THE economic effects of population growth, we have seen, may be adverse in agricultural societies maintaining rigidly unchanging techniques of production and systems of land use, but beneficial insofar as they enforce the adoption of newer and more productive systems and techniques. In industrial societies, on the other hand, where, almost by definition, techniques are being continuously improved, population increases are, in general, economically beneficial.

These conclusions however have been based, up to now, on the examination of national information and statistics. It is when we come to examine regional statistics of the growth of population and industry that we find these conclusions about the favourable economic effects of population density and population growth confirmed, indeed to an embarrassing degree. It is the regions already densely populated, and with still growing populations, which are found to be the most successful in attracting further industry and population.

It is these studies of regional growth which draw our attention to the real problems arising out of population growth in industrial countries. Such growth does not impoverish us; it enriches us economically, in the sense of providing to each of us on the average a greater abundance of the goods and services which we desire. What it does do is to create acute problems of requirements of land, for our homes, our recreation, for driving and parking our cars, for industry, and for many other uses. Under all these heads our requirements of land tend to be greater than those of our predecessors. The problems of land use and of the location of economic activities in all industrial countries are of rapidly increasing importance and complexity.

In studying the economic theory of location, one cannot help being struck by the predominance of German names (apart from Isard, generally regarded now as the leader in this field). The intellectual challenge of attempting to systematize such intractable material must have a particular appeal to the German mind. *The Economics of Location*, the most important book in this field, was published by Lösch in 1945. The possibility of a mathematical generalization of the relative numbers of towns and villages of different sizes was first discovered by Auerbach.[1] These relations were rediscovered independently, using much more extensive data, by Singer.[2] A similar generalization was made independently in 1940 by Zipf in the United States, though his formulation was much more limited. The essential theory of the reasons for the development of a hierarchy of towns and villages of different size was developed, and illustrated from contemporary data in Southern Germany, by Christaller in 1933. Two of the most important and fruitful workers on industrial location in the United States have been Chinitz and Fuchs, and in Australia Neutze, another economist of German descent.

We should also remember von Thünen, who in the 1820's developed a most original theory of the location of various types of agriculture around a consuming centre; and Weber, who developed a theory which unfortunately has attracted far too much attention, a pseudo-mathematical model whereby industries are supposed to be attracted to some sort of centre of gravity determined by the tonnages of their raw materials and products, i.e. a model determined by transport costs alone.

We may divide our problem, for convenience, into the two main sections of macro-location and micro-location. The use of these two prefixes, it is true, is not the same as their use in economic theory, where the latter refers to the analysis of the operations of the individual firm, the former to the analysis of national aggregates. In this case it is convenient to describe under the heading of macro-location the analysis of the location of population and industry as between regions and groupings of industrial towns (described as conurbations in Britain and metropolitan areas in the United States); and the term micro-location to describe in more detail how they are located within such areas.

A general description of what is happening in the modern industrial world can be given in one sentence, vast though its consequences may be. The macro-location of industry and population tends towards an ever-increasing concentration in a limited number of areas; their micro-location, on the other hand, towards an ever-increasing diffusion, or 'sprawl'.

But why, some may ask, not let these problems be solved by the free market, which has been successful in solving other economic problems? Why not let the free market put a price on land, and let those claiming it so clamorously for alternative uses decide how much they are able and willing to pay for land, and let the land be apportioned to various uses accordingly? As has been indicated in the previous chapter, the present writer is a

---

[1] *Petermann's Mitteilungen*, 1913.

[2] *Economic Journal*, June 1936. Singer (now a high official in the United Nations) was at that time a German refugee student, working in Cambridge under the supervision of the present writer.

believer of the ability of the free market to solve most (but not all) of our economic problems. But not in the matter of location and land use. There are three cogent reasons for expecting it not to be able to solve them.

The first is the exceptional slowness of adjustment. The essential concept of the free market is trial and error. You try something, you make a mistake, the consequences quickly become apparent in the form of reduced earnings, and you, or someone else, then rectifies the mistake. But can you say that this is a valid method of control in matters where you may have to wait two centuries before all the consequences of a decision are apparent? As we shall see below, this is literally the case with some location decisions.

The second reason is the existence of 'externalities'. This phrase is familiar to professional economists; but for others needs careful explanation. If A and B freely make a contract (and without either party exploiting the ignorance or weakness of the other — an important qualification of the principle of the free market from the point of view of morals) to exchange some commodity, or labour or land or capital, for a specified sum of money, then the economist generally regards the result of such free bargaining as socially beneficial. It is true that the bargain between A and B may affect C, D, E and others, if they were possible alternative sellers or buyers of the commodity or service in question. The bargain between A and B may have had the effect of preventing them from making the sale or purchase which they wished to make. But they have no ground for complaining, either from the standpoint of justice (says the moralist), or from the standpoint of the general social welfare (says the economist), so long as they were free to enter the market, without undue impediment, and to make their alternative buying or selling offers. If A and B were both aware of the existence of these competing offers (this availability of commercial knowledge, which is only possible with a good system of communications, is a necessary condition of the satisfactory operation of the free market, from the standpoints both of justice and of economics) and possessing this knowledge, A and B still decided to do the deal between themselves, then no one has any grounds for complaint.

'Externalities' arise however when the deal between A and B has a series of indirect consequences which affect the welfare of C, D, and E *without* their having an opportunity of entering the market and making competing offers. Externalities arise, so the most concise definition runs, when 'one person A, in the course of rendering some service for which payment is made to a second person B, incidentally also renders services or disservices to other persons, of such a sort that payment cannot be exacted from the benefitted parties, or compensation enforced on behalf of the injured parties'. This important development of economic theory was originated by Pigou (though the word 'externalities' came later) in 1912, when, qualifying the Marshallian tradition, he published *Wealth and Welfare*.[1]

One of the most important examples of an 'externality' in the modern world is the congestion of traffic. A customer, who does not at present drive during the rush hours, is offered the opportunity of buying a car and using it for this purpose. The garage which offers him a price for buying, fuelling and maintaining the car, and the railway which offers him an alternative means of transport, may both be making him perfectly reasonable offers from the economic point of view, fully representing both the private and the social costs incurred by them. We may go further and assume that the tax which he will pay on his car and fuel fairly represents, on the average, the cost of the road, traffic control, etc. But even so, his buying the car and using it imposes upon other road users further costs arising from the slowing down of traffic, additional use of fuel, and additional probability of accidents. The magnitude of these costs so imposed by each additional vehicle on other road users can indeed be fairly precisely estimated by traffic engineers. This is clearly a case where the other parties whose welfare is affected have no opportunity of entering the market as competing buyers or sellers, and thereby affecting the decision of the customer in question as to whether or not to buy the car. Similar 'externalities' (whose magnitude however is not precisely measurable at present) arise regarding the availability of land for recreation, the agreeableness of residential sites, and a number of other considerations affecting land use.

Another striking example of externalities is given by Berry[2] when he shows that, in the area adjacent to Chicago, no more than twenty location decisions made by major retailers during the next few years will effectively control the location of some 20,000 other retailers for the next 25 years.

Economic externalities however are more often beneficial, at any rate to the people of a particular country or region. They are then given the name of 'external economies'. The existence of these beneficial externalities may also justify some intervention against the free market allocation of resources.

The third respect in which the free market is defective in the solutions which it provides to problems of location and land use is that there appear to be cases of indeterminacy, a phrase familiar to mathematicians, and an important phenomenon in economics, even though comparatively rare.

---

[1] The enlarged editions of 1920 and later years were entitled *The Economics of Welfare*.
[2] North Eastern Illinois Planning Commission, *Metropolitan Planning Guidelines: Commercial Structure*, p. 94.

Many location and land use developments, which may have important consequences for centuries to come, arise almost by chance.

Myrdal is right in contending that the attractive power of a centre for industrial and commercial development today arises mainly out of the fact of its past growth, which started where it did and not in

'a number of other places where it could equally well or better have been started, and that the start met with success. Thereafter the ever increasing internal and external economies — in the widest sense of the word including also, for instance, a working population trained in various directions, lively communications, the feeling of growth and elbow room and the spirit of new enterprise, etc. — fortified and sustained its continuous growth at the expense of other localities and regions where instead relative stagnation or regression became the fastened pattern.'[1]

Reasons for this tendency, for already rapidly growing areas to attract more industries must also be sought, writes Hirschman,[2] in the realm of social psychology. People tend to 'sanctify and consolidate whatever accumulation of economic power and wealth has been achieved'. He boldly asserts: 'To the extent that this happens, a climate particularly favourable to further growth would actually come into existence' — quite apart from economic considerations, industrialists enjoy coming to work in such a psychological *milieu*. Explanations by historians and sociologists of social factors which favour industrial development, including the famous 'Protestant Ethic', 'instead of being the prime movers, may often be implanted *ex post*'.

Political factors also play their part. The industrial economy of Italy in the early nineteenth century was almost entirely handicraft. But at that time[3] the amount of industrial employment relative to agricultural was as high in the South as in the North. The political conquest of the South in 1861 appears to have had significant economic consequences. 'Monetary and financial centres have to follow the political headquarters . . . the very day the defeated King left Naples, the Rothschilds of Naples also left the town.'

There are therefore, in this field of location, good grounds for calling upon public authorities, making their calculations as carefully as possible, and acting with all due caution, to seek nevertheless to make and carry out decisions which will supplement the working of the free market, in some cases to anticipate movements which might otherwise only have occurred

---

[1] 'Development and Underdevelopment' Fifth Anniversary Commemoration Lectures, delivered in Cairo, 1950.
[2] *The Strategy of Economic Development*, pp. 184–5.
[3] *Economic Commission for Europe*, 1953 Report.

after extremely long delays, in other cases definitely to depart from the free market solution.

At best, however, this must only be a supplementation of the market. The complete replacement of the market in land by a system of public administration would be costly and inefficient beyond belief. The decisions which have to be taken about land use in any industrial country number literally millions every year. Not only the skill required in planning so many decisions, but also the administrative capacity to carry them out, must inevitably be lacking. The great majority of these decisions must now and always take the form of individuals or corporations selling or leasing land to each other. It is only at certain critical points that the supplementation of market forces is necessary. If every new industrial establishment, large or small, or extension of an existing establishment, had to be controlled by a system of governmental authorities and committees, the organization required would have to be large and intricate beyond belief. Moreover, we know that such government commissions would not do the job efficiently. However great the integrity and ability of their members, they would not know all the facts, and industrialists, in many cases, might conceal or distort the facts in order to make a case for a location which they preferred. The market in land must be preserved, but certain modifications introduced.

The form of action proposed[1] to deal with the undesirable present tendency towards undue concentration of industry and populations in a few limited areas, and depopulation of the remoter areas, is a system of taxes on employment in the former and subsidies to employment in the latter, the whole being worked out as a self-balancing financial project.

Hitherto we have used the adjective 'industrial' without defining it. Essential to our concept of an industrial country is the narrower concept of 'manufacture'. It is not however necessary, for the purposes of defining an industrial country, that the greater part of the working population should be engaged in manufacture. Indeed, in the wealthiest industrial communities, the proportion so engaged is low, and tending to fall further, with up to 70 per cent of the labour force, in some instances, being engaged in service industries. Nor is it a necessary concept that such a country should produce the whole range of manufactures. Some of the smaller industrial countries are highly specialized, and obtain the greater part of their requirements of manufactured goods by exchange with other countries. But nevertheless it is essential to our concept of an industrial country that it

---

[1] For further details, and examples worked out for Great Britain, see Clark, *Lloyds Bank Review*, October 1966.

should have a substantial number of efficient manufacturing industries, on whose existence indeed its economy depends.

The word 'manufacture' in turn needs definition. It is not an easy word to define. We need to exclude such operations such as building and civil engineering on the one hand, handicrafts on the other. The best definition of manufacture is that it is a continuous process, carried out on a substantial scale, of transforming commodities for ultimate sale to buyers over a wide area.

This definition by implication draws attention to an important consideration, namely the dependence of manufacture on transport. Where transport is as slow and costly as it was in the eighteenth century, only a very limited amount of manufacture can exist, and that mostly of commodities whose value is high in relation to their transport costs. Manufacture as we now know it only becomes possible after cheap transport has been made available.

Further consideration along these lines enables us to make an important classification of manufactures. Some processes, which are undoubtedly manufacture, use *materials* which are exceptionally bulky, perishable, or otherwise difficult to transport except over short distances. Examples of these are the conversion of milk into cheese, or the milling of logs or sugar beet. These are described as 'materials-oriented' manufactures, which by their nature cannot be located at any great distance from the source of their materials.

A counterpart group of manufactures supplies *products* which, because of their bulk, perishability, or for other reasons, cannot be transported for any great distance. These therefore must necessarily be 'market-oriented' manufactures, which must be located at not too great a distance from their markets. The definition here however is not quite so sharp as in the case of the 'materials-oriented' manufactures. The products of the industries usually quoted as examples of this category — brick making, printing, baking, brewing, soft drinks manufacture — are usually, it is true, sold within a short distance from where they are produced, but under certain circumstances may be transported over long distances.

Between these two there remains a third category, which in the modern world, though not so much in the past, covers most manufacturing production and employment, not restricted by unusual difficulties of transporting either the materials or the products. Such manufacturing industries are therefore freer in their choice of location. They are conveniently described by American economists as 'footloose'.

Consider now the industrial map of the world. Let us examine the location of those successful manufactures, whose existence is a necessary condition for general industrial development. We omit building and all the service industries which, like the market-oriented manufactures, must be located where their products are required. We omit handicrafts, and we omit also the materials-oriented industries, whose location is determined by the availability of supplies of agricultural, forestry or mineral products. Let us further confine ourselves to those manufactures which are efficiently and successfully carried on, as judged by their ability to sell their products in the world market; thus excluding a number of countries which have been able to develop manufactures (other than market-oriented or materials-oriented) only by creating within their own borders an artificially protected market for them.

The location of manufacturing industry, with the definition narrowed down in this manner, is found to be confined to a remarkably limited area of the earth's surface. In Western Europe, where manufacture (as we now define it) began, there is a great deal. But closer scrutiny will show how great a proportion of it lies along the 'axis' (a favourite word with geographers) running from Glasgow to Milan (with a small offshoot to Denmark and Sweden). In the United States, although in the last decade it has shown interesting signs of a much wider extension, most 'footloose' manufacture hitherto has been along the Chicago-Connecticut axis, and in Southern California. There are growing industrial zones in Russia and India, which only cover however a very small proportion of those countries' areas. Even in Japan, successful manufactures are confined to a limited area along the Tokyo–Osaka axis. The greater number of Japan's provinces are at present actually losing population.

Lösch made two very important points. The first was the tendency for regions already densely populated and growing to attract still more industry and population. The second was the extreme slowness with which such tendencies would be reversed. The present distribution of industrial population in Western Europe, he went so far as to say, was largely controlled by the pattern of population densities which had already been established in the agricultural society of the eighteenth century. This bold generalization has a great deal of truth in it, as we shall see below. But of course it must not be taken too far. It would of course be erroneous to claim that no new manufacturing region can ever develop successfully. In Europe, for instance, we see the successful extension of manufacture to Sweden. In Britain, Lancashire, a county of only agricultural population density at the beginning of the eighteenth century, became mainly industrialized in the course of that century.

On the map of the world, we also see industry developing in a number of areas which, until comparatively recently, had none. But, except perhaps in the United States, unusual efforts had to be made to do this. Japan and India started with the advantage of very high population density in the areas which they were seeking to industrialize. But in order to produce goods which they could sell in the world market they have both had to work for wages which were far lower than those of competing countries. (This refers, of course, to money wages, which determine the competitive power of exports; real wages have not been so low relative to other countries because Japanese and Indian internal prices have also been lower.) In Britain, the early and successful development of manufacture in Lancashire is often attributed by economic historians to comparatively minor factors, such as the availability of water power and the humid atmosphere suitable for spinning. In fact a large part seems to have been played here, as in nineteenth-century Japan, by the industrialist's attraction to low money wages.

Another very important point which Lösch makes is that in modern industrial countries trade unions press strongly for complete regional uniformity of wages. This desire is emotional rather than rational. Its effect is to deny to impoverished regions such opportunities as they might have had for attracting manufacture by means of low money wages (which, let it be repeated, would not necessarily have meant proportionately low real wages). Under eighteenth-century conditions, with high transport costs and little communication between regions, great differences in money wages could prevail. Arthur Young[1] gives average weekly wages of agricultural labourers in 1772, according to distances from London (Table VIII.1).

TABLE VIII.1. AGRICULTURAL WAGES IN EIGHTEENTH CENTURY ENGLAND

Under	20 miles	10/9d.
	20–60 miles	7/8
	60–110 „	6/4
	110–170 „	6/3

These were partly but by no means entirely offset by differences in prices. Bread prices were much the same everywhere, but Young records meat as costing one penny a pound more in London, and Gilboy quotes some evidence showing that clothing was cheaper in the remoter rural areas.

Ashton gives data[2] for average weekly wages (assuming a 6-day week) of urban unskilled labour (Table VIII.2).

Lancashire's attraction to employers at the beginning of the century was obvious, though by the end of the century it had become a densely

[1] Quoted by Gilboy, *Wages in 18th Century England*, 1934.
[2] *Economic History of England*.

TABLE VIII.2.   INDUSTRIAL WAGES IN EIGHTEENTH
CENTURY ENGLAND

	1700	1750
Lancashire	4/–	6/–
Oxford	7/–	7/–
London	10/–	12/–

populated and high wage area. Jewkes[1] points out that it was the cheapness of labour which attracted weaving to the North Lancashire towns, spinning having been developed in the South, in part at any rate for other reasons, including access to the sea.

From the sources quoted in Chapter III it is possible to compile a map showing, very approximately, population densities in late eighteenth-century Europe, and we can compare it with the present day (Diagrams VIII.A and VIII.B).

In broad terms Lösch's bold generalization is found to hold. Apart from the extension of industry to Sweden, exceptions in the opposite sense are the dense populations in Southern Italy, in small areas in Spain and Portugal, and above all in Ireland, which have failed to develop industrially. The reasons for these exceptions must be sought further.

On not quite so long a time scale, but making a more detailed study of small areas, a similar result was found in England.[2] The object was to compare the populations of rural areas in 1831 with those of a century later. The Census of 1831 was the first in which information was given in sufficient detail, and the last before the coming of the railway age. All such comparisons are harassed by repeated changes of administrative boundaries, calling for prolonged comparison of maps (any attempt to extend the comparison after 1931 would have broken down on this account). However, out of the counties of Hampshire, Leicestershire, Northamptonshire, Northumberland and Wiltshire it was possible to select 44 rural districts with reasonably comparable boundaries over the whole period. Of all the districts thus capable of comparison, the only ones omitted were those where there had been quite exceptional growth of non-agricultural population, generally due to mining development. These 44 districts were then ranged in descending order of agricultural population density in 1831, i.e. the number of males engaged in agriculture per unit of area of crops and grass.

---

[1] *Economic History* (Supplement to *Economic Journal*, 1930).
[2] These results were obtained in a long and patient study by Mrs. Margaret Rutherford, of the Agricultural Economics Research Institute, Oxford.

POPULATION DENSITIES PER SQUARE MILE
IN LATE 18th CENTURY EUROPE

DIAGRAM VIII.A

For each quartile were then obtained the median increases in agricultural and non-agricultural employment in the course of a century (Table VIII.3).

The more densely populated agricultural areas of 1831 did lose agricultural population more rapidly, though not strikingly so, than the less densely populated areas. But the differences in the rate of growth of non-agricultural employment are really striking. To have been already

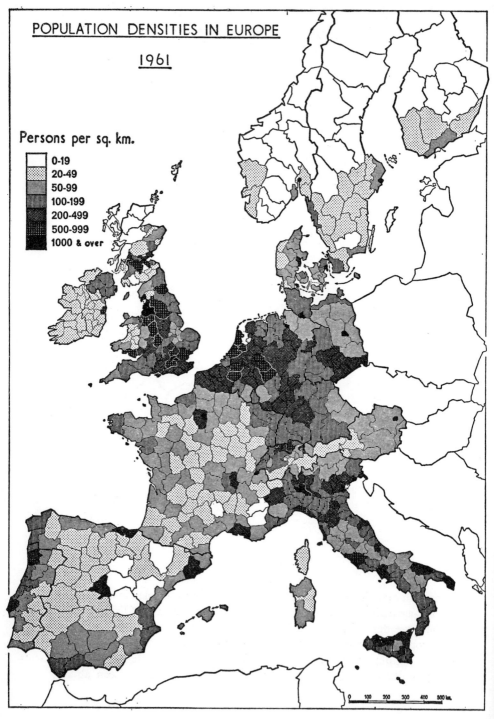

POPULATION DENSITIES IN EUROPE

1961

Persons per sq. km.

0-19
20-49
50-99
100-199
200-499
500-999
1000 & over

0 100 200 300 400 500 km.

DIAGRAM VIII.B

TABLE VIII.3. QUARTILES OF RURAL DISTRICTS ARRANGED IN DESCENDING ORDER OF AGRICULTURAL POPULATION DENSITY IN 1831

Median percentage changes 1831–1931

Men per 100 acres 1831	Number engaged in agriculture	Number engaged in non-agricultural activities
5·3	−42	+42
4·3	−42	+45
3·5	−32	+18
2·5	−35	+ 2

densely populated in the agricultural society of 1831 clearly had a bearing on the ability of rural districts to develop in the subsequent century.

We have seen how population density, and the availability of good and cheap means of transport, attract industry. But there is a very important further consideration — which may help to explain the lack of industrial growth in Ireland and Southern Italy — the most notable exceptions to Lösch's generalization about the densely populated areas of the eighteenth century being also those of the twentieth. If we have areas which are quite similar in natural resources, population density, and availability of transport, we must still nevertheless expect significant differences in their ability to attract manufacturing industry if they vary greatly in their ease of access to other industrial areas, if some are central and some are peripheral to the map of Europe. Even omitting the special cases of the market-oriented and materials-oriented industries, it remains true that every industry needs markets, and must purchase inputs. To a manufacturer choosing his location, the existence of a prosperous industrial area nearby will be *prima facie* indication of the existence of a market, certainly if he is selling directly to consumers, and probably, though less certainly, if his product consists of semi-finished goods which have to be sold to other producers. Regarding the inputs which he has to purchase, the economist may analyse them down to their ultimate elements of labour, capital, land, enterprise, etc. However, from the point of view of the individual industrialist, even a comparatively small business has to purchase a great variety of inputs — besides the labour, equipment, and raw materials directly used in production, a great range of commodities, at various degrees of fabrication, and of services, for the maintenance of his equipment, as well as for current production. The industrialist will not be concerned so much (unless his business is very large) with the quantities of these goods and services available locally, but with their availability in sufficient diversity, and obtainability in the near neighbourhood without undue delay. The aggregate population and wealth of an industrial area gives, though not a direct measure, a good practical indication of the likely availability of such a diversity of goods and services.

In practice, the only suitable regional data which we have for this analysis consist of regional statistics of population, employment, production and income. Regional income figures, where available, serve fairly well as an indication of the economic potential of a region, both as a purchaser of products from and as a supplier of inputs to industrialists in their own or adjacent regions.

The term 'potential' is borrowed from physics. If we know all the electrical charges within significant distance of any particular point, and sum the amounts of each charge divided by their distances from the point in question, we measure what we define as the 'potential' at that point. Likewise we can measure the incomes of regions adjacent to any geographical point in which we are interested, divide by their distances from the point, and sum the results to obtain its 'economic potential'. This idea was developed by Chauncy Harris, Professor of Geography at Chicago.[1] He prepared some 'potential' maps for the United States,[2] including an interesting map of the 'potentials' for purchases by farmers, which explained fairly closely the observed locations of the agricultural equipment industry.

One difficulty about using the reciprocal of distance in this manner is that the measure of potential in the middle of a densely populated and wealthy city may come out almost infinitely high. (The analagous problem does not arise in physics, because electric charges repel each other, and cannot therefore accumulate in very close proximity to each other.) Distance however is not exactly the measure which we should use. What we are concerned with is the cost, delay, risk, inconvenience, etc. of getting goods to and from another business. The costs of transport, packing, etc., are still quite substantial, even if the other business is only half a mile away. And on the other hand, as distances increase, the costs of transport do not increase in direct proportion. Both by railway and by road (though more so in the former case) transport costs contain a 'terminal' element, incurred however long or short the journey, plus a marginal element for each additional mile of travel.

Economic potentials for a number of principal positions in U.S.A. and

---

[1] The present writer was Visiting Professor at Chicago in 1952 and did some of this work in association with him.

[2] *Annals of the Association of American Geographers*, December 1954, and other papers.

Great Britain are calculated below on a formula which takes these considerations into account.

After lying dormant for some years, this idea of economic potential as a determinant of the location of industries was revived in New Zealand in an important paper by Elkan.[1] We should be able to get much the best measure of response to potential, he pointed out, in new countries, with fairly homogeneous population, whose movements therefore would not be impeded by strong local traditions and loyalties, and with relatively few old-established industries maintained in position by *vis inertiae*. Elkan's object was to calculate what was likely to happen to New Zealand manufacture if his country entered into a customs union with Australia, with results which were striking. He made use of the inverse of Harris's potential, calculating a 'market distance index', i.e. the purchasing power of each market (measured by the value of its retail sales) *multiplied* by its distance from the point under consideration, and the products aggregated. He applied this method of analysis to the six states of Australia (distinguishing in each the metropolitan area from the rest of the state); and also (again using retail sales as a measure of potential purchasing power) to the provinces of Canada (though in this case he treated the whole market of each province as concentrated in its largest city).

Elkan also introduced the valuable new idea of measuring the amount of manufacture in each state or province, not in absolute terms, but as a proportion of the state or provincial net output of primary products (agriculture, mining, fishing, forestry, hydro-electricity), which in both Australia and Canada predominated in the past, and still represent a substantial proportion of the whole national product. For Australia, the ratio of the value of net output of manufacture to that of primary industry was found to exceed 2 in the two states of highest potential (lowest 'market distance index'), Victoria and New South Wales; falling to 0·71 in Queensland and 0·75 in Western Australia. The fact that in the most distant state however, Western Australia, the ratio was a little higher, led Elkan to suggest that the relationship to economic potential might be parabolic rather than linear — distance from the leading markets, beyond a certain limit, may positively encourage certain forms of production, particularly of those goods which are comparatively difficult to transport, which begin to enjoy 'natural protection' because of high transport costs. Similar results were obtained in Canada, except that in this case the provinces fell into two groups. One group consisted of the two island provinces, Newfoundland and Prince Edward Island, together with the three 'land-locked' Prairie Provinces of Manitoba, Alberta and Saskatchewan. These provinces are

[1] *New Zealand Institute of Economic Research*, Technical Memorandum No. 8, July 1965.

much less industrialized, in relation to the value of their primary production, than the remainder. But within each group of provinces a parabolic relation between market distance index and industrial primary production ratio appears to hold. In the more industrialized group, the ratio for Quebec and Ontario is over 3, falls to 1·5 for Nova Scotia, but then rises again, with increasing distance, to 1·7 for British Columbia. Likewise, in the other group, the index shows a final upturn for the remotest province, Newfoundland.

For his own country, Elkan's final conclusions were that the ratios of industrial to primary production, which are at present 1·4 for North Island and 1·0 for South Island, would, under conditions of a customs union with Australia, fall to somewhere between 0·3 and 0·7 in both islands.

More light is thrown on the problem when we are able to analyse the composition of industries in the individual Australian states. This is not easy. In the national statistics, the structure of industry by states is only published in very broad categories. In the State statistics more detail is given, but the obligation to avoid disclosure of the figures for individual businesses has made it necessary for them to publish some of their industrial tables in combined form. A certain amount of highly approximate estimation was therefore necessary in some states. The results however were interesting.

The output of materials-oriented manufacture, in relation to primary production, does not vary very much between states, and in any case constitutes now only a small proportion of all manufacturing employment. The fact that manufacturing employment in Western Australia is higher than in the less distant state of Queensland is found to be fully explained by greater production in the market-oriented industries in Western Australia. The footloose industries, now constituting the greater part of all manufacture, are located very much in accordance with potential, without any sign of an upturn for the greatest distances (Diagram VIII.c).

Though much more industrialized than Canada, the United States also fulfils the condition of having been comparatively recently industrialized, with a homogeneous and mobile population, and with traditional established industries comparatively few (though their number is not negligible, particularly in New England).

For a country of Canada's sparse population and elongated topography, calculation of potentials by crude approximate methods may suffice. The accurate calculation of potentials for a number of points in the United States, on the other hand, would be a heavy task, even for a computer. In this case, a somewhat more refined, but still highly approximate method

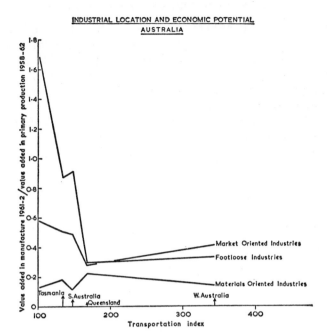

DIAGRAM VIII.c

has been used. The units of measurement are states,[1] the only exception being that a separation is made (on the basis of employment data) between Southern California and the rest of the State. In a few cases, States have been combined (e.g. New Jersey with New York). In each calculation, the contributions from states adjacent to the position in question, which contributed most to its potential, were calculated individually, but those of states at a greater distance were grouped, e.g. in calculating potentials in New England, it does little harm to treat Montana, Idaho and Wyoming as if their purchasing power were grouped at a single point.

Costs of transport were considered with arbitrary additional supplements to take account of inconveniences and delays (particularly with rail transport) in addition to direct cash costs. For any transport of goods, the minimum costs were estimated at 4·4 $/ton for journeys of 50 miles or less. To this is added a marginal cost of 3·6 cents/ton-mile for marginal cost of transport by road up to a distance of 200 miles, beyond which point it is estimated that rail transport becomes cheaper, with a marginal cost of 0·9 cents/ton-mile for the next 100 miles, 0·6 for the next, and 0·3 subsequently.

[1] Information on personal incomes by states, and each state's primary and manufacturing production, from *Survey of Current Business*, August 1965.

To the purchasing powers of the states as recorded in the form of their individual incomes, supplements were allowed to the extent of 2 per cent. of the whole to represent the purchasing power for U.S. goods of the Canadian market, and 5 per cent for all other export markets, potential being measured according to distance from the leading centres in Canada, or the nearest large sea port, respectively.

In the United States, the state ratios between manufacturing and primary production show nearly a 500-fold range. Diagram VIII.D shows that, to a considerable extent, these differences are accounted for by differing potentials.

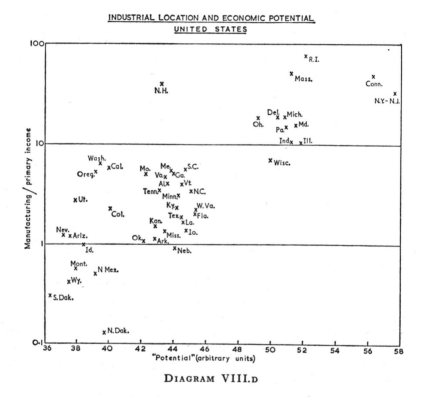

DIAGRAM VIII.D

Naturally one examines closely the principal deviations from the general line. The New York–New Jersey combination, which has the highest potential, is clearly below the line. As we shall see also from other evidence, at a certain level of industrialization and congestion countervailing forces come into play, impeding further growth.

Massachusetts, New Hampshire and Rhode Island were predominant manufacturing states in the nineteenth century. Their position above the line may be accounted for by the fact that they contain a number of old-established industries, particularly textiles, which almost certainly would not be re-established there now, if the industrialist were starting again.

On the other side of the country, California, Oregon and Washington, and to a less extent Utah, are well above the line indicated by smaller states of similar potential. It may be that when low potential (i.e. substantial distance from other main industrial centres) is offset by a local market which has already arisen above some critical size, then a fresh spurt of industrialization may take place — Los Angeles being the first and most striking example of this.

Chinitz[1] points out that it was the railway age which was really responsible for the geographical concentration of industry. Transport costs are now rising relative to manufacturing costs — between 1947 and 1954 an index number of rail freights for given weights of consignment and lengths of haul rose 41 per cent. Road transporters made the short haul and the small consignment both relatively cheaper than they used to be, and in this way favoured the small local manufacturer. He shows the percentage distribution of U.S. manufacturing output between regions at certain dates (Table VIII.4).

TABLE VIII.4.   PERCENTAGE REGIONAL DISTRIBUTION OF U.S. MANUFACTURE

	1860	1899	1929	1954
New England	30	18	12	9
Mid Atlantic	42	34	30	26
North Central	16	29	35	35
South Atlantic ⎱	8	⎰ 10	10	11
South Central ⎰		⎱ 6	7	9
Mountain and Pacific	4	4	6	10

Lösch, working in the United States during the 1930's, drew attention to the fact that many American manufacturing industries then tended to be irrationally over-centralized, with manufacturers apparently unaware of the high marginal costs which they were incurring in their transportation and selling of goods at excessive distances from the place of production. Since then, with transport costs rising still further relative to the cost of manufacturing production, and, with the size of the market also greatly expanded, many industrialists have found it worthwhile to establish branch

[1] *Traffic Quarterly*, April 1960.

plants to serve the markets which were formerly served from one plant. In this way, employment in manufacturing industries, and also in the service industries which go with them, has become considerably more decentralized. In particular, this may give us some explanation of the expansion of manufacture above the line indicated by 'potential' in some western states. Also the total volume of transport required has been found to be rising less rapidly than the real national product.

We can test our theories about the effects of distance most severely in respect of Alaska and Hawaii, which are economically part of the United States, and can trade with the mainland unimpeded in any way except by high transport costs. Their ratios of manufacturing production to primary are found to be 2·15 and 1·57 respectively. If however we treated the earnings of the Forces (excluded from the production figures) as a form of primary production, we would get much lower ratios. These would be comparable with the ratios found in the remoter mountain states on the mainland.

It has been widely held in the United States that industrial growth in some of the more rapidly developing states, particularly California, Texas, Florida and Colorado, was mainly due to the growth of market-oriented industries, which in turn had been due to the addition of large numbers of retired persons and others to the population. As we have already seen, this is not a very precise demarcation; for some industries not generally regarded as market-oriented may nevertheless act in the same manner when transport costs become exceedingly high. This view however was criticized in an important paper by Fuchs.[1] Industries which he identified as market-oriented represented only 11 per cent of all manufacturing employment in U.S. in 1954. This proportion was, as might have been expected, higher in the remoter and newly-developing states. But in California it was only 13 per cent. It was high in Colorado (23 per cent) and in Florida (32 per cent). Fuchs refined the analysis by measuring the 'comparative' gains or losses of manufacturing employment in different states and regions, i.e. the difference between their actual growth over the period 1947–54, and what their growth would have been if every state and region had developed at the average U.S. pace. The old industrial regions in the North-East, as far west as Chicago, were showing substantial comparative losses, when the South and the West were gaining. But in almost every case, except in the Mountain States and Florida, the relative part played by the supposedly market-oriented industries in the comparative gain or loss of manufacture for the whole region was of a similar order of magnitude to its part at the beginning of the period. In other words, except for the mountain regions

[1] *Review of Economics and Statistics*, May 1962.

and Florida, which are more than usually remote, the development of manufacture in the rapidly-growing states and regions includes market-oriented and footloose industries in much the same proportions as it did before. The market-oriented industries cannot therefore be regarded as the cause of the faster growth of industry in these regions.

In Britain, both industry and population are much more bound by history and tradition, and we would by no means expect a location of industry precisely in accordance with potential. In this case however *changes* in employment in manufacture over recent periods may be compared with potential.

The results[1] show that the rate of growth of employment in the largest conurbations has indeed been slowed down, to some extent by deliberate Government action; but that apart from that there is a fairly clearly marked relationship between potential and later growth of employment.

The map showing population changes in Europe during the last decade also strongly illustrates this tendency for industry to grow in areas of high potential (Diagram VIII.E).

The concept of economic potential probably explains the mechanism whereby the densely populated areas of the eighteenth century, with a few additions and deletions, became the densely populated areas of 1950. With a few exceptions, such as the south coast of France and the Pyrenees, these are also the areas rapidly gaining population in the decade 1950–60.

One of the most remarkable examples of this concentration is in Japan. Although land is very scarce in relation to population, nevertheless the majority of the rural provinces are losing population by migration to a limited number of already very densely populated industrial centres (Diagram VIII.F).

So far we have considered population and its growth by regions, of which we consider only a limited number in each country, and to whose individual characteristics some attention can be paid. We now proceed to consider individual towns and villages. Here, of course, numbers are much greater, and treatment (with very few exceptions) must be statistical, categorizing the numbers of towns and villages within certain size ranges, and some of their attributes.

The fundamental theory of the distribution of towns and villages by size was worked out by Christaller in 1933.[2] He found that his theory did fit the facts quite well as they were in his own district of Swabia, a rural area in South Germany with some scattered small industries, as it was in the 1930's. Much of his theoretical formulation, however, turned on the

---

[1] Clark, *Lloyds Bank Review*, October 1966.
[2] *Die Zentralen Orte in Sud Deutschland.*

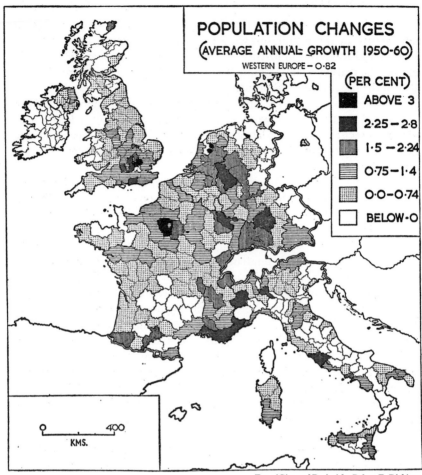

POPULATION CHANGES
(AVERAGE ANNUAL GROWTH 1950-60)
WESTERN EUROPE — 0·82

(PER CENT)
- ABOVE 3
- 2·25 — 2·8
- 1·5 — 2·24
- 0·75 — 1·4
- 0·0 — 0·74
- BELOW·0

0   400
KMS.

From 'City and Region' by Robert E. Dickinson

DIAGRAM VIII.e

supposed use of horse transport. It may be possible to re-state his theory for a time of motor transport. But it will have to be with different coefficients.

Christaller imagines a population of farmers needing first a small village which can satisfy their most frequently recurring trading needs, and which can be reached without too much travelling. Such *Marktorte*, the smallest and most widely distributed types of village, he hypothecates with a population of about 1000, and on the average only 7 km. apart.

The farmers however, and also the villagers of the *Marktorte*, have a

JAPAN—NET MIGRATION RATE BY PREFECTURE. (1955-60 average)

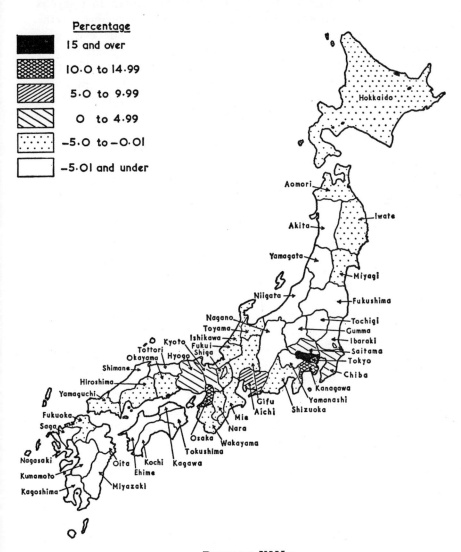

Percentage

- ■ 15 and over
- ▨ 10.0 to 14.99
- ▨ 5.0 to 9.99
- ▧ 0 to 4.99
- ⋯ −5.0 to −0.01
- □ −5.01 and under

Hokkaido

Aomori

Akita

Iwate

Yamagata

Miyagi

Niigata

Fukushima

Nagano

Toyama

Tochigi

Gumma

Ishikawa

Ibaraki

Kyoto

Fukui

Saitama

Tottori

Shiga

Tokyo

Okayama

Hyogo

Chiba

Shimane

Kanagawa

Hiroshima

Yamanashi

Yamaguchi

Gifu

Shizuoka

Aichi

Fukuoka

Mie

Saga

Nara

Osaka

Wakayama

Nagasaki

Tokushima

Kumamoto

Oita

Kochi

Kagawa

Ehime

Kagoshima

Miyazaki

DIAGRAM VIII.F

'hierarchy' of needs which can only be satisfied by larger towns. The next need beyond immediate trading requirements (remember that this is Germany!) is Government officials. So the next stage in the hierarchy is the *Amtsort*; and increasingly larger towns beyond that. The essence of Christaller's theory is that towns and villages can be at any rate roughly classified into these types; and that as we go up each step of the hierarchy we find each town or village serving about three towns or villages of the order below it. The consequence is that the relative number of towns and villages in the different orders is expressed by the powers of three.

TABLE VIII.5.   CHRISTALLER'S MODEL

		Approximate population '000	Distance apart km.	Deduced relative numbers
I	Marktort	1	7	729
II	Amtsort	2	12	243
III	Kreistadt	4	21	81
IV	Bezirksstadt	10	36	27
V	Gaustadt	30	63	9
VI	Provinzstadt	100	110	3
VII	Landstadt	500	185	1

Lösch, writing shortly afterwards, examined Christaller's theorem carefully. He was willing to support it, with the important modification that each type of town should be expected to serve on the average four rather than three of the next lower order, and that their relative numbers should rise therefore in powers of four.

Lösch defends this figure of 4 on the grounds that, if it prevails, the average distance between towns of the order n should be 2 (the square root of four) times the average distance between towns of the order $(n-1)$ — and this he finds to be true on the whole in the United States.

We have information from a number of countries making it possible for us to analyse much more closely the ranges of distance over which various types of purchases are in fact made.

For rural England in the 1930's, provided with a cheap and widespread 'bus service, but in which cars were still only used by a minority, an estimate of the distances up to which customers would be willing to travel for various types of purchases was made by Ashby[1] (Table VIII.6).

A rather more careful analysis, quoted by Lösch, was made by the Iowa State Planning Board in 1936. Referring to five villages with populations between 500 and 1,000, by that date already probably fully motorized, and

[1] Town and Country Planning Conference, October 1943.

TABLE VIII.6. MAXIMUM DISTANCES TRAVELLED FOR
PURCHASES (MILES)

	To village or small town	do. if to larger town
Tobacco, confectionery	3	
Food	8	
Banking	5	8
Pharmaceutical goods	8	10
Household equipment	10	30
Working clothing	10	
Children's clothes	10	30
Better clothing	15	30
Display clothing	50	100
Jewellery	10	150
Cheap furniture	15	50
Better furniture	50	100

at very varying distances from the nearest town, the proportions of certain requirements purchased in the town are indicated in Table VIII.7.

When distances are sufficiently large, people become willing to purchase a substantial proportion of their requirements, even of such commodities as furniture and clothing, in the local village store, rather than travel long distances.

TABLE VIII.7. PURCHASES FROM DISTANT TOWNS

Distance to nearest town in miles	8	12	15	38	49
Percent purchases made of: kitchen utensils	53	11	11	3	0
furniture	100	53	82	54	25
men's clothing	100	94	82	75	58

A really profound and original analysis of the economic and social functions of small towns of varying sizes was made by Berry, Barnum and Tennant.[1] These workers chose for their survey territory an area in South-Western Iowa which was geographically, economically and socially homogeneous (Diagram VIII.G). They ventured to categorize all settlements in five categories, ranging from regional capital to hamlet. This however was not a matter of subjective judgement, but based on the functions which each settlement was in fact observed to perform. The importance and originality of the work lay in the precise listing of their functions[2] (Table VIII.8).

[1] 'Retail Location and Consumer Behaviour', Papers and Proceedings of the Regional Science Association, 1962.
[2] In a number of cases the customary English description of various trades (e.g. public houses) has been substituted for the American.

TABLE VIII.8. CITY, TOWN AND VILLAGE FUNCTIONS

City-Level Functions

Women's Clothing
Men's Clothing
Shoes
Jewellery
Florist
Supermarket
Bakery
Wines and Spirits
Specialized Medical Practice
Solicitor
Hotel
Motel
County Government
Local Newspaper
Trade Union Office
Sales of New Cars
Sales of Used Cars
Specialized Car Repairs
Car Wrecking
Laundry
Self-Service Laundry
Shoe Repair
Plumbing
Household Equipment Repair Service
Cinema
Indoor Amusements (Billiards, etc.)
Drive-in Restaurant

Town-Level Functions

Furniture
Household Appliances
Chain Store
General Clothing
Chemist
Bank
Insurance Office
House and Estate Agency
Telephone Exchange
Dry Cleaner
Doctor
Dentist
Building Contractor
Building Materials
Radio-TV Sales and Services
Movers and Hauliers
Undertaker

TABLE VIII.8—*continued*
Veterinarian
Car Parks
Farmers' Co-operatives

Village-Level Functions
Petrol Service Station
Car Repair
Public House
Café
Grocery
Post Office
District Council Office
Church
Village Hall
Hardware
Farm Materials
Dealer in Farm Products
Farm Implements
Oil Fuel Bulk Station
Barber
Beauty Parlour

THE STUDY AREA

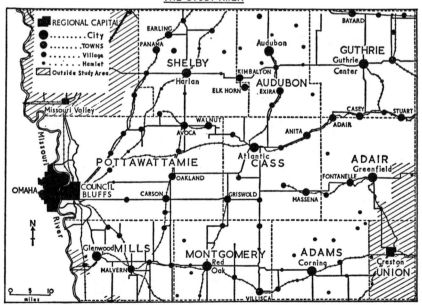

DIAGRAM VIII.G

As well as listing the functions performed, they also counted the numbers of traders performing them. In the smallest villages, while one trader may perform several functions, the number of traders may be actually less than the number of functions. But as settlements become larger one expects the number of traders to be considerably greater than the number of functions performed, i.e. a substantial degree of competition. The most valuable discovery of the authors is that the data of numbers of functions, and of numbers of traders, can be fitted tightly into a semi-logarithmic pattern, with the slopes moreover varying at points which are readily discernible, and which enable us clearly to distinguish the types of settlements categorized as hamlets, villages, towns and cities (Diagram VIII.h).

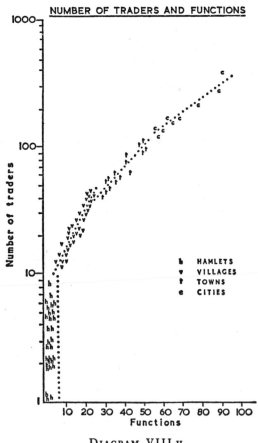

DIAGRAM VIII.h

These very small hamlets, never performing more than six or seven functions, and often with only one or two traders, fulfil the functions performed, in more densely populated areas, by larger villages. In densely and in sparsely populated rural areas the actual number of settlements per unit of area tends to be about the same, so that a farmer does not have too far to go to make his most frequent purchases, though the sizes of the settlements will be very different.

A British and an American geographer[1] made a detailed comparison of the pattern of settlement in Wisconsin, settled in the mid nineteenth century, and in Southern England, settled more than a thousand years earlier.

Contrary to the theories of some geographers and economists, who have held that a sparser population evokes a different pattern of settlement, they found that the actual geographical pattern of the settlement was very similar in the two areas. What were very different however were the populations of each order of towns and villages, and of the rural areas which they served.

TABLE VIII.9. COMPARISON OF SETTLEMENTS IN
WISCONSIN AND SOUTHERN ENGLAND

	Wisconsin	S. England
Area covered (sq. miles)	7170	6969
Populations covered ('000)		
Rural	217	998
Urban	158	1930
of which Madison	100	
Reading, Plymouth, Southampton, Bournemouth }		600 approx.

	Higher Order Centres		Lower Order Centres	
	Wisconsin	S. England	Wisconsin	S. England
Nos. of Towns	19	26	73	44
Median population of town	2515	13850	400	5080
Mean size service area (sq. miles)	129	128	32	48
Mean population of service area	2440	21080	610	7180
Mean intercentre distance (miles)	21	21	10	8

Pre-railway settlement, in both cases, was patterned on villages 4–6 miles apart. This remains the pattern still in a few districts not served by larger centres.

After his analysis of the functions of villages and towns Berry and his co-workers turned to the problem which all investigators hitherto have

[1] Brush and Bracey, *Geographical Review*, October 1955.

found so difficult, namely classifying the area and populations served. The fit in this case is not so close; but the results are clearly understandable (Diagram VIII.1).

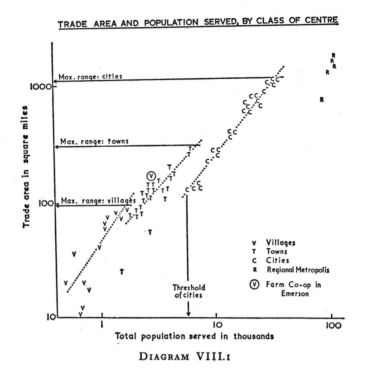

TRADE AREA AND POPULATION SERVED, BY CLASS OF CENTRE

DIAGRAM VIII.1

On this diagram hamlets are not marked; but they presumably serve, under American conditions, populations of a few hundreds. Villages may serve from anything from 10–100 square miles, but in no case a population over 1,400. Towns serve population from this level up to about 6000, the 'threshold of cities'. With some exceptions, the area served by towns is proportional to the population served by them (the slope of the logarithmic relationship is not very different from one). This means that in areas where population is dense there is *not* any discernible tendency to place towns closer together. One interesting exception is indicated for the town of Emerson, which is the centre of a farm co-operative, and for that reason serves an area unusually large in relation to its population.

In a more recent study[1] of an urban and suburban area Berry has

[1] North-Eastern Illinois Planning Commission, *Metropolitan Planning Guidelines*; Commercial Structure, p. 177.

obtained a similar diagram for the different types of shopping centre and
their functions (Diagram VIII.j).

Another very thorough study of this nature was that undertaken by
Piatier at the University of Bordeaux,[1] who enlisted the services of village
schoolmasters to analyse where the villagers made their purchases of a
large number of specified commodities.

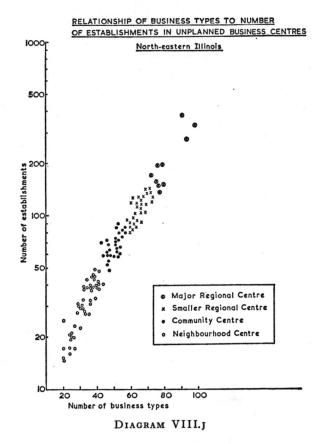

DIAGRAM VIII.j

First, however, he analysed, in a manner comparable with the Brush–
Bracey results, the service areas of different types of towns (Table VIII.10).

Some confirmation is seen of the orders of magnitude obtained by Brush
and Bracey. If Bordeaux were included as one of the centres in Gironde,
the average area served would be raised to 340 sq. km. There is no explana-

[1] *Revue Juridique et Economique du Sud-Ouest*, 1956, No. 14, 1958, No. 2, 1960, No. 1.

TABLE VIII.10. AREAS SERVED BY SETTLEMENTS

	Regional Capital	First Order Centres		Second Order Centres		Percentage of total area served by lower order centres
	Area served sq. km.	Number	Average area served sq. km.	Number	Average area served sq. km.	
Département Gironde	903 (Bordeaux)	7	261	12	62	76
Département Loir-et-Cher		3	736	13	99	44
Département Maine-et-Loire		3	279	15	72	73
Brush–Bracey results:						
Wisconsin			333		83	
Southern England			330		124	

tion, however, of the very large average area served by the first order centres in Loir-et-Cher. As is seen from the last column, this is rather an unusual area, with a big city as its centre, but on the whole sparsely populated, with more than half the area distant from towns, even from small towns, and served by villages.

Diagram VIII.K shows the populations of Bordeaux and of the first order centres, in Département Gironde, and the distances between them by main road, which of course are longer than the lineal distances.

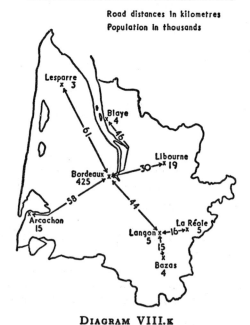

GIRONDE

AREA OF MARKET ATTRACTION MEASUREMENTS

Road distances in kilometres
Population in thousands

DIAGRAM VIII.K

TABLE VIII.11. LIMITS OF ATTRACTION (DISTANCES IN KMS.)

	In competition with Bordeaux					In competition with Langon	
	Libourne	*Arcachon*	*Langon*	*Blaye*	*Lesparre*	*La Réole*	*Bazas*
Population '000	19	15	5	4	3	5	4
Distance from larger towns (kms.)	30	58	44	46	61	16	15
Distances measured from Bordeaux (kms.):							
Bordeaux's share of food purchases over 50 per cent	10	17	6	10	8		
" " " " 20—50 per cent	10	17	6	26	25		
" " " " below 20 per cent	22	17	24	34	31		
Distance measured from smaller centre (kms.):							
Food: over 50 per cent of purchases	10	9	7	3	26	6	4
Tools: over 60 per cent of purchases	10	9	3	12		5	8
30—60 per cent "	10		10	15	10	7	11
Textiles and clothing over 60 per cent of purchases	2	2	11	5	11	6	3
30—60 per cent "	11		6	12	12	10	7
Footwear over 60 per cent of purchases	10	2	15	5	11	3	2
30—60 per cent "	15	5	5	10		6	5
Furniture over 60 per cent of purchases	7	2	10	16	10	6	4
30—60 per cent "	11		2				
Hardware over 60 per cent of purchases	10	2	5	10	8	4	2
30—60 per cent "	10	2	2	12			
Car and cycle over 60 per cent of purchases	11	13	2	6	9	7	3
30—60 per cent "		2	5				
Household equipment over 60 per cent of purchases	10	2	12	9	10	10	3
30—60 per cent "	11	2	11			5	7
Doctors and dentists over 60 per cent of purchases	2	2	2	0	0		
30—60 per cent "	10	10	12	5	0		2
Surgery over 60 per cent of purchases	6	2	2	5	10	4	
30—60 per cent "			3				
Banks over 60 per cent of purchases	10	2	12	5	10	10	
30—60 per cent "	6	10	3				
Cinema and sports over 60 per cent of purchases	5	2	2	2	10	8	3
30—60 per cent "		4	6	6	10	12	
Annual Sales over 60 per cent of purchases	11	0	2	0	0		
30—60 per cent "			6	6			

Piatier's maps, which are shown in full detail in the latter two of his publications, show precise boundaries of the areas of each settlement's market attraction, measured by its serving specified proportions of total local demand. From measuring these maps it is possible to state the distances up to which the smaller centres can compete in the direction of Bordeaux, and also sometimes the manner in which three small towns close together can compete with each other (Table VIII.11).

Regarding sales of food, Bordeaux can only dominate the market, in the sense of providing over 50 per cent of food purchases, over a radius of ten kilometres, except in the direction of Arcachon, a forested area where population is sparse and shopping centres few. The smaller towns are able to sell food over a somewhat smaller radius with the interesting exception of Lesparre, which, although it only has 3000 population, faces little competition in its somewhat isolated peninsular position.

More information is derived from a study[1] of the inland Département Charente (whose most famous town is Cognac), not so dominated by a large city as is Gironde (Diagram VIII.L).

In the first place, approximate data are given of the numbers of traders and the numbers of functions performed by all villages and hamlets down

CHARENTE

AREA OF MARKET ATTRACTION MEASUREMENTS

Road distances in kilometres
Population in thousands

DIAGRAM VIII.L

[1] *Revue Juridique et Economique du Sud-Ouest*, 1960, No. 1.

to the smallest (Diagram VIII.M). As in Berry's analysis, the logs of numbers of traders are seen to be linear in the numbers of functions — but without the number of traders in the smallest hamlets at the very low levels found in America. For a given number of functions, we find in France both a greater number of traders, and a greater rate of increase with increasing numbers of functions, than in America.

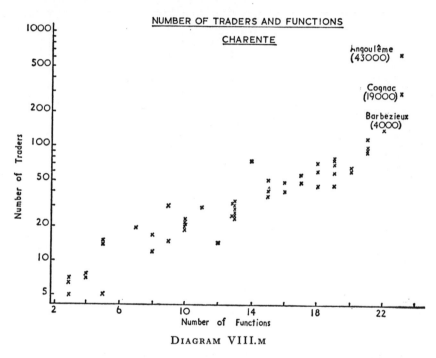

DIAGRAM VIII.M

The tabulation of distances (Table VIII.12) over which centres predominate shows, in the first instance, that there are six villages which predominate only in local food sales, and over a distance of 6 km. or less. These are not necessarily all small villages — they include Jarnac, which has 4000 population, but which has the misfortune to be situated between two major trading centres. Smaller villages such as Chalais, still more Confolens, may do a considerable amount of business because of the remoteness of competitors.

When we examine the tabulation (bearing in mind that, in some trades, the existence of an unusually good trader may considerably affect the distance over which his village trades) we notice, on the whole, no outstanding differences between the non-food commodities in the distances

TABLE VIII.12. DISTANCE (MEASURED IN DIRECTION OF NEXT LARGER CENTRE) OVER WHICH CENTRE HAS PREDOMINANCE TO THE EXTENT OF 60 PER CENT OF PURCHASES

Kms.

	Cognac	Barbezieux	Jarnac	Ruffec	La Roche-foucauld	Chateauneuf	Confolens	Chabanais	Chalais	Mansle	Aigre	Montmoreau	Blanzac	Villebois
Food	4	3	3	2	6	3	3	2	3	2	5	1	3	5
Working equipment	7	8		7		5	7		9	10				
Clothing	6	8		9			7		9	4				
Textiles	7	7		9		5	14		8	2	5			
Household linen	9	9		9		3	8		3	10				
Shoes	13	9		10		4	8		11	11	3			
Automobiles	6	3		9			2		9					
Motor cycles & cycles	9	8		9		4	8		9	5	2			
Radio & television	8	3	•	7			8		10	11	5			
Household equipment	8	3		12			8		10		4			
Gift shops	12	7		9			2		3	3	10			
Furniture	8	9		11			8		3	10				
Hardware	7	8		9			13		8	11	5			
Farm supplies	8	8		10			3		3	8				
Doctors & dentists	3	9					14		3		4			
Surgeons	2	3		2			14							
Banks	7	8		9			13		9	3				
Annual sales	7	9		10			14		4	2				
Cinemas	7	4		18			14		3	5	11			
Theatres	8	3		2			9							
Sport	3	4		10			2		3	5				

over which villages can successfully compete, except that for medical and still more for surgical services, for theatres and sport, and for the purchase of automobiles, there is a rather greater tendency to rely on the capital city of the Département. To a less extent, this tendency is seen in purchases from farm suppliers, annual sales, and gift shops. Apart from these, there is a remarkable uniformity of radius, of about 8 km., even for clothing and furniture, where more purchases from the capital city might have been expected.

So far as data are available, the impression is that for most of the non-food trades small towns serve much the same radius as they do when selling food. Only in the last four entries of the Table VIII.11 is there evidence of greater dependence upon Bordeaux, and less supply by the small towns — namely surgery, banking, recreation and annual sales (and it must be remembered that banks are used by relatively fewer people in France than in the English-speaking countries).

It may be, of course, that this is a transitional state of affairs, in a region of rural France which has not been growing rapidly. As the number of motor vehicles increases, and chain stores and other new competitors in the retailing field make their appearance, the business done by the small town retailers in non-food commodities may diminish. But this may be a slow process.

In a more motorized community a selling radius of a little below 9 km. for non-food commodities for a town of 10,000 population was also indicated[1] for Mariestadt in Sweden, where a detailed survey was made in 1958 to assess compensation arising out of the construction of a by-pass.

TABLE VIII.13.   RETAIL SALES IN MARIESTADT,
KRONOR/INHABITANT/YEAR

	Food	*Other*
Mariestadt residents	2860	2780
Population residing:		
3– 9 km. distant	470	1992
10–19 ,, ,,	60	333
20 ,, ,,	9	21
30 ,, ,,	6	53
40 ,, ,,	1	6

An ingenious new method of analysis was suggested by Olsson and Persson.[2] They defined the 'centrality' of a town by means of its actual sales of consumer durables, expressed as a proportion of the sales of such goods expected from the income of its own population. Centrality so defined, raised to the power of 0·68, gives a good measure of the average population served by such a centre. This relationship gave a better fit than did an attempt to obtain a relationship expressing distance between centres as a function of centrality (to the power of 0·33).

In Finland Tuominen[3] obtained an interesting expression giving the range of influence of a town as proportional to the square root of its number of shops.

An interesting study by the Netherlands Economic Institute[4] showed that the numbers of shops of various types in 34 Dutch towns in 1950 could be predicted ($R^2 = 0·92$) from a parabolic effect (i.e. succeeding

[1] Bengtsson, *Lund Studies in Geography*, series B, No. 24, p. 308.
[2] Regional Science Association Papers, Vol. 10.
[3] *Fennia*, Vol. 71, No. 5, 1949. Quoted *Geographical Review*, 1953, p. 415.
[4] *Onderzoek Naar de Toekomstige Behoefte aan Winkels in Ijmuiden*, 1956.

increases of income having relatively less effect) of the town's per head income, from a double-log relationship with the population of the town, and also from a double-log relationship with the distance from the nearest larger competing (sometimes called 'shadowing') town.

TABLE VIII.14. NUMBER OF SHOPS

	Exponents giving numbers of shops in towns		% change 1930–50 in numbers of shops (All Netherlands)
	In relation to population	In relation to distance from competing town	
Clothing	0·96	0·38	−26
Books, papers, etc.	0·98	0·30	−17
Food	0·99	0·19	−31
Furniture and household goods	1·15	0·30	−7
Other goods	1·57	0·42	+68

Clothing shops and newsagents tend to be a little more abundant, relative to population, in the smaller towns. The number of food shops is almost exactly proportional to population. Food is generally sold over a smaller radius than most commodities, so the number of food shops is least influenced by competition from neighbouring towns. The numbers of these first three types of shops have diminished rapidly in the course of twenty years. The type of shop whose numbers are increasing most rapidly, selling 'other goods', has a very strong tendency to concentrate in the larger towns, and also to be most sensitive to competition from 'shadowing' towns in the neighbourhood. This last type of shop also has a higher coefficient for the effect of the town's per head income than do other types of shop.

The above figures indicate fairly clearly the direction in which things are going, though the precise and radical concepts of Thijsse[1] about the future pattern of towns and villages in the Netherlands still come as a surprise. For a rural community where each family has the use of a car or motor cycle, he finds the optimum pattern in towns placed on the average 50 kilometres apart, each serving, in general, some six villages averaging 18 kilometres apart from each other or from a town. Each village would thus serve an average of 300 sq. km., which means, at Dutch rural population densities, somewhere between 9000 and 15,000, of whom at least 50 per cent, perhaps as many as 90 per cent (in areas where the prevailing type of farming does not necessarily call for the farmer to live

---

[1] Regional Science Association, Zürich Congress, 1962.

close to his livestock) may live in the village. The towns contemplated are of 100,000 population upwards.

Applying the theorem to the three north-eastern Netherlands provinces of Friesland, Groningen and Drenthe, Thijsse finds that they contain three towns, as they should, but 200 villages when they should only have 25. The recently reclaimed North-East Polder, whose villages were planned with so much fuss, was provided with 11 villages, when according to this theory it should have only three. The East Flevoland Polder, whose reclamation is now being completed, should have, according to Thijsse's theory, one town and two villages. The original plan provided for one town and ten villages, but this has been revised to one town and four villages — 'gradually the Government planners are taking the right direction', Thijsse comments. Many of the 11 villages established in the North-East Polder have in fact failed to grow.

Recent and drastic though these proposals are, the author[1] has already revised them in the light of the expectation that motor cycles may soon become obsolete, and every family have one or more cars. Under these circumstances, with a fairly dense rural population, he considers that all their trading and social needs can be served by 'villages' averaging 20–25,000 population, about 25 kilometres apart.

Graphical exploration and analysis of town size data is very difficult unless we make use of the technique of cumulating the data, and then plotting them on double logarithmic diagrams. This technique is in fact exactly analagous to the Pareto diagram for analysing the distribution of incomes which, like the distribution of towns, is also very highly skewed, with relatively very small numbers of the largest incomes. It was first discovered in 1936 by Singer, whose work was later extended by Allen.[2]

These workers were expecting to find, and did find, linear relations, as in the Pareto diagram.

An interesting theoretical analysis, suggesting why a Pareto-type distribution might be expected, has been made by Beckmann.[3]

The Christaller relation, on the other hand, shows a substantial degree of curvature when plotted on such a diagram. A study of the distribution of town and village sizes however in communities which are still predominantly rural, which were the circumstances which Christaller had in mind, does give considerable further support to this theory. The curved relationship tends to give place to the linear relationship, as we shall see later, in more industrialized countries.

---

[1] Private communication.
[2] *Bulletin of the Oxford Institute of Statistics*, 1954.
[3] *Economic Development and Cultural Change*, Chicago, April 1958.

As we are preparing logarithmic diagrams countries differing widely in total population can be included, with a vertical displacement in the case of smaller countries. The relative distribution of towns and villages of different size is measured by the slope and curvature of each country's diagram. The three predominantly rural countries thus analysed (Diagram VIII.N) show a considerable measure of agreement with the Christaller relationship (as modified by Lösch).

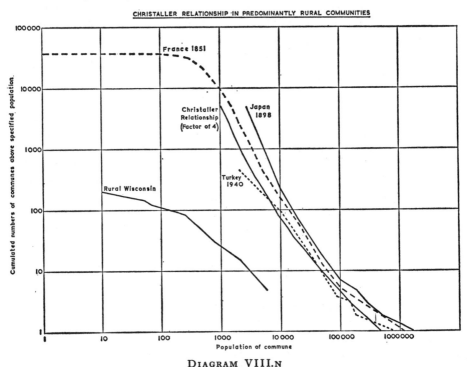

DIAGRAM VIII.N

Such curves, or straight lines, must of course come to an end (as does the Pareto curve); we cannot expect an indefinitely increasing number of villages of ever-increasing size. Christaller's analysis stops when his predetermined limit of 1000 population has been reached (as did the Japanese statistics). The interesting analysis for France as it was in 1851, covering every commune, showed that the ascending curve has definitely changed its slope by the time a population of 1000 has been reached, and has become practically horizontal (i.e. few smaller villages are to be expected) at a population of 500. The results for rural Wisconsin were obtained in the Brush–Bracey study already referred to above.

This distribution curve is clearly changing its slope by the time the population reaches 1000. But, unlike rural France, the curve does not cut out by the time a population of 500 has been reached. It goes on to cover a large number of centres of much smaller population than that, right down to a population of 10. This means that modern American farmers and their families, though they all possess one or more motor vehicles, nevertheless prefer not to have to travel over 5 miles (the mean distance apart of lowest centres was found to be 10 miles) to make their most frequently required purchases, foodstuffs, tobacco, motor fuel, hamburgers and coffee. Consequently, in areas where farm population is sparse, we still find a number of these settlements, often too small even to be called hamlets, consisting of only two or three dwellings.

Turning to the problems of a more densely populated countryside, we have some very interesting results from Jamaica[1] (Diagram VIII.o). These show how the shape of the distribution curve has changed, even in a low income country, in the course of the last 40 years. The curve for 1921 showed, on the whole, an unchanging slope until a size distinctly below 2000 population had been reached, after which it quickly became horizon-

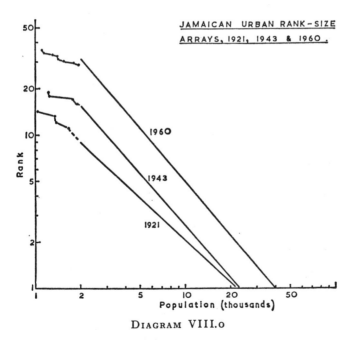

JAMAICAN URBAN RANK-SIZE
ARRAYS, 1921, 1943 & 1960.

DIAGRAM VIII.o

[1] Bruce Newling, Rutgers University, private communication.

tal. Now however the same change of slope occurs fairly clearly at a size over 2000. This measures the change in the minimum standard for size of settlements.

Some further information is available about the distribution of villages by size in low income countries[1] (Diagram VIII.P). For convenience, all the data are expressed as percentages of the total number of villages.

The patterns show considerable differences. In China there is some tendency for village sizes to congregate between 500 and 250, with comparatively few below the latter size. For both India and Africa the curves are less sharp, indicating a relatively large number of very small villages.

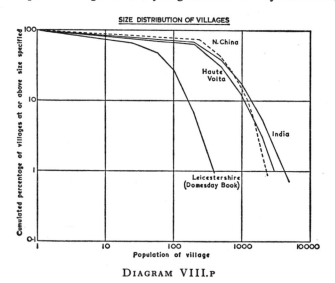

SIZE DISTRIBUTION OF VILLAGES

N. China

Haute Volta

India

Leicestershire (Domesday Book)

Cumulated percentage of villages at or above size specified

Population of village

DIAGRAM VIII.P

It is when we come to the eleventh-century England that we find the greatest difference. Leicestershire admittedly may have been one of the more sparsely populated counties. Even so, the relative prevalence of extremely small hamlets is surprising, many of them with fewer than 25 inhabitants. Paradoxically, we must conclude that eleventh-century Leicestershire must have borne, in respect of its pattern of villages and hamlets, some resemblance to the modern United States, with a number of very small hamlets serving the needs of the immediate neighbourhood. The total number for the county was 215, indicating an average service area of only 4 square miles.

[1] Gambol, *North China Villages* (data for 1920's); Jain, World Population Conference, 1965 (for India); Gerardin, *Le Développement de la Haute Volta*, ISEA Supplement 142, 1963; Russell, *Journal of Economic History*, March 1964 (Domesday book).

Analysis of the distribution of sizes of towns in industrial countries has been hampered, to an increasing degree, by the existence of what are described in Britain as 'conurbations', and in the United States as 'metropolitan areas'. These are those groups of adjacent towns which may have separate identities for purposes of administration and Census recording, but which, for economic and social purposes, fairly clearly constitute a single unit. In the past, the omission of a few suburban areas from the recorded populations of the larger cities may not have mattered very much. But as the density of industrial population has increased, and many of what were formerly separate towns have coalesced into one economic unit, these errors can become serious. Many countries, in their own Census reports, now aggregate the populations of conurbations. But valid international comparison is not possible until we have conurbations, or metropolitan areas, defined everywhere by the same convention. For this we had to wait for Kingsley Davis's extensive work of systematization at the University of California.[1]

Many countries, as we shall see, show a linear relationship when plotted on the double logarithmic diagram. The Christaller relationship, on the other hand, as it were, 'sticks its toe out' at the lower end of the slope. Contrary perhaps to first expectations, in a predominantly agricultural community such as Christaller envisaged, the relative preponderance of the capital city is much greater than it is in a more industrial community, which may be expected to have a number of large provincial centres.

In some modern communities however this primacy of the capital city has been maintained or even increased (Diagrams VIII.Q and VIII.R).

For Egypt we are fortunate in having an estimate of the distribution of town sizes in 1798, made by the invading French Army. Here the capital city had quite exceptional primacy. This primacy on the whole remains, though now shared with Alexandria. Denmark is another example of an exceptional primacy. This cannot be attributed to the small geographical area of the country, because, as we shall see shortly, several other small countries show quite different patterns.

It is better to consider Denmark still as a predominantly rural community, governed by the Christaller–Lösch relationships, in which we would expect an exceptionally large size of capital city. This relationship holds with exceptional fidelity[2] at each level of town size (Table VIII.15).

Finland provides an interesting example of a former primacy tending to disappear, and of a straight-line relationship developing. Greece on the other hand shows the primacy of Athens becoming even greater than it

[1] *The World's Metropolitan Areas.*
[2] Rallis, *Regional Science Association Proceedings*, 1962.

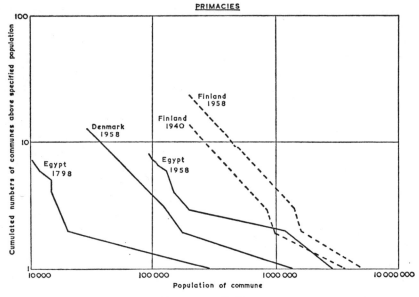

DIAGRAM VIII.Q

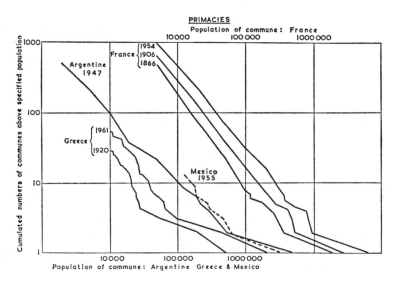

DIAGRAM VIII.R

TABLE VIII.15. DANISH URBAN PATTERN

Town rank	Number of inhabitants (thousands)	Number of towns			Distance between towns		Hinterland	
		Actual	Lösch	Proposed	Actual (km.)	Lösch (k=3)	Actual (sq. km.)	Lösch (sq. km.)
7	0·25–1	458	486	458	9	9	70	70
6	1–5	147	162	153	16	16	210	210
5	5–20	43	54	51	27	27	580	630
4	20–30	13	18	17	52	47	1,800	1,890
3	30–100	5	6	5	70	81	5,700	5,670
2	100–1000	2	2	2	140	140	13,500	17,010
1	1000 +	1	1	1	275	240	43,000	51,030

was forty years ago. In France also the relative primacy of Paris is increasing. Mexico and Argentine show exceptional primacies, which appear to be typical of Latin American countries.

It is easy to distinguish the factors which are making for the increasing primacy of Paris — the concentration of so much political, administrative, educational, and cultural authority there. Similar causes, deriving from the political and social structure of the country, not economic causes, are probably at work in Latin America, Greece and other countries.

We have also, however, interesting examples of 'counter-primacy', of countries which have imposed a relative check on the growth of their largest cities, or have removed a primacy which used to exist in the past.

In the United States in 1910 New York showed a slight but definite primacy. In the subsequent fifty years the growth of New York and Chicago Metropolitan areas has been slower than that of others. Now there prevails a definite 'counter-primacy', with a relative predominance of metropolitan areas with populations in the neighbourhood of one million (Diagram VIII.s). It may be permissible to speculate that this size suggests what may prove to be the economically optimum size for metropolitan areas in the future.

Russia and China have apparently made efforts to check the primacies of their largest cities; but even in planned economies, this does not seem to be an easy task (Diagram VIII.T). Russia shows a remarkable lack of industrial cities of middle-ranking size. (Has this been planned in order to discourage the possible growth of rival political centres?)

Switzerland, Netherlands and Belgium are countries which have made conscious and successful efforts to check the relative growth of their larger cities (Diagram VIII.U). In Switzerland now however the degree of concentration is considerably greater than it was in the nineteenth century.

One may perhaps apply the term 'oligarchy' to countries such as Japan, India and Brazil, where the towns over 100,000 population have a bigger

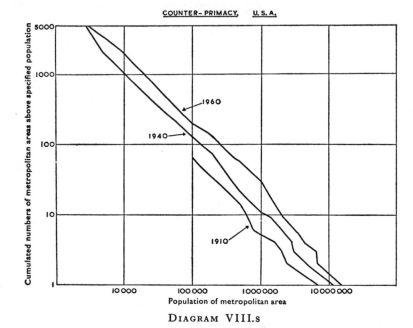

DIAGRAM VIII.s

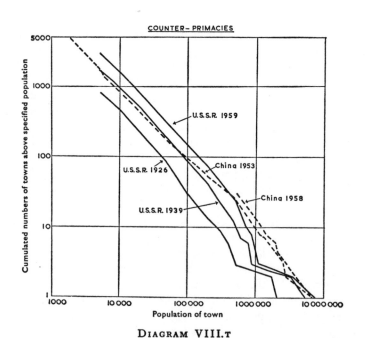

COUNTER- PRIMACIES

DIAGRAM VIII.t

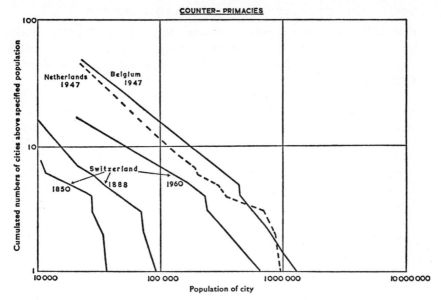

DIAGRAM VIII.u

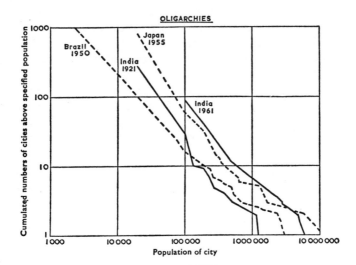

DIAGRAM VIII.v

share of the total urban population than would be expected from the straight line relationship, but where, at the same time, the primacy of the leading city is kept in check (Diagram VIII.v). Still more striking is the oligarchy of five leading cities in Australia (Diagram VIII.w).

Finally, the state of affairs in Germany (if we combine the data for East and West Germany, on the grounds that they formed part of the same economic unit until relatively recently), we find a curious situation which can only be described as a mixture of oligarchy and counter-primacy (Diagram VIII.x).

All the other countries examined can be described fairly well in terms of straight-line relationships. A tabulation of slopes is given in Table VIII.16. The lower the coefficient, the greater the relative concentration of population in the capital and large cities and *vice versa*. The nature of 'oligarchies' however is that there is a break in the slope. The point at which the break occurs (towns of approximately 150,000 population in Brazil, 500,000 in Japan and India) indicates the most relatively *disfavoured* type of town. The numbers of towns above these sizes are found to be considerably greater than would have been predicted by an extrapolation of the straight line below these sizes.

There is also an important qualification to the log-linear principle. Competing for first rank in Australia and Canada, and for second or third rank in other countries, we often find a pair or triad of cities. Such 'steps' in the curve are indicated in Table VIII.16. A theoretical explanation of this phenomenon remains to be discovered.

Our next step must be to analyse in more detail the employment structure of towns both large and small.

An important generalization on this subject was made by Linge,[1] whose object was to predict the numbers likely to be occupied in service and local market industries in Canberra, as the total population of the capital city grew. He examined the relative importance of these industries in the labour force of other small and moderate-sized towns in Australia, and made the interesting suggestion that these proportions varied in functions which were linear in the logarithm of the size of the town. Australian data however are not very numerous, and many of them refer to towns with peculiar geographic or economic characteristics. A classification of English and American data, given below, also gives relations linear in the logarithm of the size of the town, in most cases fitting fairly well, though often with slopes considerably different from those indicated for Australia. For the United States, where there is an embarrassingly abundant supply of data

[1] G. J. Linge, Australian National University, 'The Future Workforce of Canberra', National Capital Development Commission, 1960.

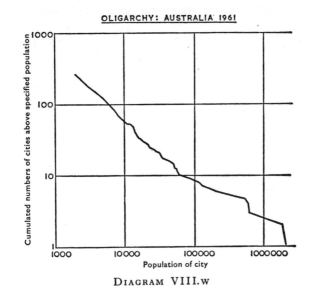

DIAGRAM VIII.w

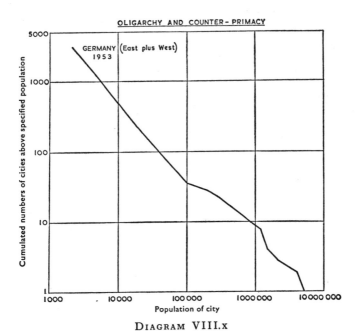

DIAGRAM VIII.x

TABLE VIII.16. SIZE-NUMBER RELATIONSHIPS FOR METROPOLITAN AREAS

		Logarithmic Slope	'Steps' (populations in m.)
Linear Relationship			
Belgium	1846	1·30	
	1890	1·15	
Canada	1956	0·87	Montreal (1·7), Toronto (1·6)
China	1958	1·24	
Italy	1959	1·23	
Yugoslavia	1953	1·19	
Pakistan	1951	0·98	
Spain	1920 (over 100,000)	1·43	
	1950	1·12	
Sweden	1950	0·87	
United Kingdom	1956	0·87	Birmingham (2·6), Manchester (2·5), Leeds (1·9), Liverpool (1·6)
Primacies (excl. primate cities)			
Argentine	1947	0·98	
Finland	1958	1·21	
France	1866	1·29	
	1906	1·19	
	1954	1·12	Lille (0·9), Lyons (0·8), Marseilles (0·8)
Oligarchies			
Australia	1961 (under 65,000)	0·95	Sydney (2·2), Melbourne (1·9),
	1961 (over 65,000)	0·62	Brisbane (0·6), Adelaide (0·6)
Brazil	1950 (under 150,000)	1·09	
	1950 (over 150,000)	0·71	Rio (3·7), Sao Paulo (3·3)
India	1921	1·36	
	1961 (under 500,000)	1·29	
	1961 (over 500,000)	0·83	
Japan	1955 (under 500,000)	1·46	
	1955 (over 500,000)	0·66	Yawata (1·7), Nagoya (1·5), Kyoto (1·4)
Counter-Primacies			
Belgium	1947 (under 600,000)	0·86	
Netherlands	1947 (under 700,000)	0·91	
Switzerland	1960 (under 200,000)	0·61	
U.S.A.	1940	1·00	
	1960 (under 1,000,000)	0·88	
	1960 (over 1,000,000)	1·29	Chicago (6·1), Los Angeles (5·6)
U.S.S.R.	1926	1·20	
	1939	1·09	
	1956 (under 500,000)	1·06	
	1956 (over 500,000)	1·68	
Oligarchy and Counter-Primacy			
Germany (West and East)	1953 (under 100,000)	1·14	
	1953 (100,000–1,250,000)	0·61	
	1953 (over 1,250,000)	1·42	

for the structure of small and medium size town employment, the study was confined to the Western States, which have the advantage of having been comparatively recently settled, being more socially homogeneous, and being probably the best available example of the economic structure of a very high income area, which may serve as an indication of the direction in which other areas or countries may move in the future.

A similar semi-logarithmic relation, for the whole of the United States, was obtained by Ullman and Dacey.[1] Their object was rather different, namely to ascertain the *minimum* employment in various service industries in each size-class of towns.[2]

A comparison of these results[3] has been made, together with some interesting results obtained for France by a different method by Carrère.[4] In towns in Australia some 65 per cent of the labour force, in the Western States of U.S.A. some 70 per cent, are found to be engaged in local service industries. The totals do not vary very much with size of town, but the figures for individual industries do, with the more specialized activities being usually relatively more important in the large towns — though there are some puzzling exceptions.

There is other evidence to show the greater relative importance, in wealthier communities, of these industries serving the local market. In Italy[5] commerce, finance and private services (i.e. excluding building, transport and Government), occupied only 45 per 1000 population in Northern Italy, 30 in Southern. Lösch in his classical study[6] found for Germany (apparently in the 1920's) a figure for all 'local market' employment of 94 per 1000 of total population, of whom 28 were in building. Nor should it be objected that this figure was affected by the existence of large low-income agricultural areas in Germany. The differences between agricultural and industrial areas were in fact very slight. For the most highly industrialized area, the Ruhr, local market employment only stood at 96 per 1000 population, including 26 building. For the low-income agricultural area of East Prussia the figures were 86 and 30 respectively.

This rise in the relative importance of local service industries as communities become wealthier has interesting but possibly disturbing consequences. A comparatively small change, either upwards or downwards, in manufacturing employment in a town, may under these circumstances be expected to cause a whole sequence of substantial consequential changes in local employment, until the ultimate effect on

[1] Proceedings of the International Geographical Union Symposium on Urban Geography, Lund, Sweden, 1960. (*Lund Studies in Geography*, Series B, No. 24).
[2] They point out that their semi-log relation, extrapolated, indicates that the proportion of employment in 'local service industries' becomes 100 per cent when we have a population of the order of magnitude of the population of the whole world, and becomes zero when we have a population of the order of magnitude of a single family. Almost too good to be true.
[3] Clark, *Journal of the Town Planning Institute*, January 1966.
[4] World Population Conference, Belgrade, 1965.
[5] Economic Commission for Europe, Economic Survey of Europe, 1953.
[6] *The Economics of Location.*

local population is many times higher than the original change. This phenomenon is known as the 'local multiplier'. The theory of it is simple — though, as we shall see, the facts do not always follow the theory with quite the certainty which is expected of them. Suppose that the arrival and setting up in employment in a town of one additional worker and his dependents, or shall we say one average income, earned in the production of manufactures or other export commodities (i.e. for sale outside the town), leads to the spending of one-third of that income on local services. The remainder 'leaks away', in the form of imports of goods and services from other areas, or of tax payments or savings whose proceeds may be spent elsewhere. If however the coefficient for spending locally is one-third of income, then we have the additional income of one unit, plus 0·333 of local incomes earned in supplying the newcomer, plus a further 0·111 earned when these local incomes are in their turn spent . . . and so on to an infinity of ever-decreasing amounts; but, according to a well-known algebraical theorem, if the fraction spent locally in each case is R, then the total amount earned, including the initial income, will be $1/(1 - R)$; in this case, the reciprocal of two-thirds, or 1·5.

Regional accounting, like most other branches of economic research, has progressed more rapidly in the United States than in other countries. An interesting review of available information was recently made by Leven.[1] In Table VIII.17 are shown, for a number of specified towns, the

TABLE VIII.17. AVERAGE PROPENSITIES OF TOWNS TO IMPORT (CALCULATED ON ASSUMED AVERAGE PROPENSITY TO SAVE OF 0·06)

	Population ('000)	Average propensity to import
Winnetka, Ill.	15	0·89
Elgin–Dundee, Ill.	60	0·62
Evanston, Ill.	80	0·85
Decatur, Ill.	110	0·52
Waterloo, Iowa	110	0·52
Sioux City, Iowa	110	0·55
Madison, Wis.	170	0·47
Fort Wayne, Ind.	205	0·52
Flint, Mich.	310	0·67
Indianapolis, Ind.	620	0·52
Milwaukee, Wisc.	1,180	0·55
New York Conurbation	16,000	0·24

[1] *Design of Regional Accounts*, Johns Hopkins University Press.

estimated proportion of locally earned incomes which will be spent on 'imports' from outside the region, including apparently national taxes, and also a general estimate for savings not invested locally, which he puts at 6 per cent of incomes.

American manufacture is larger-scale and more specialized than in Europe, and much less is for local sale. Even in the New York conurbation, the larger part of the manufacturing output is for sale outside the region.[1]

For the two small towns of Winnetka and Evanston (Table VIII.17) the 'average propensity to import' is found to be exceptionally high, and the deduced local multiplier therefore very small. These towns are at the northern edge of the Chicago conurbation, near the shore of Lake Michigan, with wealthy populations probably averaging well over one car per family, and dependent upon the rest of the conurbation not only for their goods but for most of their services — if only for the reason that town planning or 'zoning' regulations in such wealthy areas tend to impede the establishment of all but the most urgently necessary local service industries. Such towns are however a sort of *reductio ad absurdum*. A number of moderate sized towns are seen to purchase locally to the extent of nearly half their incomes, implying a multiplier of just under 2. The New York figure however implies a multiplier of 4 — any increase or decrease in manufacturing employment, in such a large area as this, may ultimately have four-fold consequences for total employment.[2] The extraordinary lack of local employment, and high dependence on imports of Winnetka and Evanston are in sharp contrast with the situation in the planned new towns adjacent to Stockholm, Vällingby and Farsta, where the development of every possible local service industry has been encouraged (amongst other reasons, with a view to reducing the volume of traffic, which is a very serious problem in Stockholm) to the point where some 40 per cent of their labour force is able to find local employment.

Due recognition should be given also to Barfod,[3] a Danish economist who did pioneer work on this problem in the 1930's. In Aarhus the average family of a manual worker employed by the oil mills, with an income of 3–4000 kroner, was estimated to spend 45 per cent of it locally (including 8 per cent going in local taxation and 14 per cent in rent). In computing the effects on the local economy of an expansion in employment in this large industrial undertaking, he introduced the further qualification that probably 10 per cent of all the salary payments, and 25 per cent of all the

---

[1] *Made in New York*, ed. Max Hall, Harvard University Press, 1959.
[2] The exceptional figure for Flint may be due to the fact that it is dependent to an unusual degree on manufacturing employment, and probably has a low average income.
[3] *Local Economic Effects of a Large-Scale Industrial Undertaking*, Humphrey Milford, 1938.

wage payments, would go to workers whose homes and spending were elsewhere. Barfod drew attention to still earlier pioneer work in this field by Johannsen in 1927 and by Wulff (a Parliamentarian) in 1896. Barfod's coefficient implies a multiplier of 1·83.

We must turn now however to more concrete measurements of the 'local multipliers', in terms of what has actually happened under various circumstances. Work in this field was pioneered by Daly, an American economist working in British data for the 1920's.[1] Daly presented his results in rather a confused form. They were in fact more interesting and convincing than appeared to him at the time. They indicate that during this decade, when the decline of the old industrial areas and the growth of the Midlands and the South-East was well under way, a local multiplier of the order of 2 applied. This multiplier predicted with considerable accuracy the changes in total employment in different regions consequent upon a rise or fall of one unit in manufacturing or mining employment. An even more interesting aspect of Daly's results was that they showed no general tendency for service employment to increase. In districts where manufacturing employment was stationary, service employment remained stationary also.

A multiplier of 2 would arise if half the incomes earned were spent on locally-provided goods and services. This seems quite a reasonable proportion for the 1920's. Subsequently, for a wealthier community, we would expect the relative dependence on locally provided services to be higher. If however we attempt to apply this principle, the elegant theory of the 'local multiplier' is found to break down. An analysis, more thorough and detailed than Daly's, of changes in employment between 1931 and 1951[2] for all the principal towns and industrial areas of Great Britain shows that the multiplier effect of 1 unit of change of employment in manufacture is only 1·4. What went wrong with the theory?

The theory of the local multiplier, like the general theory of the multiplier which plays such a large part in economics, was developed at a time of widespread general unemployment, by economists who tended to assume, without really thinking about it, that this would persist. With the general unemployment prevailing in the 1920's, the theory worked well. But with labour shortages rather than unemployment being the more usual state of affairs throughout the last twenty-five years, it has not. The inhabitants, say, of a prosperous city in the Midlands, where manufacturing employment

---

[1] *Economic Journal*, July–September 1940.
[2] These are still the latest pair of Census years for which full information is available. This analysis is being kept up to date however by information from the Ministry of Labour, which is nearly as complete as for the Census, and is of course available at more frequent intervals. Further results based on this information are to be expected shortly.

has greatly increased, have substantial spending power which, in the first instance, they would probably like to have devoted to buying the same sort of local services which their predecessors (at the same level of real income) would have bought in the 1920's. But many of these services — corner shops, comfortable pubs, washerwomen and so on — turned out just not to be available. Some substitute services were no doubt available, supplied with less agreeableness and greater efficiency. But on the whole, much of the newly available spending power turned away from services because of their expense or unavailability, and was used instead on cars, refrigerators, holidays abroad, and other commodities and services which generated little or no local employment.

It is fully to be expected that this trend will continue in the future and that local multipliers will remain low (to say nothing of the damping effect of some 30 per cent of all increases in income being taken away in direct and indirect taxation, without any comparable increase in government expenditure in expanding towns).

Another example of a very low local multiplier[1] is from the small Swedish town of Oxelösund, where a steel mill employed 783 out of a total labour force of 2,565 in 1956. An enlargement of the mill by 1960 had led to an increase in employment of 2300, taking into account both direct mill employment and constructional employment. The year-by-year increases in total employment indicate a local multiplier of only 1·2 up to 1960, but in the two subsequent years, after the main inflow of construction workers has been reduced, and replaced by an increase in the mill employment, there are indications that the multiplier, in comparison with 1956, was about 1·35. In 1959, the year in which constructional employment was at its maximum of 1640, nearly 30 per cent of the total labour force of 4725 were living outside the town, as compared with 4 per cent in 1956, and 6 per cent in 1962.

Not only for the estimation of local multipliers, but for many other purposes, we need to assemble all we can in the way of regional accounts. For low income areas they are rare indeed. Beckett's study of a Ghana village in the 1930's[2] showed that the average family of 5·9 persons had an expenditure of £28·8, of which £9·3 was on food which they had produced themselves and £4·1 on other products and services from the village; more than half their expenditure was on products obtained from outside the village, including substantial quantities of imported dried fish, their principal protein food.

A full set of estimates of the dependency of each region on inter-regional

[1] Holm, Regional Science Papers, Vol. XII, 1964 (Lund Conference, 1963).
[2] *Akosoaso*, London School of Economics, Monograph of Social Anthropology.

imports has been prepared for New Zealand by Neutze.[1] The advantages of New Zealand for such a study are that it has been recently settled by a homogeneous population who adjust themselves to nearly uniform levels of income all over the country, and that it has accurate and detailed regional information. It does differ from other countries, of course, in its high degree of dependence upon imports from abroad, amounting to some 40 per cent of the entire net domestic product, or, if we think only in terms of manufacture, nearly twice the volume of domestic manufacture. Even so, measuring the extent of inter-regional trade within New Zealand gives us interesting results.

Analysing the output of manufactures (excluding the processing of primary products), inclusive of their raw material content, we see that the Auckland region, with the largest central city, was dependent upon other regions for $10\frac{1}{2}$ per cent of its requirements for other New Zealand manufactures — and, of course, upon other countries for a substantial proportion of all its manufacturing requirements — and that this proportion rapidly increased in the case of the regions with smaller capital cities (Diagram VIII.y).

The degree of self-sufficiency of the regions in all New Zealand-produced non-agricultural goods and services, as measured by employment, was in every case of course much higher than for manufacture, because

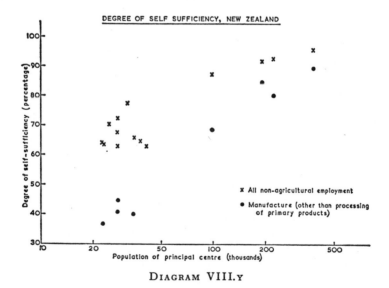

DIAGRAM VIII.y

[1] Thesis deposited in the Bodleian Library, Oxford, 1960.

these include substantial quantities of services, mainly consumed in the region where they are produced.

Direct comparison of these results can be made for a number of regions. A number of minor regions are shown in the employment comparison, but cannot be shown separately in the manufacture comparisons through lack of sub-division of the statistics, and for this purpose therefore have had to be amalgamated with the larger regions, Hamilton with Auckland, a number of minor regions with Wellington (the second city), etc.

In general, it can be said from the employment data that the degree of self-sufficiency of a region rises rapidly as the population of its capital city approaches 100,000, and continues to rise more slowly beyond that point.

Employment and population in the larger cities in France have been examined by Rochefort.[1] He enumerates systematically the specified functions expected of large cities under the four headings of commercial, financial, medical and educational, and measures their presence or absence in given cities.

His results (Diagram VIII.z) — in this case on natural and not logarithmic scales show a very considerable variability, which he proceeds to analyse. The largest provincial cities, indicated in the left-hand part of the diagram, show, he considers, a normal relationship which can be described by the points on the left-hand side of the diagram. Those cities which have, as it were, strayed over to the right can be described, if we care to do so, as over-populated in relation to the number of functions which they perform. This is because their growth as manufacturing centres, or as sea-ports, has, for one reason or another, been much greater than that of other regional centres. The eight named towns he regards as the principal regional centres of France.

The diagram on the right carries the analysis down to the smaller towns. Here the limited number of towns which are 'over-populated' in relation to the number of functions which they perform are all susceptible of explanation — Nice as a holiday centre, Grenoble as a University town, Saint-Étienne as an industrial centre, Rouen and Le Havre as ports and industrial towns, and Brest and Toulon as naval bases.

Rochefort's results were confirmed by another study[2] which set out to isolate the proportions of the labour force in large towns who were working to serve the national (including export) market (Table VIII.18).

It again appears that Lyon and the Lille district, are, as it were, 'over-populated' with manufacturing workers serving the national rather than the local market. The comparatively low figure of local employment

[1] World Population Conference, Belgrade, 1965.
[2] *Population*, March–April 1965.

RELATIONSHIP BETWEEN NUMBER OF SERVICES AND SIZE OF TOWNS IN FRANCE

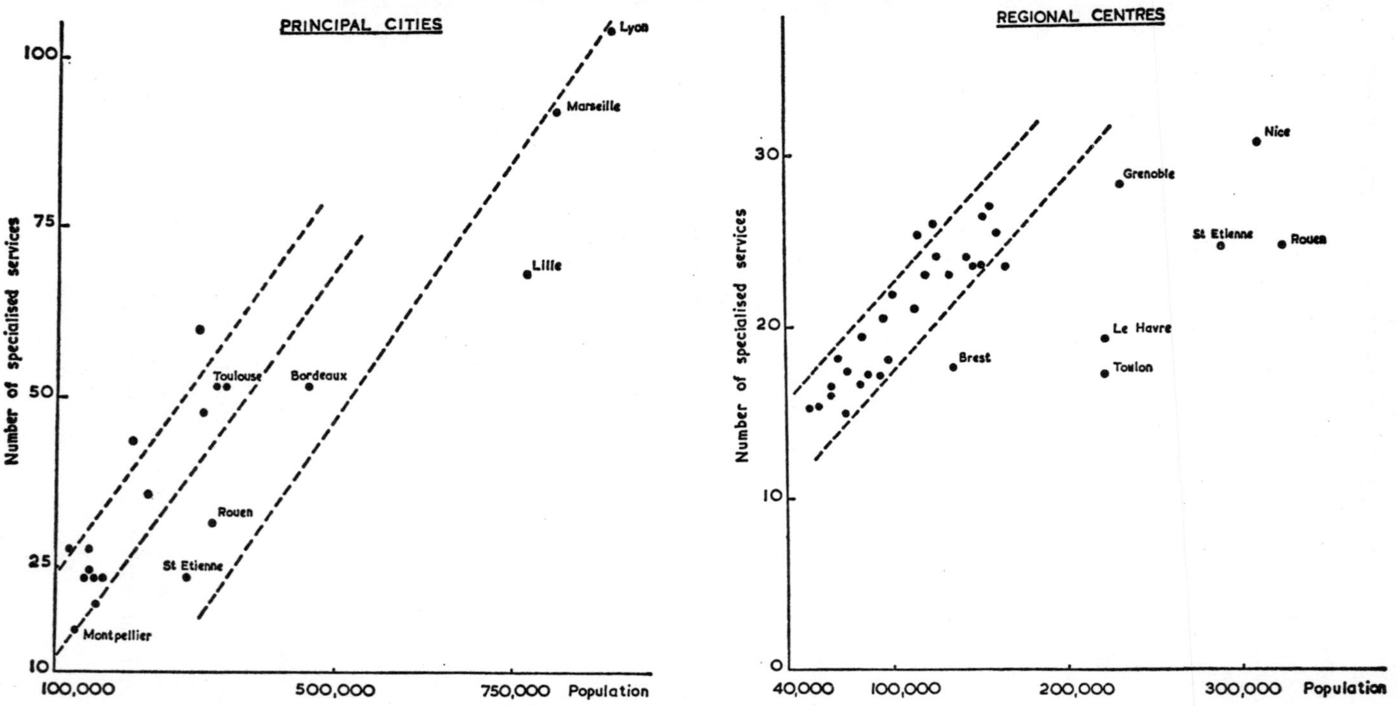

PRINCIPAL CITIES

REGIONAL CENTRES

DIAGRAM VIII.z

TABLE VIII.18. PERCENTAGE OF LABOUR FORCE WORKING
FOR NATIONAL MARKET

Paris	45·6	Average of
Lyon	48·0	Brest, Toulon, Le Havre 43·6
Lille–Roubaix–Tourcoing	51·6	
Marseille	32·3	
Bordeaux	36·1	
Toulouse	40·5	
Rouen	38·7	
Nantes	39·1	
Strasbourg	38·1	
Nice	29·7	

for Paris, which presumably has considerably higher average real income per head than the rest of France, strongly illustrates the principle that people either do without local services, or have them performed more efficiently, when they are expensive.

A world-wide review of inter-regional differences of income, a real *tour de force*, has been prepared by Williamson[1] (Table VIII.19). He develops an index of regional divergences of income, weighted according to the population of each region as follows:

Where f_i is the population of region i

   n is national population

   y_i is income per head in region i

   $\bar{y}$ is national average income per head

Then v_w (weighted measure of inequality) is defined as

$$\frac{\sqrt{\sum (y_i - \bar{y})^2 f_i / n}}{\bar{y}}$$

There is a strong general tendency for regional differences to be at their least in the advanced countries, and at their greatest in the poorest countries. There seems to be a subsidiary tendency for regional differences to be greater in countries of large geographical extent (though Puerto Rico is a striking exception).

A more interesting conclusion is reached however when he examines the trend of the v_w coefficient over time. It is found to be rising in India, Japan, and Yugoslavia, stable in Australia, France, Italy and the United Kingdom, falling in Brazil, Canada, Finland, West Germany, Netherlands, Norway, Spain, Sweden and the United States.

[1] *Economic Development and Cultural Change* (Chicago), July 1965. Part 2.

TABLE VIII.19. VALUES OF DIVERGENCE INDEX BY
COUNTRIES GROUPED APPROXIMATELY ACCORDING TO
PER HEAD INCOME

Australia	0·058	Puerto Rico	0·520
New Zealand	0·063		
Canada	0·192	Group III average	0·335
United Kingdom	0·141		
U.S.A.	0·182	Brazil	0·700
Sweden	0·200	Italy	0·360
		Spain	0·415
Group I average	0·139	Colombia	0·541
		Greece	0·302
Finland	0·331		
France	0·283	Group IV average	0·464
W. Germany	0·205		
Netherlands	0·131	Yugoslavia	0·340
Norway	0·309	Japan	0·244
Group II average	0·252	Group V average	0·292
Ireland	0·268	Philippines	0·556
Chile	0·327	India	0·275
Austria	0·225		

Williamson concludes with the broad generalization that the early stage
of economic growth are likely to increase regional income inequalities, the
higher stages to decrease them. This conclusion appears to be well
established.

CHAPTER IX

Land Use in Urban Areas

THIS problem is analysed in two stages. We consider first population densities in urban areas, or gross per head use of land for all purposes. We then consider in more detail its separate uses for residences and their private gardens, industrial and commercial sites, railways, roads, schools, public buildings, public open space, etc. Measurements are standardized to metric units of persons/hectare when measuring density; when considering specific uses of land, it is more convenient to work in the reciprocal of sq. m./person.[1]

Our measurement of urban population densities can begin with the city of Ur in ancient Babylon, which is believed to have had a population of half a million, living at a density of nearly 500 persons/hectare.[2] The ancient Greeks, on the other hand, built more spacious and beautiful cities.[3] The most crowded known was Selinus, with a gross density of 315 persons/hectare; for Athens the figure was 200, and for Corinth only 86.

Russell[4] has collected estimates of gross density for 92 mediaeval cities, at dates ranging from 1348 to 1550 (Table IX.1).

TABLE IX.1. POPULATION DENSITIES OF CITIES IN
MEDIAEVAL EUROPE

	Total area of city in hectares				
	Under 50	51–100	101–200	Over 200	Total
Persons/hectare (gross)					
Under 80	6	9	6	6	27
81–125	14	10	10	10	44
126–175	4	5	3	1	13
Over 175	2	3	2	1	8
	26	27	21	18	92

[1] 10,000 sq. m./person = 1 person/hectare = 0·405 persons/acre = 259 persons/sq. mile.
[2] Sir Leonard Woolley, *Excavating at Ur*. This was the city, which must have been the wonder of the world at the time, which Abraham was willing to leave in exchange for the austere life of a desert nomad.
[3] Doxiadis Institute, Athens, private communication.
[4] *Late Ancient and Mediaeval Population*, Transactions of American Philosophical Society, 1958.

It is clear that there was a marked tendency towards densities of about 100 persons/hectare and, rather surprisingly, the larger and more populous cities generally showed lower densities; perhaps because they could better afford the cost of more extensive walling; for we are dealing with a period when this was still considered necessary, and the inhabitants of cities had to make genuine economic sacrifices to obtain more space. Russell also analysed his figures by geographical regions of Europe, finding the strongest tendencies towards lower density along the Atlantic seaboard.

It is interesting that Beckett's study of a typical African village[1] of 1200 inhabitants showed an average gross density of 112 persons/hectare.

It must be remembered, of course, that Russell's figures refer to the two centuries after the Great Plague, and that earlier densities may have been higher. Demangeon[2] estimates density in Paris in 1329 as high as 550 persons/hectare. Judges[3] prepared a population density map for London in 1695. The parishes with the highest density were still centred on the ancient Roman landmark of the London Stone (which can be seen today facing Cannon Street Station); within a quarter-mile of this land mark, densities averaged 550 persons/hectare, falling to about 450 for the remainder of the ancient city. By the time of the first census in 1801, the ancient city centre was beginning to be occupied by commercial and public buildings, and the maximum density of residential population was found in the northern sub-registration district of the city, at a density of 630 persons/hectare. By 1851 residential density in this district had risen further to a maximum of 771. Density in the four innermost *arrondissements* of Paris had also risen to 700 persons/hectare. There is much truth in Mumford's contention[4] that the advent of the nineteenth century industrial city compelled people to live at far greater densities than had ever been known before, with consequent effects upon their health and well-being.

As late as 1931, densities of 586 persons/hectare were found in London in the Parish of St. George in the East, Stepney, and 560 in the Netherfield district of Liverpool. (Below these figures were found 361 in the Westgate Ward of Newcastle and 328 in the Medlock Ward of Manchester; the rest of urban England was below 250).

Much worse overcrowding prevailed in New York. In 1900 some parts of the Lower East Side were carrying population at a density of 1350 persons/ hectare; and there are some areas almost as densely populated now,[5] at 1230 persons/hectare (i.e. per gross hectare; they are living in very tall blocks occupying only 22 per cent of the site).

---

[1] *Akosoaso*, London School of Economics, Anthropological Monograph.
[2] *Paris, La Ville et sa Banlieue.*
[3] *Economic History Review*, October 1935.   [4] In *The Culture of Cities.*
[5] Royal Institute of British Architects Conference, 15 February 1955.

Such densities may be supported (with difficulty) by communities which possess the wealth and technique to construct very high buildings. Considerably lower gross densities may nevertheless impose greater hardship on communities which do not possess the means to build beyond two or three storeys. In Singapore[1] 300,000 of the population live at an average density of 750 persons/hectare, and 2500 persons/hectare in the worst districts. A density as high as 3000 persons/hectare has been recorded[2] for some parts of Hong Kong, under exceptional circumstances, with a great flow of immigrants entering a city narrowly constricted between mountains and sea.

The unhappy city of Calcutta now shows rapidly increasing density.[3] In the most congested central areas it has risen as shown in Table IX.2.

TABLE IX.2. PERSONS/HECTARE (GROSS) IN CENTRAL
CALCUTTA

1881	285
1901	465
1921	510
1951	840

Overcrowding in Central Calcutta is now worse (though not so very much worse) than in the worst districts of mid-Victorian London.

High densities, though not quite as high as in Calcutta, prevail in a number of Asian cities, as will be seen below.

So far we have been dealing with maximum densities; we must now consider the densities below the maxima, and how they are distributed through the urban area. The fundamental law is that density tends to fall off as a negative exponential function of increasing distance from the centre of the urban area. This was discovered by Bleicher in 1892.[4] But, like Mendel's law, it was forgotten and had to wait for rediscovery by the present writer in 1951.[5]

Where y is gross residential population density measured in persons/hectare, and x is the distance from the centre of the city in kms., then (except in the central business zone):

$$y = Ae^{-bx}$$

It will be seen that A is the density at the centre of the city, where x is zero; or rather a hypothetical density, which would be found if the observed

[1] Town and Country Planning, November 1955.
[2] Hughes, Geographical Journal, March 1951.
[3] Kar, quoted in article by Berry & others, Geographical Review, July 1963.
[4] Bleicher, H., Statistische Beschreibung der Stadt Frankfurt am Main und ihrer Bevölkerung (Frankfurt am Main, 1892).
[5] Journal of the Royal Statistical Society, 1951, Part 4.

densities were extrapolated inwards towards the centre of the city. In fact the centre of the city is mainly occupied by business and public buildings.

The coefficient b, on the other hand, which may vary very greatly between cities, is best considered as a measure of the spread or 'sprawl' of a city (an unpleasant word[1] much used by town planners to describe a phenomenon which they greatly dislike). With a high value of b the city is compact, i.e. density falls off rapidly to rural levels at quite a short distance from the centre. With a low value of b density falls off gradually and the city spreads out over a considerable distance before rural density is reached.

The coefficient b must be determined in the first instance by transport factors. Without a cheap and adequate system of transport people are very unlikely to build their city in a dispersed manner. But other factors may be important also, such as social customs. Some people prefer to live in comparatively densely aggregated cities and (particularly in the Latin countries) resent it if their homes are so far from their work places that they are unable to go home for their mid-day meal.

Integrating, we obtain a simple relationship showing that the total population of the city should be:

$$2\pi A b^{-2}$$

This, however, overstates the true population of the city[2] because it extrapolates up to the hypothetical density A in the centre of the city, and does not allow for the comparative absence of population from the central business zone. Further research, however, is required before we can estimate the order of magnitude of the adjustment that must be made on this account.

This measurement is also defective because it assumes that the city is able to spread uniformly in every direction, whereas in fact most expanding cities find expansion prevented in some directions by sea, lakes, rivers,

---

[1] Answers by Malayan candidate to question in Town Planning Institute Examination (quoted in Town Planning Institute Journal, May 1959): (a) Define the term 'urban sprawl' (b) What measures can be adopted by a local authority to control and counter 'urban sprawl'?

(a) 'Urban Sprawl' is a place where people normally spend their leisure late in the evening or early at night. Normally courting couples or young couples are very fond of having such a sprawl in such urban areas.

(b) Such a sight is sometimes embarrassing to passers-by and in order to control such sprawl the local authority could do the following (1) have the urban sprawl placed well away from the town proper — say near or in the park ways or outside the town proper vicinity. Stools (concrete) may be provided so that such couples may have complete privacy (2) enough lights be put on in such areas so that such sprawls could not take place.

[2] We are defining the word 'city' here and elsewhere to include all adjacent suburbs and other urban areas which are integrated with it economically, even though they may be recorded as separate administrative units.

swamps or mountains. Where the sea or other such obstacle subtends a comparatively uniform angle to the centre of the city, a proportionate allowance can be made.

We can say, therefore, that if a given total population is to be housed in a city, this can either be done by raising A, with b given, or lowering b, with A given, and that the latter effect is squared. In most modern cities a heavily falling value of b has made it possible to house a much larger population, with an actual fall in the central densities. Where the city is on the edge of a sea or a lake, on the other hand, much higher densities are required to house a given total population (b being given) than in an inland city — sea-ports have always been notorious for a comparatively high degree of overcrowding.

The distribution of people between high and low density residences is influenced by their incomes, present and expected work places, the number and age of their children, and also by many elements of personal choice, their comparative taste for open life or for city amenities, and the strength of their comparative dislikes for travel on the one hand, and for the dirt, noise and grime of the city on the other. Work now in progress at Nuffield

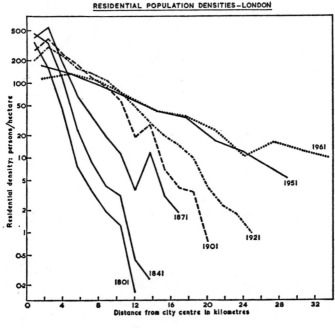

RESIDENTIAL POPULATION DENSITIES – LONDON

DIAGRAM IX.A

M

College, Oxford[1] indicates not only great differences in average incomes between different zones of the city, but also that within each zone there is a marked elasticity of demand for space occupied — this elasticity being highest at low income levels.

Out of the large number of cities for which information is available, four examples can be shown (Diagrams IX.A, IX.B, IX.C, IX.D).

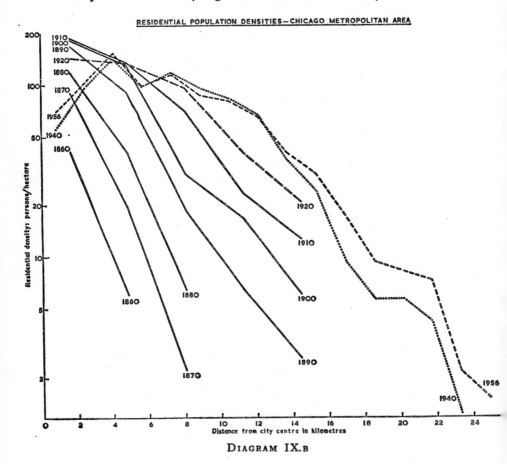

RESIDENTIAL POPULATION DENSITIES—CHICAGO METROPOLITAN AREA

DIAGRAM IX.B

The historical development of densities in London and in Chicago can be studied in detail, and shows interesting results. London in 1801 was a city with a dense population at the centre, but with density falling off very rapidly, so that four miles away almost rural conditions prevailed. 'Earth has not anything to show more fair', wrote Wordsworth, seeing London

[1] C. B. Winsten, private communication.

from Westminster Bridge in a September dawn in 1802. The packed tenements would not be visible, but the fact that

> 'Ships, towers, domes, theatres and temples lie
> Open unto the fields and to the sky
> All bright and glittering in the smokeless air'

must have given it a beauty beyond our imagination. But our descendants will be able to recreate the beauty for which man hungers, without re-creating the crowded tenements, when town planners, economists and

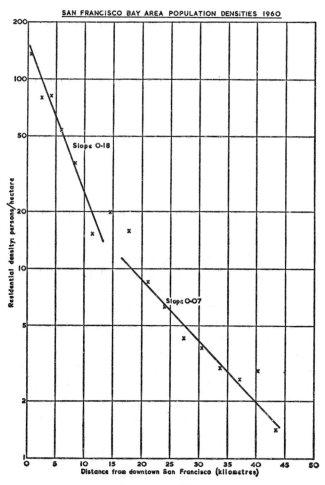

DIAGRAM IX.c

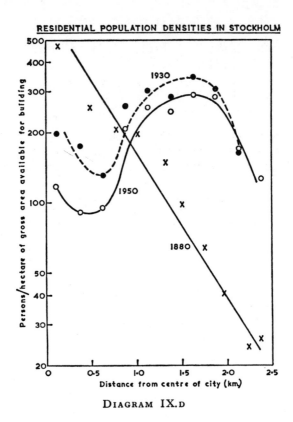

DIAGRAM IX.D

politicians have done what it is their duty to do, namely to enable people to live in moderately-sized cities, with near access to unspoiled countryside.

Between 1801 and 1841 the population of London greatly increased. During this period, when mechanical transport was not available, this increase in population had to be provided for by packing people in tighter, increasing existing densities of settlement by approximately similar proportions at all levels. Other cities in the past have also grown in this way, as some oriental cities are growing now.

When most citizens still had to depend upon walking for their personal transport, and upon costly horse transport for goods, this state of affairs can be well understood. But in London by 1871, with the use of steam transport, this situation was clearly changing. The slope of the curve had altered; the relative rate of growth of the outer districts was much higher than that of the inner, while in the innermost ring there had been an actual fall in the population since 1841, much of the space having been taken for commercial buildings, railways, etc.

From that time onward the tendency has continued. Between 1871 and 1921 all districts within a radius of two miles of the centre of the city actually lost population, while those outside this radius gained. Between 1921 and 1951 all districts within a radius of seven miles of the centre lost population. The slopes of the line have fallen from 0·78 in 1801 to 0·09 now, and central densities are far lower than they used to be.

In Chicago we see a similar process taking place, but more rapidly, and with a much greater de-population, since 1910, of the inner districts. The recent recovery of density in certain inner districts is explained by the concentration in them of the Negro population, forbidden to live elsewhere.

The Stockholm diagram is an interesting detailed study showing how in the nineteenth century (when there were comparatively few commercial buildings, and traders lived on their own premises) an almost perfect linear relation (in logarithms) prevailed, with very high densities at the centre. With the de-population of the old city centre to make room for public and commercial buildings, a new focus of maximum density has appeared about $1\frac{1}{2}$ kms. away from the old centre.

San Francisco is included as one of the rare examples of a change in slope. This is, however, understandable. Most of those living ten miles or more from the city centre have to cross the substantial water barrier of San Francisco Bay.

In Diagrams IX.A–IX.D the lines are drawn through discrete points, each of which is obtained by totalling the population of a ring lying between certain radii from the centre of the city. This technique of measurement proved to be the best when data are available for reasonably small subdivisions. When the circles are drawn on the map they do of course cut the boundaries of the wards, census tracts or other topographical units used for classifying population. An arbitrary apportionment of population between the two sectors must therefore be made every time the circle cuts a boundary. These arbitrary apportionments do not do any serious harm if the census tracts or wards are numerous and the population of each one small in relation to the total population of the ring.

An alternative technique, of plotting a simple scatter diagram to show the density of each individual ward or census tract as a function of its distance from the centre of the city, and then fitting a line to the weighted data, proved to be unsatisfactory in most cases. Where, in a few cases, data are available only in the form of a diagram, showing within what *density limits* each portion of the city lies, an alternative technique has to be used. From the centre of the city is drawn a 'spider web' of 24 radii at intervals of 15 degrees. The outer limits of any particular density range are very irregular, but they do tend very approximately to a circular shape. The distance at which each of these 24 radii cuts the outer limit can be measured and a median value taken. This technique, however, should not be used if the alternative is at all possible.

An interesting application of this latter method was made by Grytzell[1] (Table IX.3).

TABLE IX.3. MEDIAN RADII OF DENSITY ZONES, KMS.

	London	New York	Paris	Copenhagen	Stockholm
Over 100 per hectare	9·5	5·0	9·4	4·4	3·4
,, 50 ,, ,,	14·2	15·0			
,, 10 ,, ,,	24·0	35·1	18·8	6·0	7·7
,, 5 ,, ,,	30·1	45·0		8·0	9·4
,, 1 ,, ,,	40·2	65·1	34·4	17·0	18·7

We can generally summarize the situation by saying that in a city where transport costs are high, b will be high and that if, under these circumstances, a large population has to be aggregated, then inevitably density will be high. This was the position in London and Paris a century ago, and is the position in some Asian cities now. New York is unique in that central densities fell to a minimum about 1910 and after that, even though b continued to fall, began again to rise (with higher buildings).

In the modern world b has been reduced, for a number of cities, to very low levels. It appears that these lowest values can only be obtained in large conurbations, with electric railway surface transport, which after all is the cheapest form of passenger transport, e.g. London, Sydney, Manchester, Chicago; or in a city like Los Angeles, nearly all of which has recently been built on a pattern of very low density, and using private car transport. But, for one reason or another it seems to be only in the largest cities that these minimum values for b can be obtained. In more moderate-sized cities, even in the U.S.A., dependent upon more expensive bus and private car transport, much higher values of b are often found. In some cases, even under American conditions of transport (e.g. Baltimore, Bridgeport and New Orleans) the mere fact that a city is a comparatively old-established one — in other words, the existence of large blocks of old houses which it would not be economical to demolish — to this day keeps the coefficient b much higher than might have otherwise been expected.

Values of A and b for a large number of cities at various dates are given in Table IX.4.

The strikingly low b coefficients in the larger cities of Japan can probably

[1] *Svensk Geografisk Årsbok 1951.*

TABLE IX.4. VALUES OF *A* AND *b* COEFFICIENTS

A measured in persons per hectare; *b* the fall of natural logarithm of density per km. of distance

		A	b			A	b
Asia				**British Isles**			
Calcutta	1881–1951	See above	0·25	Birmingham	1921	401	0·50
					1938	201	0·29
Colombo		386	0·44	Dublin	1936	270	0·53
Djakarta	—	128	0·15	Leeds	1951	116	0·31
Hong Kong	1931	3100	0·79	Liverpool	1921	1275	0·50
Hyderabad (Pakistan)	1951	770	0·88	London	1801	1040	0·78
					1841	1080	0·58
Manila	—	280	0·11		1871	865	0·38
Nagoya	1950	116	0·27		1901	660	0·23
Okayama	1939	1390	1·76		1921	443	0·17
	1953	930	1·32		1931	475	0·17
Osaka	1950	124	0·12		1939	320	0·14
Poona	1822	290	1·18		1951	240	0·12
	1881	368	1·18		1961	205	0·09
	1953	775	0·85	Manchester	1939	143	0·18
Rangoon	1931	770	0·72				
	1951	460	0·34	**Continental Europe**			
Sholapur	1869	165	—	Aarhus	1950	279	0·96
	1938	501	0·98	Berlin	1885	1120	0·68
Singapore	1953	2550	0·37		1900	1580	0·59
Tokyo	1950	232	0·13	Budapest	1935	1080	0·56
				Copenhagen	1940	231	0·37
Australia and New Zealand				Frankfurt	1890	550	1·16
Brisbane	1901	66	0·58		1933	340	0·57
	1933	96	0·47	Oslo	1938	308	0·50
	1947	143	0·45	Paris	1817	1740	1·46
Christchurch	1911	154	1·00		1856	925	0·59
	1936	154	0·84		1896	1430	0·50
	1951	212	0·83		1931	1820	0·47
Dunedin	1911	43	0·42		1946	695	0·21
	1936	35	0·22	Stockholm	1940	425	0·48
	1951	31	0·12	Vienna	1890	660	0·50
Melbourne	1933	250	0·35	Zürich	1936	328	0·29
	1954	137	0·22				
Sydney	1911	100	0·30	**United States**			
	1947	135	0·19	Allentown	1950	58	0·35
	1954	93	0·16	Baltimore	1950	386	0·48
Wellington	1911	108	0·75	Birmingham	1950	39	0·12
	1936	96	0·53	Boston	1900	620	0·53
	1951	73	0·48		1940	174	0·19

United States		A	b	United States		A	b
Bridgeport	1950	230	0·66	Omaha	1950	54	0·30
Buffalo	1950	193	0·26	Philadelphia	1900	433	0·41
Chicago	1880	375	0·48		1940	216	0·21
	1900	386	0·25	Rochester	1950	116	0·32
	1940	275	0·13	San Francisco	1960	155	0·18
	1956	245	0·11	Seattle	1950	155	0·45
Cleveland	1940	305	0·26	St. Louis	1900	465	0·53
Dallas	1950	46	0·16		1940	135	0·27
Detroit	1950	195	0·13		1950	155	0·23
Hartford	1950	115	0·56	Washington	1948	124	0·24
Indianapolis	1950	78	0·31		1955	93	0·17
Los Angeles	1940	112	0·17	Youngstown	1950	230	0·77
Minneapolis	1950	78	0·23				
New Orleans	1950	230	0·40	Caribbean			
New York	1900	690	0·20	Kingston	1891	190	1·01
	1910	228	0·13		1911	264	0·90
	1925	314	0·13		1943	143	0·55
	1940	425	0·13		1960	158	0·33
	1950	925	0·11				

Notes

Data extracted directly from Census volumes except where indirect sources used as indicated below:

ASIA:

Calcutta: Kar, quoted Berry *et al.*, *Geographical Review*, July 1963. The *b* coefficient appears to have been unchanged throughout the period. It was measured to a distance of 8 km. in 1951, 5 km. previously.

Hong Kong: Hughes, *Geographical Journal*, March 1951. Very approximate estimate. Data are for 1931 and density may be much worse now.

Okayama: *American Journal of Sociology*, March 1955.

Poona: *Social Survey of Poona* (Gokhale Institute).

Rangoon: *Geographical Review*, 1942.

Sholapur: *Sholapur City Socio-Economic Studies*, Gokhale Institute, 1965. Population 28,000 in 1869 (at average density of 108), 200,000 in 1938.

Others from Tennant, Association of American Geographers, West Lakes Division Meeting, 1961.

AUSTRALIA:

Melbourne: Fooks, *X-ray the City!* (1933 only).

BRITISH ISLES:

Birmingham: *When we Build Again* (published in Birmingham, 1941).

Dublin: Wilson, *Geographical Review*, 1946.

Liverpool: Jones and Clark, *Journal of the Royal Statistical Society*, 1930.

London: Earlier Census data summarized in 1871 Census Population Tables.

London and Manchester: 1939 data from National Registration.

EUROPE: Data up to 1901 from Meuriot, *Des grandes agglomérations urbaines* (Paris). Very approximately estimated from shaded maps.

Aarhus: Sindel, private communication.

Budapest: *Geographical Review*, 1943.

Copenhagen, Stockholm and Paris (1946): Grytzell, *Svensk Geografisk Årsbok*, 1951.

Frankfurt: Dickinson, *City Region and Regionalism*.

Zürich: Statistisches Amt der Stadt, *Areal, Liegenschaft und Grundbesitz*, 1945.

U.S.A.: Data up to 1900 from Jefferson, *Bulletin of the American Geographical Society*, 1909.

New York: 1925, *Regional Planning Report*.

Philadelphia: 1940, Blumenfeld, *Land Economics*, 1949.

Washington: U.S. Highway Research Board Bulletin 224.

Chicago: Winsborough, University of Chicago, Dept. of Sociology. Ph.D. Dissertation.

CARIBBEAN: Newling (University of Pittsburgh) private communication.

be explained by very cheap electric railways. Calcutta has cheap tramways, and Kingston buses at a penny a mile.

Finally we may notice the remarkable variability of structure in Australia and New Zealand, with central densities increasing in Brisbane and Christchurch. In the United States, while some of the older cities still show high central densities, these are very low in some of the newer cities, as shown by Dallas and Birmingham. This contrast is interesting because, while Dallas is a wealthy city, Birmingham is a comparatively poor city with a large Negro population.

Data since 1940 are not given for Los Angeles for a reason which will be elaborated later, namely that Los Angeles is now showing a new density pattern, of which there are already interesting incipient signs in some other cities, namely for the b coefficient apparently to fall to zero (i.e. uniform density) over a large area, at a level of only about 40 persons/hectare (10,000 persons/sq. mile). At this density, a city of one million population (which, as we saw in Chapter VIII, may be the typical city now required in an industrial country) could still however be accommodated within a $5\frac{1}{2}$ mile (9 km.) radius. Outside such cities we could preserve undisturbed countryside, if we made the necessary effort to do so.

A most ingenious alternative treatment of urban density measurement, which should be followed up further, was suggested by Korzybski.[1] His method is to range all separately recorded areas within the city in order of decreasing density. For certain density limits he then computes a 'constructive radius', i.e. he measures the total area inhabited at or above the density

[1] *Population*, 1952.

specified, and computes the radius of the circle which would be required to give the same area. He again finds a linear relationship between 'constructive radius' and the logarithm of the specified density. But in this case he finds that the slopes do *not* tend to change with time. In other words, by adding constants to the logarithms of the densities, the curves for different years can be brought together. Indeed, he goes further, and brings all the data for London between 1801 and 1881, and for Paris between 1861 and 1921 almost to coincide by adding one constant for each Census. He obtained, however, not one but two clearly distinct lines. Their slopes were such to reduce density by a factor of 200 in the first 10 kilometres of 'constructive radius'; the next ten kilometres of 'constructive radius' however only reduced density by a factor of 6.

We now consider the available information showing urban land requirements by more detailed uses (Table IX.5). For this purpose our unit of

TABLE IX.5.   URBAN LAND USE SQ. M./PERSON

	Whole developed area	Residences	(of which single family)	Commercial	Light industry	Heavy industry	Railways	Roads	Parks and playgrounds	Public and Institutional Buildings
Averages of U.S. Cities:										
Central cities										
Over 250,000 population	204	82	58	8	8	10	9	50	17	19
100–250,000	325	135	116	9	8	11	17	89	19	36
50–100,000	324	121	100	9	7	9	16	108	21	35
Under 50,000	404	159	137	13	11	12	20	114	21	53
Satellite cities										
Over 25,000	234	94	72	7	32		13	63	8	16
10–25,000	536	274	256	11	8		16	132	25	68
5–10,000	870	325	309	13	21		33	288	61	126
Under 5,000	1091	300	288	34	72		49	356	33	250
Marginal requirements in U.S.	368	239		38	21		24		40	
New Towns:										
Reston (U.S.A.)	370	222		48			82			
England: Hemel Hempstead	250	120		26			46			
Harlow	152	87		15			29			
General (Best)	222	109		22			44			
General (Stone)	217	72					37	70		
Scotland — Cumbernauld	143	47		27		3	9	47		10
Planned for U.S.S.R.	12						21	14	17	
China	9·6		4				1·4	1·6	4·8	

Average use in American cities from Bartholomew, *Land Uses in American Cities*, 1955.

Marginal requirements from Niedercorn and Hearle, Rand Publication RM.3664 (obtained by regression analysis of increases in land use in a number of cities since 1940).

Marginal requirements of industrial and commercial land are stated per person engaged in those employments, not per head of the whole population. It can be assumed approximately that these represent respectively 15 and 20 per cent of the whole population; and these coefficients are used in computing marginal land use requirements per head of population.

New Towns from Best, *Town & Country Planning*, February 1964 and Stone, *Estates Gazette*, 1962.

In the new towns tabulation, roads are not separately specified except in the last entry; elsewhere they are classified with housing, industry, etc., according to the area in which they are built. There is an unexplained residue representing commercial and public buildings (except that in Reston schools and their playing fields are entered under Parks and Play-grounds). The last entry includes 16 sq. m. designated as playing fields.

Estimated requirements in U.S.S.R. and China, Botcharov and others, *Ekistics*, May 1965 (estimates for town of 250,000 population) and *Jianzhu Xuebao*, Architectural Magazine, July 1964 (ground space required for a planned factory settlement at Tientsin).

measurement must be sq. m./person (the reciprocal of persons/hectare ×
10,000).

It will be seen how greatly American land use varies with the size of the
city. Outstanding in the smaller towns is the very large amount of space
wasted (or at any rate prematurely dedicated) to roads, and it is not
surprising therefore that further developments require at the margin very
little additional land for roads. The marginal land requirement for all
purposes, however, represents a very low density, of only 27 persons/
hectare, with 65 per cent of the newly developed land being used for
residences. The marginal provision of parks and playgrounds appears low,
in comparison with that considered desirable in new towns.

The low figures for U.S.S.R. and China are striking. Apparently Chinese
planners assume that most of the traffic will be on foot or with wheel-
barrows, and that little road space is therefore required.

The space occupied in the West African village referred to by Beckett
was 89 sq. m./person, of which only 25 per cent was in the 'compounds' of
the families (houses with an enclosed patio and courtyard), the remainder
being open space and public buildings.

In the worst districts in Singapore, where people are living at a density
of 2500 persons/hectare, after allowing for roads, shops, etc. this leaves
however only 2 sq. m./person for living space.

Within a large city, as might have been expected, there are great
differences in land use according to the distance from the centre of the city.
In American cities in all areas the provision of road space is relatively
lavish, and of open space relatively meagre (Table IX.6). Chicago also gives
an analysis (Table IX.7) of uses by floor area (the classification is by the
initial digits of the zone code numbers, which correspond roughly to
distances from The Loop). Note in Table IX.7 the close proximity of the
worst housed and the best housed, near the centre of the city.

We have also an important relationship[1] showing the relatively greater
concentration of office buildings in larger cities in U.S.A. If y is square feet
of office space and x is population of urbanized area, then

$$\text{Log } y = 1 \cdot 3123 \text{ Log } x - 1 \cdot 4721 \, (1946)$$
$$\text{Log } y = 1 \cdot 3148 \text{ Log } x - 1 \cdot 4514 \, (1956)$$

These equations indicate a general increase between 1946 and 1956 in the
office space requirements of a given population. They also indicate a
concentration in the larger cities — a tenfold increase in size of city leads
to more than twentyfold increase in office space. Chicago and San Francisco

[1] Horwood & Boyce, U.S. Highway Research Bulletin 221.

TABLE IX.6. PERCENTAGE DISTRIBUTION OF LAND USE

	Residences	Roads	Open space	Car parks	Commerce	Manufacture and transport	Public Buildings
DETROIT							
Central Business District							
Core	0·4	46·9	2·8	9·1		40·8	
Outer	8·7	36·4	1·0	12·5		41·4	
1– 3 miles from centre	35·3	33·5	8·5		22·5		
3– 6 ,, ,, ,,	41·5	27·9	2·9		27·7		
6– 9 ,, ,, ,,	44·8	31·7	3·7		19·8		
9–12 ,, ,, ,,	50·7	28·1	6·4		14·8		
Over 12 miles from centre	46·0	32·7	6·0		15·3		
Whole area	45·6	30·8	5·4		18·2		
CHICAGO							
Central Business District							
(The Loop) 1956	—	36·0	—	9·0	48	2	5
0– 2 miles from The Loop	10·1	32·4	6·8		18·7	27·0	4·7
2– 4 ,, ,, ,, ,,	25·1	28·9	7·1		11·6	22·4	4·8
4– 6 ,, ,, ,, ,,	33·3	28·5	6·2		9·5	18·8	4·0
6– 8 ,, ,, ,, ,,	38·5	29·0	8·6		7·4	13·1	3·5
8–10 ,, ,, ,, ,,	42·2	28·8	8·5		5·7	10·9	3·3
10–12 ,, ,, ,, ,,	41·6	29·0	5·5		4·1	17·6	1·8
12–14 ,, ,, ,, ,,	35·5	34·0	9·1		3·6	25·4	2·3

appeared to be over-supplied with office space, Los Angeles under-supplied, and New York was 'on the line'.

Smeed[1] showed mathematically how road space requirements depend on the means of transport used. Nobody 'occupies' road space (unless he parks his car on it); but Smeed found a way of calculating the amount of additional road space which has to be provided for each person in a city, according to his method of transport. Assuming that 40 per cent of the people go to work, travelling on the average 5 miles each in the peak period, and that streets are 44 feet wide (narrow streets nearly double the space required per journey) we have the results shown in Table IX.8.

As we saw in Table IX.5, most cities make much more abundant provision than this.

We now consider some further information, which is very difficult to obtain, about the detailed distribution of work places within urban areas. In so doing, we shall also examine the indications, already mentioned, that the exponential distribution of residential densities in some cities now appears to be giving way to an almost uniform distribution, over large areas, at a density of about 10,000 persons/sq. mile, or 40 persons/hectare.

---

[1] *The Traffic Problem in Towns*, Manchester Statistical Society, 1961.

TABLE IX.7. FLOOR SPACE IN CHICAGO (MILLIONS OF SQUARE FEET)

	Manufacture	Public Utilities Transport and Communication	Retail	Commerce Service Industries	Wholesale	Public Buildings	Residences f²	Do. f²/person housed
The Loop	4·5	4·0	13·7	43·8	10·6	8·9	6·8	1360
2/3 to 2½ miles from The Loop	58·1	33·7	17·7	22·5	32·1	28·0	77·5	244
2½ – 4 "	78·0	25·8	28·5	15·9	11·8	27·7	202·0	327
4 – 6½ "	74·0	20·4	24·4	19·7	6·6	30·7	298·0	310
6½ –10 "	50·0	11·8	32·4	25·2	7·2	36·4	427·0	330
10 –13 "	26·5	5·4	12·8	6·6	3·1	17·9	183·0	243
13 –19 "	15·2	1·6	6·5	4·6	1·5	9·3	87·0	1327
19 –27 "	3·3	0·8	2·5	1·6	0·5	2·6	19·5	440

Sources for Tables IX.6 and IX.7

Detroit Metropolitan Area Traffic Study, Part I, p. 38.

Chicago Area Transportation Study, Vol. II, p. 22 and Vol. I, p. 109 (for floor areas).

This proposition appears to be established for Los Angeles (Diagram IX.E). A more detailed historical study[1] (Diagram IX.F) shows the tendency for densities in the newly built areas to ascend, and in the older areas to descend, to about 9000 persons/sq. mile.

TABLE IX.8. ROAD REQUIREMENTS (SQ. M./PERSON)

		Cars travelling 15 miles/hour	Cars travelling 10 miles/hour
44 ft. road	Car, driver only	11·0	7·8
	Car with 1·5 persons	7·2	5·2
Motorway	Car, driver only	3·9	
	Car with 1·5 persons	2·6	
	Bus	1·1	
	Foot journey	0·6	
	Railway	0·2	

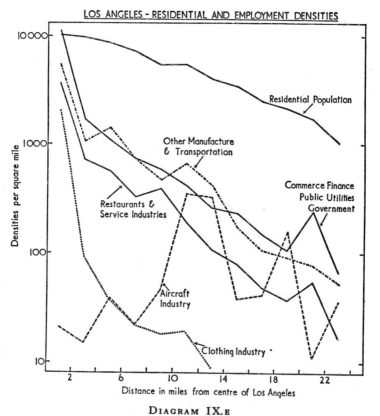

LOS ANGELES – RESIDENTIAL AND EMPLOYMENT DENSITIES

DIAGRAM IX.E

[1] Duncan, Sabagh and Van Arsdol, *American Journal of Sociology*, January 1962.

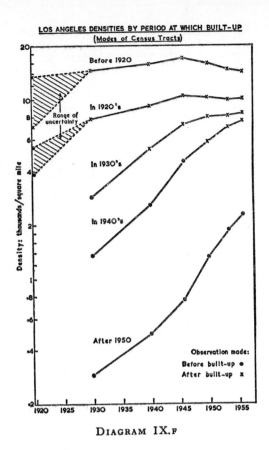

LOS ANGELES DENSITIES BY PERIOD AT WHICH BUILT-UP
(Modes of Census Tracts)

DIAGRAM IX.F

Both Chicago (Table IX.9) and Pittsburgh[1] (Diagram IX.G) are showing clear signs of 'pivoting' on a density of about 10,000 per sq. mile, the areas more densely populated than this losing and the areas more lightly populated than this gaining population. Newling has pointed out that the recent figures for London might also be interpreted as pivoting on about this density. For Kingston (Diagram IX.H), however, there are equally clear signs that the density is stabilizing at about 30,000 persons/sq. mile.

Turning to the employment data, we see that the distribution of employment in Los Angeles (Diagram IX.E) is now nearly as dispersed as the distribution of residences, though the general slope of the relationships is still downwards. One important industry, namely aircraft, has shown a positive preference for locations at a considerable distance from the centre, not only because of the large land area which it requires, but also in the

[1] Newling, private communication.

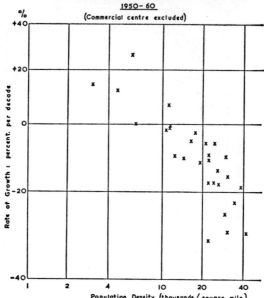

POPULATION GROWTH BY WARDS IN PITTSBURGH

1950- 60

(Commercial centre excluded)

Population Density (thousands / square mile)

(Density computed after excluding land occupied by heavy industry, railways, parks, etc.)

DIAGRAM IX.G

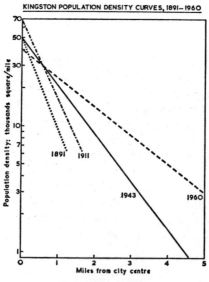

KINGSTON POPULATION DENSITY CURVES, 1891—1960

DIAGRAM IX.H

TABLE IX.9. NUMBERS[a] IN BLOCKS IN CHICAGO AT VARIOUS DENSITIES

Density Change 1950–60 (%)

Density 000/sq. m.	Increase			Decrease		
	Over 50	10–50	0–10	0–10	10–50	Over 50
30–70		3	2	12	9	
20–30		2	4	26	8	
10–20	7	20	9	25	16	
5–10	14	14	3	4	5	1
Under 5	5	7	1	4	7	

[a] Omitting blocks with population below 1000. From Dickinson, *City and Region*, pp. 138, 140: Original source from Chicago Plan Commission.

expectation that it would obtain better quality labour in these neighbour-hoods.

In an important study of New York[1] Chinitz points out that industries requiring central locations in a large urban area, and willing to pay high rents in order to obtain them, are on the one hand industries serving the immediate neighbourhood, such as bakeries and restaurants, and on the other hand industries strongly dependent on 'external economies', for example clothing and printing, which are at a loss if they cannot obtain rapid and frequent access to suppliers of the great variety of components and services which they use. In this connection we may also mention all forms of finance, which are also dependent on external economies, and in addition need frequent and rapid opportunities for face to face discussion with those with whom they have to do business.

These expected trends are observed in Los Angeles. It is of great interest to notice that the clothing industry, which now operates there very successfully, though comparatively recently established, has found it necessary to construct there also the same geographical pattern of concen-tration near the centre of the city, as in the older centres of the clothing trade, showing that in the case of this industry a high degree of concen-tration is an economic need, and not merely a historical accident.

At the International Statistical Institute Conference in 1957, where some of the above figures of residential densities were discussed, the Director of Statistics for Amsterdam pointed out that residential densities in Amsterdam, in general high, showed no significant tendency to fall with increasing distance from the centre. This he attributed to strict town

[1] *Freight and the Metropolis.*

planning legislation, which had been in force in Amsterdam for 300 years. Distribution of work places, on the other hand, gave a good exponential fit,[1] with maximum density of 450 employees/hectare and a slope of 0·74. An exponential distribution was also found for Chicago[2] with a maximum value of 212 employed/hectare, and a slope of 0·18.

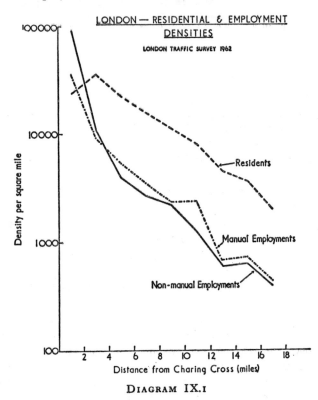

DIAGRAM IX.I

In London (Diagram IX.I) a considerable degree of centralization still prevails, and the employment-distance functions are non-linear. Outside the central area, the distributions of manual and non-manual employments are surprisingly similar.

Some features of these curves, particularly when we deal with single industries, suggest that they may be better analysed on a double log diagram (Diagram IX.J).[3] There is an interesting tendency for densities

[1] Municipal Statistics of Amsterdam, 1957, No. 3.
[2] Philip Hauser, Professor of Sociology, University of Chicago, private communication.
[3] Stockholm (method of median or mean radii for given density); for all employment Kant, *Lund Studies in Geography*, Series B, No. 24, p. 355. Employment measured per unit.

in both manufacture and wholesaling to fall precipitately once a certain lower limit has been reached. In Chicago commercial employment shows a greater concentration in the centre than does manufacturing employment, but it is distributed more widely in the suburban areas.

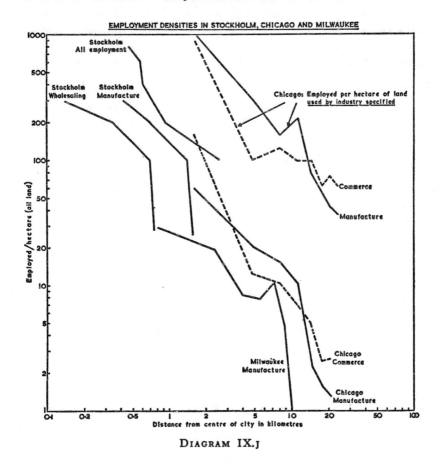

EMPLOYMENT DENSITIES IN STOCKHOLM, CHICAGO AND MILWAUKEE

DIAGRAM IX.J

The two curves on the right of Diagram IX.J for Chicago density of employment are not measured over the whole area of the ring, but measured per unit of area actually occupied by manufacture (or other activity as the case may be). As we should expect, it is those forms of commerce which can be operated in a manner economical of space which are concentrated

of gross building area. Williams–Olsson, *Stockholm Structure and Development* (data for 1941). *Chicago Area Transportation Study*, Vol. 2, pp. 22–34, and Vol. 1, pp. 20–24. The City of Milwaukee, *Industrial Location in Milwaukee County.*

at the centre. Once we are outside the two mile radius, we find a space/employment ratio only slowly changing. In manufacture the fall is more uniform. It shows a rough parallelism to the lower curve, measuring the amount of manufacturing employment per unit of total area. This means that the proportion of the total area used by manufacture does not greatly change as we move out from the centre of the city, but that the space-economical forms of manufacture are concentrated at the centre, and the space-requiring types further out; except that this concentration is less marked than it is in commerce.

Chinitz[1] was only able to divide up the New York industrial area very roughly into Manhattan, the rest of the area within approximately twelve miles radius of the centre, and the areas 12–30 miles and 30–50 miles from the centre. For each of these areas he was able to obtain, for certain industries, the proportion of the total area occupied by them, and the proportion of their employment in that area. The ratios between these two figures give a measure of the concentration of different types of industries, and also show how it is changing (Diagram IX.K). The concentration of the 'external economy' industries is clearly marked. 'National market industries' are defined as those which sell more than half of their product (measured by weight) outside the region. The local market industries are seen to show greater concentration.

Since 1929, it is seen, the concentration of wholesaling has been greatly reduced. For the other industries comparative data are only available since 1947. In every case they show a reduced concentration at the centre.

The amount of space used per employee is related to distance from the centre; but it is also strongly related to the date at which the plant was constructed. Hoover and Vernon[2] showed that the amount of space (total area of building plot) per manufacturing worker in the New York metropolitan region averaged 97 sq. m. for plants built before 1922, 186 sq. m. for plants built 1922–45, and 425 sq. m. for plants built since 1945.

One of the principal uses of information about densities of residence and of employment in different parts of an urban area is to analyse expected traffic, and to make estimates of its future growth. Traffic surveys, of a sort, are not new.[3] The city of Detroit, making some reparation for the flood of vehicles which it has loosed upon the world, pioneered in 1953 a far more complete form of traffic surveying, which is still regarded as a model (Table IX.10).

---

[1] *Freight and the Metropolis.*
[2] *Anatomy of a Metropolis*, 1959.
[3] The present writer conducted a traffic survey of the city of Brisbane as long ago as 1939. The object was to predict the traffic which would flow across a newly constructed bridge. The estimate proved considerably too low.

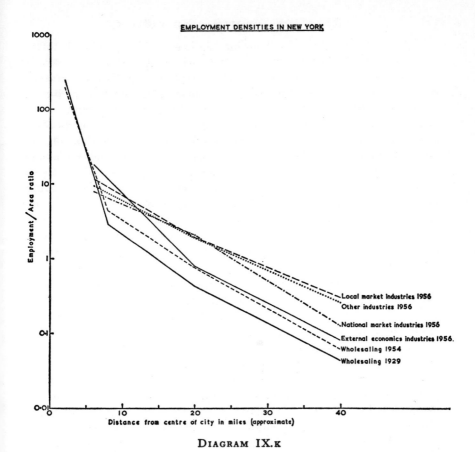

Local market Industries 1956
Other industries 1956
National market industries 1956
External economics industries 1956.
Wholesaling 1954
Wholesaling 1929

Employment/Area ratio

Distance from centre of city in miles (approximate)

DIAGRAM IX.K

TABLE IX.10. DETROIT METROPOLITAN AREA TRAFFIC STUDY, 1953

	Distance in miles from centre of city						
	0–1	1–3	3–6	6–9	9–12	Over 12	City Total
Resident population '000	21	399	784	625	626	515	2969
Resident population '000/sq. mile	6·8	32·4	18·8	7·1	6·0	1·2	
Journeys/person/day	1·28	1·19	1·58	2·08	2·16	2·22	1·86
Cars/person	0·097	0·189	0·258	0·320	0·319	0·323	0·286
Persons/dwelling	1·24	3·07	3·21	3·34	3·58	3·63	3·32
Percentage of journeys beginning or ending in zone specified which pass through congested zones	100	93·4	87·4	83·2	84·4	37·3	78·5
Percentage of journeys by public transport:							
Households with no car	80	73	66	54	53	42	62
„ „ one car		22	17	11	9	10	12
„ „ two or more cars		10	9	6	7	7	7

Surveys can be made by counting traffic at various points, and intercepting a sample of it to determine the object, origin, destination, etc. of the journey. But the most thorough (and expensive) method of surveying is to interview a substantial sample of households and inquire into all journeys of any kind (except on foot) undertaken by all members of the household during the past week. Even this method however suffers from errors of memory, and the organizers of the Detroit Survey thought this might be of the order of magnitude of 20 per cent. The principal tabulations were per 'day', i.e. the 24-hour period beginning at 4·0 a.m. Monday to Friday inclusive. The 'congested zones' were defined as those carrying over 20,000 vehicles/day. This figure was chosen because a traffic of 1600 vehicles/hour would saturate two traffic lanes, and experience has shown that rush-hour traffic *per hour* averages 9 per cent of the 24-hour total; so a zone carrying 20,000 vehicles/day may be expected to be well congested during the rush-hours.

Families living in the inner zones tend to have relatively few cars, partly because they are poorer, and partly because it is difficult to park them at night, even in the streets. Families living six miles or more from the centre approximate to the American average of one car to every three persons (the number of cars/person in rural areas will be still higher, but will include a greater proportion of older and cheaper cars). The people living in the inner areas make fewer journeys/day; partly again because they are poorer, partly because it is easier for them to reach their destinations on foot. The larger families, it is clear, are strongly attracted to the outer areas; and the innermost areas include large numbers of single person families.

One very interesting result is that people living in the outermost zone make comparatively little contribution to the pressure on the congested zones. Since the survey was taken the number of suburban shopping centres has increased, and it is probable that people living in the middle zones now cause still less pressure in the congested areas.

The analysis of floor space use is of great importance to traffic planners, giving them a finer measure of traffic generation than crude land use data (Table IX.11).

The demand for public transport, as was to be expected, is much greater from families without cars; but also, as was seen in Detroit, comes largely from the inner areas. As the outward movement of population continues, the demand for public transport, already heavily reduced, will fall still further (Table IX.12). It may be asked how people from households with no car can travel other than by public transport. The answer is, of course, as passengers in the cars of their friends and neighbours; and this method of transport is probably increasing, even for households without a car.

TABLE IX.11. PERSON-TRIPS GENERATED PER DAY (THOUSANDS)

	Chicago		Detroit — Per square mile net land use							
	Per '000 sq.ft. of floor area	Per sq. mile of net land use	Central business district	Rest of inner zone	1–3	3–6	6–9	9–12	Over 12	Whole area
Residential	3·2	31·0	470	119	42	36	27	17	9	18·6
Manufacture	2·1	31·6	98	134	59	31	24	23	5	23·6
Transport	1·9	5·5								
Commercial: Retail	7·0	116	1150	132	124	140	179	208	117	172
Service	5·4									
Industries } Wholesale	1·5									
Public buildings	3·5	33·8	605	232	57	17	29	21	11	21·1
Open space	—	2·7	—	19	6	2	5	2	1	1·9
Weighted average	3·3	24·6	975	142	47	37	32	20	10	23·0

Zones distant from centre, in miles

Chicago Area Transportation Study, Vol. I, p. 65.
Detroit Metropolitan Area Traffic Study, 1953.

TABLE IX.12. DEMAND FOR PUBLIC TRANSPORT

Average journeys per head per year by public transport in Greater London area		Urban passenger journeys per year in U.S.A. billions		Population of city	Approximate no. of journeys per head per year[a]	Percentage of population making use of public transport in U.S.[b]
1890	85	1905	5·2	Under 50,000	125	17
1901	177	1912	12·4	50–100,000		25
1911	250	1920	15·9	100–250,000		28
1921	364	1929	14·9	250,000	250	
1938	443	1939	10·4	500,000	400	⎱
1948	524	1947	18·6	1,000,000 or more	500	⎰ 43
1959	390	1959	7·8			

[a] Estimate by Pick, quoted in Garden Cities and Town Planning Association evidence to Barlow Commission, April 1938.
[b] From Automobile Facts and Figures, 1954.

The principal demand for public transport, as might have been expected, as always arisen in the largest cities. This demand is now falling rapidly in U.S.A., and has begun to fall in London.

The Chicago Area Transportation Survey estimated that with American costs, the organization of a 'bus service became unremunerative when population density fell below 25,000 per net residential square mile. The ratio between net and gross densities here is uncertain. But if we exclude large areas of open space, on the one hand, and predominantly industrial areas on the other, the amount of road, open space, public and commercial buildings in predominantly residential areas is not likely to exceed 50 per cent. This means that a population density of 12,500 per gross sq. mile (48 persons/hectare) in a predominantly residential area is likely to be the limit below which 'bus services will be unremunerative without a subsidy. Residential densities in modern cities, we have seen, are tending to stabilize well below this limit.

A survey of a number of cities[1] shows that journeys/person/day is generally within the range 1·75–2, with no significant variation with the size of the city, down to populations of 150,000. There are, however, signs of an upward tendency with time. The number of two-car families is certainly increasing. But the second car will not be used as intensively as the first. A refined analysis[2] in the town of Modesto, California (resident population 77,000 plus nearly 10,000 migratory workers at harvest season) in 1956 showed that the number of work-journeys by mechanical transport averaged about three-fifths of the numbers of earners in each household (the remainder walking, or not working that day); but that non-work journeys rose with the size of household, but more than in proportion to it (possibly an income effect). Taking the mean of 3 and 4 person families,

[1] Wingo, Transportation and Urban Land, pp. 28–34.
[2] Oi and Shuldiner, An Analysis of Urban Travel Demands, Northwestern University Transportation Centre.

mechanical transport journeys/person/day averaged 0·55 for families with
no car, an additional 0·45 on buying one car, an additional 0·18 with the
second car, and 0·15 with the third car. Here, as in Detroit, the larger
families tended to live further out. The number of journeys was almost
independent of the distance from the central business district. The demand
for public transport journeys was almost constant, irrespective of the
number of persons in the household and also of the number of cars, at
about 0·1 journeys/household/day. This demand was largely for the
transport of school children, and fell to a low level during the school
vacations.

Further analysis of the Detroit figures, size of family being held constant,
showed, as again commonsense would have led us to expect, that the
purchase of a second car is closely related to requirements for work-
journeys. In families containing three or four persons, those with two cars
have almost one work-journey/person/day more than families with one car;
families with five and more persons show an increase of 1·7 (i.e. the second
car is often used to carry more than one wage-earner to work).

In Detroit also 0·12 shopping journeys/household/day were found for
families without a car, with an additional 0·50 when they purchased a car,
and a further 0·23 when they purchased a second car. Oi and Shuldiner
were satisfied that this was not an effect of income, but simply of greater
convenience (it will be remembered that journeys on foot have been
excluded). Car journeys for social and recreational purposes, on the other
hand, show a strong income effect, rising from 0·25 journeys/household/day
for the lowest income group, and stabilizing at 1·25 for the three highest
income groups.

Recently published data for London[1] however (Table IX.13), classified
not by the size of family, but by the number of wage-earners, and by

TABLE IX.13. LONDON, 1962: ALL JOURNEYS (EXCLUDING
THOSE ON FOOT OR BY BICYCLE)/HOUSEHOLD/DAY (IN
AREAS ENJOYING NORMAL RAIL AND BUS ACCESSIBILITY)

Family income	Households with 1 resident employed			Households with 2 or more residents employed		
	No car	1 car	2 or more cars	No car	1 car	2 or more cars
Below £1000	2·06	4·05		3·54	5·74	
£1000–£2000	3·07	5·29	7·61	4·51	6·70	8·46
Over £2000		6·63	10·95		7·68	11·46

[1] London Traffic Survey, Second Report, 1966.

income, show that, for a given number of wage-earners, the second car leads to about as much additional traffic as the first, and that there is a pronounced income effect, not of course on work journeys, but on shopping, social, etc. journeys. This may be, of course, principally due to the higher income families living further away from shopping centres.

The question of price elasticity of demand for urban transport is of vital importance to those who hope to mitigate traffic congestion by various forms of 'road pricing'. Tanner[1] believes that under British conditions price elasticity is about 1 (i.e. total expenditure remains unchanged with changing prices).

A striking confirmation of Tanner's claim, in an indirect manner, comes from a travel survey in Paris in 1947.[2] Those who lived near their work usually travelled four times a day, i.e. went home to lunch, which is a more important event in a French than in an English household; and those who lived further away did not. But the average time spent on travel per day worked out at $1\frac{1}{3}$ hours alike for the 4-journey and the 2-journey workers.

The belief that price elasticity of demand for urban transport might be at or above one induced Chicago Transit Authority in 1953 to make the interesting experiment[3] of halving fares in non-rush hours. Traffic increase, however, was disappointing, and there was a net revenue loss of 5 per cent. Critics may persist that the reduction was not maintained for long enough to give time for a number of people to alter their place of residence to take advantage of the lower fares.

There have been fairly clear indications of expenditure on personal transport rising faster than income — it is difficult to say how much of this rise may have been accounted for by cars having become cheaper, relative to other goods, in recent times, and in the more economically advanced countries; and whether further reductions in the relative price of cars are still to be expected. It may be the case in U.S.A. since the mid-50's however (Table IX.14) that income elasticity of demand for urban transport has fallen a little below 1.

Oi and Shuldiner further analyse[4] the 1950 data for expenditure by size of cities (Table IX.15).

Examination of the records of the U.S. Bureau of Labor Statistics Consumption Expenditure Survey of 1950 shows that the proportion of income spent on car purchase and maintenance reached a maximum in

[1] Road Research Laboratory Technical Paper 51.
[2] Bresard, *Population*, April–June 1948.
[3] Schroeder, *Metropolitan Transit Research*.
[4] Loc. cit., p. 172.

TABLE IX.14. EXPENDITURE[a] ON PERSONAL TRANSPORT
AS PERCENTAGE OF ALL PERSONAL EXPENDITURE IN U.S.

	Local public transport	Private cars	Total
1929	1·45	7·72	9·17
1939	1·24	7·25	8·49
1949–52	0·99	10·58	11·57
1953–56	0·80	11·92	12·72
1957–60	0·65	12·01	12·66
1961–64	0·54	11·92	12·46

[a] Survey of Current Business, November 1965.

$5–6000 family income range ($3–4000 in small cities). On this indication, expenditure on cars in relation to income, even if it is now stabilizing in United States, still has a long way further to rise in almost all other countries.

TABLE IX.15. TRANSPORT AS PERCENTAGE OF
CONSUMPTION EXPENDITURE BY SIZE OF CITY

City population	Automobile	Other travel
Over 1 million	10·4	2·2
250,000–1,000,000	12·2	1·8
30,000–250,000	13·3	1·4
All cities	12·3	1·8

We get a similar indication of a rising proportionate expenditure on personal transport, as income rises, from an international comparison (Table IX.16).

Oi and Shuldiner[1] also concluded that price elasticity was almost zero under American conditions, even in the 1930's.

TABLE IX.16. EXPENDITURE ON PERSONAL TRANSPORTATION
AND COMMUNICATION (UNITED NATIONS DEFINITION)
AS PERCENTAGE OF ALL PRIVATE CONSUMPTION, 1955–58

United States	14·3
Canada	13·4
Sweden	12·1
United Kingdom	8·8
Italy	7·8
France	7·5
Norway	7·1
Finland	6·5
Netherlands	4·3

[1] Loc. cit., pp. 161–5. They quote Bureau of Labor Statistics, Family Expenditure in Selected Cities, 1935–6, Vol. VI, Bulletin 648, 1940 (white families).

Automobile cost averaged for the whole country 3·04 cents/vehicle-mile run; but in Atlanta and Providence it averaged only 2·70, in Denver and Portland 3·40. In these cities, however, there were, at given income levels, no discernible deviations from the national mean of mileage run.

Analysing five principal cities, they concluded that there has been, however, a substantial income elasticity of demand. The large differences between the cities require us to accept the results with caution. The medians of cities indicate that automobile expenditure rose from 8·4 per cent of all consumption expenditure in 1935 to 9·7 per cent in 1950, while income elasticity of demand for automobiles remained at about 1·5. Income elasticity of demand for local public transport was only about 0·2 in 1935.

The price effect may have been obscured by the cheapening of private transport relative to public in recent years (between 1935 and 1955 the former rose[1] 82 per cent in price, the latter 103 per cent). Some recent results,[2] (more encouraging to those who have hopes of making use of price elasticities) were quoted by *Chicago Area Transportation Study*. The time required to travel by public transport between the central business district and various outlying areas, expressed as a multiple of the time required for automobile travel, may be as high as 3, or as low as 0·6. This ratio, raised to the power of − 1·85 and multiplied by 41·1, gives the expected percentage of journeys made by public transport, with quite a good fit. An equally good fit, however, is obtained by raising relative *price* to the power of − 0·89, and multiplying by 7·4.

A study by the Netherlands Economic Institute[3] (Table IX.17) showed that in a small town (population 63,000) price elasticity of demand for public transport was higher and income elasticity lower than in larger cities. Much of this 'demand', in long-term analysis, arises out of people's choice of place of residence.

TABLE IX.17. ELASTICITY OF DEMAND FOR TRANSPORT
IN THE NETHERLANDS

	Price elasticity	Income elasticity
Amersfoort	− 1·3	0·8
The Hague	− 0·7	2·4
Amsterdam	− 0·8	2·0

With the increasing concentration of population in large urban areas, their rising incomes, their strong tendency to buy and use more cars, and

[1] *Monthly Labor Review*, August 1956.
[2] Mortimer, Highway Research Bulletin 203 (1958).
[3] *Die entwikkeling van het locaal personenvervoer in Amersfoort*, 1955.

the declining use of public transport, are we not heading for a complete seize-up? Is it not urgently necessary to provide some restored and modernized form of public transport, even at great expense, which will take at any rate a substantial proportion of cars off the roads during the rush hours? This was the decision reached, albeit by a very small majority, by the electors of the San Francisco neighbourhood in 1963 — though admittedly this is an exceptional case, with wide water barriers concentrating traffic on two long bridges. It is a decision which Los Angeles is expected to take at any moment — so we have been told for some years now, though at the point of final decision there always seems to be still some disagreement among the experts as to what really is a satisfactory form of urban public transport under modern conditions. It was a decision reached by President Kennedy and Congress, when a very large sum was voted to be held available as subsidies for the authorities of any metropolitan area who installed an efficient modern public transport system. But this was an example of the tendency sometimes noticed amongst politicians, to act first and think afterwards. When the President's expert committee reported, in 1962, after the decisions had already been taken, the report caused a sensation in transportation circles.[1] An improved electric railway system, they reported, of the kind demanded for many cities, was only justified, in the United States, in the case of New York. For all other cities, the most economical method of carrying the rush-hour traffic was not by rail but by bus — but with the important qualification that the buses should be allowed segregated tracks, clear of other traffic.

Apart from this main theme, the authors take some vigorous side-swipes at some important obstacles to urban transport, which have nevertheless become deeply embedded in the American Way of Life. In the first place, if everyone drove a small car, the rush-hour capacity of the highways would be increased 30–40 per cent. In the United States (as elsewhere) the driving of taxis for hire is rigidly licensed, with the object of obtaining an adequate and secure livelihood for professional taxi drivers, who are strongly organized, and also, as the authors frankly point out, of securing graft for municipal politicians. If any and every car owner were free to carry passengers for reward whenever he was willing to do so, charges much lower than the present regulated taxi rates would prevail, and a great many people would use such services rather than bring their own cars into the city. Finally, the authors point out, much of the pressure on traffic facilities is caused by the highest income group, who mostly work near the

---

[1] *Technology and Urban Transport*; Meyer–Kain–Wohl Report (the two former being economists, the latter an engineer). Originally circulated in duplicated form; incorporated in a recent book, *The Urban Transportation Problem*.

centre of the city and live a great distance away. Many of these families, in return for the saving of travel time, would be quite willing to pay the high rents demanded for accommodation near the centre of the city, were it not for one consideration, namely the outstanding badness of the city schools in central areas, and the very high charges made by private schools. The authors admit that the idea of subsidizing fee-charging private schools in these areas would be a real affront to American political principles. Nevertheless, it might, by encouraging high income families to reside in central areas, make a substantial contribution to the traffic problem — and also help to restore land values in the central areas, a matter of much concern to civic authorities, as well as to private investors.

Turning to the main theme, the authors point out that the popular belief about city centres being flooded by ever-increasing numbers of daily peak-hours travellers is at variance with the facts. There has been a considerable displacement of employment away from the central areas, and in many cities the numbers entering them are falling (Table IX.18).

A more detailed study, year by year, has been made for Chicago. If we assume that the numbers entering the Central Business District between 7 and 9.30 a.m. gives an indication of those actually employed there, this figure was at a maximum of 298,000 in 1948, falling to 238,000 by 1961. The numbers entering later, presumably mostly for purposes other than employment in the area, numbered 73,000 in 1948, and only 44,000 in 1961. Unfortunately, in spite of propaganda by the Transit Authority to the contrary, they all tend to leave the Central Business District in the peak hours.

One other popular legend also has to be discredited. The average time required to traverse a given route in Los Angeles is now less, not more, than it was in 1936.

TABLE IX.18. CITY CENTRE TRAFFIC

	Period of comparison	Percentage change in numbers leaving Central Business Districts during evening peak hours	Percentage change in population of metropolitan areas
Chicago	1950–61	−1	+20
Dallas	1946–58	+14	+50
Detroit	1947–53	−9	
Los Angeles	1941–61	0	+125
Minneapolis	1947–61	−16	
New York	1948–56	−10	
Philadelphia	1940–60	0	+35
San Francisco	1947–59	+10	+30

The authors also strongly contravert the widely held view that it is only the existence of public transport which makes possible high density, either of residence or of employment, in the centre of the city. These high densities, and also the existence of the public transport system, should both be regarded as consequences of the age of the city. When we look at the density patterns of those cities which have grown up in comparatively recent years, we see the force of this argument.

Traffic entering Central London between 7 and 10 a.m., on the other hand,[1] continues to increase, and is now over 1,300,000 daily. But only 10 per cent of this is by private transport. In the public transport sector, surface and underground railways are of rapidly increasing importance, buses of decreasing importance, and trams and trolleybuses now abolished.

Hamburg has 220,000 workers in its central business district,[2] of whom 73 per cent use public transport, 10 per cent walk, 11 per cent use cars and 6 per cent use cycles or motor cycles.

Returning to the United States, we can list the metropolitan areas in order of the volume of traffic which has to be carried out of these central business districts during peak hours (Table IX.19).

TABLE IX.19. PEAK HOUR TRAVEL OUT OF CENTRAL BUSINESS DISTRICTS FOR ALL METROPOLITAN AREAS WITH POPULATION EXCEEDING 500,000

Over 800,000	New York
200–250,000	Chicago
150–200,000	Philadelphia
100–150,000	Boston, Los Angeles, San Francisco
75–100,000	Cleveland, Detroit, Atlanta, Pittsburgh, New Orleans, St. Louis, Baltimore
50–75,000	Dallas, St. Paul, Minneapolis, Providence, Ft. Worth, Milwaukee
Below 50,000	Miami (17,000), Cincinatti, Rochester (34,000), Seattle, Kansas City (12,000)

The problem of New York is clearly out of comparison with that of other cities, accentuated as it is by the water barriers. Regarding the other cities, Meyer, Kain and Wohl report that a volume of passenger traffic as high as 250,000 passengers/hour could be carried by buses using eight lanes of highway specially reserved for them, 150,000 passengers/hour with five lanes.

---

[1] *The Paper Metropolis*, Town and Country Planning Association.
[2] Tuchic, *Traffic Quarterly*, January 1964.

It now remains to estimate costs by the three alternative forms of transport, namely surface railway, bus running on segregated tracks, and private automobile. Costs are calculated on the principle of debiting to each form of transport all costs, whether incurred by the transport operator or by public authorities, including maintenance, interest and amortization on the whole highway or track used. Furthermore, the whole of these costs are debited to the rush hour traffic, all of which is assumed to pass in two hours each way daily. (This assumption that traffic during the rest of the day can make no contribution to capital costs is perhaps a little unfair to the automobile, but reasonable for rail and bus transport.) The calculations are based on highways constructed to take the required volume of traffic (presumed known) at 35 miles/hour. Automobile costs include the provision and operation of parking space. The average automobile is assumed to provide 1·9 usable seats.

TABLE IX.20. COSTS OF ALTERNATIVE FORMS OF
TRANSPORT (CENTS/SEAT/MILE)

Passengers/hour		50000	40000	30000	20000	10000	5000
Railway	6 miles	11·3	11·6	12·5	13·4	16·2	21·2
	10 ,,	8·1	8·6	9·3	10·4	13·1	18·4
	15 ,,	6·7	6·7	7·9	8·8	11·7	17·1
Bus	6 miles	9·5	9·6	9·7	10·1	11·1	14·8
	10 ,,	6·2	6·3	6·4	6·8	8·9	13·8
	15 ,,	4·6	4·7	4·8	5·5	8·2	14·7
Automobile	6 miles	17·1	17·2	17·2	16·6	16·8	16·6
	10 ,,	13·4	13·6	13·7	13·7	13·1	13·0
	15 ,,	11·5	11·5	11·5	11·7	11·1	11·1

For traffic flows of 5000 passengers/hour or less, and for distances of ten miles upwards, the individual automobile proves to be the lowest-cost form of transportation. But in all other circumstances the bus is considerably the cheapest. As the volume of traffic increases, the difference between the bus and the railway is slowly narrowing. A very large volume of traffic, of New York dimensions, is required to justify the actual construction of railways — apart, that is to say, from continuing to operate those already constructed in the past.

So much for the rush-hour traffic. But what of the people who still find it cheaper or more convenient to use their own cars, irrespective of the congestion and difficulties which they cause to others? We could have no clearer case than this of economic 'externalities' discussed at the beginning of Chapter VIII. In this case the 'externality', the slowing down and cost to all other traffic imposed by one additional vehicle coming on to the roads in certain circumstances, can be precisely numerically measured.

A formula showing how increasing the number of vehicles reduces average speed was developed by Wardrop.[1] This formula is not intended to apply in uncongested conditions, i.e. if average speed exceeds 24 miles/hour.

Vehicles/hour (both directions) $= 3(31 - v)(w - 6) - 430$
where v is average speed in miles/hour and w width of road in feet

The effect of speed upon the costs (exclusive of any taxes imposed on the vehicle or its fuel) incurred by the individual vehicle operator (i.e. apart from any costs which he imposes on others) have been estimated[2] and are as follows:

Costs net of tax in pence/mile $= 4 \cdot 1 + 224/v$
where v is speed in miles/hour.

Smeed[3] derived a formula showing (on the assumption that the relation between speed and traffic flow was linear) the 'public costs' imposed by given low speeds.

These formulae have been used by Roth,[4] Hewitt[5] and others to work out the most economically appropriate 'congestion tax' which might be imposed under various circumstances. The imposition of such a tax on congested roads was proposed by Pigou[6] as long ago as 1920. Modern engineers have available a whole array of devices, once the political decision is made to impose a congestion tax, which will make it possible to tax travel or parking in congested areas, varying the rates between streets or between times of day if required, by impulses sent to a sealed meter in the car from cables in the road, or by other devices. When traffic is moving at 15–18 miles/hour, Hewitt calculated for the congested[7] town of Slough an economically optimum tax rate of 2·8–3·1 pence/mile. For the same town, on the assumption of 15/miles/hour speed, Smeed computed 4·9. For Central London, with an assumed speed of 10 miles/hour, Hewitt's

[1] *Operation Research Quarterly*, March 1954.
[2] Charlesworth & Paisley, *The Work Assessment and Returns from Road Works*, London, Institution of Civil Engineers, 1959.
[3] *The Traffic Problem in Towns*, Manchester Statistical Society, 1961.
[4] Review of the International Statistical Institute, 1963. Paper also obtainable from the University of Cambridge, Department of Applied Economics.
[5] *Economica*, February 1964.
[6] *The Economics of Welfare*.
[7] Before the recent completion of the motorway which by-passes it.

formula gives 9 and Smeed's as much as 14 pence/mile. Hewitt proposes that parking should be charged 9–12 pence/hour; and buses and heavy commercial vehicles four times the proposed rates for cars.

Bruce Johnson makes an attack on the problem on American data.[1] He prefers to think in minutes/mile, i.e. the reciprocal of speed. It may be approximately true, over a considerable range, that speed is a linear function of the volume of traffic. But the relationship between vehicles/hour and this reciprocal is always curved, and the curvature increases rapidly. At approximately 5 minutes/mile (12 miles/hour) the relationship becomes vertical, i.e. no higher rate of vehicle flow is possible than that which prevails at this speed. If an increasing number of vehicles attempt to use the road, the result is lower average speed and a finally reduced flow of vehicles/hour (Diagram IX.L).

For the effect of speed on cost he uses a formula devised in the Chicago Area Transportation Survey, which is considerably lower than the British

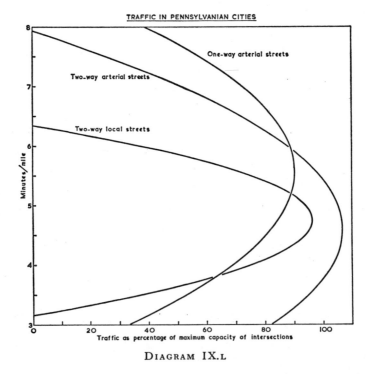

TRAFFIC IN PENNSYLVANIAN CITIES

DIAGRAM IX.L

[1] *Econometrica*, January–April 1964. Data quoted from the Highway Research Board, Bulletin No. 303.

formula, because it excludes all the fixed costs of the automobile (it is assumed that the average American family will possess one in any case).

Operating costs in cents/mile = 1·829 + 0·132 minutes/mile
(reciprocal of speed)

He then works out a schedule of economically optimal taxes at various speeds on two types of road (Table IX.21). For reasons given above, such a tax should approach infinity as speed falls to 12 miles/hour.

TABLE IX.21. OPTIMAL TAX CENTS/MILE

Speed miles/hour	Arterial one way road	Arterial two way road
35	0	0·9
30	0	1·5
25	0·1	2·6
20	1·3	4·8
19	1·7	5·7
18	2·2	6·8
17	2·8	8·4
16	3·5	11·1
15	4·6	16·3
14	6·2	31·8
13	9·0	Infinite

Such calculations must of necessity include a term for valuing the time of the driver and occupants of the vehicles. This is sometimes calculated by ingenious methods based on observation of the circumstances under which people use time-saving toll roads, and the amount which they are willing to pay for them. This method, Johnson believes, is gravely biased; other things being equal, or even some way from equality, people, he thinks, have a preference for the new toll roads — they seem to enjoy the drive on them for its own sake. He values time at 0·5 $/person/hour, or 0·9 $/vehicle/hour, assuming 1·8 average occupancy.[1]

There have been other conflicting estimates on this question of the value of the saving of time. Fretar[2] estimated $1.20 per car hour (presumably to represent the average of about 1·5 persons travelling per car), from statistics of tolls which passengers were willing to pay in order to save time. Lawton,[3]

---

[1] The Chicago Area Transportation Survey, Vol. III, p. 9, quoted five different estimates which give a median value of 1·4 $/automobile/hour. They make a lower estimate of average occupancy and value time at approximately 0·9 $/person/hour.

[2] *Traffic Quarterly*, 1948.

[3] *Traffic Quarterly*, January 1950. For light, medium and heavy trucks he also estimated 1·9, 3·2 and 5·4 $/hour respectively.

however, estimated from tollbridge experience a figure of \$2·28 — this represented mostly traffic at rush hours. For longer journeys he preferred a figure of \$1.10 per hour, deduced from experience on the Merritt Parkway out of New York.

If Johnson is right, these figures may be biased upwards by people's preference for new toll roads. They should not, however, feel any preference for different ways of crossing the English Channel. Barry[1] reached a figure of only 0·24 \$/hour from comparing these.

This latter result is compatible with more leisurely English ways and lower incomes than in the United States. As real incomes go up, the valuation put on lost time should rise. This point was very neatly illustrated by Beesley[2] in a study which he was able to make of various grades of the British Civil Service.

TABLE IX.22.   VALUATION OF TIME ACCORDING TO INCOME

	Average earnings		Valuation per hour spent in public transport as % of hourly earnings
	£/Year	shillings/hour	
Clerical grade	650	6·5	30
Executive grade	850	9·0	35
Higher grades	—	—	42–50

In Sweden,[3] a high-income country, passengers tend to value loss of time at $1\frac{1}{2}$ \$/hour; economists prefer to estimate \$1. Australians, however, are not believed by their governments to show the American preference for new roads; the toll[4] for a new express-way saving half an hour on the Sydney–Newcastle road (built at a cost of \$A.$7\frac{1}{2}$m.) is at the rate of only 0·45 U.S. \$/hour.

There are other methods of estimating the value of lost time, including its indirect effects, such as illness and fatigue. Ernest Bevin, as Minister of Labour, made a very interesting statement[5] (unfortunately the evidence from which he was speaking cannot be traced) as follows: 'When you can get a person from home to factory in half to three-quarters of an hour as against one to two hours, you increase production by 9 to 10 per cent.'

On this reckoning, an hour's travel time costs as much as 0·45 hours of product, in fatigue and mental stress. A careful study[6] made on the Philips

[1] *Traffic Quarterly*, April 1961.
[2] *Economica*, May 1965.
[3] Classon, 1963, quoted *Traffic Quarterly*, July 1965, p. 429.
[4] *Australian News*, 23 December 1965.
[5] *Hansard*, 27 November 1940, Vol. 367, p. 294.
[6] Quoted by Kathe Liepmann, in *The Journey to Work*.

Lamp workers at Eindhoven in the Netherlands by Schut showed that each additional hour's travel per day imposed a cost in fatigue and sickness measured at 2 per cent of earnings, and in increased labour turnover (a cost falling on the employer) of 1 per cent. He concluded in general that the 'indirect costs' of travel amounted to as much as 60 per cent of the direct costs.

Now comes the final crux of the problem from the point of view of the traffic engineer or city planner. If we can foresee the density of residential settlement in certain parts of the city, and the density of places of employment (or of shops, or of other destinations of journeys) in others, can we predict the volume of traffic between them?

Many have attempted to do this by means of 'gravity models'. By analogy with the law of gravity in physics, it is assumed that the volume of traffic between two areas is proportional to the product of their population, divided by the square of the distance between them. An important early study in this field was made in Munich in 1952.[1] In this case an exponent of − 1·7 was preferred to the inverse square law; another study[2] proposed a coefficient of − 2·6. The original studies were based simply on the populations of the two zones; more refined studies have set out to estimate, e.g. work journeys from the product of the residential population in the zone of origin and the amount of employment in the zone of destination, etc.

These ideas have been considerably refined by Lowry (Table IX.23) using detailed data from Pittsburgh.[3] He had before him detailed frequency distributions of lengths of work journeys. Defining as P the cumulated

TABLE IX.23. VALUES OF dP/dr :

For work journeys		for Shopping, etc.	
Managerial and Professional	$35/7r^{-1.08}$	Food, drugs, personal services $(0\cdot5107 - 0\cdot7400r + 0\cdot2699r^2)^{-1}$	
Clerical and Sales	$37\cdot2/r^{-1.12}$	Schools, public buildings $(0\cdot1208 - 0\cdot1670r + 0\cdot0643r^2)^{-1}$	
Craftsmen and Operatives	$48\cdot5/r^{-1.47}$	Eating, drinking, financial services, other retail $(0\cdot0655 - 0\cdot0595r + 0\cdot0227r^2)^{-1}$	
Labourers, Domestic Service Workers	$60\cdot1/r^{-1.85}$	Dept. stores, furniture, appliances, professional $(0\cdot0664 - 0\cdot0442r + 0\cdot0156^2)^{-1}$	
All	$43\cdot9/r^{-1.33}$		

[1] Feuchtinger & Schlums, *A Study Concerning the Arterial Road System in the Munich Area.*

[2] Ikle, *Traffic Quarterly,* April 1954.

[3] Rand Corporation, Memorandum RM 4035 RC, pp. 67 and 70.

percentage of journeys to work to or below a distance *r* measured in miles, he found that dP/dr could be fitted as a function of *r*. Different social groups however showed different exponents; managerial and professional workers were least deterred by distance, labourers most. Another set of equations, in a different form, show journey-length functions according to object of journey.

This refined study perhaps represents the limit to which 'gravity models' can be carried — and by now they do not bear much resemblance to the simple law of gravity.

We may perhaps be permitted to go back to physics to obtain an analogy for quite a different form of law, which is coming to be known as the Principle of Alternative Opportunities.[1] The physical analogy is the law describing the distribution of lengths of paths of molecules in a gas. The logarithm of the number of paths *to or beyond* a given length is found to be inversely proportional to the length.

This principle was first applied in social science in 1940 by Stouffer, in analysing the length of the journeys made by migrants.[2] In this case the controlling variable is not distance, but the number of 'intervening opportunities', measured, in the case of migration, by the population resident within the distance specified. To try to introduce distance into one's explanatory formula, Stouffer pointed out, merely confuses the main relationship, which is between movement and opportunities. This radically new principle, we shall see later, is true, though only within certain limits, for traffic movements in an urban area. The application of this method to traffic was first proposed by Schneider, a member of the staff of the Chicago Area Transportation Survey. Schneider's proposed formula was tried out for analysis of the journeys made by residents in a few sample areas of Chicago, and gave some interesting results.

Although there are now throughout the world a great many data about daily journeys to work, it is unfortunately rare (this qualification applies to all the United States Census data) for the destinations to be sufficiently disaggregated to make any analysis on these lines possible. The form in which journeys to work were tabulated in the British Census of 1951 for the component boroughs of Greater London and adjacent areas did, however, make such analysis possible, albeit in a highly approximate manner.[3]

The general conclusion to be drawn is that, of all those residing within

[1] For the most recent formulation of the Alternative Opportunities Equations, and the technique of the practical use in Chicago, see Chicago Area Transportation Survey (130 N. Franklin St. Chicago) Research News, 31 December 1965.
[2] *American Sociological Review*, December 1940.
[3] Clark and Peters, *Traffic Quarterly*, January 1965.

twelve miles of Charing Cross, some 35–40 per cent of the residents of each borough obtain work close to, mostly within walking or cycling distance of their homes. The remainder, however, are distributed among work places according to Schneider's formula (Diagram IX.M).

The preparation of such a diagram is laborious. In this case, a series of rings has to be drawn with the Borough of Kensington in the centre. The proportion of all available employments in the Greater London area lying

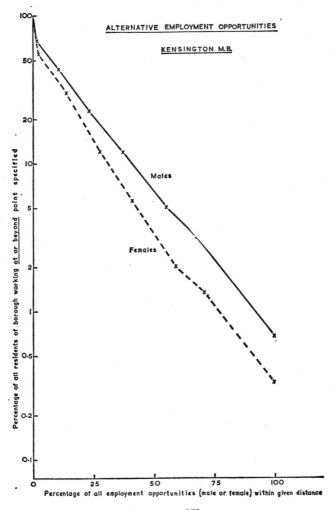

DIAGRAM IX.M

within the boundary of each succeeding ring then has to be measured, and gives us the points on the horizontal scale. The logarithm of the number of Kensington residents working at or beyond such distances gives us the vertical scale. It was Kain who suggested the separate analysis for male and female workers, revealing different slopes — women distributed themselves among alternative opportunities of employment in the same manner as men, but with a greater relative preference for jobs nearer home, as was indeed to be expected, in view of their lower earnings.

A series of tests on the data for a number of boroughs shows that, within the radius specified, the effects of distance can indeed be ignored, and that the amount of movement is fully explained by the alternative opportunities principle.

If it were possible to obtain travel diagrams for different occupational groups, as Lowry did in Pittsburg, it is probable that we should find very differently sloped relationships.

However beyond about twelve miles from Charing Cross, where employment opportunities are less thick on the ground, the relationship ceases to hold. Distance begins to matter, and a much larger proportion will find work in the immediate neighbourhood.

It remains to relate all the phenomena so far observed above to the creation (or destruction) of land values in urban areas.

A theory was first proposed by Winkler,[1] that land values were at their highest in the centre of the area, and that with increasing distance from it they fell off, not exponentially, as does population density, but in a double logarithmic relationship.

One interesting example of this has been observed, at Okayama in Japan[2] (Diagram IX.N).

These land value relationships had established themselves in a city which had to be almost completely re-built after war-time bombing. They nevertheless bear a strong resemblance to the relationships prevailing in 1939. These relationships must therefore be the product of contemporary social forces, and not historical accident.

Despite this good fit for the double log principle, land value data in most other cases are found to follow different rules (Diagram IX.O).

The different currencies have been converted to dollars, approximately, on the basis of their purchasing power rather than their exchange rate values.

It will be seen that in several cities, while a central business zone with

---

[1] Winkler proposed this relationship in a discussion at the Municipal Statistics Section of the International Statistical Institute in 1957.

[2] Hawley, *American Journal of Sociology*, March 1955. 24·4 yen of 1939 purchasing power/tsubo (3·4 sq. m.) may be equated to $1 of 1964 purchasing power/sq. ft.

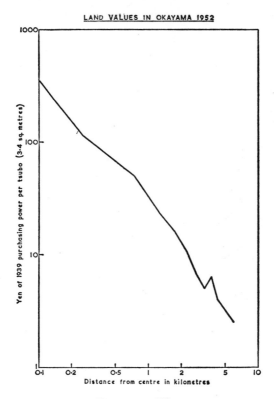

LAND VALUES IN OKAYAMA 1952

DIAGRAM IX.N

comparatively high land values remains, outside this there is a strong tendency for land values to flatten out at a fairly uniform level. Just outside the central business zone indeed they may show a heavy fall. There are some such areas in Chicago whose real value now, allowing for changes in the purchasing power of money, is less than it was in 1870.

The very low values in Perth in Australia may appear surprising. These are largely explained by the system of taxation of land values which prevails in some (but not all) of the Australian States. Such taxes, levied on the imputed selling values of the vacant land, have the effect of reducing the price of land in the ratio (rate of tax)/(rate of tax + rate of interest). This can be demonstrated in a very simple piece of algebra (Table IX.24), which most people nevertheless find very puzzling; but also in fact, by what has happened to land values in the States imposing such taxation.

It was not possible to include New York in Diagram IX.o, because the City is so strangely shaped, and has two centres; a business centre on

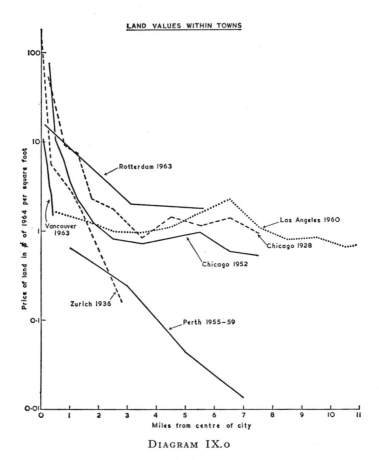

DIAGRAM IX.0

Wall Street, and what was once a high point of residential values (though now it is becoming a business centre also) on Park Avenue. Nevertheless there have been some remarkable tendencies at work there. The highest

TABLE IX.24. EFFECTS OF LAND TAX ON PRICE OF LAND

Rate of tax on land	t
Rate of interest	i
Current selling value of land	V
Full selling value of land before tax	F
Full economic rent of land before tax	E

$$\text{Then} \quad F = E/i$$
$$V = (E - tV)/i$$
$$\text{i.e.} \quad V = E/(t + i)$$
$$\text{and} \quad V/F = i/(t + i)$$

land values now found in New York and area are the rate of 400 $/sq. ft.[1]
An interesting book prepared in 1911[2] gives detailed maps of land values in
these areas, in 1911 dollars, which had 3·67 times the purchasing power of
1964 dollars. The maximum value shown was 400 $/sq. ft. for a site in Wall

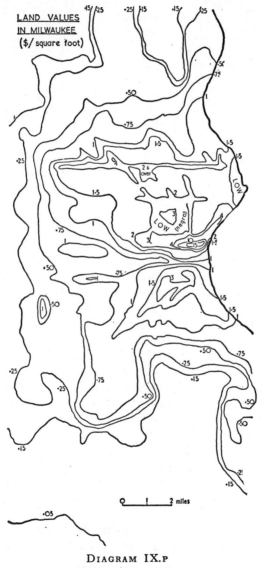

LAND VALUES
IN MILWAUKEE
($/ square foot)

DIAGRAM IX.P

[1] *Fortune*, September 1964, p. 199.   [2] Hurd, *Principle of City Land Values.*

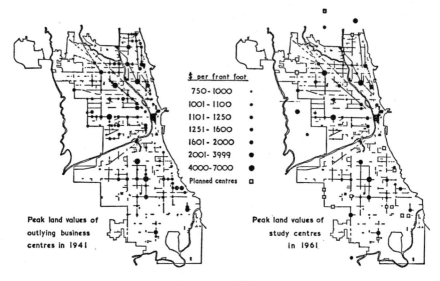

$ per front foot

750 - 1000 ·
1001 - 1100 ·
1101 - 1250 ·
1251 - 1600 ·
1601 - 2000 ●
2001 - 3999 ●
4000 - 7000 ●
Planned centres □

Peak land values of outlying business centres in 1941

Peak land values of study centres in 1961

DIAGRAM IX.Q

Street, and land prices over $100 were paid by those who wished to be within easy walking distance (about 250 yards) of the financial centre. A mile away, however, the median price was still about $12. High prices, up to 90 $/sq. ft. also prevailed on the sites surrounding Central Park; but fell off very rapidly towards the East Side. These, however, represent real values much higher than those of today.

Measuring site values as merely a function of distance from the centre of the city is, however, an unsatisfactory procedure.

In most cities the formation of land values is highly irregular, along the principal business streets, with remarkable islands of low values in some areas. Full land value maps for cities are still scarce. A map of Milwaukee (Diagram IX.P) brings out the nature of the distribution.

Maps of Chicago (Diagram IX.Q) indicate very clearly how site values rise along the principal shopping streets, with particularly high values at certain street corners. Comparison of 1961 and 1941 show clearly however that these shopping centres are tending to become more concentrated and the areas of high values fewer.

A more recent study by Yeates[1] (Diagram IX.R) shows how the situation has almost inverted itself since 1910. Then there was a comparatively

[1] *Economic Geography*, January 1965.

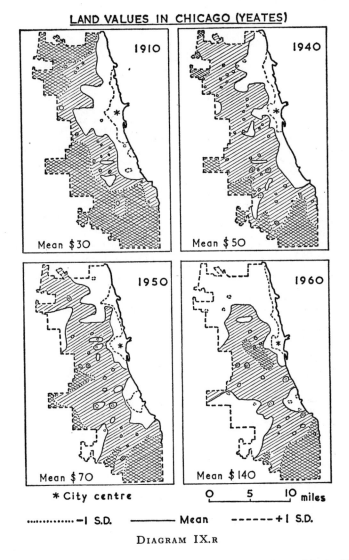

LAND VALUES IN CHICAGO (YEATES)

1910 — Mean $30
1940 — Mean $50
1950 — Mean $70
1960 — Mean $140

* City centre

0   5   10 miles

.... -1 S.D.   ——— Mean   ------ +1 S.D.

DIAGRAM IX.R

regular zone of high values[1] near the centre of the City, with rapidly de-creasing values outside it. The old high value areas have in most cases lost their value, and in some cases have reached very low values, while new high value areas have appeared in the further suburbs.

[1] City mean values shown per square foot, with contour lines for differences from mean of + 1 and − 1 standard deviations.

Index